FINANCIAL ANALYSIS:
Practical Tools for Making Effective Financial Decisions in Business

DIANA R. HARRINGTON

THOMSON
LEARNING

*Financial Analysis: Practical Tools for Making
Effective Financial Decisions in Business*
by Diana R. Harrington

COPYRIGHT © 2002 by South-Western, a division of Thomson Learning. The Thomson Learning logo is a registered trademark used herein under license.

All Rights Reserved. No part of this work covered by the copyright hereon may be reproduced or used in any form or by any means—graphic, electronic, or mechanical, including photocopying, recording, taping, or information storage and retrieval systems—without the written permission of the publisher.

ISBN: 0-324-15376-7

Printed in Canada
1 2 3 4 5 04 03 02 01

For more information contact South-Western, 5191 Natorp Boulevard, Mason, Ohio, 45040 or find us on the Internet at http://www.swcollege.com

For permission to use material from this text or product, contact us by
- **telephone: 1-800-730-2214**
- **fax: 1-800-730-2215**
- **web: http://www.thomsonrights.com**

Library of Congress Cataloging-in-Publication Data
Harrington, Diana R.
  Financial analysis: Practical tools for making effective financial decisions in business / Diana R. Harrington.
      p. cm.
  Includes bibliographical references and index.
  ISBN 0-324-15376-7
    1. Corporations—Finance. I. Title.

HG4026 .H34 2000
658.15--dc21

00-036547

The author would like to dedicate this book to her daughter Maya Anna Maria del Carmen Harrington and her Papa.

PREFACE

Financial Analysis is designed to provide an overview of the key concepts in and practical tools for making effective financial decisions in business today. This book emphasizes the financial impact of business decisions on a company's value now and in the future.

The author uses examples of actual business situations to demonstrate how managers can use financial tools, concepts, and theories to improve decision making and enhance business performance. The author's direct, no-nonsense approach to the basics of finance and current financial concepts is especially useful for non-financial managers who want to understand financial analysis in the global economy.

PRACTICAL TOOLS FOR CREATING VALUE

Financial Analysis does not present abstract financial theory or rigorous mathematical proofs; rather, it examines the practical tools for creating value. The focus throughout the book is on the manager's role in enhancing the value of the company. Managers can create value through the financial decisions they make, and thorough financial analysis can assist them in making better decisions—decisions that enhance the firm's attractiveness to outside investors. Value creation, and the role that proper financial analysis plays in helping managers to make value-enhancing decisions, is the topic of this book.

Acknowledging the multinational character of the financial arena in which managers operate, *Financial Analysis* contains explanations of important concepts in international finance. It maintains a global perspective on financial analysis with an equal number of domestic and international examples and includes a discussion of international financial statements and the financial impact of changes in foreign exchange rates on managers' decisions.

In addition to these features, *Financial Analysis* also contains the following:

- **Up-to-Date Content:** The sections on risk management, real options analysis, and inflation are current.
- **Helpful References:** Selected references at the end of each chapter encourage further reading and research on key topics.
- **Self-Testing Study Questions:** Study questions and problems at the end of each chapter allow you to practice using the tools discussed in the chapter.
- **Solutions to Study Questions:** Suggested solutions to the end-of-chapter study questions and problems are provided in the appendix, allowing you to assess your own understanding and application of the concepts.

Whether you are a financial manager or a non-financial professional, this book will enhance your knowledge of important financial tools and concepts. It is designed to serve both as an introductory text for professionals who want to gain basic information about financial analysis and as a reference tool for managers who want to refresh their skills.

ABOUT THE AUTHOR

Diana R. Harrington is the Donald P. Babson Professor of Applied Investment Management and the Babson Distinguished Professor of Finance at Babson College in Wellesley, MA. She has wide experience as a consultant on issues of finance and financial strategy and provides executive education for a number of companies. She has worked with practicing finance professionals and with managers in many other functional areas. Her current research is on the impact of 401K retirement plans on the financial health of companies.

Dr. Harrington has written numerous books and articles, including *Corporate Financial Analysis: Decision in a Global Environment* (currently in its 6th edition), *The New Stock Market* (with Fogler and Fabozzi), *Case Studies in Financial Decision Making, Modern Portfolio Theory, The Capital Asset Pricing Model, Arbitrage Pricing Theory: A User's Guide*, and the article "Capital Budgeting" in *Handbook of Modern Finance*.

Prior to her tenure at Babson College, she was a faculty member at the Darden Graduate School of Business at the University of Virginia for 16 years, attaining the rank of Full Professor. She has held Visiting Professorships at the Kellogg School at Northwestern University and at the Tuck Graduate Business School at Dartmouth College and is on the boards of a number of mutual funds.

CONTENTS

CHAPTER 1
Analyzing Corporate Performance   **1**
I. Who Needs to Analyze Corporate Performance?   2
II. Financial Statements   3
    1. Statement of Earnings   3
    2. Statement of Financial Position   5
    3. Statement of Cash Flows   5
    4. Statement of Changes in Shareholders' Equity   8
    5. Financial Statement Footnotes   10
III. Analysis of Financial Statements   12
    1. Profitability Analysis Using Ratios   14
    2. Profitability Analysis Using Common-Size Statements   18
    3. Profitability Using Growth Rates   19
    4. Asset Utilization Ratios   22
    5. Capitalization Ratios   30
    6. Sustainable Growth Rate   38
    7. Market Ratios   42
    8. Return Versus Risk Performance Ratios   46
IV. Comparative Ratio Analysis   50
    1. Historical Comparisons   51
    2. Comparisons to Other Companies   53
    3. Comparisons with Others in the Industry   54
V. Summary   55
    Appendix 1A Cross-Border Ratio Analysis   63

CHAPTER 2
Forecasting Future Needs   **88**
I. Cash Budgets   89
II. Projected Financial Statements   96
    1. Developing Projections Directly   96
    2. Developing Financial Statement Forecasts from Cash Budgets   99
III. Projecting Financial Statements in Highly Uncertain Conditions   99
IV. Analyzing Assumptions   103

		1. Historical Comparisons	104
		2. Sensitivity Analysis—One Scenario	107
		3. Sensitivity Analysis—Three Scenarios	109
		4. Probability Analysis	110
	V.	Multi-Currency Financial Statements	111
		1. The Importance of Exchange Rates	111
		2. Exchange Rate Theories	112
		3. How Exchange Rates Affect Forecasts	114
	VI.	Summary	118

CHAPTER 3
Managing Working Capital — 126

I.	The Working Capital Cycle		126
	1. The Impact of Inflation		128
	2. The Impact of Sales Growth		128
	3. The Impact of Variable Sales Demand		130
II.	Cash Management		132
	1. Managing Receipts		132
	2. Managing Disbursements		133
	3. Investing Cash Balances		133
III.	Managing Other Working Capital Requirements		135
	1. Accounts Receivable		135
	2. Inventories		136
IV.	Financing Working Capital		137
V.	Summary		140

CHAPTER 4
Valuation 1: Capital Budgeting — 146

I.	Cost-Benefit Analysis of Proposed Investments	147
	1. Cash Benefits	148
	2. Cash Payments	148
II.	Evaluating Incremental Costs and Benefits	152
	1. Mutually Exclusive Investments: The Breakfast Proposal	153
	2. Mutually Exclusive Investments: Salad, Sushi, and Pasta Bar Proposal	155
III.	Choosing Among Investments	156
	1. Simple Valuation Methods	156
	2. Dealing with the Timing of Cash Flows: Discounting Techniques	160
	3. Ranking Projects	169
IV.	Assessing and Incorporating Risk	169
	1. Defining Risk	169
	2. Changing the Discount Rate	170
	3. Risk Categories by Investment Type	171

	4. Danger of Raising Discount Rates: New Products and New Processes	172
	5. Cash Flow Manipulation to Incorporate Risk	172
	6. Multi-Scenario Analysis	173
	7. Upside Risk Analysis—Contingent Claims Analysis	176
V.	Other Considerations in Creating Value	178
	1. The Impact of Taxes and Depreciation on Value	178
	2. Including Investment-Size Considerations	182
	3. Incorporating Expected Inflation	183
VI.	Summary	185
	Appendix 4A Real Options and Capital Investing	190
	Appendix 4B Tax Codes and Depreciation in Highly Inflationary Environments	203

CHAPTER 5
Valuation 2: Acquisitions and Divestitures — 205

I.	Present Value Analysis of Cash Flows	211
	1. Calculating the Value of an Acquisition Without Synergy	211
	2. Calculating the Marginal Benefit of an Acquisition with Synergy	214
	3. The Value of Redundant Assets	217
	4. Calculating the Marginal Benefit of an Acquisition with Growth	218
	5. Terminal Value	218
	6. Inflation and Growth	221
II.	Valuation Using Market Multiples	223
	1. Earnings Multiples	223
	2. Other Multiples for Valuation	227
III.	Other Valuation Techniques	228
	1. Book Value	229
	2. Liquidation Value	229
	3. Replacement Cost	230
	4. Market Value	230
	5. Dividend Discount Valuation	231
	6. Relationship between Earnings, Cash Flow, and Dividend Discount Models of Valuation	232
	7. Cross-Border Acquisitions	233
IV.	Summary	234

CHAPTER 6
The Required Rate of Return on Equity — 239

I.	What Is a Shareholders' Required Return?	239
II.	Capital Market Basics	240

III.	Cash Flow Valuation Models	246
	1. The Dividend-Discount Method	246
	2. Discounted Cash Flow Models	253
	3. Implicit Required Return on Equity	255
IV.	Capital Market Estimations—Risk Premium Models	255
	1. The Stock-Bond Yield Spread	256
	2. The Capital Asset Pricing Model	257
	3. Using the CAPM	266
V.	Other Concerns in Determining Required Return on Equity	267
	1. New Equity Issues	267
	2. Cost of Retained Earnings	267
	3. Preferred Stock	268
VI.	Required Return on Equity for Private, Non-U.S., or Companies Experiencing Change	268
VII.	Summary	270

CHAPTER 7
Obtaining Outside Capital — 275

I.	The Value of Leverage	276
II.	Sources of Debt Financing	283
III.	Determining the Cost of Debt	287
IV.	RICHS Analysis	291
	1. Risk to Lenders	294
	2. Income	299
	3. Control	306
	4. Hedging and Speculating	308
	5. Greenway's Financing Decision	315
	6. Leasing	315
V.	Leverage in Acquisitions	317
VI.	Summary	317
	Appendix 7A The Weighted-Average Cost of Capital and Free Cash Flow Valuation	322
	Appendix 7B Adjusted Present Value: The Case of the Leveraged Acquisition	334

APPENDIX
Solutions to Study Questions — 339

INDEX — 391

CHAPTER 1
Analyzing Corporate Performance

Over the past decade, our world has changed more profoundly and more rapidly than we could ever have believed. Not only have political systems been challenged and changed, but many of the basic notions on which we have based personal and corporate financial decisions have been contested. Companies now have to compete with others from all over the world for customers and for suppliers of labor, goods, and capital. The markets for goods and capital have become increasingly integrated, and will continue to do so.[1] At the same time, the Internet has added both challenges to existing systems for doing business and opportunities to create totally new ways to market, sell, manage, communicate, and inform. Information that was once privately held or held only by experts now is widely available with the click of a computer mouse, and communications are virtually instantaneous. The Internet has made business truly global, and we have just begun to see the possibilities and implications for doing business using it. What is certain is that managers of companies have to be flexible, creative, and pay close attention to the world around them.[2]

These changes have profoundly affected all our lives, and it is important for corporate managers, shareholders, lenders, customers, and suppliers to understand the past and future performance of the companies on which they rely. All who depend on a company for products, services, or a job must be informed about the company's ability to meet their demands over time as the world changes and businesses adapt.

This chapter's purpose is to provide the basic tools that any individual can use to begin an analysis of business performance and strength. These tools are often mathematical and are simple to calculate, but they require some experience to use well. Your skill in using them will increase with experience.

---

[1] In fact, we have been seeing the formation of economic cartels. The first of these was in the European Common Market, where much more complete economic integration culminated in Europe in 1992 and in currency integration in 1999. In addition, other economic unions, such as NAFTA and MERCOSUR, have been or are forming in South and North America and Asia.

[2] In fact, one of the biggest changes management must face is in the rapid introduction of substitute products and methods of delivery that have been created by the Internet.

I. WHO NEEDS TO ANALYZE AN ENTERPRISE'S PERFORMANCE?

All kinds of people need insight into business performance:

Customers: The company's customers are concerned with the company's viability as a vendor of goods or services. Qualified vendors are able to fulfill both their contractual obligations and the customers' needs, and will be able to provide product innovations and future service for their products.

Suppliers: Suppliers provide the resources that a company uses:

Goods and services: Individuals and companies that provide goods and/or services to a company are concerned with whether the company can pay its obligations on time and whether it will continue to be a customer. These suppliers also include those who work for the company, supplying labor.[3]

Capital: Money is a good that is provided to businesses by lenders and by shareholders. Lenders are concerned with the company's ability to pay the interest, repay the loan, and abide by the loan covenants (the requirements) during the time that the loan is outstanding. Shareholders (the company's owners and potential owners) are interested in evaluating the skill of the company's management and in determining the financial strength of a company as they think about the company's future and its value.[4]

Employees: Employees are a special group of suppliers. They supply the labor needed by the company, and because of their intimate relationship with the company they need to better understand the forces affecting it. The future of their company, the industry, and their jobs depends upon them understanding the company's potential and contributing to its innovation.

The topic of this chapter is evaluating and interpreting a company's historical financial performance. First, you will be introduced to the basic financial statements provided by companies. Second, you will be shown how to calculate and interpret ratios created from information contained in the company's financial statements. Finally, using three simple ratios, you will see how to relate corporate financial performance to the shareholders' response to past and anticipated performance. The chapter uses information from an actual com-

---

[3] In the 1980s and 1990s, a significant number of the largest U.S. companies with publicly traded stock changed ownership. Many of these ownership changes also resulted in serious reductions in their work forces. In the late 1990s the increasing number of cross-border mergers had serious implications for employees in many countries.

[4] The value of a company is determined by many things—its earning power, the sustainability of its earnings, the riskiness of the business it is in, and how management conducts the business. Each of these topics will be explored in this book.

pany operating in the United States, and the appendix to this chapter shows you how to extend this analysis to companies operating in different countries.[5]

Remember, the past performance of a company, as shown in its financial statements, may help predict future performance. However interesting past performance may be though, managers and analysts really are more interested in what will happen in the future. Chapter 2 will describe how historical statements and analysis of those statements can be used to help forecast the future. To start this analysis let's look first at the raw material we have to work with: the various financial statements that most companies provide to their internal and external analysts.

II. FINANCIAL STATEMENTS

The types of financial information published in financial statements vary among countries, each of which has different requirements for disclosure of information. Most industrialized countries require that financial statements disclose sufficient data to allow a meaningful analysis of performance. Regulations in the United States, the United Kingdom, other Commonwealth countries, and the European Union require the most complete disclosure. The growing trend of major international companies to raise funds in foreign capital markets has meant that these multinational companies provide at least the minimum level of financial information expected by investors in the countries where they are raising capital.

In all countries, public disclosure requirements apply only to publicly owned companies.[6] Privately owned companies—companies owned by a small group, such as management or a family—may not be required to disclose any financial information to the public. However, some groups, such as lenders or private investors, often have access to financial statements from privately owned companies.

In the United States, publicly owned companies are required to prepare four financial statements: statements of earnings, of financial position, of cash flows, and of changes in shareholders' equity. Typically, these statements are prepared quarterly.

1. Statement of Earnings

The **statement of earnings**, also known as the **income statement** or **profit and loss statement**, shows the total revenues earned and the total expenses in-

---

[5] In this chapter we will use U.S. companies because many of you are based in the United States, or deal with U.S.-based companies. Thus you are more familiar with U.S. accounting principles. A truly useful and comprehensive analysis of a company should, however, include the performance of its worldwide components and competitors. For that, a knowledge of other countries' accounting standards is needed. A brief discussion of this topic appears in the appendix to this chapter.

[6] Publicly held companies are those whose equity (common stock) is traded in the capital markets.

curred to generate these revenues during a specific period of time. The difference between revenues and expenses is termed **net income** (also known as earnings, profit, or margin) or **net loss** for the period.

This statement of earnings summarizes all revenue or expense transactions during a specified period of time, the reporting period. A **quarterly report** includes the transactions made during a three-month reporting period. An **annual report** includes all income and expense items for a year.[7] Exhibit 1-1 is an example of an annual statement of earnings.[8] It is the 1998 statement for Hannaford Bros. Co., a U.S. supermarket chain.[9] The company is involved in the distribution and retail sale of food, prescription drugs, and related products through supermarkets and combination stores. Hannaford is a multi-regional food retailer, with 148 supermarkets located throughout Maine and New Hampshire, and in parts of Vermont, Massachusetts, New York, Virginia, North Carolina, and South Carolina, primarily under the names Shop'n Save, Sun Foods, and Wilson's. Its private bands are under the labels of Shop'n Save, Bonnie Maid, and Green Meadow. During 1998 Hannaford remodeled stores in

EXHIBIT 1-1 Hannaford Bros. Co.

CONSOLIDATED STATEMENT OF EARNINGS FOR THE YEARS ENDED DECEMBER 31 (in thousands)

Summary of Operations:	1998	1997
Sales and other revenues	$3,323,588	$3,226,433
Cost of sales	2,480,346	2,427,287
Gross margin	843,242	799,146
Selling, general, and administrative expenses	664,357	635,355
Impairment loss		39,950
Operating profit	178,885	123,841
Interest expense, net	26,577	26,425
Earnings before income taxes and minority interest	152,308	97,416
Income taxes	57,661	37,769
Net earnings	$ 94,647	$ 59,647

---

[7] For many companies the year end coincides with the end of the calendar year; for others the year end is chosen to coincide with an appropriate time in its business cycle. For instance, for a seasonal business the year end might be when inventories and accounts receivable are low.

[8] Note that expenses, or negative numbers, are identified by parentheses in some financial statements. In others, for instance, in Hannaford's statement of earnings, the reader is expected to know that expenses are deductions. As a reader of financial statements you will become accustomed to the variety of reporting schemes.

[9] Note that the Hannaford financial statements used in this chapter's examples use the term **consolidated**. This means that subsidiaries owned by Hannaford are operated and treated as if they were fully integrated into the company's activities.

the northeast where Wal-Mart was expected to enter the grocery business, opened eight new stores, and continued to invest in HomeRuns®, its home delivery business operating primarily in the Boston area. The company also operated 100 pharmacies within its supermarkets and combination stores and sold goods to independent wholesale customers.

2. Statement of Financial Position

The **statement of financial position** is also referred to as the **balance sheet**. This statement reports the corporation's assets, liabilities, and owners' equity at a particular date in time, which is usually the end of the reporting period. The corporation's assets must equal or balance the funds used to purchase the assets (hence the term balance sheet). Funds provided by lenders are recorded on the balance sheet as liabilities; funds provided by shareholders are recorded as owners' equity, or shareholders' equity for publicly held corporations.

The statement of financial position, the balance sheet, differs from the statement of earnings in that it reports the firm's status at a point in time, the end of the reporting period. While the statement of earnings reports on the flow of transactions or funds, the statement of financial position reports on the resulting financial status. Thus a quarterly report specifies the status of the assets, liabilities, and owners' equity at the end of a quarter; an annual report indicates status at the conclusion of the reporting year. The Hannaford statements of financial position, or balance sheets, for the years ended 1998 and 1997 are presented in Exhibit 1-2. Note that Hannaford Bros. Co.'s fiscal year is the same as the calendar year.

3. Statement of Cash Flows

A company generates new financial resources in several ways: by borrowing additional funds, issuing new owners' equity, retaining the period's earnings, and/or decreasing assets (for instance, selling excess equipment). The resources thus generated can be used to increase assets by purchasing new equipment, decrease liabilities by paying off loans, or decrease owners' equity by paying a dividend or repurchasing outstanding shares. Previously known as the **statement of changes in financial position** or **funds flow statement**, the **cash flow statement** reports the amounts of cash generated by the company during the period, as well as the disposition of cash. The difference between the sum of the sources of cash and the sum of its uses is typically reported as a change in cash, as used by Hannaford, or as a change in net working capital.[10]

The cash flow statements for 1998 and 1997 from the 1998 Hannaford Bros. Co. Annual Report are shown in Exhibit 1-3.

Another handy way an analyst can determine the changes that occurred over the period is to create a **statement of sources and uses**. This statement is

---

[10] **Net working capital** is current assets minus current liabilities.

EXHIBIT 1-2 Hannaford Bros. Co.

STATEMENT OF CONSOLIDATED FINANCIAL POSITION (in thousands)

	1/2/1998	1/3/1997
Assets		
Current assets:		
Cash and cash equivalents	$ 59,722	$ 57,663
Accounts receivable, net	22,869	14,918
Inventories	201,219	188,767
Prepaid expenses	6,116	7,801
Deferred income taxes	5,952	6,912
Total current assets	**295,878**	**276,061**
Property, plant, and equipment, net	823,368	777,909
Leased property under capital leases, net	54,911	58,516
Other assets:		
Goodwill, net	63,517	67,552
Deferred charges, net	25,074	28,724
Computer software costs, net	19,318	16,551
Miscellaneous assets	2,472	1,877
Total other assets	**110,381**	**114,704**
Total assets	**$1,284,538**	**$1,227,190**
Liabilities and Shareholders' Equity		
Current liabilities:		
Current maturities of long-term debt	$ 19,296	$ 18,155
Obligations under capital leases	2,108	1,873
Accounts payable	186,626	182,252
Accrued payroll	27,254	25,526
Other accrued expenses	23,873	24,553
Income taxes	442	2,829
Total current liabilities	**259,599**	**255,188**
Deferred income tax liabilities	28,859	18,265
Other liabilities	38,734	41,171
Long-term debt	220,130	235,850
Obligations under capital leases	73,866	75,687
Shareholders' equity:		
Common stock, par value $.75 per share Authorized 110,000 shares; 42,338 shares issued.	31,754	31,754
Additional paid-in capital	109,664	115,130
Preferred stock purchase rights	423	423
Retained earnings	525,344	456,063
Total equity	667,185	603,370
Less common stock in treasury	3,835	2,341
Total shareholders' equity	**663,350**	**601,029**
Total liabilities and shareholders' equity	**$1,284,538**	**$1,227,190**

EXHIBIT 1-3 Hannaford Bros. Co.

STATEMENT OF CONSOLIDATED CASH FLOWS
AS OF DECEMBER 31 (in thousands)

	1998	1997
Cash flows from operating activities:		
Net income	$ 94,647	$ 59,647
Adjustments to reconcile net income to net cash provided by operating activities:		
Impairment loss	0	39,950
Depreciation and amortization	96,739	93,953
Decrease (increase) in inventories	(12,452)	2,891
Decrease (increase) in receivables and prepaids	(6,202)	599
Increase (decrease) in accounts payable and accrued expenses	2,986	440
Increase (decrease) in income taxes payable	(2,387)	297
Increase (decrease) in deferred taxes	11,554	(7,815)
Other operating activities	(1,081)	(446)
Net cash provided by operating activities	183,804	189,516
Cash flows from investing activities:[11]		
Acquisition of property, plant, and equipment	(135,904)	(152,862)
Sale of property, plant, and equipment	9,156	6,143
Increase in computer software costs	(7,262)	(6,205)
Decrease (increase) in deferred charges	911	(4,054)
Net cash used in investing activities	(133,099)	(156,978)
Cash flows from financing activities:[12]		
Principal payments under capital lease obligations	(1,740)	(1,788)
Proceeds from issuance of long-term debt	20,000	26,600
Payments of long-term debt	(34,580)	(14,418)
Issuance of common stock	11,048	9,648
Purchase of treasury stock	(18,008)	(14,379)
Dividends paid	(25,366)	(23,043)
Net cash (used in) provided by financing activities	(48,646)	(17,380)
Net increase in cash and cash equivalents	2,059	15,158
Cash and cash equivalents at beginning of year	57,663	42,505
Cash and cash equivalents at end of year	**$ 59,722**	**$ 57,663**

not one that you will find in an annual report, just a rather straightforward way for an analyst to determine where money went and where it came from. To create this statement the analyst simply compares the current statement of financial position with that of the previous reporting period. This analysis can highlight the changes that have occurred in the company's financial position

---

[11] Activities having to do with managing resources.
[12] Activities having to do with funding assets.

and can be especially useful when no cash flow statement is readily available. Such an analysis is shown in Exhibit 1-4. Note, we have summed the sources and uses to show that they are equal. If they are not equal, check your analysis. They must be equal.

Both the cash flow statement and our analysis of sources and uses show that Hannaford has been investing heavily in property, plant, and equipment and inventories. Most of these investments were made from the company's own profits, though deferred taxes provided some resources.

4. Statement of Changes in Shareholders' Equity

This report is called the **statement of changes in shareholders' equity** or the **statement of retained earnings**. It provides additional details on the composition of the owners' equity accounts for the company, and shows how much the company earned in the period, how much of it was paid out, and how much was retained on the shareholders' behalf. This statement also shows any shares repurchased and reports any new shares the company issued.

The purpose of this statement is to highlight changes in owners' equity or retained earnings that have occurred during the reporting period. This statement is similar to the cash flow statement; however, it focuses specifically on changes within the owners' equity segment of the balance sheet. In the statement there are several columns reporting the annual changes in various equity accounts.

- **Common stock.** This is the number of shares issued and held by the company's shareholders, its owners. The shares are recorded at a par value, or face value, of the stock. For Hannaford common stock the par value is $0.75.
- **Additional paid-in capital.** This is the amount above par value the shareholders paid for their shares when the company first issued them.
- **Preferred stock.** Preferred stock is stock that typically has a predetermined dividend that must be paid before any common shareholders receive dividends. Normally the owners of the shares have no voting rights.
- **Purchase rights.** Purchase rights are the right to purchase stock, usually preferred stock and usually at a set price and/or time. These rights may be issued in conjunction with a financing arrangement or merger. For Hannaford the rights are associated with an agreement whereby certain shareholders are given the right to keep the proportion of their ownership of the company the same, even when the company issues new shares.
- **Retained earnings.** This is the amount of the net income kept or retained by the company after all dividends are paid. This is the shareholders' income put to use in the company for their future benefit.
- **Treasury stock.** These are shares that the company is authorized to issue but has not sold to current or potential shareholders. These may also be shares that have been sold and repurchased by the company.

II. Financial Statements

EXHIBIT 1-4 Hannaford Bros. Co.

STATEMENT OF SOURCES AND USES (in thousands)

Assets	1998	1997	Uses	Sources
Current assets:				
Cash and cash equivalents	$ 59,722	$ 57,663	$ 2,059	
Accounts receivable, net	22,869	14,918	7,951	
Inventories	201,219	188,767	12,452	
Prepaid expenses	6,116	7,801		$ 1,685
Deferred income taxes	5,952	6,912		960
Total current assets	295,878	276,061		
Property, plant, and equipment, net	823,368	777,909	45,459	
Leased property under capital leases, net	54,911	58,516		3,605
Other assets:				
Goodwill, net	63,517	67,552		4,035
Deferred charges, net	25,074	28,724		3,650
Computer software costs, net	19,318	16,551	2,767	
Miscellaneous assets	2,472	1,877	595	
Total other assets	110,381	114,704		
Total assets	$1,284,538	$1,227,190		
Liabilities and Shareholders' Equity				
Current liabilities:				
Current maturities of long-term debt	$ 19,296	$ 18,155		1,141
Obligations under capital leases	2,108	1,873		235
Accounts payable	186,626	182,252		4,374
Accrued payroll	27,254	25,526		1,728
Other accrued expenses	23,873	24,553	680	
Income taxes	442	2,829	2,387	
Total current liabilities	259,599	255,188		
Deferred income tax liabilities	28,859	18,265		10,594
Other liabilities	38,734	41,171	2,437	
Long-term debt	220,130	235,850	15,720	
Obligations under capital leases	73,866	75,687	1,821	
Shareholders' equity:				
Common stock, par value $.75 per share Authorized 110,000 shares;				
42,338 and 42,338 shares issued.	31,754	31,754		
Additional paid-in capital	109,664	115,130	5,466	
Preferred stock purchase rights	423	423		
Retained earnings	525,344	456,063		69,281
Total equity	667,185	603,370		
Less common stock in treasury	3,835	2,341	1,494	
Total shareholders' equity	663,350	601,029		
Total liabilities and shareholders' equity	$1,284,538	$1,227,190		
Total sources or uses			**$101,288**	**$101,288**

Exhibit 1-5 shows the statement of changes in shareholders' equity for Hannaford from its 1998 Annual Report.

You can see that Hannaford issued shares each year to fulfill obligations to the employee benefit plans, and that the retained earnings—the proportion of the net income retained by the company—grew each year.

5. Financial Statement Footnotes

In addition to the data contained in the financial statements, companies also include significant financial information in notes to the statements. These footnotes typically contain further information about the items on the balance sheet and income statement. Most companies provide further information about taxes, details about debt, contingent liabilities, leases, nonconsolidated subsidiaries, foreign exchange impacts, employee benefit plans, and depreciation schedules for property, plant, and equipment. Most unusual items also are normally described in the footnotes. To give you an example from the Hannaford statements, in December 1997 Hannaford reported an impairment loss. This loss was to recognize the loss of operating cash flows and the probable loss of the book value of assets for stores that Hannaford closed but had not yet sold.

Because specific accounting policies can have a significant impact on the performance reported in financial statements, companies usually include in the footnotes an explanation of the major accounting procedures used in preparing the statements. For instance, in 1998 the U.S. Accounting Standards Board, the group that determines accounting policies in the United States, required that software developed by a company for its own use be capitalized and depreciated. In the past these costs had been shown as an expense when the money was spent.[13] You will see these capitalized expenses on the 1998 income statement for Hannaford.

Some of these footnoted items can be very important. Stock analysts spend considerable time in trying to understand and value the impact of un- or underreported items. For instance, it was not until late 1992 that U.S. companies were required to report the present value of the cost of providing nonpension-related post-retirement benefits, such as health care, for their employees. Previously, U.S. companies reported the costs of these benefits as they were paid or when the employee retired, not as they were earned during the employee's career. This accounting change had a significant impact on the earnings of many U.S. companies at the time. Canny stock analysts had estimated

---

[13] Expensing the costs means that the full cost is reported on the income statement in the period when the expense is incurred. Capitalizing the expense means that the cost is turned into an asset on the balance sheet and depreciated (reported as an expense) on the income statement over a period of years. Changing from an expense to a capitalized and depreciated asset reduces the reported expenses in the year in which the asset is purchased or created (and thus increases income and taxes) and spreads out the expenses, income, and tax reduction over several years. As you will see later in this book, the time value of money makes a current tax reduction more valuable than an equivalent tax reduction in the future.

EXHIBIT 1-5 Hannaford Bros. Co.

CHANGES IN SHAREHOLDERS' EQUITY (in thousands)

	Common Stock		Additional Paid-In Capital	Preferred Stock Purchase Rights	Retained Earnings	Treasury Stock	
	Shares	Amount				Shares	Amount
Balance, December 30, 1995	$42,298	$31,724	$121,974	$423	$364,556	$ 410	$ 12,250
Net earnings					75,205		
Cash dividends on common stock					(20,302)		
Shares issued to certain shareholders per agreement	20	15	484				
Shares issued under employee benefit plans	20	15	(3,059)			(468)	(14,129)
Treasury stock purchases						(58)	(1,879)
Balance, December 28, 1996	42,338	31,754	119,399	423	419,459		
Net earnings					59,647		
Cash dividends on common stock					(23,043)		
Shares issued to certain shareholders per agreement							
Shares issued under employee benefit plans			(4,269)			399	13,917
Treasury stock purchases						(400)	(14,379)
						(59)	(2,341)
Balance, January 3, 1998	42,338	31,754	115,130	423	456,063		
Net earnings					94,647		
Cash dividends on common stock					(25,366)		
Shares issued to certain shareholders per agreement							
Shares issued under employee benefit plans			(5,466)			392	16,514
Treasury stock purchases						(418)	(18,008)
						(85)	(3,835)
Balance, January 2, 1999	$42,338	$31,754	$109,664	$423	$525,344		

the size of the earnings impacts on companies most affected and determined how it would impact the value of the companies and made buy and sell recommendations based on their findings.[14]

Included in the notes to the financial statements of all companies in countries that abide by international accounting standards is information about their accounting standards and policies. For purposes of brevity, the notes to the Hannaford Bros. Co. financial statements have not been reproduced here.[15]

III. ANALYSIS OF FINANCIAL STATEMENTS

When analyzing financial statements, keep in mind the purpose of the analysis. Since different analysts are interested in different aspects of a corporation's performance, no single type of analysis is appropriate for all situations. However, there are several general factors the analyst should bear in mind when reviewing data on financial statements.

First, all financial statement data are historical. Although one may make projections based on such data, the accuracy of these projections depends both on the forecaster's ability and the continued pertinence of the historical relationships to current or future operations and to industry and economic conditions.

Second, historical data are collected and reported on the basis of particular accounting principles. These accounting principles and rules vary from country to country. Even within a country or an industry several approaches to specific issues may be allowed at one time, and these approaches may change over time. One example is the price at which a company can transfer an item out of inventory (reported on the balance sheet) into cost of goods sold (reported on the income statement) when a product is sold. Exhibit 1-6 shows the inventory balance that would be reported on the balance sheet and the expense in cost of goods sold as well as the resulting income and taxes from using three different inventory methods. The inventory methods are descriptively named FIFO, LIFO, and average cost. Each of these indicates the price at which inventory is transferred out of inventory into cost of goods sold when goods are made and sold. FIFO transfers goods at the first price, LIFO at the price of the last purchase, and average cost at the average cost of the items in inventory. To understand the difference this can have on the balance sheet and income statement items, including taxes and profits, you need only look at Exhibit 1-6. From this

---

[14] Chapter 5 will discuss another big change: the change in merger accounting from pooling to purchase accounting that will occur at the end of 2000.

[15] To see the full financial report, you may log on to Hannaford's web site, www.hannaford.com, or obtain it in the form of the 10-K, the company's annual report to the Securities and Exchange Commission. That data is available from the SEC web site www.SEC.gov, or can be reached via links from many financial web sites. Some of these sites are listed at the end of this and other chapters.

III. Analysis of Financial Statements

EXHIBIT 1-6 Inventory Methods and the Impact on Earnings

Balance Sheet Impacts		Inventory Method		
Date	Action	First-In, First-Out (FIFO)	Last-In, First-Out (LIFO)	Average Cost
Jan. 1	Buy 10 units at $10 each	$ 100.0	$ 100.0	$ 100.0
Jan. 15	Buy 10 units at $15 each	150.0	150.0	150.0
Jan. 15	Inventory value	250.0	250.0	250.0
Jan. 16	Use 10 units in manufacturing, sell item and move inventory cost to cost of goods sold	(100.0)	(150.0)	(125.0)
Jan. 16	Inventory balance	$ 150.0	$ 100.0	$ 125.0
Income Statement Jan. 1–Jan. 16				
Revenues from sale of 10 units at $25		$ 250.0	$ 250.0	$ 250.0
Cost of goods sold		(100.0)	(150.0)	(125.0)
Operating income		150.0	100.0	125.0
Other expenses		(75.0)	(75.0)	(75.0)
Net income before taxes		75.0	25.0	50.0
Taxes (@ 34%)		(25.5)	(8.5)	(17.0)
Net income		$ 49.5	$ 16.5	$ 33.0

exhibit you can see that the choice of inventory method can make quite a difference, and can distort comparisons between companies with different methods. You need to look only at the inventory balance and net income figures to see the magnitude of the differences that come only from the accounting method. Over time the results are identical.

Before drawing conclusions over time or between companies, the analyst must be aware of the choices that exist and determine what approach is being used. Although in many countries notes to financial statements summarize some of the significant accounting principles, the analyst should be aware of the impact that accounting methods and changes in them can have on the reported performance of a company. Because obtaining information on the differences that exist in accounting principles between countries can be difficult to obtain and tedious to absorb, we have included an appendix to this chapter, "Cross-Border Ratio Analysis," to aid the reader. In addition, there are sources for this information listed at the end of the appendix.

Third, because of the variability of seasonal funds flows and requirements in some businesses, the analyst should be aware of the timing of the reporting. For some companies in highly seasonal or cyclical industries, comparisons of results from different reporting periods should be approached cautiously.[16]

---

[16] One thing that could be done is to compare ratios at the same time from year to year, or to adjust the numbers for seasonal peaks and troughs.

Despite these concerns, an analyst can develop an insightful examination of a corporation's financial performance. The most common method of analyzing financial statements is the use of ratios. These ratios are simple mathematical relationships between various items on financial statements. This chapter will describe the most commonly used ratios. In addition to the commonly used ratios described and demonstrated in this chapter, most analysts develop and use specialized ratios to examine specific companies or industries. While you need to be able to compute the ratios, the important analytical skill is in determining which ratios to use in each case and interpreting the results: the ratios, by themselves, are relatively meaningless. Only by comparing ratios over time and between companies—and by determining the underlying causes of the differences among them—does ratio analysis help the shareholder, lender, employee, analyst, portfolio manager, or manager gain insight into corporate performance.

The key ratios commonly used for analyzing the internal performance of a company can be categorized into four groups: (1) profitability ratios, (2) asset utilization or efficiency ratios, (3) capitalization or financial leverage ratios, and (4) market ratios. For each group there is a key ratio that summarizes the company's performance in that area. These key ratios can be combined to determine the rate at which the company can grow in the future without major changes—the sustainable rate of growth.

Let's first turn to the company's profits, and how to gauge it.

1. Profitability Analysis Using Ratios

Analysts use a number of methods to determine the relative profitability of a company. The key ratio is called the **return on sales** (ROS), which relates a company's net earnings or income to its sales.[17] This ratio is also referred to as **net profit ratio** or **profit margin**. Using data from the Hannaford Bros. Co.'s annual financial statements, this ratio is calculated as follows.[18]

$$\text{Return on sales} = \frac{\text{Net income}}{\text{Net sales}}$$

$$= \frac{\$94,647}{\$3,323,588}$$

$$= 0.0285 \text{ or } 2.85\%$$

This ratio tells us what percentage of each dollar of revenue is available for the owners (the shareholders) after all the expenses are paid to other suppliers. For Hannaford the net income is $0.0285 for every $1.00 of revenue.

---

[17] Net sales are generally net of discounts, returns, and allowances to customers. If no net sales figure is reported, analysts use total sales or revenues.

[18] The 1998 Hannaford Bros. financial data will be used in the remainder of the chapter to illustrate calculation of ratios. Note that because the financial statements report performance in thousands of dollars, all the numbers in this chapter are in thousands, unless otherwise noted.

III. Analysis of Financial Statements

Within every industry there is variation: some companies are more profitable than others; some industry segments have superior earnings; some countries provide better profit environments than do others. In an industry that is domestic and international, and consists of small, large, and specialized grocers, Hannaford operates as a large U.S. grocer. Hannaford's ROS of 2.9 percent is better than the 2.5 percent average for large U.S. grocers but lower than the return of 3.1 percent for specialty grocers. The specialty grocers are the health-food oriented grocers like Whole Foods and Wild Oats, grocers that do not compete on price alone. Foreign grocers had the lowest performance in 1998 with an ROS of 2.3 percent. While the differences seem small, on a percentage basis being in the right segment and country can make quite a difference. By the way, these differences were not only for 1998.

The differences between companies in different industries are even more dramatic. Exhibit 1-7 shows the ROS for a number of industries in the United States in 1998. As you can see, there is a wide range of profit margins among industries operating in one country. The profitability of companies differs among industry groups and depends on their competitive situations. For example, grocery stores, like Hannaford, operate with very low profit margins because competition in this industry tends to be based on low prices.[19] On the other hand, profit margins in industries with highly differentiated products are generally much higher, and the volume of sales of each item can be much lower.

In addition to the differences in ROS among industries, profitability can change for any company or industry over time. Hannaford, and most grocers,

EXHIBIT 1-7   1998 Return on Sales—Various U.S. Industries

	Return on Sales
Airline transport	0.3%
Apparel manufacturers	8.8
Asset management	19.9
Brewers	−2.7
Computer manufacturers	3.1
Computer peripherals	−6.3
Direct marketing	−1.0
Electric housewares	7.7
Forest products	3.0
Furniture and fixtures	4.8
Newspapers	15.4
Steel manufacturing	3.5
Temporary service agencies	1.7
Tires and rubber goods	5.9
Hannaford	2.9

SOURCE: Data from Morningstar *Principia Pro for Stocks*.

---

[19] To cover all costs, and make a profit for shareholders, high volume is typical in this industry.

have a relatively steady ROS over time: over 10 years the ROS varied from 2.2 percent in 1992 to a high of 2.9 percent in 1993 and 1998.[20] Cyclical companies usually have much lower returns on sales at the bottom of a business cycle when costs tend to be high, but prices have been kept low in an effort to lure the few buyers that exist. At the top of a cycle, companies are able to raise or maintain their prices and, since they are operating close to capacity, fixed costs per unit tend to be low.[21] The automobile industry is an example of a cyclical industry. Exhibit 1-8 shows the profits of one of its major participants, General Motors, since 1989. The impact of the business cycle on the profitability of this company is clear. This example demonstrates how important it is for the analyst to know and understand the nature of a company's business to properly interpret ratios.

The return on sales is the key profitability ratio. This ratio tells the analyst what proportion of the revenues remain after all expenses are met. However, when the analyst sees significant changes in the ROS over time or relative to other companies, more information is needed: the analyst needs to examine what contributed to the return on sales. Looking at the expenses can do this.

Companies make and sell products in many ways. Companies with low profit margins may have high costs of production; high marketing, selling, or

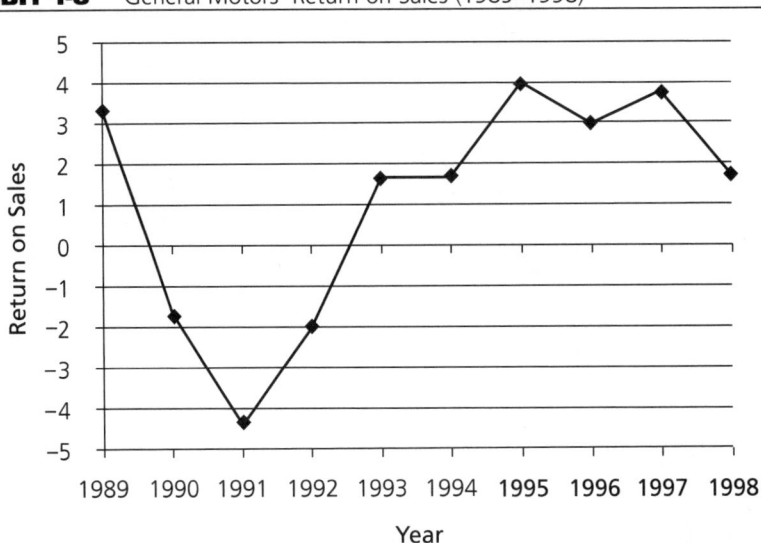

EXHIBIT 1-8   General Motors' Return on Sales (1989–1998)

[20] This ignores the unusual charge in 1997 that dropped the ROS from almost 3 to 1.8 percent. The adjustment is useful to show the operating realities.

[21] The relationship between fixed and variable costs is known as break-even analysis. This analysis shows at what level of sales revenues the company's fixed and variable costs are fully covered, with no profit.

research expenses; or a combination of these. Changes in profitability reflect changes in some or all of these costs. Thus, as a first step in understanding the sources of profitability, many analysts look at the profit a company earns after direct costs of production. This ratio is called the **gross margin** or **gross profit**. Gross margin is net revenues minus cost of goods sold.

$$\text{Gross margin} = \frac{\text{Gross profit}}{\text{Net sales}}$$

$$= \frac{\$843{,}242}{\$3{,}323{,}588}$$

$$= 0.2537 \text{ or } 25.37\%$$

For Hannaford, the gross margin was 25.4 percent. This means that 74.6 percent of every dollar of revenue Hannaford earned was used to cover the direct costs of producing or obtaining the products it sold. Because the net profit margin was 2.9 percent, the rest of the company's profits, 22.5 percent, went to cover all other expenses such as the costs of administration, including interest on debt, research and development, and taxes.

Another ratio can be used to determine the relative profitability of a company after all costs except taxes: **operating profit/sales**. Operating profit or margin is gross profit minus operating expenses such as selling, general, and administrative expenses.

$$\text{Operating profit/Sales} = \frac{\text{Operating profit}}{\text{Net sales}}$$

$$= \frac{\$178{,}885}{\$3{,}323{,}588}$$

$$= 0.0538 \text{ or } 5.38\%$$

Hannaford's gross margin or profit was 25.4 percent; the operating margin was 5.4 percent. The difference between the two, 20 percent, was the portion of net sales that Hannaford spent on nonproduction-related expenses. This portion can vary substantially over time and among companies. How much a company spends on nonproduction-related expenses depends, among other things, on the importance of new product development and the efficiency of corporate headquarters.

Analysts who want to know how profitably a company produces and markets its goods, not how inexpensively it finances itself, may calculate yet another ratio, **EBIT/sales**. **EBIT** stands for earnings before interest and taxes.

$$\text{EBIT/Sales} = \frac{\text{Earnings before interest and taxes}}{\text{Net sales}}$$

$$= \frac{\$178{,}885}{\$3{,}323{,}588}$$

$$= 0.0538 \text{ or } 5.38\%$$

You will note that Hannaford's EBIT/sales is the same as its operating profit/sales ratio because Hannaford had no other nonoperating-related expenses except taxes and interest charges.

The final profitability ratio that is in widespread use, particularly among stock analysts, is **EBITDA**. Actually the ratio is **EBITDA/sales** or EBITDA/revenues, with EBITDA standing for earnings before interest, taxes, depreciation, and amortization. Using this ratio the analyst attempts to eliminate all the outside influences and timing effects on the company's profitability figure. Thus financing costs, interest, depreciation, timing of the capital expenses as dictated by tax authorities, and taxes are ignored in calculating EBITDA. For Hannaford, operating profit was $178,885, but this included depreciation expenses of $96,739. The EBITDA was the sum of the two, $275,624.[22]

$$\text{EBITDA/Sales} = \frac{\text{EBITDA}}{\text{Sales}}$$

$$= \frac{\$178,885 + \$96,739}{\$3,323,588}$$

$$= \frac{\$275,624}{\$3,323,588}$$

$$= 0.0829 \text{ or } 8.29\%$$

The EBITDA ratio is one that has gained widespread acceptance among financial analysts, especially investment analysts, as they attempt to find a ratio that represents real cash earnings, earnings not impacted by such things as the differences in tax treatment of assets.[23] It is also believed that this ratio is more comparable for companies using different accounting practices or when comparing companies that use different accounting systems. In an increasingly global world where analysts follow industries with companies operating under different accounting and tax rules, a ratio that reduces the tax/accounting-induced differences is a very valuable tool.[24]

2. Profitability Analysis Using Common-Size Statements

Another approach analysts use to examine the profitability and expenses of a company is called the **component percentage analysis**. The results of this

---

[22] The EBIT figure comes from the income statement in Exhibit 1-1. Since Hannaford does not report depreciation on the income statement as a separate item, the depreciation figure comes from the consolidated cash flow statement (Exhibit 1-3).

[23] This ratio is used as a proxy for cash earnings. This is similar to the cash flow figure discussed extensively in Chapters 4, 5, and 7. The canny analyst will calculate EBITDA eliminating depreciation and interest impacts and EBIT.

[24] Few analysts really want to know all the different accounting and tax rules in every country where they research companies. While an analyst with accounting/tax rule knowledge may understand the business performance better or uncover hidden liabilities or assets, the fact is that quick comparisons are important, and EBITDA helps the global analyst do the job better.

analysis are called **common-size statements**. To calculate component percentages, the analyst simply relates each cost or profit reported on the income statement to that period's revenues or sales.[25] Such an analysis is useful when looking at the company's performance over time. A component analysis of the Hannaford income statements for 1997 and 1998 is shown in Exhibit 1-9. While ratios may tell an interesting story, this analysis shows in detail the cost-revenue relationships for the company.

3. Profitability Using Growth Rates

Of great interest to those looking at a company's financial performance is how rapidly various items are growing, in particular revenues and profits. Indeed, these particular growth rates have their own names: top-line growth for revenues, and bottom-line growth for profits. Like the common-size statements we can look not only at the growth of the revenues and profits, but at each of the expense items as well.[26] In Exhibit 1-10 you can see the result of the growth rate analysis for Hannaford over the last five years. In particular, you will notice the dramatic drop that occurred in profits in 1997. The reason is not readily obvious, but recall that in 1997 Hannaford took an "impairment loss" and did so in no other year.[27] Had Hannaford not taken the impairment loss in

EXHIBIT 1-9   Hannaford Bros. Co.

PERCENTAGE COMPONENTS FOR STATEMENT OF EARNINGS (dollars in thousands)

Summary of Operations:	1998 Dollars	1998 Percentage	1997 Dollars	1997 Percentage
Sales and other revenues	$3,323,588	100.00%	$3,226,433	100.00%
Cost of sales	2,480,346	74.63	2,427,287	75.23
Gross margin	843,242	25.37	799,146	24.77
Selling, general, and administrative expenses	664,357	19.99	635,355	19.69
Impairment loss	0	0.00	39,950	1.24
Operating profit	178,885	5.38	123,841	3.84
Interest expense, net	26,577	0.80	26,425	0.82
Earnings before income taxes and minority interest	152,308	4.58	97,416	3.02
Income taxes	57,661	1.73	37,769	1.17
Net earnings	$ 94,647	2.85%	$ 59,647	1.85%

---

[25] This form of ratio analysis also can be used to examine the composition of various items on the balance sheet. The comparison is of each asset, liability, or equity account with the total assets.

[26] This is particularly easy with a computer spreadsheet approach.

[27] This was a loss taken in advance of what management believed were certain losses from the sale of acquired stores.

EXHIBIT 1-10   Hannaford Bros. Co.

GROWTH RATES OF INCOME STATEMENT ITEMS, 1994–1998

Summary of Operations:	1998	1997	1996	1995	1994
Sales and other revenues	3.0%	9.1%	15.2%	12.1%	11.5%
Cost of sales	2.2	8.2	14.9	12.9	12.0
Gross margin	5.5	11.8	15.9	9.5	10.2
Selling, general, and administrative expenses	4.6	11.9	18.1	9.9	9.5
Operating profit	44.4	−15.6	8.1	8.0	12.7
Interest expense, net	0.6	19.0	14.6	−9.3	10.5
Earnings before income taxes and minority interest	56.3	−21.8	7.0	11.6	13.2
Income taxes	52.7	−23.4	6.7	9.9	11.9
Net earnings	58.7	−20.7	7.1	12.7	9.8

1997, profit growth would have been over 32 percent, and the dramatic profit growth of 1998 would have been a negative 5 percent.

This growth rate analysis shows how well the company is progressing, and how well it is keeping the expense and profit items in line with each other. You can also look at the growth rate of asset and liability accounts using this same type of analysis. Growth rate analysis is quite telling, and is particularly useful when we use the past as a basis for forecasting the future. We will do this in Chapter 2. However, you must take care: the growth rate analysis could be flawed. Various outside influences can dramatically impact the growth rates and lull the unsuspecting analyst into a false sense of robust growth. There are two outside influences worth noting particularly. They are growth by expansion or acquisition, and inflation.

The growth by acquisition or expansion can mask natural growth, growth that comes as a result of growing sales alone. For example, can we tell how well Hannaford was actually growing at its existing locations? Is growth coming from the purchase of new stores? It is difficult to tell since they were adding stores. Analysts have used a variety of ways to determine the rate of natural growth: sales per square foot and same-store sales. **Same-store sales**, sales from stores owned in both periods, has become a widely used way to discuss this natural growth independently of expansion and acquisition. Hannaford calls it "identical store sales" and reports that the sales growth in stores owned in both years was 1.3 percent. This is in contrast to total sales growth of 3 percent in 1998.

The second and perhaps the most insidious problem in understanding growth is inflation. Let's demonstrate what inflation can do to a simple analysis and its interpretation. Exhibit 1-11 shows the income statement for a company with and without inflation's impacts exposed. The figures with inflation are called **nominal**; those without are **real**.

III. Analysis of Financial Statements

EXHIBIT 1-11 Growth Analysis With and Without Inflation—Hypothetical Company

In Currency	2000	1999	1998	1997	1996
Revenues	293	266	242	220	200
Cost of goods sold	(190)	(173)	(157)	(143)	(130)
Gross income	103	93	85	77	70
Selling, general, and administrative expenses	(73)	(67)	(61)	(55)	(50)
Operating income	30	26	24	22	20
Taxes	(12)	(11)	(10)	(9)	(8)
Net income	18	15	14	13	12

Nominal Growth Rate	2000	1999	1998	1997
Revenues	10%	10%	10%	10%
Cost of goods sold	10	10	10	10
Gross income	10	10	10	10
Selling, general, and administrative expenses	10	10	10	10
Operating income	10	10	10	10
Taxes	10	10	10	10
Net income	10	10	10	10

Real Growth Rates				
Revenues	−2%	0%	3%	5%
Cost of goods sold	−2	0	3	5
Gross income	−2	0	3	5
Selling, general, and administrative expenses	−2	0	3	5
Operating income	−2	0	3	5
Taxes	−2	0	3	5
Net income	−2	0	3	5
Inflation	12%	10%	7%	5%

Factoring out inflation-driven growth gives us quite a different view of a company's real growth over this period. If we had not included the impacts of inflation, we might have believed this company was growing at a steady 10 percent. However, it was not. The numbers masked a deterioration in all categories. After inflation, our hypothetical company actually declined in the final year of our example. This is critical to know and would have been missed if we had not done our analysis in real terms.

How extensive such an analysis of real growth should be depends, in part, on how the analyst will use the results and how extreme the conditions were. In 1999, when U.S. inflation had been at record low levels for some time, such an analysis seems extraneous. It is not when change is rapid or general or specific inflation is high.[28] However, the U.S. is not all of the world, and high inflation does exist in countries around the world. Furthermore, while general inflation is low, inflation in such things as wages may be ready to escalate. Thus, while inflation is not so interesting at the moment, moments change, conditions change, and the understanding of different kinds of analysis is always very useful.

4. Asset Utilization Ratios

Once the analyst has examined the company's expenses and profits, the next area of interest is the assets. A company typically acquires assets for use in producing sales revenues and ultimately, profits. **Asset utilization ratios** indicate how effectively or efficiently a company uses its assets. These asset utilization ratios are called **efficiency** or **turnover ratios**. The information needed to calculate these ratios is taken from both the statement of earnings and the statement of financial position.

To start, the analyst would look at how efficiently the company is using all its assets. The ratio used to do this is the **total asset turnover** (TATO). This ratio measures what also is called **operating leverage**.

$$\text{Total asset turnover} = \frac{\text{Net sales}}{\text{Assets}}$$

$$= \frac{\$3,323,588}{\$1,284,538}$$

$$= 2.587 \text{ or } 259\%[29]$$

Hannaford's sales were 259 percent of its year-end 1998 assets. Is this good or bad? You will need to consider the kind of business in which the company operates before drawing a conclusion. The nature of the grocery industry dictates a high utilization of assets: its inventory contains a large percentage of perishables that must be sold quickly. Other industries are inherently different. Compare Hannaford's ratio to that of other U.S. industries shown in Exhibit 1-12. The differences in asset utilization, that is, capital intensity, are dramatic.[30]

---

[28] To use an example from late 1999: In September 1999, Taiwan had a massive earthquake. While the initial news was about the devastation and the cost in human suffering, the news in the financial press rapidly turned to computer-chip scarcity. A significant portion of the world's computer chips were sourced from this one island, and the impact on the industry and the cost of chips, the inflation story, was unknown. This was one of the things that contributed to the precipitous drop in the U.S. stock market in mid-September 1999.

[29] We report this and all ratios, except the price/earnings ratio, as a percentage. Some analysts and reporting services report some ratios as a multiple. For instance, you might see 2.59X or 259 percent reported for the total asset turnover ratio. Obviously you must be consistent in your analysis and when using data from another source.

[30] **Capital intensity** is the degree to which capital goods—property, plant, and equipment— rather than labor are used to produce products. If products are produced with a high level of labor and little capital investment, the production process is called **labor intensive**.

EXHIBIT 1-12 1998 Return on Assets—Various U.S. Industries

	Return on Sales	Total Asset Turnover	ROA
Airline transport	0.3%	1.6x	0.5%
Apparel manufacturers	8.8	1.9	16.7
Asset management	19.9	0.7	13.9
Brewers	−2.7	0.8	−2.2
Computer manufacturers	3.1	1.9	5.9
Computer peripherals	−6.3	1.3	−8.2
Direct marketing	−1.0	2.4	−2.4
Electric housewares	7.7	1.2	9.2
Forest products	3.0	0.8	2.4
Furniture and fixtures	4.8	1.7	8.2
Newspapers	15.4	0.7	10.8
Steel manufacturing	3.5	1.9	6.7
Temporary service agencies	1.7	3.4	5.8
Tires and rubber goods	5.9	1.3	7.7
Hannaford Bros.	2.9	2.6	7.5

SOURCE: Data from Morningstar *Principia Pro for Stocks*.

However, if you think about it, the differences are not surprising. For example, you might have suspected that manufacturing companies would need considerable assets to produce their product, and you can see that they do. Supermarkets, at least on this list, turn out to be quite asset efficient.

For the rookie analyst, a little care must be taken in calculating this ratio. For instance, if the company has had a large increase or decrease in its assets during the year, average assets might be a better figure to use than period-end total assets.[31] There is one other note of caution when making comparisons: be certain that the ratios are calculated in a similar fashion when comparing data provided by others or over time. While a consistent use of average assets is preferable, most reported ratios are based on the year-end asset figure. For Hannaford the problem is mute: the company had only a modest change in assets over the year. Thus, for Hannaford, the analyst may use either ending or average assets to calculate the total asset turnover ratio.[32]

Using the total asset turnover ratio alone does not lead the analyst to any firm conclusions about a company's efficiency. However, when the information is joined with information about the nature of the business, the industry, and economic conditions, the skilled analyst can gain real insight.[33] In spite of its

---

[31] Since we are comparing the size of the asset base at a point in time with income or with revenue earned over time, a good analyst will determine whether significant changes in the accounts did occur over the period and, if so, how to adapt the ratios.

[32] In some cases the beginning, ending, and average numbers are all needed to tell a complete story.

[33] Hannaford's financial performance will be compared across time and with others in its industry later in this chapter.

limitations, TATO has another very useful property: by multiplying TATO by ROS, we can calculate the **return on assets** (ROA).

$$\text{Return on assets} = \text{Return on sales} \times \text{Total asset turnover}$$
$$= \frac{\text{Net income}}{\text{Net sales}} \times \frac{\text{Net sales}}{\text{Assets}}$$
$$= \frac{\text{Net income}}{\text{Assets}}$$

Using this relationship for Hannaford, the ROA is calculated as follows:

$$\text{ROA} = \text{ROS} \times \text{TATO}$$
$$= 0.0285 \times 2.587$$
$$= 0.0737 \text{ or } 7.37\%$$

One can, of course, calculate the ROA directly:

$$\text{ROA} = \frac{\text{Net income}}{\text{Assets}}$$
$$= \frac{\$94,647}{\$1,284,538}$$
$$= 0.0737 \text{ or } 7.37\%$$

By understanding this relationship, you can see why capital-intensive companies have lower returns on assets, all other things being equal, than do service companies with fewer assets. The asset efficiencies and the returns on assets for various industries are shown in Exhibit 1-12.

Two industries typify the cost of being capital intensive. Asset management, the most capital intensive of the list, actually has a lower ROA than its ROS. For the next most capital intensive, brewers, that is an advantage: the negative ROS is not greatly impacted by the operating leverage. Temporary service agencies demonstrate the reverse. They have a low ROS, but high operating leverage and low investment in capital assets results in a greatly enhanced ROA.

After examining the overall asset efficiency of a company, you, or any analyst, will probably want to delve into the way the company uses some or all of its assets.[34] This is particularly true if you find the asset efficiency to be different from what was expected or has changed over time. If it is different, what should be the logical next step? The next step is to look at the assets themselves. Let's start with the biggest assets.

---

[34] All this analysis is like detective work. When you find a clue you are urged to dig deeper. Some analysts say it is like peeling an onion: the more layers you remove the more there are, until you are crying.

III. Analysis of Financial Statements

For most companies, especially manufacturers and retailers, inventory is a very large asset. This asset can get out of control. The ratio that will help you understand how the company has used its inventory is the **inventory turnover ratio**.

$$\text{Inventory turnover} = \frac{\text{Cost of sales}}{\text{Inventory}}$$

$$= \frac{\$2{,}480{,}346}{\$201{,}219}$$

$$= 12.33 \text{ times or } 1{,}233\%$$

This ratio indicates the percentage of Hannaford's inventory that was sold and replaced during the reporting period, in this case one year. Since Hannaford is a grocery chain we would expect the inventory turnover to be rapid, and it is: about once each month. Other industries are typified by long inventory turnovers. You can think of why jewelry stores, with their high-value infrequently sold inventory, and liquor producers, with their long-maturation process, might have very slow inventory turnovers.

As with every ratio there are some nuances. This is the case with the inventory turnover. First, like the total asset turnover ratio, if inventory grew substantially during the year, average inventory may be a more accurate denominator for the ratio. Second, the numerator should be cost of sales rather than net sales: cost of sales does not include the profit portion of net sales and leaves only the production costs.[35] Third, you may want to look beyond a total inventory analysis. Finally, it is important to remember that the quality of the information contained in this ratio depends on how the company values its inventory.

Let's look a bit more closely at two of these nuances. First, let's look beyond the total inventory, the figure reported by Hannaford. Other companies, like manufacturers, report their inventories at each stage of the production process: raw materials, work-in-process, and finished goods.[36] An analysis of these pieces can be very instructive. If finished goods rose, what might be the cause of rapid increases in the finished goods inventory? It could come from falling sales or an inventory buildup before a seasonal peak. If the raw materials balance rose, what might be the cause of a rapid buildup of raw materials? It could come from stockpiling in advance of potential shortages or price increases, or from an overabundance of obsolete inventory. The total inventory figure may mask these rapid changes.

The second inventory-related item we should take into account concerns the way in which inventory is valued. Every company must choose a way to

---

[35] If the net sales total were used, and the company had high prices relative to costs, the ratio would be higher than the actual inventory turnover.
[36] Hannaford does not since it is not a manufacturer.

value its inventory. You might think this is easy, but in fact it can make quite a difference in the company's performance. In Exhibit 1-6 you saw the impact of different inventory methods on net income and taxes. While the example is for a rather static environment over a short period of time, imagine the same inventory valuations with rapidly changing costs when goods are kept in inventory for a long time. Clearly, the method of inventory valuation is important in times of high or rapidly changing rates of inflation and deflation, and changes in the prices of raw materials due to changes in technology or supplier power.

Keeping these caveats in mind, a high inventory turnover ratio indicates that the company is using its financial resources efficiently by maintaining low inventories. Hannaford's inventory turnover is relatively quick.[37] The nature of some companies' production processes—for instance, aircraft manufacturers—makes achieving a high inventory turnover ratio impossible, while others, like grocery stores, deal in more perishable items and thus would be expected to have a rapid turnover of inventory.

This inventory turnover ratio also can be expressed in terms of the number of days goods are held in inventory using the following approach.

$$\text{Days' inventory} = \frac{\text{Inventory}}{\text{Cost of sales}} \times 365^{[38]}$$

$$= \frac{\$201{,}219}{\$2{,}480{,}346} \times 365$$

$$= 29.6 \text{ days}$$

This same analysis can be done for each of the different kinds of inventory.

Because Hannaford has a TATO ratio that is lower than its inventory turnover ratio, we will want to look at how efficiently other assets are being utilized by the company. For instance, it would make sense to look at the **accounts receivable**, the sales made for credit for which payment has not been received. The ratio of **accounts receivable to net sales** indicates the relative proportion of the company's sales made on credit and still outstanding at the end of the reporting period.

$$\text{Accounts receivable/Net sales} = \frac{\text{Accounts receivable}}{\text{Net sales}}$$

$$= \frac{\$22{,}869}{\$3{,}323{,}588}$$

$$= 0.0069 \text{ or } 0.69\%$$

---

[37] You might have expected a grocer's turnover to be more rapid since it stocks and sells perishables. However, the perishables—dairy, produce, and meat—account for only a portion of what is sold in the modern grocery store.

[38] We use 365 days as the calendar year. While some analysts choose to reduce it by the five legal U.S. holidays, since assets are held by the company all 365 days regardless of the work habits of the employees, 365 is the appropriate number.

III. Analysis of Financial Statements

As you can see, of the sales made by Hannaford in 1998, approximately 0.7 percent remained unpaid at the end of the year.[39] This is certainly what we would have expected from a grocery store chain where virtually all sales are made for cash or paid for with credit or debit cards.

Creative analysts developed a variation of this ratio that converts the percentage of sales into the length of time the average account receivable is unpaid or outstanding. Many find **days' sales outstanding** or the **receivables collection period** easier to interpret and more informative than the accounts receivable/net sales ratio. To calculate the days in receivables, simply multiply the accounts receivable/net sales ratio by the number of days in the year.

$$\text{Days' sales outstanding} = \frac{\text{Accounts receivable}}{\text{Net sales}} \times 365$$

$$= \frac{\$22,869}{\$3,323,588} \times 365$$

$$= 2.5 \text{ days}$$

Obviously, companies that sell their products on credit, such as furniture manufacturers, will have long collection periods. Grocery chains, like Hannaford, that offer little or no credit will have low receivables and very short collection periods: Hannaford's customers paid their bills in an average of 2.5 days.[40] Given the nature of the supermarket industry, the extremely low days' sales outstanding is not surprising. Of course the analyst will want to look at the trend in accounts receivable over time and how the company is doing relative to others in the industry.[41]

Management and lenders may want to look closely at the receivables. In some companies most customers pay on time, but some are slow to clear this account. This is especially true with problem companies or in problem economies. To deal with this lenders and management may want to look at an **aging of accounts receivable**: the accounts receivable are broken into groups by the length of time the account has been overdue. This is a particularly useful way to understand abnormally long collection periods when the ratio is skewed by a single large account that has been overdue for a long time. It requires internal information, so it is best used by corporate analysts or lenders with considerable inside information.

Not only are assets of interest, but the analysts may be interested in the efficiency with which the company manages its short-term liabilities.[42] For in-

---

[39] Had we wanted to know the average accounts receivable outstanding over the year, we could have used average accounts receivable in the ratio.
[40] Credit and debit card charges clear to the company's benefit almost immediately.
[41] The analyst should also determine what normal credit terms are for the company and industry. Most companies that offer credit have standard credit terms such as 2/10 net 30. This means that there is a 2 percent discount for bills that are paid within 10 days, but the full amount is due within 30 days. When such policies exist, the actual accounts receivable ratios should be compared to the terms that are offered.
[42] Some analysts consider this a leverage ratio.

stance, the company's suppliers might wonder how much the company owes to its suppliers in relation to what it purchased from them. To determine this, the ratio of **accounts payable to purchases** would be used. Since most external analysts do not have access to the amount the company purchases over any period, the ratio of **accounts payable to cost of sales** is typically substituted.

$$\text{Accounts payable/Cost of sales} = \frac{\text{Accounts payable}}{\text{Cost of sales}}$$

$$= \frac{\$186{,}626}{\$2{,}480{,}346}$$

$$= 0.0752 \text{ or } 7.52\%$$

Another way to see how promptly the company is paying its obligations is to measure the **payables payment period**.

$$\text{Payables payment period} = \frac{\text{Accounts payable}}{\text{Cost of sales}} \times 365$$

$$= \frac{\$186{,}626}{\$2{,}480{,}346} \times 365$$

$$= 27.5 \text{ days}$$

Hannaford pays its suppliers much more slowly than its customers pay Hannaford. Companies that use their suppliers as a major source of funding, such as Hannaford, will have longer payables payment periods.[43]

For companies with seasonal sales, care must be taken when calculating this ratio as well as when calculating days' sales outstanding and the inventory turnover ratio. When a company's sales have grown substantially over a period or the company has seasonal sales, using the annual cost of sales may inflate or deflate the ratios and provide an unrealistic look at the actual patterns experienced by the company. In such situations some analysts calculate monthly ratios based on the cost of sales for that month, or an average for several months during the same season, rather than using the annual figure.

In addition to, or in place of, these ratios, the analyst may perform a **component percentage analysis** of the company's balance sheet. In this analysis, also known as a common-size statement, each asset, liability, and equity account balance is compared with the total asset figure.[44] This analysis is especially useful for comparing changes over time. Such a component analysis is shown in Exhibit 1-13.

---

[43] In Chapter 2 we discuss the working capital cycle. This cycle includes the disparity between the payment from customers and to suppliers as a source of working capital for a company. The difference for Hannaford is 25 days. This is the time Hannaford keeps its suppliers' capital (does not pay its accounts payable), 27.5 days, less the time it takes its customers to pay their bills, 2.5 days.

[44] A variation of this component-size analysis is to compare each asset to the sales for the year. This allows the analyst to see what relationships exist between sales and the assets.

EXHIBIT 1-13 Hannaford Bros. Co.

COMPONENT ANALYSIS OF BALANCE SHEET ITEMS AS OF DECEMBER 31, 1997 AND 1998 (dollars in thousands)

Assets	1998 Dollars	1998 Percentages	1997 Dollars	1997 Percentages
Current assets:				
Cash and cash equivalents	$ 59,722	4.65%	$ 57,663	4.70%
Accounts receivable, net	22,869	1.78	14,918	1.22
Inventories	201,219	15.66	188,767	15.38
Prepaid expenses	6,116	0.48	7,801	0.64
Deferred income taxes	5,952	0.46	6,912	0.56
Total current assets	295,878	23.03	276,061	22.50
Property, plant, and equipment, net	823,368	64.10	777,909	63.39
Leased property under capital leases, net	54,911	4.27	58,516	4.77
Other assets:				
Goodwill, net	63,517	4.94	67,552	5.50
Deferred charges, net	25,074	1.95	28,724	2.34
Computer software costs, net	19,318	1.50	16,551	1.35
Miscellaneous assets	2,472	0.19	1,877	0.15
Total other assets	110,381	8.59	114,704	9.35
Total assets	$1,284,538	100.00%	$1,227,190	100.00%
Liabilities and Shareholders' Equity				
Current liabilities:				
Current maturities of long-term debt	$ 19,296	1.50%	$ 18,155	1.48%
Obligations under capital leases	2,108	0.16	1,873	0.15
Accounts payable	186,626	14.53	182,252	14.85
Accrued payroll	27,254	2.12	25,526	2.08
Other accrued expenses	23,873	1.86	24,553	2.00
Income taxes	442	0.03	2,829	0.23
Total current liabilities	259,599	20.21	255,188	20.79
Deferred income tax liabilities	28,859	2.25	18,265	1.49
Other liabilities	38,734	3.02	41,171	3.35
Long-term debt	220,130	17.14	235,850	19.22
Obligations under capital leases	73,866	5.75	75,687	6.17
Shareholders' equity:				
Common stock, par value $.75 per share Authorized 110,000 shares; 42,338 and 42,338 shares issued.	31,754	2.47	31,754	2.59
Additional paid-in capital	109,664	8.54	115,130	9.38
Preferred stock purchase rights	423	0.03	423	0.03
Retained earnings	525,344	40.90	456,063	37.16
Total equity	667,185	51.94	603,370	49.17
Less common stock in treasury	3,835	0.30	2,341	0.19
Total shareholders' equity	663,350	51.64	601,029	48.98
Total liabilities and shareholders' equity	$1,284,538	100.00%	$1,227,190	100.00%

Note: Some percentages totals may not add due to rounding.

You can see that Hannaford has had little change over the two years. In fact, it is only in the capital accounts where much has occurred at all.

Now that we have investigated the profitability and asset efficiency of the company, the next step is to see how the company has been financed. In the common-size balance sheet we saw some changes in the way the company was financed, and earlier we could have deduced from the low interest expense reported in the income statement that Hannaford either had little debt or that its debt was inexpensive. Let's see which is the case.

5. Capitalization Ratios

Capitalization or **financial leverage ratios** provide information about the sources the company has used to finance its investment in assets. The term **financial leverage** is used to indicate the impact debt financing has on the returns of the company to its owners, the shareholders. When the income generated by investment in assets is greater than the cost of debt, the equity holders will benefit from financing an increased amount of assets through borrowing. This is called leverage or, in some countries, particularly the U.K., **gearing**. Later we will see how financial leverage or gearing affects the return on equity. First, let's see how we measure a company's financial leverage.

The majority of the financial leverage ratios are based on information from a company's balance sheet. Of primary interest to a company's owners is how much of the company they have financed. To measure this we can use the **assets to equity ratio**. Because we want to know the company's position at the end of the year, we do not use averages of the accounts over the year. Instead, we use the balance at the end of the year.[45] For Hannaford, this ratio is calculated as follows:

$$\text{Assets to equity} = \frac{\text{Assets}}{\text{Shareholders' equity}}$$
$$= \frac{\$1,284,538}{\$663,350}$$
$$= 1.936 \text{ times or } 193.6\%$$

If the assets to equity ratio were 100 percent, the company would be totally financed by its owners. A higher ratio shows that a company finances some of its assets with debt—it is leveraged. The assets to equity ratio shows the proportion of the firm financed by its owners. When it is combined with ROA, we can find the return that shareholders earned on the book value of their investment in the company, the **return on equity** (ROE).[46]

---

[45] Once again, if the equity and/or assets have changed dramatically over the year or at any point in the year, we may need to calculate averages or to calculate the ratio at several points during the year to get a full picture of what happened.

[46] The **book value** is the value of the total equity reported on the statement of financial position, the balance sheet.

III. Analysis of Financial Statements

$$\text{Return on equity} = \text{ROS} \times \text{TATO} \times \text{Leverage}$$

$$= \frac{\text{Net income}}{\text{Net sales}} \times \frac{\text{Net sales}}{\text{Assets}} \times \frac{\text{Assets}}{\text{Equity}}$$

This can be reduced to

$$= \text{ROA} \times \text{Leverage}$$

Or

$$= \frac{\text{Net income}}{\text{Assets}} \times \frac{\text{Assets}}{\text{Equity}}$$

Or

$$= \frac{\text{Net income}}{\text{Equity}}$$

For Hannaford, the return on equity is calculated as follows:

$$\text{ROE} = \text{ROS} \times \text{TATO} \times \text{Leverage}$$
$$= 0.0285 \times 2.587 \times 1.936$$
$$= 0.1427 \text{ or } 14.27\%$$

We can use this set of ratios to test a potential change in operating or financial strategy. For instance, what if the company had been financed with more debt—for example, its assets to equity ratio was 300 percent? The ROE would have been 22.1 percent, 1.5 times its current level.[47] If the company had been financed by shareholders alone, the return on equity would have been 7.4 percent, exactly the same as the company's return on its assets. Finally, you can see that if the total asset turnover (TATO) and the assets to equity ratio were 100 percent, the ROS, ROA, and ROE all would be the same—2.85 percent.[48] The fewer assets a company uses to generate sales, and the more debt it uses to finance those assets, the higher the return shareholders can earn.

Financial leverage is a powerful thing. The impact of leverage on shareholders' return can be seen by looking at Exhibit 1-14. This exhibit shows the graph of the return on equity with different asset/equity levels. The returns can vary from a positive 10 percent to a loss of 10 percent, and are dramatically changed by financial leverage: the higher the company's financial leverage, the more the return on equity can vary as the return on assets changes.

You can also see the impact of financial leverage on the various industries shown in Exhibit 1-15. For example, the airline industry had a 0.3 percent return on sales, but a return on equity of 3.0 percent. This came as a result of the combined impacts of high operating leverage and very high financial leverage.

---

[47] This is determined by multiplying the ROS of 2.85 percent by the TATO of 258.7 percent by an asset to equity ratio of 300 percent.

[48] Here I have used the extremes, but you can test any number of different combinations.

EXHIBIT 1-14 Return on Equity at Different Levels of Financial Leverage

In contrast, low operational and financial leverage kept the brewers from experiencing greater losses.[49]

EXHIBIT 1-15 Industry Average Financial Leverage and Return on Equity, 1998

	Return on Sales	Total Asset Turnover	ROA	Assets/ Equity	ROE
Airline transport	0.3%	1.6x	−0.5%	6.3x	3.0%
Apparel manufacturers	8.8	1.9	16.7	2.2	36.8
Asset management	19.9	0.7	13.9	2.7	37.6
Brewers	−2.7	0.8	−2.2	1.5	−3.2
Computer manufacturers	3.1	1.9	5.9	2.4	14.1
Computer peripherals	−6.3	1.3	−8.2	2.3	18.8
Direct marketing	−1.0	2.4	−2.4	2.3	−5.5
Electric housewares	7.7	1.2	9.2	2.7	24.9
Forest products	3.0	0.8	2.4	3.2	7.7
Furniture and fixtures	4.8	1.7	8.2	2.1	17.1
Newspapers	15.4	0.7	10.8	3.0	32.3
Steel manufacturing	3.5	1.9	6.7	2.2	14.6
Temporary service agencies	1.7	3.4	5.8	2.3	13.3
Tires and rubber goods	5.9	1.3	7.7	2.1	16.1
Hannaford	2.9	2.6	7.5	1.9	14.3

SOURCE: Data from Morningstar *Principia Pro for Stocks*.

---

[49] However, if the brewers had a positive profit, the leverages would not have greatly enhanced the ROE. This is the up- and downside of operating and financial leverage.

III. Analysis of Financial Statements 33

Since Hannaford's assets to equity ratio is 194 percent, it has significant debt—in fact, 94 cents of debt for every dollar of equity. Is it too much? To determine whether this level of leverage is high, it will be useful to look at other capitalization ratios.

Shareholders are not the only people interested in the way a company finances itself. Lenders, who may provide a large portion of the company's capital resources, are especially interested in the way the company is capitalized. While they could certainly deduce their position from the ratio of assets to equity, they have developed ratios that show their position directly.[50] Two commonly used lender-perspective ratios are **long-term debt to equity** and **long-term debt to total assets**. For our Hannaford example, the first is calculated as follows:

$$\text{Total long-term debt to equity} = \frac{\text{Total long-term debt}}{\text{Equity}}$$

$$= \frac{\$315,400}{\$663,350}$$

$$= 0.4755 \text{ or } 47.55\%$$

And the second is calculated as follows:

$$\text{Total long-term debt to assets} = \frac{\text{Total long-term debt}}{\text{Assets}}$$

$$= \frac{\$315,400}{\$1,284,538}$$

$$= 0.2455 \text{ or } 24.55\%$$

Note that both these ratios used as long-term debt not only the long-term debt ($220,130), but also capital leases ($73,866), current maturities of the debt ($19,296), and the current capital lease obligations ($2,108). The capital leases were included because they constitute a long-term, contractual obligation that has many of the same features and obligations of debt.[51] Some analysts use only the long-term debt and do not include either the capital leases or the current maturities of either the long-term debt or the capital leases. Others omit the current portions, but include both the long-term debt and capital leases. The decision of what to use is up to the analyst, and reflects both the analyst's

---

[50] Debt/Assets is simply [1 − (Equity/Assets)].
[51] In determining the long-term debt of a company, analysts often disagree about the items to include. All the previous calculations included the capitalized leases and the current portions of long-term debt and capitalized leases. You might also include deferred taxes, long-term contingent liabilities, or other long-term liabilities. If these items are included, they must be included consistently throughout any analysis and comparisons. Whenever using ratios from a commercially available source, it is important to know what data is used in the calculations and how the calculations were performed. Not every source uses the same data or methodology.

concerns and the economic situation. It is critical with this ratio to observe how it is calculated when using others' data.

Another ratio looks only at the long-term debt, and does not include debt-like accounts. The long-term debt could be compared to equity, but in this ratio it is compared to the total capital of the company. The **long-term debt to total capital ratio** uses as total capital the sum of the long-term debt and equity used to finance the business. The ratio for Hannaford is calculated as follows:

$$\text{Long-term debt to total capital} = \frac{\text{Long-term debt}}{\text{Long-term debt} + \text{Equity}}$$

$$= \frac{\$220{,}130}{\$220{,}130 + \$663{,}550}$$

$$= 0.2491 \text{ or } 24.9\%$$

This ratio is sometimes confused with the total long-term debt to total assets ratio. Including all debt-like accounts that ratio would be 32.2 percent.

The appropriate size of capitalization ratios depends upon the perspective of the analyst, the nature of the company, and its situation. Lenders such as bondholders and bankers typically prefer low debt ratios, which provide greater security for their loans. Since equity investors' returns are improved by more leverage, shareholders generally prefer more leverage. This leverage provides a higher return on equity if the company is profitable.[52] Issues involved in determining the appropriate amount of debt—the appropriate capital structure—are discussed in Chapter 7.

Lenders and other sources of short-term capital—for instance, suppliers of goods to the company—also want to know how the company will meet its obligations. Since some companies use significant amounts of short-term debt to finance their operations, three ratios have been found to be useful for examining the situation: total liabilities to assets, the current ratio, and the acid-test ratio.[53] For Hannaford, the first of these, **total liabilities to assets**, is as follows:

$$\text{Total liabilities to assets} = \frac{\text{Total liabilities}}{\text{Total assets}}$$

$$= \frac{\$621{,}188}{\$1{,}284{,}538}$$

$$= 0.4836 \text{ or } 48.36\%$$

---

[52] High degrees of financial leverage also, in times of decreased revenues and profits, result in low or negative returns on equity. This is a dilemma. Lenders want less risk to preserve the principal; the shareholders want more risk since their downside is limited to zero but their upside is theoretically limitless. The managers want to do what is best for the owners, although not at the risk of their jobs. This is what economists call an agency problem: different interested parties, shareholders versus agents, have different interests.

[53] In this case we include the accounts payable as short-term debt. While they are not interest-bearing obligations, as is debt, the company has incurred the obligation. You may choose not to include them.

III. Analysis of Financial Statements

Over 48 percent of Hannaford's assets have been financed by lenders, including trade creditors, rather than by shareholders.

By any ratio we choose to use, Hannaford is a somewhat leveraged, or geared, company. Let's see if the leverage is of critical concern. One way to test the danger is to see if it can pay off its most immediate obligations if it were forced to do so.

The **current** and **acid-test ratios** measure the company's ability to pay its current liabilities using current assets. These ratios, also called **liquidity ratios**, reflect the size of short-term obligations. Hannaford's current ratio is calculated as follows:

$$\text{Current ratio} = \frac{\text{Current assets}}{\text{Current liabilities}}$$

$$= \frac{\$295{,}878}{\$259{,}599}$$

$$= 1.1398 \text{ or } 113.98\%$$

A current ratio greater than one is preferable.

Companies with high liquidity ratios are considered more liquid than those with low liquidity ratios: their short-term assets are greater than their short-term liabilities.[54] Being more liquid generally means that a company is better able to pay off its short-term obligations than is its less liquid peers. Hannaford is a relatively liquid company: its current ratio is 1.14 times or 114 percent. This means that Hannaford could pay off its current liabilities using the proceeds from its current assets alone. There is one catch, however. Some current assets are not as easy to turn into the cash as others. The current asset that is often hardest to turn into cash is inventory, and for Hannaford the single largest asset is inventory.

Since Hannaford's single largest current asset is its inventory, we can use another ratio, the **acid-test ratio**, also called the **quick ratio**, to test its real liquidity. This ratio is just like the current ratio, except we eliminate the assets that are not readily and rapidly turned into cash. In addition to eliminating the inventory, we can also exclude prepaid expenses and deferred income taxes since neither would be available to cover current liabilities. To follow the example of Hannaford, its quick or acid-test ratio is calculated as follows:

$$\text{Acid-test ratio} = \frac{\text{Cash + Marketable securities + Accounts receivable}}{\text{Current liabilities}}$$

$$= \frac{\$59{,}722 + 0 + \$22{,}869}{\$259{,}599}$$

$$= 0.3181 \text{ or } 31.81\%$$

---

[54] Short-term investments can be investments in such things as marketable securities. Some anaysts call these "near cash" since they are usually easily converted into cash in a very short period of time.

The acid-test ratio tells us that if Hannaford had to pay all its current liabilities at one time, it would have to rapidly liquidate its inventories or turn to some other sources of financing. In Hannaford's defense, its inventories are rather salable and turn over rather quickly, hence a low quick or acid-test ratio is not likely to concern management or Hannaford's lenders. However, for companies where inventory turnover is quite slow, such as jewelers or liquor manufacturers, the acid-test ratio is much more important than the current ratio in determining the company's short-term payment capacity. In understanding both the current and quick ratios, skill and insight are an analyst's best allies.

Determining what constitutes a good or bad level of liquidity depends on who is analyzing the current or acid-test ratio. A banker who has made a short-term loan would like both ratios to be high, because the banker believes they indicate that the company has sufficient current assets to pay all current liabilities, including the current portion of the bank's loan. On the other hand, the company's management might prefer lower ratios, in the belief that they show the company has minimized funds invested in current assets that may yield low returns. Companies with rapid turnovers of receivables and inventories generally need a smaller liquidity cushion, and thus can have lower current and acid-test ratios than those with slower turnovers.

All these capitalization ratios show the relative ability of a company to repay the principal (what is owed) of its short- and long-term debt obligations. However, the ability to repay principal is only one of the concerns lenders have. In fact, it may be the lesser of two concerns: whether the company can repay the principal, and whether the company can pay the interest on the debt. Because the lender's product is debt, and to make a profit the product must be "sold," lenders are concerned less with actual repayment of the principal than with the company's ability to repay it if requested. Companies that have the ability to repay the debt make good candidates for loans, if they can pay the interest on the debt.

Lenders have developed several ratios to test the borrower's ability to pay interest. These are called **coverage ratios**. They test the company's ability to pay interest, interest and principal, or interest, principal, and other contractual obligations.[55] These ratios are called **debt-service ratios** when the ratio measures the ability to pay interest plus principal payments.

Over the long term, interest must be paid out of funds generated by company operations. Because earnings are usually the primary source of funds to service debt obligations, a frequently calculated coverage ratio is **EBIT coverage**. In most cases we include both the interest on the debt and capitalized interest on the leases in the interest expense figure. This was done for Hannaford using data from the annual report footnotes for capitalized lease interest expense.

---

[55] These are called coverage ratios because they measure the company's ability to cover the interest payments on its debt.

$$\text{EBIT coverage} = \frac{\text{Earnings before interest and taxes}}{\text{Interest expense}}$$

$$= \frac{\$178,885}{\$26,577}$$

$$= 6.7308 \text{ times or } 673.08\%$$

Note that Hannaford's EBIT, not net income, was used in calculating this ratio: both interest and its tax effect are deducted from EBIT in calculating net income. Since interest is a pretax expense the EBIT is the appropriate figure. With a ratio of 673 percent, Hannaford is able to pay its interest easily.

Analysts use a number of variations on the coverage ratios to determine the ability of a company to meet its interest obligations. For instance, an analyst might add depreciation, a noncash expense, to EBIT in estimating the coverage ratio.[56] This ratio is called the **cash flow coverage ratio**. The depreciation figure comes from Exhibit 1-3.

$$\text{Cash flow coverage} = \frac{\text{EBIT} + \text{Depreciation}}{\text{Interest expense}}$$

$$= \frac{\$178,885 + \$96,739}{\$26,577}$$

$$= 10.3708 \text{ times or } 1037.08\%$$

If a company has depreciation, the ratio for cash flow coverage will always be larger than that for EBIT coverage. Other cash flows might be added or subtracted from the EBIT to determine the cash available to pay interest expenses.

While interest coverage is of primary concern, lenders also require that principal payments be made to retire or reduce the debt principal. Unlike interest costs these payments are not deductible for tax purposes, so they must be paid with after-tax funds. To determine the ability of the company to meet both interest and principal payments, the ratio of **debt-service coverage** is used. In this ratio, principal repayments are adjusted to a before-tax basis to compensate for their lack of tax deductibility. The principal payment obligations and marginal tax rates for a company can be found in the notes to financial statements. Since Hannaford has capital leases with required annual payments, these are included in the principal payments shown below.

$$\text{Debt-service coverage} = \frac{\text{Earnings before interest and taxes}}{\text{Interest} + [\text{Principal payments}/(1 - \text{Tax rate})]}$$

$$= \frac{\$178,885}{\$26,577 + [(\$1,740 + \$34,580)/(1 - 0.38)]}$$

$$= 2.10 \text{ times or } 210\%$$

---

[56] In case your accounting is hazy, depreciation is a way to spread the tax impact of capital asset investments, not the reflection of a cash expense in the year it is reported. Thus, while it is shown as an expense, it does not reflect an outflow of cash.

Note that for Hannaford, both the interest and debt-service coverage ratios are well above their logical minimums, 100 percent. In fact, even when principal payments, including capital lease obligations are included, the company can cover its obligations, at least its debt obligations, more than two times.

These two basic ratios, interest coverage and debt-service coverage, can be adapted for other contractual or noncontractual obligations, such as preferred stock dividends, using EBIT or cash flow in the numerator. Each variation of these two basic ratios gives a somewhat different view of the company's ability to meet its contractual and/or perceived obligations. It is up to the analyst to determine which ratio gives a better view, and to be certain that any comparisons are based on the same methodology.

Lenders and lessors like coverage ratios to be high. Shareholders, seeking higher returns, prefer the ratios to be low. The best level for each of the ratios depends on the nature of the business, the economic situation, and the willingness of the owners or managers to take risk. For Hannaford, while the financial leverage ratios are relatively high, the company is well able to cover its interest and debt service, with ample room to spare. Its EBIT is not highly variable, and its business is relatively stable. It does not appear as if the company is likely to sustain an unexpected or cyclical downturn, thus making the risk of missing payments quite low. As a consequence, Hannaford seems well able to manage its current level of debt. Lenders should take comfort in their position, while shareholders reap the benefits of leverage on their returns.

6. Sustainable Growth Rate

By combining return on sales, total asset turnover, and leverage, you saw that we can calculate the shareholders' return on equity. Whether the shareholders receive all the returns immediately or not depends upon the dividend payment policy of the company. As illustrated in Exhibit 1-16, some of the returns may be sent to the shareholders in the form of cash dividends, while the rest are retained by the company to fund future growth on behalf of the shareholders.[57]

To measure the proportion of the earnings paid out to shareholders we can use the **dividend payout ratio** (DPO). The amount of dividends paid out to the common equity shareholders is shown in the statement of cash flows, Exhibit 1-3.

$$\text{Dividend payout} = \frac{\text{Dividends paid}}{\text{Net income}}$$

$$= \frac{\$25,366}{\$94,647}$$

$$= 0.268 \text{ or } 26.8\%$$

---

[57] Indeed some may be used to repurchase shares, thus making the remaining shareholders' proportional share of the company increase. One note—recently the share repurchases made by some companies have come quite regularly. Stock analysts have begun including the share repurchases in a recalculated dividend yield called the "all-in-yield." They believe this better represents the true dividend-related return the company provides to its shareholders.

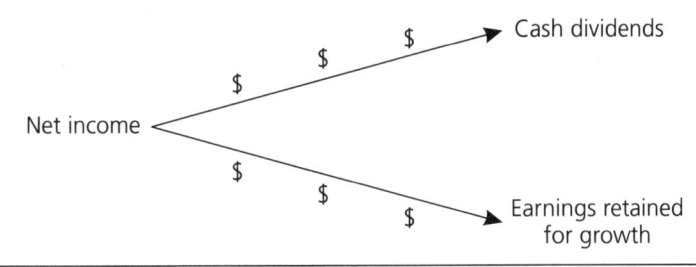

EXHIBIT 1-16 Disposition of Net Income to Shareholders

```
                        $        $  → Cash dividends
                   $
Net income <
                   $
                        $
                                 $  → Earnings retained
                                      for growth
```

The proportion of earnings retained for use by the firm, the **earnings retention ratio**, is simply the opposite of the payout ratio:

$$\text{Earnings retention} = \frac{\text{Net income} - \text{Dividends}}{\text{Net income}}$$

Or

$$= 1 - \text{Dividend payout ratio}$$
$$= 1 - 0.268$$
$$= 0.732 \text{ or } 73.2\%$$

This means that of its 1998 earnings, Hannaford kept 73 percent to reinvest for the shareholders' future benefit. The payout ratio is determined by company policy in the light of economic conditions and industry practice.

The retention ratio is interesting in itself since it tells us about the company, its age, the conditions in the industry, and its prospects for growth. The ratio has another useful result when combined with the ROS, TATO, and leverage ratios.[58] By multiplying them, we can determine the maximum rate at which the company can grow using internally generated funds. This rate is called the **sustainable growth rate** (SGR) or the **self-sustainable growth rate** (SSGR). In doing this analysis we must assume that the key ratios all stay the same; that is, as earnings are retained, they are matched with enough new debt to keep the ratio of assets to equity the same, and neither the TATO nor the ROS ratio changes. The SGR is calculated as follows:

$$\text{SGR} = \text{ROS} \times \text{TATO} \times \text{Leverage} \times \text{Retention ratio}$$

$$= \frac{\text{Net income}}{\text{Sales}} \times \frac{\text{Sales}}{\text{Assets}} \times \frac{\text{Assets}}{\text{Equity}} \times \frac{\text{Earnings retained}}{\text{Net income}}$$

---

[58] Most companies do not pay out more in dividends than they earn during a year. Hannaford has a long-standing policy of never cutting dividends. If management is faced with a year with depressed earnings it can either change the dividend policy or pay out more in dividends than the company earned. To pay out more in dividends than its current year's earnings, a company could do one of three things: borrow, sell assets, or sell new common stock.

$$= \frac{\$94{,}647}{\$3{,}323{,}588} \times \frac{\$3{,}323{,}588}{\$1{,}284{,}538} \times \frac{\$1{,}284{,}538}{\$663{,}350} \times \frac{\$69{,}281}{\$94{,}647}$$

$$= 0.0285 \times 2.587 \times 1.936 \times 0.732$$

$$= 0.105 \text{ or } 10.5\%$$

This ratio may also be calculated using the following shortcut:

$$\text{SGR} = \text{ROE} \times (1 - \text{DPO})$$
$$= 0.1427 \times (1 - 0.268)$$
$$= 0.105 \text{ or } 10.5\%$$

If Hannaford's ratios stay the same in the future as they were in 1998, the company can grow at 10.5 percent: Hannaford can grow its revenues, expenses, profits, assets, liabilities, and equity by 10.5 percent on the basis of its internally generated funds.

By segmenting the sustainable growth rate into the four sources of growth—profitability, asset efficiency, leverage, and profit retention, we can look at each of the four factors that affect the growth rate. This approach provides for a clear diagnosis of past financial performance. In addition, understanding this concept and an analysis of the SGR components can allow an analyst or manager to determine what would happen if the company had followed a different strategy for any component. Thus, if the sustainable growth rate turned out to be lower than expected or desired, management could review the various components to determine the areas in which the company was underperforming. Exhibit 1-17 shows the components and sustainable growth rates for several different industries. There is a wide range of sustainable growth rates. To understand how useful this information is, let's look specifically at Hannaford.

Based only on its 1998 sustainable growth rate, Hannaford could grow at a rate of approximately 10.5 percent per year, that is, it could grow its sales, assets, liabilities, dividends, and so forth. If Hannaford management wanted the company to grow at a faster rate, it would have to change something. Management could use the ratios that underlie the sustainable growth rate to understand what it could do. The most obvious candidate for change would be to cut the dividend: if Hannaford had cut its entire dividend in 1998, its sustainable growth rate would have been 14.3 percent, the same as the return on equity.[59] The other possibilities for change are the profit margin, the efficiency of its assets, or even its financial leverage.[60] Changing these usually takes considerable time and effort, even when the change is possible.

---

[59] Cutting the dividend is an action taken with extreme reluctance by directors and management. The reason is that they believe that it signals to the marketplace (the current and potential security holders) that the company is in some difficulty. Thus they believe that stock and bond prices will react negatively.

[60] In order to have a SSG of 14.3 percent, and changing financial leverage alone, the asset to equity ratio would have to rise to 265 percent. If only the operating leverage changed, it would have to increase to 354 percent. By changing only the ROS, management would have to find price increases or cost reductions that increase the ROS to 3.9 percent.

III. Analysis of Financial Statements

EXHIBIT 1-17 Industry Average Retention Ratios and Sustainable Growth Rates, 1998

	Return on Sales	Total Asset Turnover	ROA	Assets to Equity	ROE	Retention Ratio	Sustainable Growth Rate
Airline transport	0.3%	1.6x	0.5%	6.3x	3.0%	96.4%	2.9%
Apparel manufacturers	8.8	1.9	16.7	2.2	36.8	60.8	22.4
Asset management	19.9	0.7	13.9	2.7	37.6	69.5	26.1
Brewers	-2.7	0.8	-2.2	1.5	-3.2	0.0	0.0
Computer manufacturers	3.1	1.9	5.9	2.4	14.1	94.5	13.4
Computer peripherals	-6.3	1.3	-8.2	2.3	-18.8	94.6	-17.8
Direct marketing	-1.0	2.4	-2.4	2.3	-5.5	92.8	-5.1
Electric housewares	7.7	1.2	9.2	2.7	24.9	69.4	17.3
Forest products	3.0	0.8	2.4	3.2	7.7	55.3	4.2
Furniture and fixtures	4.8	1.7	8.2	2.1	17.1	28.1	4.8
Newspapers	15.4	0.7	10.8	3.0	32.3	76.2	24.6
Steel manufacturing	3.5	1.9	6.7	2.2	14.6	60.8	8.9
Temporary service agencies	1.7	3.4	5.8	2.3	13.3	60.8	8.1
Tires and rubber goods	5.9	1.3	7.7	2.1	16.1	66.4	10.7
Hannaford	2.9	2.6	7.5	1.9	14.3	73.2	10.5

SOURCE: Data from Morningstar *Principia Pro for Stocks*.

All the ratios we have looked at thus far concern the health of the company. How have its owners been faring? What have they gotten for owning the stock? What has been their return and what has happened to their share price?

7. Market Ratios

In addition to ratios that are calculated using only data from the company's financial statements, analysts often calculate ratios using information from the market for publicly owned companies' stock. These ratios facilitate analyzing the company's financial market performance because the company's internal performance should and will be reflected in the capital market's evaluation. Since the return on investment for an equity owner may come primarily from changes in the market price of the equity, these ratios are of particular interest to the shareholders of a company. Equity investors purchase shares of common stock in the company, thus most market ratios are calculated on a per-share basis. A typical starting point for market analysis is **earnings per share** (EPS). Hannaford's 1998 earnings per share was $2.24.[61]

$$\text{Earnings per share} = \frac{\text{Net income}}{\text{Number of common shares outstanding}}$$

$$= \frac{\$94{,}647}{42{,}338}$$

$$= \$2.24$$

Other ratios are based on the market price for a share of common stock. In early January 1999, the share price for Hannaford was $53.00. Using this price, several useful ratios can be calculated. The first is the **price/earnings** or **P/E ratio**.

$$\text{Price/Earnings} = \frac{\text{Market price per share}}{\text{Earnings per share}}$$

$$= \frac{\$53.00}{\$2.24}$$

$$= 23.7 \text{ times}$$

Note that the P/E ratio normally is not cited as a percentage but as a multiple: Hannaford's price was over 23.7 times its earnings. This ratio can be used to evaluate the relative financial performance of the stock. Most analysts be-

---

[61] There are many versions of earnings per share. What we have shown here is the primary earnings per share. We might also have fully diluted earnings per share, the EPS after all options are exercised. Hannaford's EPS is for fiscal year 1998. We could also have shown the calendar year EPS if the calendar and fiscal year were different, or the EPS for the TTM, the EPS for the trailing 12 months: the 12 months from the reported date of the earnings per share. When using EPS be sure you know how it is calculated.

lieve that it gives an indication of how much investors are willing to pay for a dollar of the company's earnings, and it provides a scaled measure that allows market value comparisons of companies with different earnings levels.

Typically, investors expect companies with high P/E ratios to grow, to have more rapid increases in dividends in the future than companies with low P/E ratios because earnings retained now will feed the company's growth.[62] Additionally, companies with higher sustainable growth rates are expected to have higher P/E ratios. Looking at Exhibit 1-18, you can see for yourself whether there is a relationship.

Comparing price to earnings is the traditional way of relating the market price to the shareholders' return at any point in time. However, earnings are impacted by many things that do not have anything to do directly with the operations of the company—for instance, its financial structure. To circumvent any misunderstandings that might come from differences in financial structures between companies or over time, many analysts use **market price/EBIT multiple**.

$$\text{Price/EBIT} = \frac{\text{Market price per share}}{\text{EBIT per share}}$$

$$= \frac{\$53.00}{\$178{,}885/42{,}338}$$

$$= 12.5 \text{ times}$$

EXHIBIT 1-18 Industry Average ROE and Market Measures

	ROE	Price/ Earnings	Price/ Sales	Price/ Cash Flow	Market/ Book Value
Airline transport	3.0%	21.7x	0.8x	11.7x	3.8x
Apparel manufacturers	36.8	14.8	1.1	0.2	2.7
Asset management	37.6	23.0	4.2	15.8	3.2
Brewers	−3.2	18.9	1.0	12.4	1.1
Computer manufacturers	14.1	37.0	2.2	27.2	13.0
Computer peripherals	−18.8	42.8	1.8	26.1	4.2
Direct marketing	−5.5	26.3	1.0	37.1	3.5
Electric housewares	24.9	16.0	1.2	18.9	3.8
Forest products	7.7	34.2	1.0	8.4	2.5
Furniture and fixtures	17.1	58.1	0.6	21.9	2.0
Newspapers	32.3	20.2	2.1	17.5	3.8
Steel manufacturing	14.6	50.7	0.4	8.1	1.0
Temporary service agencies	13.3	17.8	0.4	6.5	2.8
Tires and rubber goods	16.1	13.9	0.8	12.2	1.9
Hannaford	14.3	23.7	0.7	11.7	3.4

SOURCE: Data from Morningstar *Principia Pro for Stocks*.

---

[62] This is true for all but cyclical companies: a high P/E ratio can indicate that earnings are at their cyclical low; a low P/E ratio can occur when companies are doing their best, at the cyclical peak.

Another ratio that is of increasingly widespread use is **market price/EBITDA**. Earlier in this chapter we discussed the EBITDA and you saw how it removed the timing impacts of depreciation as well as financing costs. That ratio for Hannaford is:

$$\text{Price/EBITDA} = \frac{\text{Market price per share}}{\text{EBITDA per share}}$$

$$= \frac{\$53.00}{(\$178{,}885 + \$96{,}739)/42{,}338}$$

$$= 8.1 \text{ times}$$

Stock market analysts are increasingly relying on market price to EBITDA and revenues ratios as a way to level industry and country accounting differences.

Since earnings can be impacted by accounting and tax requirements, analysts, particularly stock analysts, have found ways to look at the price being paid for a share relative to other features of corporate performance. Two of these are in widespread use. The first is the **market price/revenues ratio**.[63] For Hannaford, the market price is 68 percent of the revenues.

$$\text{Price/Sales} = \frac{\text{Market price per share}}{\text{Revenues per share}}$$

$$= \frac{\$53.00}{\$3{,}323{,}588/42{,}338}$$

$$= 0.675 \text{ times}$$

This ratio, or multiple, has seen a resurgence of use in valuing technology, especially Internet stocks since most have no earnings. Take care when revenues include funds unrelated to the company's business, such as interest income.

The second is the **market price/cash flow ratio**. While cash flow can be defined in many ways, ways discussed in later chapters, most analysts use the simple approach of simply adding back to net income the noncash charges for the period. The most typical noncash charge is depreciation. Hannaford's depreciation was $96,739, or $2.29 per share.

$$\text{Price/Cash Flow} = \frac{\text{Market price per share}}{\text{Cash flow per share}}$$

$$= \frac{\$53.00}{\$2.24 + \$2.29}$$

$$= 11.7 \text{ times}$$

For companies with significant noncash charges, analysts believe this ratio better reflects the true underlying earning power of the company. This is particu-

---

[63] Note, these are in such common use that most analysts leave out the market in market price.

III. Analysis of Financial Statements

larly true for companies with limited earnings, or companies in early stages of development. Exhibit 1-18 shows the price/earnings, price/revenues, and price/cash flow ratios for various industries.

To determine whether management has created and is expected to create value for its shareholders we can use the **market-to-book value ratio**. This ratio relates the market value (market price) per share of common stock to the book value or net worth per share. A market-to-book value ratio greater than 100 percent indicates that shareholders are willing to pay a premium over the book value of their equity. The book value per share of a company is calculated by dividing shareholders' equity on the statement of financial position or balance sheet by the number of shares outstanding.

$$\text{Market-to-book value} = \frac{\text{Market value per share}}{\text{Book value per share}}$$

$$= \frac{\$53.00}{\$663,350/42,338}$$

$$= \frac{\$53.00}{\$15.67}$$

$$= 3.38 \text{ times}$$

As you can see, Hannaford's shareholders are happy about how management has used their investment, since they place a publicly traded value on their equity 338 percent higher than the capital they invested. Had they believed that management had squandered what it had been given, the MV/BV ratio might well have been below 100 percent. Market-to-book values, price/earnings ratios, and returns on equity for a number of industries are shown in Exhibit 1-18.[64] None of these industries show a ratio below parity, but let us keep in mind that 1998 and 1999 were perceived to be market highs, and if true, these ratios would be at historic levels.

There are some interesting relationships you can see. For instance, steel manufacturers have the lowest market price/book value, but a relatively high ROE, while computer peripherals have one of the highest market price/book value and a highly negative ROE. What is going on? Don't the shareholders recognize a good ROE? In fact, these numbers force you to consider the future, which is just what the capital markets were doing. The markets see a dim future for steel companies and a much brighter one for the computer industry.

One other ratio used by stock analysts and investors is the **dividend yield**. This indicates the return on a share of stock provided by the current dividend payment.

---

[64] The analyst should keep in mind that book values result from specific accounting conventions that require the use of historical values for assets. When historical values do not reflect the current economic value or earning potential of these assets, the use of replacement cost or inflation-adjusted valuations may result in a more meaningful ratio of market-to-book value.

$$\text{Dividend yield} = \frac{\text{Dividends per share}}{\text{Market price per share}}$$

$$= \frac{\$0.60}{\$53.00}$$

$$= 0.011 \text{ or } 1.1\%$$

Hannaford's shareholders received a 1.1 percent dividend yield. By way of comparison, at that time a broad group of large U.S. company stocks, the Standard and Poor's 500, were yielding 1.1 percent. Again, since the stock market was at record highs, this yield was well below its long-term average.

The dividend policy of a company tends to be related to its industry, its maturity, and its need for future equity investments. Companies that are in mature industries that need to have loyal shareholders tend to pay higher dividends. Those in new industries where there are significant needs for financing future opportunities tend to pay little or no dividends. Paying out a dividend is related to the company's need for investment capital.

In recent times the dividend yield has not fully reflected the full payout to shareholders for many companies. These companies buy back outstanding stock, thus allowing the investor who wants cash to sell some shares, rather than being forced to receive a dividend.[65] In the case of regular share repurchase plans, stock analysts have combined the share repurchase with actual dividends paid to create an "all-in-dividend yield" measure. Since Hannaford did not buy back shares and had no regular buy-back plan, this ratio is irrelevant. For some companies, the share repurchases are the most significant cash for shareholders, especially those that want regular cash payments from their shares.

Of course, dividends are only part of the return investors expect from their investment in common stock; the remainder comes from the potential growth in future dividends that results from wise investment of the profits retained by the company. Usually companies with higher dividend yields are expected to have lower growth in future dividends. Since they are paying more of their earnings out in the form of current dividends, these companies typically have growth rates lower than their sustainable growth rates. Companies with lower current dividends usually are retaining more of their profits for future growth. This is reflected in their sustainable growth rates.

8. Return Versus Risk Performance Ratios

There is another ratio that has gained widespread use. It is called the **spread** or **economic value added**. This ratio is designed to give the analyst a measure of how well the company is doing without the distortions of accounting conven-

---

[65] This is particularly useful when the tax rate on dividends is higher than it is on capital gains.

tions, and taking the capital providers into account. While there are differences in the ways that this ratio is calculated, in general it is:

$$\text{Spread} = \text{Return on equity} - \text{Required return on equity}$$

To calculate the "spread" we must have an estimate of the investors' required ROE, also called the cost of equity and labeled R_e. For Hannaford, the required ROE, the R_e, is 9.6 percent.[66] For a company like Hannaford, the spread would be 4.7 percent. This is a very positive spread.[67]

$$\text{Spread} = 14.3\% - 9.6\%$$
$$= 4.7\%$$

Many analysts adapt this measure. For instance, some use an adjusted return on equity, adjusting the earnings for transactions that affect accrual accounting earnings, such as depreciation, accounting adjustments, and investments.[68] For Hannaford, the analyst might add back to the net income of $94,647 the depreciation of $96,739 and adjust by changes in such things as accounts receivable, inventories, accounts payable, and property, plant, and equipment. The result would be an adjusted ROE of 13.3 percent, and a spread of 3.7 percent.

To show the usefulness of this ratio, we can compare the spread to the market-to-book value ratio. This comparison suggests that investors can see beyond accrual accounting to the real value being created by the company, and reflect this value in the stock price (as reflected in the market-to-book value ratio). Since Hannaford's management, at least in 1998, had a positive spread, we would expect investors to be pleased. The market-to-book value is 338%. This shows that investors recognized the value that Hannaford management created.

The average spreads for a variety of industries are shown in Exhibit 1-19. The first set of numbers that should catch any analyst's eye are those for the computer peripherals industry. What is going on when the spread is so negative and the market value/book value the highest? Either the numbers are wrong or investors have high expectations for the future of this industry: the 1998 ROE does not reflect their hopes for the future ROE. The steel industry stands in stark contrast. The ROE exceeds that which investors require, but investors are not willing to pay more than the book value per share for the stock. Why? Prospects for this industry at the end of 1998, a period of global overcapacity and increasing use of substitute products, is, at best, uncertain. This analysis of the spread and shareholders' expectations makes sense and, more importantly, provides insight into performance and shareholders' optimism about future performance.

---

[66] We discuss how to calculate R_e in Chapter 6.
[67] Since we compare the earned ROE with an expected ROE, the R_e, we can also call this a risk-adjusted return: the shareholders take risk into account in determining the required return.
[68] We discuss how such adjustments can be made in Chapter 4.

EXHIBIT 1-19 Industry Average Market-to-Book Values, Price/Earnings Ratios, and Sustainable Growth Rates, Shareholder Spreads 1998

	Sustainable Growth Rate	P/E	MV/BV	ROE	Required Return (R_e)	Spread
Airline transport	2.9%	21.7x	3.8x	3.0%	12.3%	−9.3%
Apparel manufacturers	22.4	14.8	2.7	36.8	10.8	25.9
Asset management	26.1	23.0	3.2	37.6	12.4	25.2
Brewers	0.0	18.9	1.1	−3.2	9.4	−12.6
Computer manufacturers	13.4	37.0	13.0	14.1	12.7	1.4
Computer peripherals	−17.8	42.8	4.2	−18.8	12.7	−31.5
Direct marketing	−5.1	26.3	3.5	−5.5	11.6	−17.1
Electric housewares	17.3	16.0	3.8	24.9	11.5	13.4
Forest products	4.2	34.2	2.5	7.7	10.4	−2.7
Furniture and fixtures	4.8	58.1	2.0	17.1	10.8	6.3
Newspapers	24.6	20.2	3.8	32.3	10.3	22.0
Steel manufacturing	8.9	50.7	1.0	14.6	10.4	4.3
Temporary service agencies	8.1	17.8	2.8	13.3	11.3	2.0
Tires and rubber goods	10.7	13.9	1.9	16.1	10.7	5.4
Hannaford	10.5	23.7	3.4	14.3	9.6	4.7

SOURCE: Data from Morningstar *Principia Pro for Stocks* and other sources.

Even better than numbers is the graphic relationship that is shown in Exhibit 1-20. Here the spread and market/book value ratios of a number of U.S. industries are plotted.[69] If there is a relationship between the returns generated by a company and investors' enthusiasm, we should find the higher the ROE, the higher the MV/BV ratio. This is the case, but there are exceptions. This ratio is for one year at a time and reflects, in the main, investors' optimism or pessimism about the future *at that point in time*. It is interesting to note that investors can use this kind of analysis to target over- and undervalued industries. The undervalued industry candidates are those below the diagonal line. Those above the line have high relative market values, although the middle of 1998 was a time of high market valuations in the United States, thus making this analysis less useful at that time.

EVA® analysis is a conceptually similar but proprietary version of the spread analysis we just discussed. In essence a charge for capital costs, the cost of debt and equity, is subtracted from the net operating profit. As with the adjusted spread, it seeks to estimate the economic profit above the capital investors' required minimum. To use this method, a variety of balance sheet and income statement items are adjusted to better reflect the surplus or residual income that remains after deducting the cost of borrowing or using shareholders'

---

[69] These are not the same industries as those shown in the previous exhibits. The previous exhibits included industries to illustrate the points of difference in ratio analysis. Exhibit 1-20 contains a broad representation of U.S. industries.

EXHIBIT 1-20 The Spread and Market/Book Value for a Variety of Industries—1998

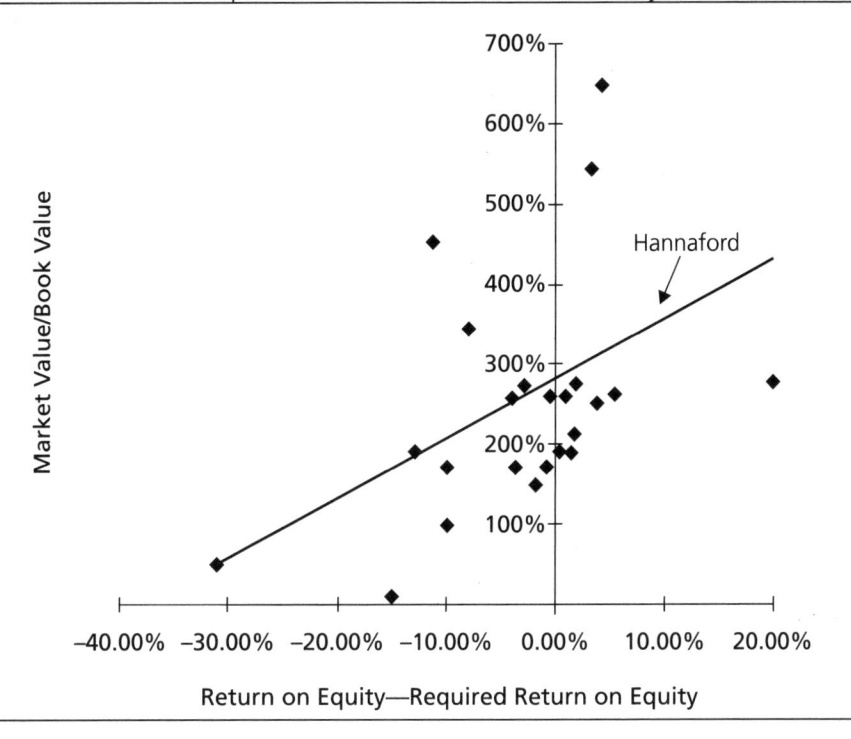

[Scatter plot: Y-axis labeled "Market Value/Book Value" ranging from 0% to 700%; X-axis labeled "Return on Equity—Required Return on Equity" ranging from -40.00% to 20.00%. Hannaford data point labeled near the trend line.]

capital. The cost of the company's capital is also called the weighted average cost of capital, the WACC.[70] In formula form the EVA® is

$$\text{EVA}^\circledR = \text{Invested capital} \times (\text{ROIC} \times \text{WACC})$$

Or

$$\text{EVA}^\circledR = \text{Invested capital} \times (\text{Return on invested capital} \times \text{Weighted average cost of capital})$$

Where:
- ROIC = NOPLAT/Beginning of year invested capital × 100%
- NOPLAT = Operating profits of the company with taxes adjusted to a cash basis
- WACC = The capital structure weighted average marginal costs of debt and equity.

NOPLAT earnings are earnings before interest charges and are adjusted for noncash charges—charges that have no impact on the economic, real earnings

---

[70] Required return on capital, the WACC, is discussed in Appendix B of Chapter 7.

of the company in that period. Adjustments would be made for such things as the current value of future employees' benefits and the goodwill that comes from an acquisition.[71] The required return on capital is the return that capital providers require the company to earn on their investments. Exhibit 1-21 shows the spread, the ROE – R_e, and EVA® estimates. In some cases the differences between the spread and EVA® spread estimates are very small. In other cases, for instance copper and aerospace, the differences are substantial.

This discussion of ratios is not intended to be all-inclusive. Rather, it is intended only to illustrate the types of ratios that may be calculated to provide the analyst or manager with insights into the performance of the corporation. Any number of ratios can be computed; the important thing is to determine what information is relevant to the problem at hand, and then to undertake the appropriate analysis.

IV. COMPARATIVE RATIO ANALYSIS

While we have discussed many ways of looking at the performance of a company, actually calculating the ratios or percentages is relatively simple. The crit-

EXHIBIT 1-21 EVA® and Spreads for Selected Industries[72]

	Spread	EVA® Spread	
	Return on Equity – Cost of Equity	Return on Capital – Weighted Average Cost of Capital	Difference
Advertising	2.3%	4.8%	–2.5%
Aerospace	3.0	3.8	–0.8
Cement	–6.7	5.6	–12.3
Basic chemicals	8.3	9.9	–1.5
Copper	–7.8	4.9	–12.7
Financial services	4.5	–2.2	6.7
Grocers	7.7	6.9	0.8
Internet	–23.0	–15.4	–7.6
Tobacco	9.4	18.0	–8.5

---

[71] We will discuss goodwill in Chapter 5. In essence it is the part of the purchase price of an acquisition above the value of the assets acquired. It cannot be written off against taxes. It is a feature of the purchase method of accounting for an acquisition.

[72] This is just a selection of the group of industries analyzed by A. Damodoran and reported on http://equity.stern.nyu.edu/~adamodar. The following table shows the means, the averages, for the two spreads, the differences between them and the standard deviations, the average variations, around the means for the sample of 79 industries.

	ROE – R_e	EVA®	Difference
Mean	2.4%	4.9%	–2.5%
Standard deviation	6.5%	6.9%	7.8%

IV. Comparative Ratio Analysis

ical ingredient in a successful analysis is the analyst's interpretation of these figures. To interpret the ratios, analysts generally compare a company's performance to that (1) from various time periods, (2) of one or more companies in the same industry, and (3) of the average performance of the industry. To ensure comparability of the results, and to be able to explain the differences in performance among various time periods or companies, the analyst must thoroughly understand the company, its products, marketing techniques, organization, the industry, and the way the ratios were calculated. Furthermore, the financial statements used to prepare the various ratios must be based on comparable accounting procedures or properly adjusted statements.

Using the Hannaford Bros. Co. financial statements as an example, we can see how much more we can discover about the company's performance by making such comparisons.

1. Historical Comparisons

The easiest first step in making historical comparisons is to do a full analysis of the components in the company's sustainable growth rate over time. This analysis, showing the five relevant ratios for Hannaford from 1994 to 1998, is given in Exhibit 1-22.

Hannaford's 1997 performance was its worst in the past five years. What happened? An analysis of the component percentages of Hannaford's financial statements can help us determine the source of the change.

Exhibit 1-23 makes just such a comparison for the income statement. This comparison shows that cost of sales was the largest component of the company's expenses and that it increased at the end of the period. However, Hannaford had decreases in selling, general, and administrative costs, and interest expense remained relatively flat. The combination of these changes improved the return on sales from a low of 1.9 percent in 1997 to 1998's high of 2.9 percent.

If you look behind these numbers, you would see that Hannaford acquired Wilson's Supermarkets in 1994, and opened more than 20 new stores over the course of 1994 and 1995. Moreover, Hannaford had increased its net selling square footage by more than 75 percent. A key driver behind this growth was an increase in the number of combination stores operated by Hannaford.

EXHIBIT 1-22   Hannaford Bros. Co.

SUSTAINABLE GROWTH RATE COMPONENT ANALYSIS					
	1998	1997	1996	1995	1994
Return on sales	2.8%	1.8%	2.5%	2.7%	2.7%
Total asset turnover	258.7	262.9	249.9	267.0	261.1
Assets to equity	193.6	204.2	208.0	185.4	193.1
Earnings retention	72.8	61.3	72.8	74.7	73.9
Sustainable growth rate	10.4	6.1	3.6	3.4	3.6

EXHIBIT 1-23 Hannaford Bros. Co.

COMPONENT PERCENTAGES FOR CONSOLIDATED INCOME STATEMENTS

	1998	1997	1996	1995	1994
Sales and other revenues	100.0%	100.0%	100.0%	100.0%	100.0%
Cost of sales	74.6	75.2	75.8	76.0	75.4
Gross margin	25.4	24.8	24.2	24.0	24.6
Selling, general, and administrative expenses	20.0	19.7	19.2	18.7	19.1
Impairment loss	0.0	1.2	0.0	0.0	0.0
Operating profit	5.4	3.9	5.0	5.3	5.5
Interest expense, net	0.8	0.8	0.8	0.8	0.9
Earnings before income taxes and minority interest	4.6	3.1	4.2	4.5	4.6
Income taxes	1.7	1.2	1.7	1.8	1.8
Net earnings	2.9	1.9	2.5	2.7	2.8

Combination stores, similar to so-called supercenters, offer expanded lines of general merchandise, videos, and other services in addition to the traditional all-department supermarket. The company viewed the key benefit to combination stores as being a higher revenue per square foot than basic supermarkets.[73] These increases in sales and profits were accomplished despite intense supermarket and expanded supercenter competition from Sam's Club, BJ's Wholesale, and Price/CostCo. While Hannaford opened stores, it also closed stores with potential losses and reported these potential losses as impairment losses. The Annual Report stated the losses were "related to supermarket assets and associated costs for stores that were closed in January 1998 and being held for sale or disposal" and "supermarket assets the Company continued to use in its operations." If Hannaford had not taken this loss in 1997, the ROS would have been 2.8 percent.[74] As you can see, a little detective work showed that the decline in 1997 ROS was related to earlier growth, not to a decline in prices or an increase in its cost of normal operations.

Another way to gain insight into the pattern of performance is to examine the growth in various accounts over the same periods. Since looking at the magnitude of raw data can mask the changes in various accounts, **percentage change analysis** can be used to determine the relative change in an item (expense, income, asset, or liability) over time. The percentage changes can be compared with the changes in related items over the same time period. Exhibit 1-24 shows this analysis for Hannaford. As you can see, this analysis shows the change in each account each year. Obviously, the 1997 numbers are at variance with the rest of this 5-year history. This also makes the change from 1997 to

---

[73] Revenue per square foot is one of the industry-specific ratios we discussed earlier.
[74] The impairment loss would be added back to operating earnings, and the taxes would be recalculated to result in the 2.8 percent ROS.

IV. Comparative Ratio Analysis

EXHIBIT 1-24 Hannaford Bros. Co.

YEAR-TO-YEAR STATEMENT OF EARNINGS PERCENTAGE CHANGES

	1998	1997	1996	1995	1994
Sales and other revenues	3.0%	9.1%	15.2%	12.1%	11.5%
Cost of sales	2.2	8.2	14.9	12.9	12.0
Gross margin	5.5	11.8	15.9	9.5	10.2
Selling, general, and administrative expenses	4.6	11.9	18.1	9.9	9.5
Impairment loss					
Operating profit	44.4	−15.6	8.1	8.0	12.7
Interest expense, net	0.6	19.0	14.6	−9.3	10.5
Earnings before income taxes and minority interest	56.3	−21.8	7.0	11.6	13.2
Income taxes	52.7	−23.4	6.7	9.9	11.9
Minority interest and accounting change					
Net earnings	58.7	−20.7	7.1	12.7	9.8

1998 difficult to use. A skillful analyst would adapt the numbers to operating numbers by eliminating the impairment losses. The adapted net earnings change from 1997 to 1998 would have been about 13 percent. This is in line with what Hannaford had achieved in 1995 and its recent history.

2. Comparisons to Other Companies

Looking at one company's ratios, even across time, only gives us a limited view into the company's performance. We need to see how the company has done in contrast to other companies. Because financial requirements and uses of funds differ among industries, it is important that companies chosen for comparison first be limited to those within the same industry. Such an analysis is shown in Exhibit 1-25. Data for Winn-Dixie, another company in the supermarket industry, are compared with data for Hannaford.

For two companies in the same industry there are major differences. These differences would be of interest to management as well as potential investors. First, Hannaford's profit margin is almost twice that of Winn-Dixie, a company that operates much like Hannaford, but concentrates its stores in the southeastern and southwestern United States. The second obvious difference between the two is the asset turnover: Winn-Dixie's asset turnover is much higher than that of Hannaford. Even with these differences, the combination of Winn-Dixie's lower profit margin and higher turnover result in a ROA that is very close to that of Hannaford.[75]

---

[75] This is a clear example of where it is important to look beyond the summary data: If you judged performance by ROA above, you would fail to grasp the relative strength of Hannaford compared to Winn-Dixie.

EXHIBIT 1-25 Comparison of Hannaford Bros. Co. to Winn-Dixie Stores, Inc., 1998

	Hannaford	Winn-Dixie
Return on sales	2.9%	1.5%
Total asset turnover	258.7	440.0
Return on assets	7.4	6.5
Assets to equity	193.6	220.0
Return on equity	14.3	14.5
Dividend payout ratio	26.8	95.3
Retention ratio	73.2	4.7
Sustainable growth rate	10.5	0.7

The other major difference between the two grocery chains is the retention ratio. Winn-Dixie pays out most of its earnings, Hannaford does not. As a consequence, from returns on equity that are almost identical, Winn-Dixie's sustainable growth rate is almost zero. This means that if Winn-Dixie seeks to grow, it must obtain capital from outside sources while Hannaford can fund considerable growth with its own retained profits. These are big and important differences. They have serious implications for each company's strength, its ability to grow and to weather adversity.

3. Comparisons with Others in the Industry

Comparisons can include several companies or all of those in the relevant industry. Typically, industry-wide comparisons are based on industry averages. These averages are available from several sources that collect and publish the data. Exhibit 1-26 compares the 1998 Hannaford data with 1998 industry averages.[76] Because of financial differences in companies of differing sizes, analysts commonly select from the industry a sample of companies that correspond in size with the target company. In Exhibit 1-26 you see Hannaford compared to others based on asset and revenue size, as well as the whole U.S. grocery industry.

Hannaford is a small company, particularly in the global context. In the rapidly rationalizing industry worldwide, the companies listed in Exhibit 1-27 were the major companies in 1999.[77]

An analysis of the data indicates that Hannaford's performance compares favorably with that of the industry no matter how the industry is defined. Its cost of goods sold was lower than the industry average, giving Hannaford a higher after-tax profit margin of 2.85 percent as compared with just over one

---

[76] These are the most recent data available. Because of the delay in collecting and compiling the data, industry data often lag behind individual companies' reported financial information.

[77] An example of this rationalization, Carrefours and Promodes, two very large grocery chains in France, announced a merger in early September 1999.

EXHIBIT 1-26 Comparison of Hannaford Bros. Ratios with Those of the U.S. Industry, 1998

	Smaller Supermarkets			All Supermarkets
	Hannaford	By Revenues	By Assets	
Return on sales	2.85%	0.2%	0.8%	0.5%
Total asset turnover	258.7	250.0	230.0	140.0
Return on assets	7.4	0.5	1.8	0.7
Assets to equity	193.6	250.0	240.0	300.0
Return on equity	14.3	1.3	4.4	2.1
Dividend payout	26.8	49.5	39.7	31.3
Retention ratio	73.2	50.5	60.3	68.7
Sustainable growth rate	10.5	0.6	2.7	1.4

percent for the industry. Even more important in an industry where mergers are occurring, its ability to grow without as many demands on outside sources is superior to the averages.

An analyst should assess a number of other things in looking at a company. If the performance being analyzed occurred over a period during which there was a significant change in industry or economic conditions (for instance, inflation or global economic change), the analyst might want to look at the company's relative performance.

V. SUMMARY

Using the major external sources of financial information, the financial statements, an analyst can learn a great deal about the financial performance of a

EXHIBIT 1-27 Global Grocery Companies Ranked by Size

Ranking	Name	Country	Sales
1	Wal-Mart	U.S.	$123.2
2	Metro	Germany	49.0
3	Kroger	U.S.	38.6
4	Intermarche	France	36.6
5	Ahold	Netherlands	34.9
6	Carrefour	France	33.9
7	Auchan	France	23.6
8	Leclerc	France	23.1
9	Promodes	France	20.9
10	Casino	France	14.8

SOURCE: from Samer Iskandar, "Supermarkets Set to Unveil Giant Merger in France," *Financial Times*, August 30, 1999, p. 1.

company through comparative ratio analysis. Calculating a ratio is not a difficult skill. The analysis is much like detective work, where clues are sought from the data. These clues often require further digging. It is in the choice of ratios and the interpretation of the results where skill is required.

Proper interpretation requires an understanding of the company as well as of the environment. Critical issues that need to be considered are general economic conditions, the competitive situation, and the business and financial strategies of the company. All of these factors, individually and in combination, affect the financial results for the company and the value that will be earned by the company's owners, its shareholders.

SELECTED REFERENCES

Sources of industry data and financial ratios are found in current issues of:

Dun & Bradstreet, *Industry Norms and Key Business Ratios.*

Robert Morris Associates, *Annual Statement Studies.*

Troy, Leo. *Almanac of Business and Industrial Financial Ratios.* Englewood Cliffs, NJ: Prentice Hall.

The concept of sustainable growth is discussed in:

Copeland, Tom, Tim Koller, and Jack Murring. *Valuation: Measuring and Managing the Value of Companies.* New York: John Wiley & Sons, 1990.

Higgins, Robert C. "How Much Growth Can a Firm Afford?" *Financial Management*, Fall 1977, pp. 7–16.

Rappaport, Alfred. *Creating Shareholder Value.* New York: The Free Press, 1986.

Van Horne, James C. "Sustainable Growth Modeling," *Journal of Corporate Finance*, Winter 1987, pp. 19–25.

For information about spread and EVA® analysis, see:

Stern, Joel M., G. Bennett Stewart III, and Donald H. Chew, Jr. "The EVA® Financial Management System," *Journal of Applied Corporate Finance*, Summer 1995, pp. 32–47.

Ehrbar, Al. *Stern Stewart's EVA: The Real Key to Creating Wealth.* New York: John Wiley & Sons, 1998.

Grant, James. "Foundations of EVA® for Investment Managers," *Journal of Portfolio Management*, Fall 1996, pp. 41–48.

Stewart, G. Bennett III. *The Quest for Value.* New York: Stern Stewart & Co. with Harper Collins Publishers, Inc., 1998.

For further information on ratio analysis, see:

Bodie, Zvi, and Robert Merton. *Finance.* Upper Saddle River, NJ: Prentice Hall, 2000, chap. 3.

Brealey, Richard A., and Stewart C. Myers. *Principles of Corporate Finance.* 4th ed. New York: McGraw-Hill, 1991, chap. 27.

Brigham, Eugene F., Louis C. Gapenski, and Michael Ehrhardt. *Financial Management.* 9th ed. Fort Worth, Texas: The Dryden Press, 1999, chap. 2.

Damodoran, Aswath. *Corporate Finance.* New York: John Wiley & Sons, 1997, chap. 4.

Fraser, Lyn M. *Understanding Financial Statements: Through the Maze of a Corporate Annual Report.* Reston, VA: Reston Publishing, 1985.

Gordon, Gus. *Understanding Financial Statements.* Cincinnati, OH: South-Western Publishing Co.

Ross, Steven A., Randolph W. Westerfield, and Jeffrey F. Jaffe. *Corporate Finance.* 5th ed. Homewood, Ill.: Irwin McGraw Hill, 1999, chap. 2.

Web Sites of Interest:

Ratios on a variety of publicly traded companies can be found on numerous web sites including:

www.freeedgar.com for Securities and Exchange Commission filings.

www.hoovers.com as a source of company and industry profiles.

In addition, many companies have their own web sites. These can be found through various search engines, or through a site like www.askjeeves.com.

For information on EVA® analysis, see:

http://www.equity.stern.nyu.edu/~adamodar/

STUDY QUESTIONS

1. Melissa Hampton was reviewing the recent performance of the EASY Chair Company, a company with a reputation for producing high-quality home furniture. Over the years, the name EASY had become synonymous with a kind of chair called a recliner. By 2000, the company was producing a variety of home furnishings, including reclining sofas, sleep sofas, living room cabinets, upholstered furniture, and solid-wood dining room furniture. In the past decade, the company had also entered the office furniture business by producing office systems and patient seating for clinics and hospitals. To determine the impact that diversification and expansion had on EASY, Ms. Hampton collected the following data for the company:

EASY CHAIR COMPANY
FINANCIAL DATA
(dollars in millions)

	2000	1999	1998	1997	1996
Sales	$592.3	$553.2	$486.8	$420.0	$341.7
Net income	$28.3	$27.5	$26.5	$24.7	$23.0
Dividends per share	$0.5	$0.5	$0.4	$0.4	$0.4
Number of shares	17.9	17.9	18.3	18.4	18.3
Total assets	$361.9	$349.0	$336.6	$269.9	$233.0
Total equity	$214.6	$194.3	$178.8	$165.3	$147.0

a. How had EASY's sustainable growth rate changed over time? What caused any changes you found?

b. The home furniture industry had the following ratios over the same time. How did EASY compare with the industry?

HOME FURNITURE INDUSTRY RATIOS

	2000	1999	1998	1997
Return on equity	15.12%	15.54%	15.31%	15.74%
Retention rate	71.00	71.00	71.00	72.00
Sustainable growth rate	10.73	11.03	10.87	11.33

2. Perplexed by the declining profit margin and the rate of growth of EASY's net income, Melissa Hampton pressed the company management for more detailed information. The management asks you, one of EASY's financial analysts, to compute component and percentage changes for the following statements and determine if there were any positive or negative trends.

EASY CHAIR COMPANY
INCOME STATEMENT
(in millions)

	2000	1999	1998	1997
Net sales	$ 592.3	$ 553.2	$ 486.8	$ 420.0
Cost of sales	(430.4)	(397.8)	(352.1)	(289.8)
Gross profit	161.9	155.4	134.7	130.2
Selling, general, and administrative expenses	(111.6)	(106.9)	(91.4)	(85.5)
Income from operations	50.3	48.5	43.3	44.7
Interest expense	(7.2)	(7.6)	(4.0)	(1.9)
Other income	2.5	3.1	2.7	2.1
Income before taxes	45.6	44.0	42.0	44.9
Taxes	(17.3)	(16.5)	(15.5)	(20.3)
Net income	$ 28.3	$ 27.5	$ 26.5	$ 24.6

3. Ms. Hampton was not satisfied with EASY's performance. She believed that the company could achieve the following ratios:

EASY CHAIR COMPANY
MS. HAMPTON'S TARGET RATIOS

Dividend payout	45.0%
Market price	$15.00
Dividend yield	5.2%
Number of shares outstanding	18,000
Return on equity	13.7%
Long-term debt/equity	27.3%
Current ratio	551.0%
Acid-test ratio	407.3%
Profit margin	5.1%
Gross margin	27.6%
Return on assets	9.4%
Inventory turnover	733.3%
Operating profit	8.7%
Accounts receivable collection period	92.5 days
Accounts payable payment period	28.7 days
Tax rate	34.0%

Using Ms. Hampton's target ratios for EASY, complete the following financial statements:

EASY CHAIR COMPANY
MS. HAMPTON'S REVISED FINANCIAL STATEMENTS

Income Statement
Sales _____
Cost of sales _____
  Gross profit _____
Selling, general, and administrative expenses _____
  Operating profit _____
Interest _____
  Earnings before taxes _____
Taxes _____
    Net income _____

Balance Sheet
Cash _____
Accounts receivable _____
Inventory _____
  Total current assets _____
Net property, plant, and equipment _____
    Total assets _____
Accounts payable _____
Other current liabilities _____
  Total current liabilities _____
Long-term debt _____
  Total liabilities _____
Owners' equity _____
    Total liabilities and owners' equity _____
Dividends per share _____

4. As the new financial analyst for Peterson's Chemicals, you have been asked to analyze the profitability problems encountered during the last two years. Current financial statements and selected industry averages are as follows:

PETERSON'S CHEMICALS
FINANCIAL STATEMENTS
(dollars in millions)

Income Statement	2000	1999
Sales	$ 1,478	$ 1,435
Cost of goods sold	(1,182)	(1,076)
Gross profit	296	359
Selling and administrative expenses	(443)	(445)
Operating profit	(147)	(86)
Interest expense	(27)	(29)
Net income	$ (174)	$ (115)

Balance Sheet	2000	1999
Cash and equivalent	$ 120	$ 76
Accounts receivable, net	432	437
Inventory	324	284
Other current assets	37	38
Total current assets	913	835
Plant, property, and equipment	300	375
Total assets	$ 1,213	$ 1,210
Accounts payable	$ 500	$ 412
Other current liabilities	309	98
Total current liabilities	809	510
Long-term debt	178	300
Total liabilities	987	810
Owners' equity	226	400
Total liabilities and owners' equity	$ 1,213	$ 1,210

Using your analysis of the financial statements, how does Peterson's compare to the following industry averages?

CHEMICAL INDUSTRY AVERAGES

	Industry Ratios
Current ratio	150%
Acid-test ratio	90%
Receivables collection period	65 days
Payables payment period	60 days
Debt/equity	110%
Return on assets	7%
Return on equity	19%

5. Peterson's management has decided to reexamine the company's short-term credit policies. The chief financial officer estimates that reducing the receivables collection period to 78 days would result in a sales decrease of 3 percent. The purchasing department reports that by reducing the payables period to 68.5 days, discounts would be available that would reduce the cost of goods by 9 percent. Initially the cash required to finance these changes would come from additional long-term debt, resulting in a debt to equity ratio of 100 percent. As an analyst:

   a. determine whether Peterson's Chemicals would have been profitable if management had made these changes at the beginning of 2000.

   b. determine how the ROE and ROA would have been affected.

   c. prepare new financial statements to reflect these changes.

6. Lacey Harmoniski had just moved to the Endura Republic as a part of a business school summer internship. His mentor and supervisor, Mr. Rickki, had handed him THE FASTNER CO. income statements and asked him to analyze them. His mentor was proud of the progress the company had made. Lacey knew that the analysis would show how well the joint fastener company had done over the past five years, and that his analysis was his introduction to a company of which his mentor was proud. Mr. Rickki had described the economic environment as one that was difficult: inflation had been high and variable. The company, he said, had coped with the inflation, and prospered.

   a. Calculate common-size statements for the income statements of THE FASTNER CO. On the basis of this analysis, determine how well the company did.

THE FASTNER CO.
INCOME STATEMENTS
(currency in millions)

	1999	1998	1997	1996	1995
Volume (in units)	54,518	55,631	54,540	54,000	50,000
Revenues	10,119	8,294	6,480	4,800	4,000
Cost of goods sold:					
Labor	2,255	1,762	1,456	1,120	1,000
Material	4,588	3,584	2,636	1,856	1,600
Gross profit	3,276	2,948	2,388	1,824	1,400
Marketing expenses	873	715	559	414	345
Administrative expenses	539	435	334	244	200
Operating profit	1,864	1,798	1,495	1,166	855
Taxes	615	593	493	385	282
Net Income	1,249	1,205	1,002	781	573

b. What was the price per unit of the goods being sold by THE FASTNER CO.?

c. Mr. Rickki has asked that Lacey calculate and comment on the growth rates of the various items on the income statement. Lacey asks that you draft the report. Please do so.

d. In spite of the fact that Mr. Rickki had not asked, Lacey decided to put one of his new business school tools to use: an analysis of real growth rates. In addition to the nominal growth rates of the various items, please help him by calculating and commenting on the real growth rates the company has achieved over the past four years. Inflation was as follows:

	1999	1998	1997	1996
Inflation	28%	26%	40%	12%

e. Draft a report to Mr. Rickki stating your conclusions regarding how well THE FASTNER CO. has done.

APPENDIX 1A
Cross-Border Ratio Analysis[1]

One problem that can arise in ratio analysis is the problem of comparability: ratios cannot be used to compare two companies or industries if the accounting principles used by one company are different from those used by another. This is true whether the accounting impacts the value of an asset, a liability, income, or an expense. Thus it is important to understand the accounting principles that are being used, and to take those differences into account in analyzing financial statements.

Understanding the general accounting principles U.S. firms use can be difficult, but once the accounting rules are learned and understood, the task of comparing companies is relatively straightforward. U.S. accounting rules allow some discretion about how some items are valued, such as inventory, and the method of accounting must be described in the footnotes to the financial statements. Thus differences between the rules used by different companies can be noted and taken into account.

When comparing the financial statements of companies from different countries, the analyst has a much harder job. Accounting standards vary widely from country to country and, until recently, companies in many countries were not even required to disclose the accounting principles on which their financial reports were created.

Various accounting groups around the world have attempted to harmonize the accounting rules and principles used around the world. The result of these efforts is the *International Accounting Standards*, published by the International Accounting Standards Committee.[2] The rules of the IASC are voluntary.[3]

In making industry comparisons, analysts choose to deal with accounting differences in two ways. First, many analysts simply ignore companies that operate using accounting principles from another country. This, however, is a

---

[1] This appendix was prepared with James Parrino, Babson College, with assistance from Virginia Soybel, Babson College, and Gary S. Schieneman, Smith New Court, New York.

[2] For information about the Committee and the accounting standards it has developed and proposed, go to its web site at www.iasc.org.uk.

[3] These standards are being followed by public companies in most countries and have resulted in disclosure of the accounting principles on which the statements are prepared. In addition, the IASC is generating common accounting principles. The rules set forth by the IASC do not meet the reporting standards of the U.S. Securities and Exchange Commission, and were rejected in late 1999 as incomplete by the U.S. Financial Accounting Standards Board.

dangerous approach. As world commerce becomes increasingly global, the analyst might ignore a major competitor, a significant industry participant, or a potentially interesting investment opportunity.

The second approach is quite different: analysts examine the companies in an industry but ignore differences in the methods of accounting. This approach purports to give the analyst a view of the global industry, but as you will see, it can be very distorted. The error in this approach is amply demonstrated by Exhibit 1A-1, which shows non-U.S. company data that have been adjusted to meet U.S. generally accepted accounting principles (GAAP).[4] This exhibit reveals how big an impact on reported performance a change in accounting principles can have.[5] It is important to note that we do not suggest that one accounting system is superior to another, even though it may be. The point of this appendix is that different systems result in different reported performance, and the analyst must take these differences into account. This exhibit is not intended as a criticism of any accounting system, only a demonstration of the dangers that await the unwary.

In this appendix we discuss the various ways in which a company can account for various items on its financial statements. The appendix is not meant to be an exhaustive compilation of these differences, but to open the reader's

EXHIBIT 1A-1 Telecommunications Equipment Producers, 1986: Financial Statement Changes to Adjust to U.S. Generally Accepted Accounting Principles

Company	Change in		Return on Assets		Return on Equity	
	Net Income	Equity	Reported	Adjusted	Reported	Adjusted
Mitel, Canada	7.4%	−20.1%	−10.0%	−9.4%	−22.6%	−21.1%
Bell, Canada	−15.3	−6.9	4.9	4.2	14.0	12.6
Sumitomo Electric	−5.9	−2.3	2.6	2.4	8.7	8.4
Siemens	40.1	30.7	2.8	4.0	11.1	12.6
Philips	−11.0	−12.4	1.9	1.8	6.3	6.2
Ericsson	16.2	17.9	1.5	1.8	8.2	8.1
British Telecom	14.9	−32.5	9.0	10.0	20.7	40.0
GEC	−1.0	2.0	8.4	8.3	16.6	16.2
Racal	−19.6	50.4	3.6	2.6	10.5	6.6
Standard Telephone and Cables	−27.1	60.1	8.4	4.8	22.0	9.4
NEC, U.S.	N.A.	N.A.	0.6	6.0	3.0	3.0

SOURCE: Speech given by Gary S. Schieneman, Smith New Court, to Association for Investment Management and Research and the European Federation of Financial Analysts Societies, November 1991, London, England.

---

[4] Generally accepted accounting principles (GAAP) means accepted by the accounting organization operating in that jurisdiction. It does not mean that any particular set of principles is generally accepted around the world.

[5] While this data is from the end of the 1980s, the same holds true today. This is one of the best comparisons that has been done, and dramatically points out the range of differences.

mind to the world of global accounting and its implications for analyzing performance.

I. ACCOUNTING PRINCIPLES BACKGROUND

Why do differences in accounting principles exist? There are many reasons that differences exist, but the primary ones are:

1. **Culture.** Accounting standards reflect a society's attitude toward business. Countries that have a distrust of business will usually require strict disclosure, and companies will be given few choices about how to do their accounting. This factor has a major impact on the accounting standards.
2. **Level of economic development.** Accounting systems generally reflect the level of economic development in the economy.
3. **Legal requirements.** Accounting systems are developed to serve the needs of those who will use the financial statements. In general, accounting systems are either mandated by law or by an institution that represents the accounting profession.[6] In countries with legally mandated systems, the government plays a dominant role in the development of the rules, and little or no differences exist between the financial and tax accounting systems. The goal is to control the corporation and collect taxes. Nonlegalistic systems are generally developed to serve groups interested in the company's performance, such as lenders and shareholders.

The accounting principles used throughout the world are relatively few. Any accounting system must report a company's liabilities and assets, its expenses and revenues.[7] In addition, every accounting system must deal with problems created by foreign operations and inflation. Once an analyst understands the basic principles, understanding the rules for any country becomes manageable. There are many items that change from system to system. The major differences concern how to account for the value of research and development, investment securities, inventories, fixed assets, leases, deferred taxes, bad debts, and acquisitions and goodwill. In addition, asset valuation and the

---

[6] In the United States, this group is the American Institute of Certified Public Accountants, and its Financial Accounting Standards Board changes the rules. The International Accounting Standards Board is developing global standards. However, each country has its own rules. A detailed description of the accounting rules for each country can be obtained from the body that regulates accounting in that country.

[7] The impact of depreciation on earnings and company value, as well as the particular changes that can occur in asset revaluation when there is very high inflation, are discussed in Chapters 2 and 4.

effects of inflation also will be discussed.[8] Let us begin by seeing how big the differences can be, and how the differences can impact performance. Let's look at research and development expenses.

II. RESEARCH AND DEVELOPMENT

If you are just becoming familiar with the accounting rules of one country, then how significant these accounting principle-based differences can be might not have been obvious to you. As an example of how distortions can occur, let's look at a concrete example.

In most countries, all research and development costs, except for software, are expensed. However, that is not true in all countries. Some consider research and development an investment made in the company's future, and therefore treat it as an investment. Exhibit 1A-2 shows the ways research and development are treated in six countries.

As with any investment, research and development (R&D) can be capitalized by adding its cost to the balance in the long-term asset account and amortizing it over time or expensing it in the year it is spent. Panel A of Exhibit 1A-3 shows the impact on the financial statements of capitalizing and amortizing R&D, and the statements if research and development is expensed.[9] Panel B shows the key ratios that result from the two sets of statements. The companies shown in this exhibit are identical, except that one expenses its 20,000 in R&D on its income statement and the other capitalizes it on its balance sheet. You will note that the key ratios are affected by this accounting principle difference. In fact, the impact is even felt in the sustainable growth rates: the company that expenses R&D has a very low SGR, while the capitalizing company's SGR is higher. Remember, these companies are identical in every way except in the accounting for R&D.[10]

EXHIBIT 1A-2 Methods for Accounting for Research and Development Expenses

	Canada	France	Germany	U.K.	Japan	U.S.
May be expensed in the year spent, but can be capitalized		X				
Expensed in the year spent, but can be capitalized					X	
Expensed in the year spent	X		X	X		X

---

[8] As you read the rest of this appendix, remember that the differences in performance that come from using different accounting principles often are the result of differences in when a particular item (e.g., research and development) is reported and/or the actual value of what is being reported (e.g., how to translate foreign exchange or how to account for inflation).

[9] Recently we have also seen the capitalizing of advertising expenses by some U.S. companies.

[10] The question of whether they are identical or not actually depends on the tax code that impacts the amount of taxes that each would pay. Here we assumed the same rate of taxes.

EXHIBIT 1A-3 Impact of Expensing or Capitalizing Research and Development Expenses

Panel A (in units of currency):

	Expensing Research & Development	Capitalizing Research & Development
Income Statement		
Revenues, net	100,000	100,000
Cost of sales	(45,000)	(45,000)
Gross margin	55,000	55,000
Other costs and expenses:		
General and administrative	(20,000)	(20,000)
Depreciation and amortization	(7,500)	(9,500)
Research and development	(20,000)	—
Total costs and expenses	7,500	25,500
Earnings before interest and taxes	7,500	25,500
Net interest	(1,000)	(1,000)
Earnings before taxes	6,500	24,500
Income taxes	(2,145)	(8,085)
Net income	4,355	16,415
Balance Sheet		
Assets		
Cash and equivalents	10,000	10,000
Receivables, net	45,000	45,000
Inventories	35,000	35,000
Total current assets	90,000	90,000
Gross property, plant, and equipment	400,000	420,000
Accumulated depreciation	(150,000)	(150,000)
Net property, plant, and equipment	250,000	268,000
Total long-term assets	250,000	268,000
Total assets	340,000	358,000
Liabilities and Owners' Equity		
Accounts payable	75,000	75,000
Income taxes payable	10,000	10,000
Accruals	3,000	3,000
Total current liabilities	88,000	88,000
Long-term debt	125,000	125,000
Total liabilities	213,000	213,000
Common equity	127,000	145,000
Total net worth	127,000	145,000
Total liabilities and net worth	340,000	358,000
Other information:		
Number of shares	1,000	1,000
Dividends per share	2.50	2.50
Earnings per share	4.36	16.42

EXHIBIT 1A-3 *(continued)*

Panel B:

	Expensing Research & Development	Capitalizing Research & Development
Sustainable Growth Analysis		
Earnings/Revenue	4.4%	16.4%
Revenue/Assets	29.4	27.9
Earnings/Assets	1.3	4.6
Assets/Equity	267.7	246.9
Return on equity	3.4	11.3
Dividend payout ratio	57.4	15.2
Sustainable growth rate	1.5	9.6

Obviously the difference between these two methods of accounting for R&D is the timing of the expenses for tax purposes—when the money spent is reported on the income statement. For the company that expenses R&D, it impacts the income statement in the year the R&D is done. The capitalizing company spreads out the impact over time. This difference in timing is at the root of most of the differences in accounting principles, and thus it is a useful thing to keep in mind.

The R&D example also shows how big an impact on financial performance different accounting methods can have. To understand the relative performance of two companies operating under different accounting principles, we must adjust the statements to a common standard.

In our increasingly global world, where a company of interest might be operated from a country other than the analyst's, it is important to know the accounting rules for that country. Accountants in a country know their own accounting rules and usually do a good job of keeping track of changes in them. Analysts unfamiliar with the accounting rules must understand in detail the accounting rules that govern the company they are analyzing. Sometimes the differences in accounting rules between countries can be difficult to discover.[11] For the analyst who wants to analyze the performance of an industry, memorizing the rules for each of several countries is a difficult task. For the novice, nonaccountant analyst, the task is impossible.

This is not to suggest that there is nothing to be done. There are some basic choices that must be made in creating an accounting system, and understanding those differences will help the analyst begin the task of analysis. In general, the main differences are in standards for valuing assets and liabilities and recording revenues and expenses. This appendix gives you some simple rules

---

[11] Increasingly, the differences in accounting principles are available on web sites. For the particular country's accounting rules, try a query through www.askjeeves.com.

about differences in accounting principles that will enable you to begin to analyze companies from different countries. However, the appendix is designed only to give you a basic introduction to the differences that exist. It will not make you an expert in any accounting system. For those whose company or clients depend upon the quality of the analysis, much more expertise is needed.

III. CONSOLIDATION

One of the first things that the analyst must determine is what is included in the financial statements. A financial statement can be **consolidated**, combining each of the accounts (such as balance sheets and income statements) from the company's various operations and subsidiaries, or not. When the subsidiaries' accounts are not consolidated, the ownership of the subsidiaries' operations is shown as an investment on the parent's balance sheet. The subsidiary investment shows the net value of the subsidiaries.

Consolidated statements can be confusing: by including in one statement financial data from different businesses, it can be hard to draw conclusions about the company's performance. For example, many U.S. auto manufacturers own both auto production operations and a subsidiary that finances dealer inventory and consumer vehicle purchases.[12] Their statements are the merging of data from a production operation and a lending institution, and the ratios resemble neither. Auto manufacturers are not the only companies with these diverse consolidated operations. Accounting rules in many countries do not allow consolidation. Consolidation is allowed in the United States.

IV. INVENTORY

A company invests in all kinds of assets. One asset that can be accounted for in a number of different ways is inventory. If the cost of any item held in inventory (e.g., raw materials used in manufacturing a product awaiting sale) changes from the time it is purchased to the time it is used to produce the goods for sale, the method of inventory valuation impacts the financial statements.[13] There are several methods that can be used to value inventory.[14]

---

[12] For example, General Motors and GMAC, and Ford and Ford Motor Credit.

[13] All inventory accounting methods assign the same value to inventory when it is purchased and when it is transferred to cost of goods sold if no change has occurred in the cost of the items in inventory from the time of its purchase to the time of its sale.

[14] Several more exotic methods of inventory valuation are used in a limited number of countries, for instance, base stock, latest purchase price, and next-in, next-out. These methods are not as widely used, however, as those described in the text. The interested reader should consult the references listed at the end of this appendix or other sources for a further explanation and accounting rules for the country of interest.

1. **First-in, first-out** (FIFO): the cost attributed to the item removed from inventory is based on the cost of the oldest item in inventory.
2. **Last-in, first-out** (LIFO): the cost attributed to the item removed from inventory is based on the cost of the most recently purchased item in inventory. LIFO is not permitted in most countries. Among large industrialized nations it may be used in the United States, Japan, and Germany. A variation of this is the lower-of-cost-or-market value. For many assets this latter method is used worldwide. These assets include many financial assets such as marketable securities and investments in other types of securities.
3. **Weighted-average cost**: the cost attributed to the item removed from inventory is based on the average cost of the items in inventory.
4. **Specific identification**: the cost attributed to the item removed from inventory is the price paid for the specific item when it was purchased. This is the most accurate of the historically based methods, but it is expensive to maintain a record of prices. Thus it is used for very large and expensive items held in inventory.

Exhibit 1A-4 shows an example of how a company's cost of goods sold and inventory accounts would look at the end of its first year of operations under two different inventory accounting methods, LIFO and FIFO. These methods result in quite different outcomes and illustrate the accounting results that come from inventory valuation methods. For the analyst, the inventory method chosen determines the allocation of the inventory's value between the income statement (cost of goods sold) and the balance sheet (inventory). Furthermore, the method chosen impacts either the cost of goods sold or inventory. One is a more accurate reflection of its actual economic value. For example, when prices for an item have risen, LIFO attributes a realistic cost to the income statement's cost of goods sold, but leaves the balance sheet's inventory undervalued. When prices are declining, the reverse would be true.

The differences that can result in the inventory and cost of goods sold values are significant, and the problem for the analyst can be seen when looking at performance ratios. The ratios that result from using each of the four main inventory accounting methods are summarized in Exhibit 1A-5.

V. INFLATION

Thus far the differences in the ratios are the result of differences in accounting methods. Inflation distorts both the financial information and the actual performance of a company. Let's use an example to see how the distortions can occur before discussing how the data might be adapted for comparability.

Exhibit 1A-6 (page 73) shows the monthly income statements for a company operating in a world where inflation is 25 percent.[15] From an analysis of

---
[15] This is moderately high inflation, but by no means as high as inflation can be.

EXHIBIT 1A-4 Inventory Valuation Method's Impact on Inventory and Cost of Goods Sold (as of December 31 in units of currency)

Panel A

Assume	Transaction
January 1	Purchase 1,200 units for 1.00.
April 1	Purchase 200 units for 0.50.
July 1	Sell 600 units.
October 1	Sell 600 units.

Panel B

	LIFO	FIFO
Income Statement		
Revenue	1,500	1,500
Cost of goods sold	(1,100)	(1,200)
Selling, general, and administrative expenses	(100)	(100)
Operating profit	300	200
Depreciation	(50)	(50)
Research and development	(50)	(50)
Earnings before income taxes	200	100
Interest	(50)	(50)
Earnings before tax	150	50
Taxes	(60)	(20)
Net income	90	30
Balance Sheet		
Assets		
Cash	50	90
Accounts receivable	250	250
Inventory	200	100
Property, plant, and equipment, net	400	400
Other assets	100	100
Total assets	1,000	940
Liabilities and Equity		
Accounts payable	250	250
Long-term debt	400	400
Deferred tax	0	0
Common equity	100	100
Retained Earnings:		
Beginning of year	160	160
Net income	90	30
Retained earnings, end of year	250	190
Total equity	350	290
Total liabilities and equity	1,000	940

* For simplicity, taxes for reporting purposes equal the actual tax liability. Differences in taxes are accounted for by changes in cash.

EXHIBIT 1A-5 Ratios That Result from Different Methods of Inventory Valuation

Method	ROS	Sales/Assets	Assets/Equity	ROE
LIFO	6%	150%	286%	26%
FIFO	2	159	324	10
Weighted average	18	92	248	41
Specific identification	6	103	303	19

the company's performance you would conclude that the company's sales had grown. However, the unit volume of 10 units per month had not grown over the whole time. You might falsely conclude that the company had such market power that it raised its prices every year by 25 percent, if you did not know that the company was in an inflationary environment. How fast had the company really grown? Inflation has distorted our view of the real performance.

We can compensate for the problem of inflation by thinking and forecasting in real (adjusted for inflation) terms instead of nominal (unadjusted for inflation) terms. To see how the company actually performed, the real and nominal statements are shown in the last two columns of Exhibit 1A-6. Revenues started at 100 and reached 1,455 by the end of the 12 months, in nominal terms. In real terms, however, there had been no change at all: the value of revenues was still 100.

This straightforward example assumes that revenues and all costs rise with inflation, but if this is true it is only reflected when the proper method for accounting for inventory is used.[16] Even when an appropriate method of inventory valuation is used, the inventory account could be seriously misvalued. This example demonstrates that inflation can cause major distortions in reported financial performance. It is these distortions that the analyst must attempt to understand.[17]

Inflation can distort both the income statement and the balance sheet in a variety of ways, and accounting systems in different countries deal with the problem in different ways. Some ignore the problem, while others have devel-

---

[16] Both LIFO and the latest-purchase methods are more likely to compensate for the problems created by inflation than either FIFO or weighted-average cost. This is because they transfer goods from inventory to cost of goods sold at more current prices, and the resulting income better represents what the company actually earned. However, the inventory is not valued realistically. If a company uses a method such as FIFO in a time of inflation, unless inventory is turned over very rapidly, the cost of inventory charged to cost of goods sold misstates its current cost and results in a misstatement of income.

[17] In spite of the fact that accountants like to believe that financial statements can be made to reflect financial performance, in times of high inflation financial statements do not provide reliable information. As an example of the problem consider how you might adapt revenues to real terms when inflation over a short time span is highly variable (for instance, 20 percent in the first half of a month and 75 percent in the second half) and affects various revenue and expense items differently.

EXHIBIT 1A-6 Impact of Inflation on Revenues, Costs, and Unit Volume

NOMINAL INCOME STATEMENTS—25% INFLATION
(in units of currency)

	Nominal													Real
	0	1	2	3	4	5	6	7	8	9	10	11	12	12
Revenues	100	125	156	195	244	305	381	477	596	745	931	1,164	1,455	100
Costs	(50)	(62)	(78)	(97)	(122)	(152)	(191)	(239)	(298)	(372)	(465)	(582)	(727)	(50)
Gross income	50	63	78	98	122	153	190	238	298	373	466	582	728	50
Other costs	(20)	(25)	(31)	(39)	(49)	(61)	(76)	(95)	(119)	(149)	(186)	(233)	(291)	(20)
Earnings before taxes	30	38	47	59	73	92	114	143	179	224	280	349	437	30
Taxes	(15)	(19)	(23)	(29)	(37)	(46)	(57)	(72)	(89)	(112)	(140)	(175)	(218)	(15)
Net income	15	19	24	30	36	46	57	71	90	112	140	174	219	15
Unit volume	10	10	10	10	10	10	10	10	10	10	10	10	10	10
Real revenue	100	100	100	100	100	100	100	100	100	100	100	100	100	100

oped sophisticated methods to correct for the distortions created by inflation.[18] The inflation-adjustment methods are, however, variations of two approaches: general price-level or specific price-level adjustments.

1. General Price-Level Adjustments

General price-level adjustments are also called constant dollar accounting. This method adjusts for decreases in the value of the currency that accompany inflation.[19] Conceptually, adjustments are made so that the revenues, expenses, assets, and liabilities are reported in units of the same purchasing power. **Purchasing power** reflects the units of currency needed to buy the same quantity of goods from one time to the next. This is an inflation-adjusted currency value. The first column of Exhibit 1A-7 shows the statements that would be reported in the absence of adjustments for inflation. Because the company shown in this exhibit experienced 20 percent inflation over the period, the ratios do not really tell us the actual performance of the company in any useful way. Columns 2 and 3 provide general price-level-adjusted statements for the same period, the first adjusting the income statement and the second adjusting the balance sheet.

2. Specific Price-Level Adjustments

This method, also called **constant cost accounting**, focuses on specific asset values rather than a general change in purchasing power caused by inflation. Rather than using historical costs, the replacement value of the asset is used. This value can be determined by multiplying the historic value by an index reflecting subsequent inflation.[20] For example, the index used for fixed assets might be an appraisal or a construction-cost index that shows gain in prices due to inflation. Any gain or loss as a result of the revaluation would be reported either as an inflation gain or loss on the income statement, or directly to the retained earnings account on the balance sheet. Exhibit 1A-7 Column 4 shows the result of specific price-level adjustments to the income statement and Column 5 shows the impact if the adjustments are reported to the balance sheet.

The general price-level adjustments can be quite different from those calculated using a general inflation index. Thus it captures the changes that specifically change the price of one asset or asset category. General price-level adjustments or specific price-level adjustments can be used separately or together, and can be used on some or all of the items on the financial statements.

---

[18] In countries that have had high inflation for long periods of time, accountants have more sophisticated approaches to adjusting financial statements for inflation. Brazil, Israel, and Argentina, for example, have well-developed inflation accounting systems.

[19] The example in Exhibit 1A-6 shows the impact of inflation on the value of the currency.

[20] In general, this index will be a government-calculated index reflecting the changes in wholesale or consumer prices. Just how the index is calculated varies from country to country, and even can vary over time.

EXHIBIT 1A-7 Effect on Financial Statement of Different Accounting Methods for Inflation (in units of currency)

Income Statement	No Adjustment	Constant Dollars Income Statement Adjustments*	Constant Dollars Balance Sheet Adjustments†	Specific Cost Income Statement Adjustments‡	Specific Cost Balance Sheet Adjustments**
Revenues, net	1,000	1,000	1,000	1,000	1,000
Cost of sales	(600)	(600)	(600)	(600)	(600)
Other	(100)	(100)	(100)	(100)	(100)
Gross margin	300	300	300	300	300
Depreciation and amortization	(50)	(60)	(60)	(53)	(53)
Research and development	(50)	(50)	(50)	(50)	(50)
Earnings before interest and taxes	200	190	190	197	197
Net interest	(50)	(50)	(50)	(50)	(50)
Earnings before taxes	150	140	140	147	147
Income taxes (@ 40%)	(60)	(56)	(56)	(59)	(59)
Inflation gains (losses)	—	100	—	40	—
Net income	90	184	84	128	88

Balance Sheet					
Assets					
Cash and equivalents	50	54	54	51	51
Receivables, net	250	250	250	250	250
Inventories	200	200	200	200	200
Net property, plant, and equipment	400	470	470	417	417
Other assets	100	120	120	120	120
Total assets	1,000	1,094	1,094	1,038	1,038

EXHIBIT 1A-7 (continued)

Balance Sheet	No Adjustment	Constant Dollars Income Statement Adjustments*	Constant Dollars Balance Sheet Adjustments†	Specific Cost Income Statement Adjustments‡	Specific Cost Balance Sheet Adjustments**
Liabilities and Net Worth					
Accounts payable	250	250	250	250	250
Long-term debt	400	400	400	400	400
Common equity	100	100	100	100	100
Retained earnings:					
Beginning of year	160	160	160	160	160
Net income	90	184	84	128	88
Inflation adjustments	—	—	100	—	40
End of year	250	344	344	288	288
Total equity	350	444	444	388	388
Total liabilities and equity	1,000	1,094	1,094	1,038	1,038
Ratios					
Return on sales	9.0%	18.4%	8.4%	12.8%	8.8%
Sales/assets	100.0	91.4	91.4	96.3	96.3
Return on assets	9.0	16.8	7.7	12.4	8.5
Assets/equity	285.7	246.4	246.4	267.4	267.4
Return on equity	25.7	41.4	18.9	33.0	22.7

* Inflation constant dollar application to long-term assets, holding gains (losses) flow through income statement, general price index = 1.2, depreciation based on revalued assets (net PP&E = 400 × 1.2 minus the change in depreciation).
† Inflation constant dollar application to long-term assets, holding gains (losses) flow directly through to balance sheet, general price index = 1.2, depreciation based on revalued assets (net PP&E = 400 × 1.2 minus the change in depreciation).
‡ Inflation specific cost application to long-term assets, holding gains (losses) flow through income statement, general price index = 1.2, depreciation based on revalued assets, PP&E appraised at 417 (PP&E = 420 minus change in depreciation).
** Inflation specific cost application to long-term assets, holding gains (losses) flow directly through to balance sheet, general price index = 1.2, depreciation based on revalued assets, PP&E appraised at 417 (PP&E = 420 minus change in depreciation).
NOTE: For simplicity, financial taxes for reporting purposes (40%) equal the actual tax liability. Difference is taxes are accounted for by changes in cash.

An analyst familiar with the two basic adjustment techniques is capable of interpreting the specific approach used in any country.

The problem that the accountant faces when there is inflation is how to adjust for inflation and how to do so in a way that can be understood.[21] This section has provided a particularly brief introduction to the problem of understanding performance at a time of inflation. You need to be wary of inflation since it can compromise the value of the information contained in the financial statements.

Inflation not only changes the financial statements of the company but can radically change the very way it conducts its business. In highly inflationary environments financial profits often become much more important than operating profits: production becomes the servant to speed, distribution methods may depend upon how and when the product is priced rather than the most efficient method of distribution; the work of the employees on pay day becomes how to preserve personal wealth rather than how to do their jobs. Inflation has fascinating consequences.

VI. THE IMPACT ON STATEMENTS OF NONDOMESTIC TRANSACTIONS

Few companies operate solely in one country. Many buy supplies or sell products outside their domestic environments, and many hold assets or have liabilities in several countries. These transactions provide special challenges for accountants and particular problems in statement comparability for analysts. For assets and liabilities held outside the domestic environment, the problem is how to translate the value from the local currency into that in which the company's statements are reported: assets and liabilities held or owed in a foreign country must be reported in the company's home currency. For revenues and expenses, the problem is how to report transactions that occur outside the company's domestic environment into the company's home currency.[22] All foreign currency problems occur because the company's statements are reported in just one currency, its home currency.

1. Foreign Exchange Transactions

The method of accounting for foreign transactions and foreign-held assets can have a significant impact on the financial performance reported for a company. Unfortunately, accountants have devised no simple set of ways for dealing with these situations; thus the analyst must be particularly alert to the accounting

---

[21] If inflation is not taken into account, distortions in accounting occur that can result in real changes in managers' behavior. For instance, consider the United States in the late 1970s, when managers turned to more service-oriented operations rather than asset-based investments since the inflation-induced depreciation drag was considerable.

[22] An example of the problem is a credit sale. A change in exchange rates between the two countries will result in a loss or gain. The loss or gain will be for the seller if the product is priced in the buyer's home currency.

rules that are used by any company being analyzed. To gain a perspective on the ways different countries choose to deal with the problem of foreign exchange transactions is to take what is called a transaction perspective.

One-Transaction Perspective. Accountants using this approach assume that gains or losses from changes in exchange rates should not be separated from the actions that initiated them—for instance, making sales abroad. Let us demonstrate this with an example.

> Assume that a U.S. company buys raw materials from a company in the United Kingdom for £375 when the dollar/pound exchange rate is \$1.60/£1.00. At that time, the company's financial statements would show \$600 of inventory and \$600 in accounts payable. If, on April 1, the exchange rate is \$1.75/£1.00, the financial statements would show an additional \$56.25 in inventory and \$56.25 in accounts payable [(1.75\$/£ × £375) − (1.60\$/£ × £375)]. With no further exchange rate changes, when the company pays for the goods, accounts payable and cash will be reduced by \$656.25. When the inventory is sold, the cost, including any costs attributable to exchange rate changes, is charged to cost of goods sold and is reflected on the income statement.[23]

This method has a significant drawback: exchange rate gains and losses are combined with the actual cost of the company's supplies. This factor limits the comparability of the information.[24] When using this method, the analyst is left with the question: Did skillful management of the company or did exchange rate fluctuations create the performance?

Two-Transaction Perspective. The two-transaction perspective is designed to provide information so the analyst can determine whether a company's performance was based on its managers' ability to manage or from gains or losses in exchange rates. The two-transaction perspective separates the value of the event (in our example, the purchase of materials) from any subsequent exchange rate gains or losses, by creating two new accounts. On the balance sheet the account is *loss/gain on foreign exchange*, and on the income statement the entry is *foreign exchange gains or losses*. To see how these statements would differ from those using the one-transaction perspective and from those of a company with no foreign purchases, see Exhibit 1A-8.[25]

---

[23] Any exchange rate changes that occur before the accounts payable are paid are reported to cost of goods sold, even if the goods have already been used in the manufacture of the company's products and the products have been sold.

[24] This method is not used in the United States. It is used in other countries, for instance, in Brazil.

[25] The example transaction would be accounted for by showing 600 in inventory and 600 in accounts payable on January 1. On April 1, when the exchange rate changed, 56.25 would be added to accounts payable, and 56.25 to an account called "loss on foreign exchange." When the inventory is sold, on the balance sheet the inventory is reduced by 600 and loss on foreign exchange by 56.25; when the goods are paid for, accounts payable and cash are reduced by 656.25 and the income statement reflects a cost of goods sold of 600 and a foreign exchange loss of 56.25. All numbers are in units of currency.

EXHIBIT 1A-8 Effect of Different Accounting Methods for Foreign Exchange Transactions* (in units of currency)

	No Transactions	Foreign Exchange Method One-Transaction	Foreign Exchange Method Two-Transaction
Income Statement			
Revenue	1,000	1,000	1,000
Cost of goods sold	(600)	(656)	(600)
Selling, general, and administrative expenses	(100)	(100)	(100)
Operating profit	300	244	300
Depreciation	(50)	(50)	(50)
Research and development	(50)	(50)	(50)
Exchange rate gain (loss)	—	—	(56)
Earnings before interest and taxes	200	144	144
Interest	(50)	(50)	(50)
Earnings before taxes	150	94	94
Taxes	(60)	(36)	(38)
Net income	90	56	56
Balance Sheet			
Cash	50	14	14
Accounts receivable	250	250	250
Inventory	200	200	200
Property, plant, and equipment, net	400	400	400
Other assets	100	100	100
Total assets	1,000	964	964
Accounts payable	250	250	250
Long-term debt	400	400	400
Common equity	100	100	100
Retained earnings:			
Beginning of year	160	160	160
Net income	90	54	54
End of year	250	214	214
Total equity	350	314	314
Total liabilities and equity	1,000	964	964
Ratios			
Return on sales	9.0%	5.6%	5.6%
Sales/assets	100.0	103.7	103.7
Return on assets	9.0	5.8	5.8
Assets/equity	285.7	307.0	307.0
Return on equity	25.7	17.8	17.8
Operating profit margin	30.0	24.4	30.0

* Figures reflect assumptions in this appendix. For simplicity, financial tax for reporting purposes (40 percent) equals the actual tax liability. Differences in taxes are accounted for by changes in cash.

2. Foreign Exchange Translation

When a company holds assets and liabilities in different countries there is another sort of reporting problem. It is not that we have to account for a transaction, but that the value of nondomestic assets and liabilities are changed by changes in exchange rates. These changes in values must be reflected on the balance sheet. Multinational companies, with divisions or subsidiaries in other countries, have long dealt with this problem. However, as more companies operate in more than one country, the problem becomes more urgent and widespread.

The object of accounting is to develop financial statements that reflect the company's situation fairly and makes them understandable to and useful for investors, creditors, and managers. Since it would be impossible to understand statements where different currencies are just added together, the value of all foreign assets and liabilities are translated into the company's home currency. Whatever method of translation is used, the company must report both how it chose the exchange rate and how it accounted for exchange rate gains and losses.

There are three basic translation methods used for these translations: current/noncurrent, monetary/nonmonetary, and current.

1. **Current/noncurrent method.** In this method, assets and liabilities are grouped according to their maturity. Current assets and liabilities are translated at the date of the company's balance sheet; those that are noncurrent are translated at the rate in effect at the time of the transaction itself—for instance, when the liability was incurred or the asset purchased.
2. **Monetary/nonmonetary method.** Using this approach, assets are put into monetary or nonmonetary groups. **Monetary** or **financial assets and liabilities** are such things as cash receivables, payables, and long-term debt. In fact, you can think of them as any account that must be stated at current market value and must be translated at the exchange rate in effect at the date of the financial statement. **Nonmonetary assets** are translated at the rate in effect when the transaction first occurred, for instance, when a plant was purchased. A variation of this approach, called the **temporal method**, is used in the United States and other countries when accounting for the translation effects of foreign subsidiaries in high inflation countries.
3. **Current method.** This method is the easiest and most widely used method. All assets and liabilities are translated as of the date of the financial statements.[26]

---

[26] One curious problem that plagues historic, adjusted statements is whether they were adjusted for exchange rate changes or inflation, and what the inflation index or exchange rate was that was used. As a consequence, it is difficult to understand or reconstruct the statements later.

Generally, all income statement accounts are translated at the average of the exchange rate prevailing over the period reported.[27] After the accounts are translated to reflect the effect of foreign exchange rates, a gain or loss is computed. There are two ways to account for foreign exchange translation gains or losses. Using the first method, a foreign exchange loss or gain would be shown as a separate income or expense item, thus affecting the income statement directly. The second method charges the gain or loss against the retained earnings account on the balance sheet. Exhibit 1A-9 shows the impact on a company of different methods of accounting for foreign exchange translations.

Translation gains and losses are not real losses as are transaction gains and losses. They are estimates of what the fair value would be if the asset was sold or a liability retired at the time the financial statements were prepared. The translated income statement shows an approximation of the revenues and expenses as if they had been incurred in the home currency. Although these figures are purely estimates, they do have a profound impact on financial statements and on measures of financial performance.

These are only some of the accounting principles that can profoundly impact both how information is reported and how it is analyzed. These reporting differences also impact the way that managers manage.

VII. CONCLUSION

When a company operates in more than one country, whether it is selling or sourcing products or holding assets or liabilities, the analysis of financial statements becomes more complex. The ways a company can account for various income statement and balance sheet items is long, varies from country to country, and discretion exists within a country.

Exhibit 1A-10 provides a list of the various ways in which a company can account for each of the items discussed in this appendix. It is not an exhaustive list of differences in accounting principles throughout the world, but it does reflect the primary areas about which an analyst should be concerned when comparing the financial performance of companies from different countries. Exhibit 1A-11 provides a list of the ways in which various countries account for the major items discussed here. This list does not deal with every account or possibility, only with the most important and universal. Furthermore, due to changes in accounting rules, these rules should be verified before undertaking an analysis since the rules can change. The intention in providing these exhibits is to highlight the basic differences between accounting methods, and to indicate how a company from that country would deal with these major items. Exhibit 1A-11 is a simple matrix and does not substitute for the more detailed analysis the professional analyst should undertake.

---

[27] The rationales are that revenue and expenses are received and paid fairly evenly over the year and that exchange rates changed gradually. This assumption is often erroneous, however.

EXHIBIT 1A-9 Effects of Different Accounting Methods for Foreign Exchange Translations

		Income Statement Changes			Balance Sheet Changes		
	U.S. Dollars	Current/Noncurrent (yen)	Nonmonetary/Monetary (yen)	Current Rate (yen)	Current/Noncurrent (yen)	Nonmonetary/Monetary (yen)	Current Rate (yen)
Income Statement							
Revenue	$ 1,000	¥145,000	¥145,000	¥145,000	¥145,000	¥145,000	¥145,000
Cost of goods sold	(600)	(87,000)	(87,000)	(87,000)	(87,000)	(87,000)	(87,000)
Selling, general, and administrative expenses	(100)	(14,500)	(14,500)	(14,500)	(14,500)	(14,500)	(14,500)
Operating profit	300	43,500	43,500	43,500	43,500	43,500	43,500
Depreciation	(50)	(8,250)	(8,250)	(6,750)	(8,250)	(8,250)	(6,750)
Research and development	(50)	(7,250)	(7,250)	(7,250)	(7,250)	(7,250)	(7,250)
Exchange rate gain (loss)	—	(8,500)	(1,500)	(10,000)	—	0	—
Earnings before interest and taxes	200	19,500	26,500	19,500	28,000	28,000	29,500
Interest	(50)	(7,250)	(7,250)	(7,250)	(7,250)	(7,250)	(7,250)
Earnings before taxes	150	12,250	19,250	12,250	20,750	20,750	22,250
Taxes	(60)	(4,900)	(8,900)	(4,900)	(8,300)	(8,300)	(8,900)
Net income before inflation adj.	90	7,350	10,350	7,350	12,450	12,450	13,350
Inflation gains (losses)	—	—	—	—	—	—	—
Net income	$ 90	¥ 7,350	¥ 10,350	¥ 7,350	¥ 12,450	¥ 12,450	¥ 13,350
Balance Sheet							
Cash	$ 50	¥ 6,750	¥ 6,750	¥ 6,750	¥ 6,750	¥ 6,750	¥ 6,750
Accounts receivable	250	33,750	33,750	33,750	33,750	33,750	33,750
Inventory	200	27,000	33,000	27,000	27,000	33,000	27,000
Property, plant, and equipment, net	400	66,000	66,000	54,000	66,000	66,000	54,000
Other assets	100	16,500	16,500	13,500	16,500	16,500	13,500
Total assets	$ 1,000	¥150,000	¥156,000	¥135,000	¥150,000	¥156,000	¥135,000

EXHIBIT 1A-9 (continued)

	U.S. Dollars	Income Statement Changes			Balance Sheet Changes		
		Current/ Noncurrent (yen)	Nonmonetary/ Monetary (yen)	Current Rate (yen)	Current/ Noncurrent (yen)	Nonmonetary/ Monetary (yen)	Current Rate (yen)
Accounts payable	$ 250	¥ 33,750	¥ 33,750	¥ 33,750	¥ 33,750	¥ 33,750	¥ 33,750
Long-term debt	400	66,000	66,000	54,000	66,000	66,000	54,000
Common equity	100	16,500	16,500	13,500	16,500	16,500	13,500
Retained earnings:							
Beginning of year	160	26,400	26,400	26,400	26,400	26,400	26,400
Net income	90	7,350	13,350	7,350	12,450	12,450	13,350
Other	0	—	—	—	(5,100)	900	(6,000)
Total equity	350	50,250	56,250	47,250	50,250	56,250	47,250
Total liabilities and equity	$ 1,000	¥150,000	¥156,000	¥135,000	¥150,000	¥156,000	¥135,000
Ratios							
Return on sales	9.0%	5.1%	7.1%	5.1%	8.6%	8.6%	9.2%
Sales/assets	100.0	96.7	92.9	107.4	96.7	92.9	107.4
Return on assets	9.0	4.9	6.6	5.4	8.3	8.0	9.9
Assets/equity	285.7	298.5	277.3	285.7	298.5	277.3	285.7
Return on equity	25.7	14.6	18.4	15.6	24.8	22.1	28.3

EXHIBIT 1A-10 Common Methods of Accounting around the World

Method	Balance Sheet Effect	Income Statement Effect
Inventory		
a. FIFO	Inventory value based on recent prices	Cost of goods sold based on obsolete prices of inventory units sold
b. LIFO	Inventory value based on obsolete prices	Cost of goods sold based on recent prices
c. Weighted average	Inventory value based on weighted-average prices for purchases during the current fiscal year	Cost of goods sold based on weighted-average costs for inventory units sold during the current fiscal year
d. Specific identification	Inventory value based on actual historical cost of each item purchased	Cost of goods sold based on actual historical cost of each inventory item sold
e. NIFO	Inventory value based on obsolete prices	Cost of goods sold based on current market prices of inventory units sold
f. Latest purchase price	Inventory value based on current market prices	Cost of goods sold based on obsolete prices for inventory units sold
g. Lower of cost or market	Inventory value based on lower of cost or market value	Cost of goods sold based on higher of cost or market value
Inflation		
a. Constant dollar, flow-through method	Various assets and liabilities revalued using a general price-level index	Inflation gains (losses) included in reported income
b. Constant dollar, balance sheet method	Various assets and liabilities revalued using a general price-level index; inflation gains (losses) recorded directly to the equity section of the balance sheet	Income statement does not reflect changes in profits caused by inflation
c. Specific cost, flow-through method	Various assets and liabilities revalued based on specific appraisals or specialized indices	Inflation gains (losses) included in reported income
d. Specific cost, balance sheet method	Various assets and liabilities revalued based on specific appraisals or specialized indices; inflation gains (losses) recorded directly to the equity section of the balance sheet	Income statement does not reflect changes in profits caused by inflation

EXHIBIT 1A-10 *(continued)*

Method	Balance Sheet Effect	Income Statement Effect
Inflation		
e. No adjustments	Balance sheet accounts do not reflect changes in value caused by inflation	Income statement does not reflect changes in profits caused by inflation
Foreign Exchange Transactions		
a. One-transaction perspective	Receivables or payables are adjusted to reflect changes in the exchange rate prior to completion of the transaction	Gains (losses) from changes in exchange rates not separately recorded, but included with the other income statement accounts; the gain (loss) is only recorded if the transaction is completed
b. Two-transaction perspective	Receivables or payables adjusted to reflect changes in the exchange rate prior to completion of the transaction	Gains (losses) from changes in exchange rates reported as a separate item on the income statement, and reflect changes in the exchange rate prior to completion of the transaction
Foreign Exchange Translation		
a. Current/ Noncurrent	Current assets and liabilities translated at the current exchange rate (balance sheet date); noncurrent assets, liabilities, and equity accounts translated at the rates in effect when each transaction occurred	Revenue and expenses translated using the average exchange rates for the period; depreciation expenses normally translated at the rate in effect when the asset was purchased; foreign exchange translation gains (losses) usually recorded in the current year in either a balance sheet reserve account or directly to the income statement
b. Monetary/ Nonmonetary	Monetary assets and liabilities translated at current rates; nonmonetary assets, liabilities, and equity accounts translated at historical rates	Same as current/noncurrent method
c. Current rate	All assets and liabilities translated at the current exchange rate; capital stock translated at the rate in effect when the stock was issued; ending retained earnings becomes the balancing item	Same as current/noncurrent method

EXHIBIT 1A-11 Accounting Methods Available in Selected Countries§§

Country	Inventory	Inflation	Foreign-Exchange Translation	Foreign-Exchange Transaction
United States	a, b, c, d	e	c	b
United Kingdom	a, c, e	e	c	b
Germany	a, b, c, e	e	a, b, c*	b†
France	a, e	d, e	b, c	b‡
Spain	a, b, c, d	e	b, c	b
Japan	a, b, c, d, e	e	b§	b
Singapore	a, b, c, d	e	b, c	b
Canada	a, c, d, e	e	b, c	b"
Mexico	a, b, c	a, c	c**	b**
Brazil	a, b, c	a, d	b, c	a

* No specific requirements exist in German law or accounting principles as to which method must be used. The requirement is that whatever is chosen must be used consistently.
** There are no published accounting principles or regulations to account for the effects of foreign currency but companies generally follow U.S. accounting practices.
† No gains are recognized.
§ Noncurrent monetary items are carried at historical rates.
" Unrealized gains (losses) on long-term monetary items are deferred until the transaction is completed.
§§ Refer to Exhibit 1A-10.
‡ Losses may be deferred until the transaction is completed.

It should be clear by now that an analyst cannot simply compare companies operating from different countries. Differences in accounting alone can make the financial statements of two companies incomparable. The analyst must move beyond the simple comparisons to adjusting for the significant accounting differences. To do this there are three steps a good financial analyst will take:

1. Define the economic event that caused the accounting transaction.
2. Determine the accounting principle that governed the transaction.
3. Determine when the event will be or was reported on the financial statements.

As hard as it may be, whenever performance must be judged and the company operates outside the analyst's home-base economy or operates in several different countries, the analyst takes on the challenges of international accounting.

SELECTED REFERENCES

Afteman, Allan B. *International Accounting, Financial Reporting and Analysis*. Boston, Mass.: Warren, Gorham & Lamont, 1995.

Ball, Ray. "Making Accounting International: Why, How, and How Far Will It Go?" *Journal of Applied Corporate Finance*, Fall 1995, pp. 19–29.

Belkaoui, Ahmed. *Multinational Management Accounting*. New York: Quorum Books, 1991.

Carlsberg, Bryan. "FAS #52—Measuring the Performance of Foreign Operations," in *New Developments in International Finance*, Joel M. Stern and Donald Chew, Jr., eds. New York: Basil Blackwell, 1988, pp. 97–104.

Coopers & Lybrand (International). *International Accounting Summaries*. 2nd ed. New York: John Wiley & Sons.

Lessard, Donald, and David Sharp. "Measuring Performance of Operations Subject to Fluctuating Exchange Rates," in *New Developments in International Finance*, Joel M. Stern and Donald Chew, Jr., eds. New York: Basil Blackwell, 1988, pp. 121–133.

Moffett, Michael. "Issues in Foreign Exchange Hedge Accounting," *Journal of Applied Corporate Finance*, Fall 1995, pp. 82–94.

Nobes, Christopher. *International Classification of Financial Reporting*. New York: St. Martin's Press, 1984.

Quick, Graham. *Global Reporting: A Guide*. London: Extel Financial Limited, 1989.

Shapiro, Alan C. *Multinational Financial Management*. 6th ed. New York: John Wiley & Sons, 1999, chaps. 8–11.

Stewart, Bennett. "A Proposal for Measuring International Performance," in *New Developments in International Finance*, Joel M. Stern and Donald Chew, Jr., eds. New York: Basil Blackwell, 1988, pp. 105–120.

Stickney, Clyde, and Roman L. Weil. *Financial Accounting*. 9th ed. Fort Worth, TX: The Dryden Press, 2000, chap. 4.

CHAPTER 2
Forecasting Future Needs

Forecasts are critical to evaluating future courses of action. To make useful forecasts, analysts must have the technical skill to forecast and the interpretive ability to understand the future. All forecasting depends upon the skill of the individual making the forecast, and skill comes from both knowledge and experience. A financial analyst must have skill in interpreting and understanding the company's past and current strategy and performance. The quality of an analyst's forecasts depends upon understanding the forces—technological, competitive, and economic—that will affect the company in the future. The accuracy of any forecast depends on proper interpretation of historical data, and the identification and extrapolation of the forces that will affect the company's performance.

No one can forecast the future accurately. Yet every day we make decisions that require forecasts: buy stock, invest in Brazil, build a new plant, introduce and market a new product. All these decisions depend upon our interpretation of the future. To forecast the future, the analyst must make assumptions about what will happen. These assumptions are critical to creating forecasts and to understanding the scenarios behind the forecasts. The skilled analyst knows that these assumptions must be detailed and explicit. An inability to recognize the assumptions that have been made and failure to test them can result in tenuous or obscure forecasts, or forecasts that can be derailed by unforeseen changes in the company, industry, and/or economic conditions.

The forecasts discussed in this chapter are financial in nature. They represent the expected activity and condition of the company over time and at various points in the future, expressed in financial terms. These financial forecasts are the explicit details about what is expected from the way a company creates its products or services.

There are a variety of forecasts financial analysts can make. External analysts typically make forecasts to anticipate a company's performance. For example, a stock analyst may try to determine what returns might be expected from an equity investment in a company and whether its stock is attractive. A lender would try to determine whether a company would generate sufficient cash to remain solvent and repay its obligations. Internal analysts, on the other hand, are often concerned with forecasting financial needs so managers can plan future operations and investments. This chapter's primary focus will be on the types of analyses used by internal corporate managers. These forecasts often rely on information unavailable to external analysts.

Financial analysts for a company turn forecasts for the company's future into two types of financial statements. For a view of the near future, a method known as cash budgeting is most often used. When the forecasts are longer term, projected financial statements are developed.[1] Both will be discussed, and some ways to test the assumptions used in creating the forecasts will be described.

I. CASH BUDGETS

A **cash budget** specifically focuses on the cash account of the company. The cash budget is a forecast of the cash receipts and cash disbursements the company will make. The objective is to identify whether sufficient cash will be available to meet the financial needs or whether there is excess cash that can be invested. This cash-based approach differs significantly from the common method of accounting in corporations, the accrual method. **Accrual accounting** attempts to match the revenues earned with the expenses incurred during a specific period, without regard to actual cash receipts or disbursements. The cash budget looks only at when cash is received or spent.

A cash budget can be made for a whole company, a division, and/or a business unit, or even for an individual or family. To determine whether there is extra cash or a need for more cash, the analyst compares the expected cash receipts with the anticipated cash disbursements. The difference between cash receipts and disbursements reveals either an excess of cash or a need for additional cash for that particular period.

Whether a company has excess cash or a need for cash depends upon the timing of cash receipts and disbursements. If a company prices its products to break even or make a profit, and if the cash payments for its sales are received at the same time it makes payments for its production costs, it will not need additional cash. However, credit sales, seasonal demand, and other factors can combine to cause mismatches between disbursements and receipts. These mismatches result in the need for cash or more cash than is needed to run the business.[2] Because of these timing differences, a cash budget is an essential planning tool for management.[3]

---

[1] Some finance texts and finance professionals call forecasted financial statements pro forma. However the word *pro forma* means restated for different conditions. Here we are not restating statements but making forecasts.

[2] The need for cash can create serious problems. For example, when a company does not have enough cash to meet its payroll, the employees cannot cash their paychecks, resulting in problems for the employees and a general decrease in confidence in the company. Extra cash does not cause the same problem. However, failing to invest the excess means a loss of income and less value for the shareholders.

[3] A cash budget requires considerable information, much of which is available only within the company. Hence, it is primarily a management tool, not a tool used by outside investors to assess the value of an investment.

There are three steps in creating a cash budget:

1. *Choose an appropriate time period for the forecast.* For the typical company a cash budget for monthly cash flows is normal. However, in industries with highly volatile cash flows or during times of high inflation or rapid economic or industry change, cash budgets may be for weekly or even daily cash flows. Not surprisingly, in some highly inflationary environments, companies have been known to prepare hourly cash budgets.
2. *Choose a suitable length of time over which to forecast.* The forecast horizon depends on the firm's situation. If monthly cash budgets are suitable, a 12- or a 24-month forecast would be appropriate. Cash budgets based on shorter time periods are usually developed for correspondingly shorter forecast horizons.
3. *Determine what critical assumptions underlie the forecast.* Most forecasts begin with an assumption about the sales volume. The forecast for sales should be developed in light of the company's current market share, its product line, and its current and future competition. Once the sales forecast has been made, the analyst can use history, along with expected changes in the future, to determine what other assumptions underlie the forecasts. A good place to start is with an historic performance analysis, like that described in Chapter 1. For most cash budgets, asset, liability, and expense levels will be related to the forecasted level of sales. Thus the expected relationships between sales and the assets and expenses are important and need to be stated explicitly.

The cash budget includes forecasts for cash and credit sales, and credit and inventory policies. It results in a series of schedules to determine the cash receipts and disbursements for each period.

To demonstrate how to create a cash budget, let's develop one for Tulipline Fashions, Inc., a wholesale distributor of tennis and swimming clothing and accessories. Although Tulipline sustained some losses during its initial operations, management expects that continuing operations will be profitable. The company has been in existence for only two years, and the owner has relied on a bank loan of $50,000 to offset the financial drain caused by the early losses. Although sales are expected to increase annually by 10 percent, the necessity of extending credit to customers for long time periods causes severe cash problems during the peak summer sales season. To determine the severity of the problem, monthly cash budgets, commencing on September 1, 2000 and extending through August 2001, are prepared.

The first assumption in creating a cash budget is the level of sales: much of the activity of the company depends upon the sales level. Tulipline management might have used information about customers, from its sales force, the industry, other companies, and trade organizations, to forecast sales growth of 10 percent. Starting with a forecast for sales growth of 10 percent, management makes the remaining assumptions. Management may use its experience or the experience of others in the industry to make the remaining forecasts. The assumptions made by Tulipline's management are listed in Exhibit 2-1. Based on these assumptions, the expected sales volume, cash and credit sales, accounts receivable collections, and purchases of merchandise for each of the 12 months of the cash budget period are shown in Exhibit 2-2. In addition, since Tulipline sells mostly in credit, credit sales are included for July and August 2000. These are used to forecast the collections of credit sales in September and October.

As you look at the cash budget and the other forecasts that follow, note that in making forecasts the years increase going to the right. Historic financial statements most often show the most recent year to the left, as was shown in Chapter 1. Do not be confused. It is just one of the odd conventions to which you will become accustomed.

If Tulipline made all of its sales and purchases in cash, everything would be easy. However, it does not. Because of this we must estimate the impact on its cash position of delays in receiving payments from customers and making payments for what it owes. The following describes how to create the schedules, starting with the forecasts for September.

1. To determine the accounts receivable for September 30, add to the August 31 accounts receivable balance of $246,100 to the credit sales for

EXHIBIT 2-1 Tulipline Fashions, Inc.

CASH BUDGET ASSUMPTIONS

1. *Sales.* Sales, shown in Exhibit 2-2, are seasonal with the peak occurring during the summer months. Sales are expected to increase about 10 percent per year.
2. *Cash and credit sales.* Ten percent of the sales are for cash. Credit terms for Tulipline's customers are net 60 days, and customers meet the credit terms.
3. *Cost of goods sold.* Supplies are purchased the month prior to need. Cost of goods sold is 73 percent of sales.
4. *Accounts payable.* Suppliers require payment in 30 days.
5. *Selling, general, and administrative expenses.* Selling, general, and administrative expenses are 14 percent of sales. These expenses are paid in the month in which they are incurred.
6. *Fixed operating expenses.* Fixed operating expenses are $6,500 per month. This does not include $500 per month for depreciation.
7. *Lease and interest payments.* Lease and interest payments are $3,000 per month. This is a simplifying assumption since interest expense will depend upon the actual amount borrowed.
8. *Taxes.* The company has tax loss carryforwards: no tax payments need be made in 2000–01. The fiscal year begins in September.
9. *New equipment.* New equipment will be purchased in March 2001 for $25,000, and must be paid for two months later.
10. *Credit line.* The bank will allow a credit line of no more than $50,000. This allows the company to borrow up to $50,000 as needed.
11. *August 31 cash balances.* Tulipline has a $9,000 cash balance at the end of August 2000. Its accounts payables are $70,100 and receivables are $246,100.
12. *Dividend payments.* No dividends will be paid.

EXHIBIT 2-2 Tuplipline Fashions, Inc.

FORECAST FOR SALES, PURCHASES, AND COLLECTIONS

2000	Sales	Cash Sales	Credit Sales	Collection of Accounts Receivable	Purchases
July	$ 151.9	$ 15.2	$ 136.7	N.A.	N.A.
August	121.5	12.1	109.4	N.A.	$ 70.1
September	$ 96.0	$ 9.6	$ 86.4	$ 136.7	$ 54.8
October	75.0	7.5	67.5	109.4	40.2
November	55.0	5.5	49.5	86.4	32.9
December	45.0	4.5	40.5	67.5	25.6
2001					
January	35.0	3.5	31.5	49.5	32.9
February	45.0	4.5	40.5	40.5	51.1
March	70.0	7.0	63.0	31.5	76.7
April	105.0	10.5	94.5	40.5	105.9
May	145.0	14.5	130.5	63.0	131.4
June	180.0	18.0	162.0	94.5	120.5
July	165.0	16.5	148.5	130.5	98.6
August	135.0	13.5	121.5	162.0	115.2
Total 9/2000 to 8/2001	$1,151.0	$115.1	$1,035.9	$1,012.0	$885.8

N.A. = Not applicable

September. From the total subtract the accounts receivable collected: the credit sales from the prior 60 days. Do this for each month. The result is shown in Exhibit 2-3.

2. To determine the total receipts, add to the cash sales for September to that month's collections on accounts receivable from the accounts receivable schedule in Exhibit 2-3. Do this for each month. The result is shown in the receipts panel in Exhibit 2-5. Tulipline has no receipts other than from its sales.
3. To determine the payments, begin with the August 31 accounts payable balance of $70,100. Add to the balance the purchases for September (73 percent of October's sales), and subtract the payments on the accounts payable. The payments are the purchases from the prior month. Do this for each month. The complete schedule is shown in Exhibit 2-4.
4. The disbursements schedule, also shown in Exhibit 2-5, is the sum of the accounts payable payments from Exhibit 2-4, and the other disbursements listed in Exhibit 2-1. Remember, depreciation is not a cash expense.
5. The cash account is determined by adding to the August 31 cash balance the September receipts and deducting the September disbursements. The result of doing this for each month is shown in Exhibit 2-6.

I. Cash Budgets

EXHIBIT 2-3 Tulipline Fashions, Inc.—2000–01 Accounts Receivable Schedule (in thousands)

	September	October	November	December	January	February	March	April	May	June	July	August
Beginning accts. receivable	$246.1	$195.8	$153.9	$117.0	$90.0	$72.0	$72.0	$103.5	$157.5	$225.0	$292.5	$310.5
Credit sales	86.4	67.5	49.5	40.5	31.5	40.5	63.0	94.5	130.5	162.0	148.5	121.5
Collection—accts. receivable	136.7	109.4	86.4	67.5	49.5	40.5	31.5	40.5	63.0	94.5	130.5	162.0
Ending accts. receivable	$195.8	$153.9	$117.0	$90.0	$72.0	$72.0	$103.5	$157.5	$225.0	$292.5	$310.5	$270.0

EXHIBIT 2-4 Tulipline Fashions, Inc.—2000–01 Accounts Payable Schedule (in thousands)

	September	October	November	December	January	February	March	April	May	June	July	August
Beginning accts. payable	$70.1	$54.8	$40.2	$32.9	$25.6	$32.9	$51.1	$76.7	$105.9	$131.4	$120.5	$98.6
Purchases	54.8	40.2	32.9	25.6	32.9	51.1	76.7	105.9	131.4	120.5	98.6	115.2
Payments	70.1	54.8	40.2	32.9	25.6	32.9	51.1	76.7	105.9	131.4	120.5	98.6
Ending accts. payable	$54.8	$40.2	$32.9	$25.6	$32.9	$51.1	$76.7	$105.9	$131.4	$120.5	$98.6	$115.2

Note: Shaded cells indicate beginning balances from the balance sheet.

EXHIBIT 2-5 Tulipline Fashions, Inc.—2000–01 Monthly Cash Budget (in thousands)

	September	October	November	December	January	February	March	April	May	June	July	August
Receipts												
Cash sales	$ 9.6	$ 7.5	$ 5.5	$ 4.5	$ 3.5	$ 4.5	$ 7.0	$ 10.5	$ 14.5	$ 18.0	$ 16.5	$ 13.5
Collections on accts. receivable	136.7	109.4	86.4	67.5	49.5	40.5	31.5	40.5	63.0	94.5	130.5	162.0
Total receipts	$146.3	$116.9	$91.9	$72.0	$53.0	$45.0	$38.5	$51.0	$77.5	$112.5	$147.0	$175.5
Disbursements												
Accts. payable payments	$ 70.1	$ 54.8	$40.2	$32.9	$25.6	$32.9	$51.1	$ 76.7	$105.9	$131.4	$120.5	$ 98.6
Selling, general, and admin. expense	13.4	10.5	7.7	6.3	4.9	6.3	9.8	14.7	20.3	25.2	23.1	18.9
Operating expenses	6.5	6.5	6.5	6.5	6.5	6.5	6.5	6.5	6.5	6.5	6.5	6.5
Lease and interest expenses	3.0	3.0	3.0	3.0	3.0	3.0	3.0	3.0	3.0	3.0	3.0	3.0
New equipment	—	—	—	—	—	—	—	—	25.0	—	—	—
Tax payments	—	—	—	—	—	—	—	—	—	—	—	—
Total disbursements	93.0	74.8	57.4	48.7	40.0	48.7	70.4	100.9	160.7	166.1	153.1	127.0
Receipts less disbursements	$ 53.3	$ 42.1	$34.5	$23.3	$13.0	$ (3.7)	$(31.9)	$(49.9)	$(83.2)	$ (53.6)	$ (6.1)	$ 48.5

EXHIBIT 2-6 Tulipline Fashions, Inc.—2000–01 Cash Account Balance (in thousands)

	September	October	November	December	January	February	March	April	May	June	July	August
Beginning cash balance	$ 9.0	$ 62.3	$104.4	$138.9	$162.2	$175.2	$171.5	$139.6	$ 89.7	$ 6.5	$(47.1)	$(53.2)
Receipts less disbursements	53.3	42.1	34.5	23.3	13.0	(3.7)	(31.9)	(49.9)	(83.2)	(53.6)	(6.1)	48.5
Ending cash balance	$62.3	$104.4	$138.9	$162.2	$175.2	$171.5	$139.6	$ 89.7	$ 6.5	$(47.1)	$(53.2)	$ (4.7)

Notes: Shaded cells indicate beginning balances from the balance sheet. Negative cash balance indicates a need for financing.

Using this cash budget, we can see that Tulipline would need $47,100 additional cash in June and a total of $53,200 in July. The need is relatively short term as we can see: the need declines to $4,700 by the end of August. This short-term need for funds is typical of companies with seasonal sales, and most, Tulipline included, have a significant cash balance at the beginning of the next selling season.

This cash budget gives Tulipline management important information. The company has a credit limit of $50,000, but this is not enough to meet the needs in July. Management has two choices. It can change its marketing plan, thus reducing the need for sales-driven cash, or go to the bank and negotiate an increase in the credit line to accommodate the need. Since the forecast shows that the funds are needed because of the nature of the business, not because of poor planning or bad management, management should go to the bank well before the funds are needed. By extending the cash budget for one month, management can show the bankers that Tulipline's cash need is a temporary supplement needed only to meet its seasonal requirements during the summer months. Graphically, Exhibit 2-7 shows the cash balance and vividly demonstrates the impact on financing needs that can come solely from selling a product with seasonal demand.

We have not mentioned the positive cash balances that Tulipline has for most of the year. What should Tulipline management do? Be pleased with the cushion, or plan for its use? The real question is, Just how much reserve cash should Tulipline keep? The liquidity a company requires depends on its operating practices and the environment in which it operates. Companies operating

EXHIBIT 2-7 Tulipline Fashions, Inc.—2000–01 Monthly Cash Balance (in thousands)

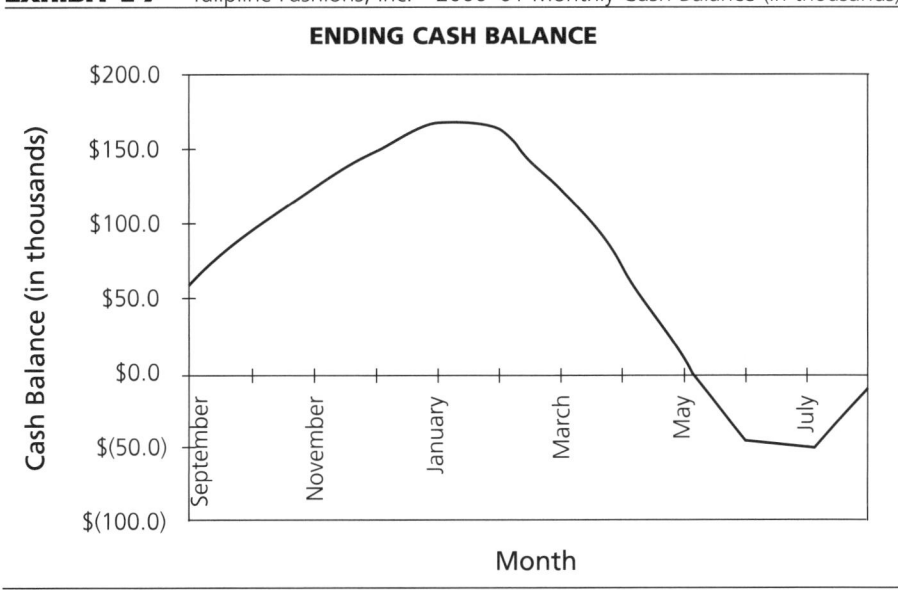

in more volatile environments, with greater uncertainty about such things as sales, collections, and costs, need to maintain a higher cash balance than those operating in more stable economic conditions. Obviously, the more difficult it is to forecast future events, the greater the need to maintain a high cash reserve for unforeseen needs. One thing to note—the cash reserve need not be maintained as an actual cash balance. Adequate liquidity protection can be established with a line of credit with a bank.[4] Other kinds of companies need actual cash. Companies with retail operations, for instance, companies like Hannaford—the grocery store chain we analyzed in Chapter 1, need cash for daily store transactions.

II. PROJECTED FINANCIAL STATEMENTS

Cash budgets are used to track the ebb and flow of accounts, particularly the cash account. Management uses cash budgets the same way you track your own cash receipts and disbursements: to make certain that money is available when needed, and that excess cash is invested. The cash budget is a management tool, not a way to determine whether the company is profitable and healthy over the longer term. Most managers, stock analysts, and investors would rather see forecasted financial statements, the income statement and balance sheet, for that insight.

1. Developing Projections Directly

Forecasted financial statements, like normal financial statements, provide aggregate accrual information either over the forecast period for the income statement, or at a point in time for the balance sheet. You could also think of a projected financial statement as a summary of the information contained in the cash budget. Cash budgets provide the details, while financial statement forecasts provide information in the more familiar accrual-based accounting format.[5] Although financial statement forecasts could be prepared weekly or monthly, as was our cash budget, they are usually created for the same periods as those reported historically—as quarterly or annual forecasts.

Like cash budgets, making a financial statement forecast requires defining one or more critical variables and the relationships of other variables to the critical variable(s). The relationships that underlie the forecast, and assumed by

---

[4] A line of credit allows a company to borrow up to a preset limit at any time the credit line is in force. To provide such a credit line, the bank will charge a fee for what is borrowed, and a fee for keeping the credit facility available.

[5] Projected income statements forecast earnings and expenses for the period; projected balance sheets forecast assets and liabilities at the conclusion of the period; projected cash flow statements forecast funds changes over the period.

the analyst, should be explicit and written, just as they should with the cash budget.[6]

When you want to forecast how well a company will do in the future you can use a simple extension of ratio analysis on which to base the forecasts. The first step in this process is to determine the historical relationships among financial statement accounts for previous years, just as we did in Chapter 1 for Hannaford. These relationships, expressed as ratios, are then adjusted to account for expected future events and trends. Finally, the analyst forecasts the various accounts on the basis of these adjusted ratios. As is the case with cash budgets, the first projection to be made is the sales or revenues. In most cases, other accounts are then forecasted on the basis of their expected relationship with sales. Using Tulipline Fashions for our example, let's develop the forecasted financial statements.

Our first statement will be the income statement. All of what we need to make the forecast is found in Exhibits 2-1 and 2-2. The forecast, along with notes about the sources of the data, is shown in Exhibit 2-8. The net income is expected to be $29,700.

The balance sheet for Tulipline is a bit more difficult to create than the income statement. One reason is that the forecasted balance sheet rarely balances. One of two things can happen. Either the assets will be larger than the liability and equity accounts, indicating a need for additional financing if the asset strategy is to be followed, or the liability and equity accounts will exceed the assets. An excess of assets indicates that the company has additional sources of

EXHIBIT 2-8   Tulipline Fashions, Inc.

2001 INCOME STATEMENT (in thousands)

Sales	$1,151.0	Sum of September 2000–August 2001 sales, Exhibit 2-2.
Cost of goods sold	(840.2)	Assumption 3, Exhibit 2-1.
Gross income	310.8	Calculated.
Expenses:		
Selling, general, and administrative	(161.1)	Assumption 5, Exhibit 2-1.
Fixed operating	(78.0)	Assumption 6, Exhibit 2-1.
Depreciation	(6.0)	Assumption 6, Exhibit 2-1.
Lease and interest	(36.0)	Assumption 7, Exhibit 2-1.
Net income before taxes	29.7	Calculated.
Taxes	0.0	Assumption 8, Exhibit 2-1.
Net income	$ 29.7	Calculated.

---

[6] We will continue to argue for explicit, written, and detailed assumptions. These are easier to follow, interpret, change, and return to later.

capital that may be used to increase assets or reduce liabilities and equity. One easy way to deal with this problem of balance is to include a "net financing needed" account on the projected balance sheet. This might be called a "plug" account because it is not a real account since it is used only to create the balance. If the amount in this account is positive, additional financing is needed. If the amount is negative, the company has excess funds, and additional capital is available for investment. As you can see in the balance sheet in Exhibit 2-9, Tulipline needs at least $4.7 million at the end of August 2001.[7] This is the same figure calculated in the cash budget. Since the assumptions underlying both are the same, the amounts should be the same.[8]

EXHIBIT 2-9 Tulipline Fashions, Inc.

BALANCE SHEETS DIRECTLY FORECASTED AS OF AUGUST 31
(in thousands)

	Actual 2000	Forecasted 2001	
Assets:			
Cash	$ 9.0	0.0	
Accounts receivable	246.1	$270.0	The sum of July and August 2001 credit sales from Exhibit 2-2.
Inventories	89.0	134.6	Inventory from year-end 2000 + purchases from July 2000–August 2001, less cost of goods sold.
Total current assets	344.1	404.6	
Net equipment	42.0	61.0	Equipment from year-end 2000 plus new equipment less depreciation (Exhibit 2-1 assumptions 6 and 9).
Total assets	$386.1		
Trial balance		$465.6	
Liabilities and Equity:			
Notes payable	$ 10.0	$ 10.0	No change.
Accounts payable	70.1	115.2	August 2001 purchases from Exhibit 2-2.
Total current liabilities	80.1	125.2	
Long-term debt	100.0	100.0	No change.
Equity	206.0	235.7	Equity from year-end 2000 plus net income from income statement in Exhibit 2-8.
Total liabilities and equity	$386.1		
Trial balance		$460.9	
Net financing needed		$ (4.7)	Negative number here would indicate that there is a need for cash, the firm must borrow at least this amount.

---

[7] The statement is built using the assumptions from Exhibits 2-1 and 2-2 and the net income figure from Exhibit 2-8.

[8] The cash budget and balance sheet give us the same forecast for what the company will need for August 2001. However, the balance sheet shows only that date; the cash budget shows us the full year, month by month. If we had only looked at the balance sheet, we might miss the larger need in the months preceeding August.

It is essential to remember that the reliability of all forecasts depends on the assumptions. While these forecasts are simple, even they must be adapted for anticipated company and market conditions. More sophisticated forecasting approaches may be used if warranted.

2. Developing Financial Statement Forecasts from Cash Budgets

Cash budgets and financial statements are related. In fact, if you have a cash budget, you can derive the financial statement forecasts directly from it. To create the financial statements from a cash budget, you need two things: the balance sheet at the beginning of the forecast period and the cash budget. With these two statements you can create an end-of-period income statement, balance sheet, and a sources and uses of funds or cash flow statement. Once again we will use Tulipline as an example to demonstrate this process.

To forecast the September 1, 2000 to August 31, 2001 income statement we use the assumptions from Exhibit 2-1. This is identical to the process we used in creating Exhibit 2-8 and the result is identical, and will not be repeated here. For the balance sheet, the process is different.

We will use the balance sheet for August 31, 2000, the beginning of the forecast period, and information from the cash budget to create the projected balance sheet for August 31, 2001. The resulting balance sheet is shown in Exhibit 2-10. This exhibit details the sources of the data and the changes that are expected to occur in the various accounts over the forecast period. Exhibit 2-11, the sources and uses of funds, summarizes the changes over the forecast period.

These financial statement forecasts are the basis on which stock analysts, portfolio managers, shareholders, lenders, and managers make decisions and test possibilities. Thus it is important to understand them and the assumptions on which they rest. The best way to be able to interpret forecasts made by others is to be skilled at making forecasts yourself.

Although projections do not provide the level of detail about the ebbs and flows in the cash account that is shown in the cash budget, they do show the cash balance at the end of the forecast period: they indicate the company's financing needs at the end of the period. For companies that do not experience a significant change in cash during a year, this approach to forecasting their cash requirements is usually adequate. Because cash budgets are more time-consuming to prepare, most managers elect to develop financial statement projections directly rather than on the basis of a cash budget.

III. PROJECTING FINANCIAL STATEMENTS IN HIGHLY UNCERTAIN CONDITIONS

A number of critical assumptions underlie the financial forecasts we made for Tulipline Fashions, Inc. Making assumptions is very difficult, even in circum-

EXHIBIT 2-10 Tulipline Fashions, Inc.

BALANCE SHEETS FROM CASH BUDGET AS OF AUGUST 31
(in thousands)

	Actual 2000		Forecasted 2001
Assets			
Cash	$ 9.0	From cash budget, Ex. 2-6.	$ (4.7)
Accounts receivable	246.1	From accounts receivable schedule, Ex. 2-3.	270.0
Inventories	89.0	2000 balance plus purchases of $885.8, less cost of goods sold of $840.2.	134.6
Total current assets	344.1		399.9
Net equipment	42.0	2000 inventory plus new equipment of $25, less depreciation of $6.	61.0
Total assets	$386.1		$460.9
Liabilities and Equity			
Notes payable	$ 10.0	No change.	$ 10.0
Accounts payable	70.1	From accounts payable schedule, Ex. 2-4.	115.2
Total current liabilities	80.1		125.2
Long-term debt	100.0	No change.	100.0
Equity	206.0	2000 balance plus net income of $29.7 from the income statement, Ex. 2-8.	235.7
Total liabilities and equity	$386.1		$460.9

EXHIBIT 2-11 Tulipline Fashions, Inc.

SOURCES AND USES STATEMENT SEPTEMBER 2000 TO AUGUST 2001
(in thousands)

Sources	
Decrease in cash	$13.7
Increase in accounts payable	45.1
Net profits	29.7
Total sources	$88.5
Uses	
Increase in accounts receivable	$23.9
Increase in inventories	45.6
Increase in net equipment	19.0
Total uses	$88.5

stances that generate relative confidence. Analysts usually feel most confident when they make forecasts for companies that:

1. Are in a reasonably stable industry.
2. Have a strong position in their industry.

3. Are not making many changes to:
   a. the products they sell,
   b. the methods used for production, and
   c. the sources of financing.
4. Are in reasonably stable economic and political environments.

Tuliplane operated in a relatively certain environment. However, many companies operate in situations that are challenging. While understanding the historical performance of companies that operate in highly volatile environments can be difficult, forecasting their future performance can seem impossible. As an example let's use a company operating in a country where the economic environment has been quite volatile.

Terra Blanca bound paper into notebooks for use by schools and businesses. The late 1990s were a difficult time for the company. First, the country where it operated was on an economic roller coaster, with inflation reaching very high levels. Second, because of declines in individual and government incomes, sales of products had not met management's expectations. In addition, since some of the material Terra Blanca used to make its products came from outside the country, and those prices were not frozen by government mandate, costs had been difficult to control. The financial performance of the company for 1997 through 1999 is shown in Exhibit 2-12. As you can see, performance was erratic. This is most obvious when you look at the common-size statement (Panel B) and the growth rates in the various expense items (Panel C). You should note the strange profit figure in 1997. In that year the net financing income, income from financial transactions, dwarfed the sales.

Management, believing that planning was essential even though it had to be flexible, continued to make forecasts in spite of the volatility of the business and economy. However, management was confronted with a difficult problem: historical data was so erratic that it did not provide much information to use as a basis for estimating the future. What should they do?

After looking at the past to understand how the economic environment had impacted Terra Blanca, the next thing management did was to assess the environment in which the company would be operating in the future. Recent events had led Terra Blanca management to believe that the economy was under control and that a period of stability was evident and had been under way since late 1999. In this case management determined that the current situation was normal enough to use it as a basis for making forecasts. Explicit forecasts were made for inflation, as well as for the way in which Terra Blanca's business would react to the economic environment. Their analysts' forecasts are shown in Exhibit 2-13.

Several things about the Terra Blanca financial statements, and those for companies in similar environments, are quite different from those shown for companies in more stable environments. First, for Terra Blanca, inflation was high and had an uneven impact on revenues and costs. Second, operating profits in an uncertain and inflation-prone environment can be negative because of

EXHIBIT 2-12 Terra Blanca Sociedad Anonima

HISTORIC INCOME STATEMENT DATA
(in thousands of currency units)

Panel A:	Currency		
	1997	1998	1999
Sales	10,100	38,500	68,540
Cost of goods sold	(20,100)	(49,450)	(82,800)
Gross profit	(10,000)	(10,950)	(14,260)
Operating expenses	(6,500)	(38,450)	(48,840)
Operating profits	(16,500)	(49,400)	(63,100)
Net financing costs	73,010	77,900	66,400
Profit before taxes	56,510	28,500	3,300

Panel B:	Percentages		
Sales	100%	100%	100%
Cost of goods sold	−199%	−128%	−121%
Gross profit	−99%	−28%	−21%
Operating expenses	−64%	−100%	−71%
Operating profits	−163%	−128%	−92%
Net financing costs	723%	202%	97%
Profit before taxes	560%	74%	5%

Panel C:		Growth Rates	
Sales		281%	78%
Cost of goods sold		146%	67%
Gross profit		10%	30%
Operating expenses		492%	27%
Operating profits		199%	28%
Net financing costs		7%	−15%
Profit before taxes		−50%	−88%

declines in demand brought on by decreases in real income, or because of price freezes instituted by the government to reduce inflation rapidly. Third, inflationary environments provide profit-making opportunities for companies that have cash to invest: net financing costs turn into lending profits rather than interest expenses, and the profits from financial transactions can offset product/market losses. As you can see, as inflation dropped Terra Blanca's profits from financial transactions declined. At that point, you will note that the company stops making financial gains and borrows cash, incurring financing costs. This situation is not unusual in inflationary environments.

One solution to the complexity of making high inflation forecasts might be to make the forecasts in real, net of inflation, terms. The statements in Exhibits 2-12 and 2-13 are nominal, and include inflation. Creating real statements would be a good plan if, and only if, inflation impacted all the forecasted items

IV. Analyzing Assumptions

EXHIBIT 2-13   Terra Blanca Sociedad Anonima

FORECASTED FINANCIAL STATEMENTS
(in thousands of currency)

	2000	2001	2002	2003	2004
Sales	99,109	130,625	149,174	176,324	208,415
Cost of goods sold	(67,394)	(73,150)	(82,046)	(88,162)	(104,207)
Gross profit	31,715	57,475	67,128	88,162	104,208
Operating expenses	(69,376)	(88,825)	(71,604)	(79,346)	(83,366)
Operating profits	(37,661)	(31,350)	(4,476)	8,816	20,842
Net financing costs	48,000	28,450	(22,100)	(16,000)	(12,000)
Profit before taxes	10,339	(2,900)	(26,576)	(7,184)	8,842
Assumptions					
Real annual sales growth rate	2.0%	5.0%	8.0%	12.0%	12.0%
Gross profit/sales	32.0	44.0	45.0	50.0	50.0
Operating expenses/sales	70.0	68.0	48.0	45.0	40.0
Inflation rate per month	3.0	2.0	0.5	0.5	0.5
Inflation rate per year	42.6	26.8	6.2	6.2	6.2
Taxes/profit before taxes	42.0	42.0	42.0	42.0	42.0
Nominal annual sales growth rate	44.6	31.8	14.2	18.2	18.2

identically. Unfortunately, this is rarely true. Costs can escalate faster than inflation, some costs may lag inflation, revenues may first go up with inflation and then stabilize, and the income from invested cash, the financial gains, might rise at quite a different rate indeed. Since costs and revenues can be affected by inflation in different ways, real statements do not solve the problem of forecasting in an inflationary environment. Management must determine how inflation will impact their company and its financial forecasts, taking no shortcuts.

Terra Blanca provides a somewhat more complex forecasting problem that we had seen before. It is not harder than making forecasts for Tulipline, it is just more complex and requires keen market and economic intelligence.

IV. ANALYZING ASSUMPTIONS

Projections require assumptions. If the assumptions are not valid, then the subsequent forecasts are valueless. Whether an assumption is valid or not is recognizable only after the fact. Still, we want to be certain that our assumptions are realistic representations of a likely future. To test the reasonableness of an assumption several procedures have been used. The methods generally do one of two things: test for reality or demonstrate how the change in an assumption will impact a forecast. Rather than just describe the various ways you can gain perspective and confidence about assumptions, let's use an example.

Design Supplies, Inc. is a distributor of drafting and architectural supplies and software. The equity investment was provided by the owner/manager of the company, and a friend provided the remainder of the funding of $200,000 as a no-interest loan. The lender, a friend who considered herself more a silent partner than a lender, recently requested that she become involved in the operations of the company. However, she is willing to be paid off, or will remain silent as long as there are real prospects for having her entire loan repaid in the near future. The original agreement was that the owner/manager would fully repay the debt at the end of 2003. The owner/manager hopes that Design Supplies will provide sufficient funds to allow him to do so.

To determine whether adequate funds will be available for a buyout, the minority owner has developed a five-year forecast. Exhibits 2-14 and 2-15 show the income statements and balance sheets for the previous three years and the projected statements for five more years. The assumptions used in developing the forecasts are shown at the bottom of the exhibits.

From the forecasts, it appears that the company will generate sufficient funds by 2003 to allow the owner/manager to fully pay off the debt. You will note, as should the owner, that while the total of these accounts is sufficient to pay off the partner, doing so would leave the company with a small amount of cash for operations. The owner will have to plan to have sufficient cash for operations when the loan is repaid.[9]

If you are the friendly lender these forecasts look good, if you can wait until 2004. However, before accepting that the loan can be paid off five years from now, you would certainly want to understand the assumptions on which the forecasts are based. A reasonable way to look at the assumptions would be to compare Design Supplies' forecasts to its own recent performance.

1. Historical Comparisons

Just as ratios are used to examine the historical performance of a company, so too can they be used to test whether assumptions about future performance are reasonable. For Design Supplies, such a comparison is shown in Exhibit 2-16. There are several things you might note: real and nominal sales growth is expected to be higher than the previous year, and operating expenses and current assets are expected to be lower. If you were the lender, would you feel confident in these forecasts?

Let's look first at the sales growth. Is it too optimistic? As the lender you might note that the forecasted sales growth is above that obtained in 1999, but below what was experienced in 1998. This increase may assume a decline in inflation and an increase in the real rate of growth. In addition to the very im-

---

[9] You certainly must have noted that all we have planned for, thus far, was to pay off the lender's $200,000. What if the lender was expecting interest? If the lender was expecting only 6 percent return on her loan, the full value of the loan plus interest could not be repaid until 2004. If the interest rate were higher, it would take even longer.

IV. Analyzing Assumptions 105

EXHIBIT 2-14 Design Supplies, Inc.—Historic and Forecasted Income Statements (in thousands)

	Actual			Forecasted			
	1997	1998	1999	2000	2001	2002	2003	2004
Sales	$1,094	$1,360	$1,402	$1,612	$1,854	$2,132	$2,452	$2,820
Cost of goods sold	(792)	(980)	(984)	(1,128)	(1,298)	(1,492)	(1,716)	(1,974)
Gross profit	302	380	418	484	556	640	736	846
Operating expenses	(244)	(290)	(351)	(376)	(402)	(430)	(460)	(492)
Profit before taxes	58	90	67	108	154	210	276	354
Taxes	(15)	(30)	(14)	(36)	(51)	(70)	(92)	(118)
Net profit	$ 43	$ 60	$ 53	$ 72	$ 103	$ 140	$ 184	$ 236

Assumptions
Sales will grow at 15 percent.
Gross margin will be 30 percent of sales.
Operating expenses will grow at 3 percent plus the expected 4 percent rate of inflation.
Taxes will be 33.3 percent of profit before taxes.

EXHIBIT 2-15 Design Supplies, Inc.—Historic and Forecasted Balance Sheets (in thousands)

	Actual			Forecasted			
	1997	1998	1999	2000	2001	2002	2003	2004
Assets								
Cash	$ 45.0	$ 54.0	$ 60.0	$ 64.2	$ 68.7	$ 73.5	$ 78.6	$ 84.2
Accounts receivable	118.0	168.0	165.0	177.4	204.0	234.5	269.7	310.2
Inventory	309.0	320.0	365.0	403.1	463.5	533.1	613.0	705.0
Other current assets	46.0	52.0	75.0	80.3	85.9	91.9	98.3	105.2
Total current assets	518.0	594.0	665.0	725.0	822.1	933.0	1,059.6	1,204.6
Fixed assets, net	13.0	19.0	14.0	14.0	14.0	14.0	14.0	14.0
Total assets	$531.0	$613.0	$679.0	$739.0	$836.1	$947.0	$1,073.6	$1,218.6

(continued)

EXHIBIT 2-15 *(continued)*

	Actual			Forecasted			
	1997	1998	1999	2000	2001	2002	2003	2004
Liabilities and Equity								
Accounts payable	$ 41.0	$ 61.0	$ 73.0	$ 80.6	$ 92.7	$ 106.6	$ 122.6	$ 141.0
Other current liabilities	3.0	5.0	6.0	6.0	6.0	6.0	6.0	6.0
Total current liabilities	44.0	66.0	79.0	86.6	98.7	112.6	128.6	147.0
Long-term debt	200.0	200.0	200.0	200.0	200.0	200.0	200.0	200.0
Common stock	150.0	150.0	150.0	150.0	150.0	150.0	150.0	150.0
Retained earnings	137.0	197.0	250.0	322.0	425.0	565.0	749.0	985.0
Total equity	287.0	347.0	400.0	472.0	575.0	715.0	899.0	1,135.0
Trial balance	531.0	613.0	679.0	758.6	873.7	1,027.6	1,227.6	1,482.0
Net financing needed (excess funds)	—	—	—	(19.6)	(37.6)	(80.6)	(154.0)	(263.4)
Total liabilities and equity	$531.0	$613.0	$679.0	$739.0	$836.1	$ 947.0	$1,073.6	$1,218.6
Total excess funds plus cash	$ 45.0	$ 54.0	$ 60.0	$ 83.8	$106.3	$ 154.1	$ 232.7	$ 347.5

Assumptions
Receivables will be 11 percent of sales.
Inventory will be 25 percent of sales.
Cash and other current assets will increase at 3 percent plus the expected 4 percent inflation rate.
Accounts payable will be 5 percent of sales.
Other current liabilities will not change.
New fixed asset investments will equal depreciation.

EXHIBIT 2-16 Design Supplies, Inc.

COMPARISON OF ACTUAL RESULTS AND FORECAST ASSUMPTIONS

	Actual			Forecast
	1997	1998	1999	2000–04
Sales growth	N.A.	20%	11%	15%
Inflation	N.A.	6	6	4
Real sales growth	N.A.	14	5	11
Receivables/sales	11%	12	12	11
Inventory/sales	28	24	26	25
Payables/sales	4	5	5	5
Gross margin	28	28	30	30
Operating expense growth	N.A.	19	21	7

N.A. = Not Applicable

portant assumptions about inflation and real growth, the forecast for operating expense decline is dramatic. This reduction in operating expenses coupled with lower inventories and receivables constitute a forecast for a tightly controlled company that is growing. These forecasts may be overly optimistic.[10]

There are many other ways managers and analysts have used to gain more confidence in their forecasts. Statistical tools such as regression analysis allow the analyst to project mathematical relationships based on several past periods of data. While this method provides the security of quantitative rigor, it may be false security if the analyst has good reason to expect future relationships between various accounts to differ from their historical patterns.

2. Sensitivity Analysis—One Scenario

One variable at a time. A valuable means of analyzing the assumptions is called **sensitivity analysis**. This process examines how the change in an assumption will change the forecasts. If changing a particular assumption has little impact on the forecasts, then the assumption is not considered critical. If changing one assumption causes a major change in the projected statements, then it is considered a critical variable that warrants further analysis and careful monitoring.

There were two assumptions, sales growth and operating expenses/sales, that were optimistic in the Design Supplies' forecasts, but are they critical? If you were the lender you would want to know what might happen to the loan repayment if sales were lower or the operating expenses were higher. To look

---

[10] One way to get some perspective would be to look at others in the industry. While we will not make the comparison here, recall that when comparing companies you must be certain that the companies to be compared are similar; that is, they should be in the same industry and have similar operating and marketing strategies. If such strictly comparable companies cannot be found for evaluation, then the analyst should adapt the comparison companies' ratios as needed.

at this we could make two new forecasts, one with lower sales and the other with higher operating expenses.

A simple change would be to forecast sales growth at the level achieved in 1999: 11 percent. With a sales growth rate of 11 percent there would be $252,900 cash available to repay the lender in 2004, but less than needed by 2003. We could expand this test of the sales growth rate by calculating the excess cash available at a variety of sales growth levels. This is done most easily in a computer spreadsheet. Even better than looking at a series of spreadsheets, we could graph the results. Such an analysis and the resulting graph for Design Supplies is shown in Exhibit 2-17. Here you can see that if sales growth is much under 10 percent, the investor's $200,000 note cannot be paid off in 2004. Clearly, whether the lender can be fully repaid in 2004 depends upon Design Supplies' growth being at least that achieved in 1999.

Operating expenses were another of the critical assumptions, and it turns out that it is even more critical to our lender than sales growth. Let's look at what happens if the operating expenses change. If the operating expenses grow at the rate of sales (not a really crazy assumption), Design Supplies not only cannot pay off the lender, but also will need more funds. This is shown in Exhibit 2-18. This type of analysis can be done on any of the other critical assumptions.

Although sensitivity analysis is a fairly simple concept it can give us lots of insights. As attractive as it is, however, it is rather time-consuming to execute properly. If the forecasts incorporate many assumptions the analysis could take considerable time and effort. To ease this process, analysts attempt to simplify

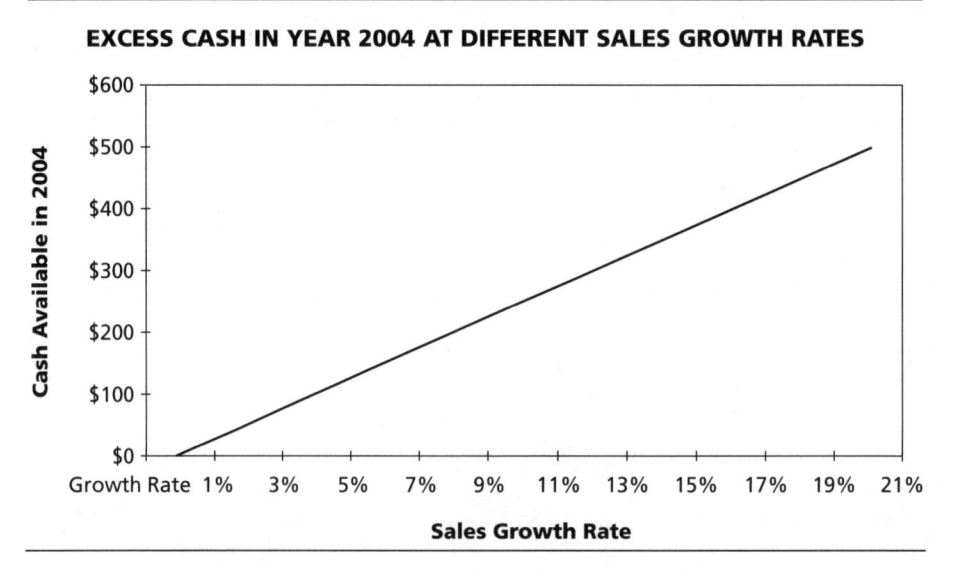

EXHIBIT 2-17 Design Supplies, Inc.

EXCESS CASH IN YEAR 2004 AT DIFFERENT SALES GROWTH RATES

EXHIBIT 2-18 Design Supplies, Inc.

TOTAL EXCESS FUNDS PLUS CASH, OPERATING EXPENSES GROW WITH SALES (in thousands)

	2000	2001	2002	2003	2004
Sales	$ 1,612	$ 1,854	$ 2,132	$ 2,452	$ 2,820
Cost of goods sold	(1,128)	(1,298)	(1,492)	(1,716)	(1,974)
Gross profit	484	556	640	736	846
Operating expenses	(404)	(464)	(534)	(614)	(706)
Profit before taxes	80	92	106	122	140
Taxes	(27)	(31)	(35)	(41)	(47)
Net profit	$ 53	$ 61	$ 71	$ 81	$ 93
Net financing needed (excess funds)	(1)	23	49	78	112
Total excess funds plus cash*	$ 65	$ 46	$ 25	$ 0	$ (28)

*Cash and net financing come from balance sheets, created as Exhibit 2-15 but not reproduced here.

the assumptions and to estimate which factors will have a critical impact on the results. The sensitivity analysis is then confined to these factors.

As an alternative some analysts analyze only negative outcomes. Their reasoning is that while optimistic relationships may occur and create problems, those problems are easier to deal with than the problems pessimistic outcomes create. By focusing only on the downside risks, a range of potential negative results are forecasted. In some cases, however, negative results arise from upside factors. For example, a large increase in sales may appear positive, but it could also result in an increased need for working capital, a need that should be foreseen and planned.

3. Sensitivity Analysis—Three Scenarios

The risk of looking at the impact of only one variable at a time is that simplifying some critical assumptions may be ignored. To concentrate on the key factors, analysts frequently design different **scenarios**, different sets of assumptions about the future. A widely used technique of scenario analysis combines three different sets of values for the crucial assumptions: most likely, optimistic, and pessimistic. The original forecast, or scenario, is usually the **most likely scenario**. The optimistic and pessimistic forecasts are not the same as the absolute best and worst cases that can be imagined. We want to focus on scenarios with a real likelihood of happening, not those that are only remotely possible.

What might be these three probable scenarios for Design Supplies? The critical variables and the resulting excess cash available to repay the lender are shown in Exhibit 2-19. In this exhibit you can see three scenarios. You might

EXHIBIT 2-19 Three Scenarios for Design Supplies, Inc. Forecasts

	Pessimistic	Most Likely	Optimistic
Sales growth	11%	15%	20%
Inflation	6	4	2
Real sales growth	5	11	18
Gross margin	27	30	32
Operating expense growth	7	7	12
Cash and other assets growth (real)	3	3	3
Receivables/sales	12	11	11
Inventory/sales	28	25	24
Payables/sales	4	5	5
Excess cash in 2004	$(45.44)	$347.3	$456.12

disagree about which factors should be changed and by what degree. That is the prerogative of the analyst. What should be clear from this exhibit is the degree to which the outcome depends upon the assumptions, and that some assumptions are more critical than are others.

Computer-based financial modeling systems have been developed that greatly increase the analyst's ability to undertake sensitivity analysis. The analyst can determine the most significant relationships and the effect that potential changes might have on performance. Not only can the modeling systems perform the calculations rapidly, they also facilitate the use of probability analysis.

4. Probability Analysis

Probability analysis is an extension of sensitivity analysis. There are three steps in doing probability analysis. First, forecast a range of possible outcomes. Second, estimate the likelihood that each will occur. Finally, combine the probabilities for each factor with the range of outcomes. As an example, we might take the three scenarios shown in Exhibit 2-19 and make estimates of the likelihood each will occur. For instance, management might expect the most likely scenario to have a 50 percent chance of occurring, while the other two are only 25 percent probable. The weighted outcome is $276.3. This is not the most likely outcome but the **expected value**—the weighted average of the outcomes.[11]

More powerful than scenario-based probability is estimating the potential range and likelihood for each of the critical variables in the forecasts. For example, the analyst might estimate that a 7 percent sales growth has a probability of 15 percent; a 10 percent sales growth, 70 percent; and a 15 percent sales growth, 15 percent; and so on for each item. By combining these probabilities with those estimated for other variables—such as cost of goods sold and rates

---

[11] A more complete probability analysis is shown in Chapter 4.

of inflation—the analyst can calculate the overall probabilities of all possible outcomes. This series of calculations, called a **simulation**, provides more useful information than do projections relying on a single or point estimate for each variable. As you might guess, this is painstaking analysis, unless you have a computer with spreadsheet software. A simulation package makes this kind of analysis even easier. For the reader interested in doing such an analysis, suggested readings are listed at the end of the chapter.

V. MULTI-CURRENCY FINANCIAL STATEMENTS

The forecasts for Tulipline Fashions and Design Supplies were made in dollars, because the companies operated only in the United States. But what if a company made or sold products in more than one country or sourced materials outside its domestic environment, like Terra Blanca? How would the forecasts change? What would be different about a company that was owned by another company in another country? How would those forecasts change?

The first question concerns the proper currency in which to forecast, and the second is how to adapt the forecasts for multiple currencies. The answer to the first question is, forecast in the currency in which the cash will be spent and received. For Tulipline Fashions, that would be U.S. dollars, and for Terra Blanca, its home currency. Before we can answer the second question we need to understand how exchange rates operate.

1. The Importance of Exchange Rates

The globalization of the economic world forces us to recognize that few companies operate in only one currency. A company may owe suppliers, sell products, or get or pay dividends or interest to owners or lenders in other countries. This exposure to foreign currencies introduces a special problem when making forecasts—exchange rates. To make financial forecasts, analysts must forecast receipts and disbursements in whatever currency they occur. If the company is expected to change any of its receipts or disbursements into another currency, the analyst must forecast when the transfer will occur and the currency exchange rate that will be in effect at that time. Thus, to make cross-border forecasts, an analyst must have a basic understanding of foreign exchange markets, of how exchange rates affect their forecasts, and of what makes exchange rates change.[12] However, an analyst forecasting the financial performance of a company with currency exposure must understand the accounting issues, as well as foreign exchange rates and how they change. So how are exchange rates determined and how do they change?

---

[12] In the Appendix to Chapter 1, we discussed how foreign exchange transactions and translations are handled by accountants. In this chapter our concern is transactional.

2. Exchange Rate Theories

An exchange rate is the rate at which one currency can be exchanged for another. This is the rate at which the demand for and supply of a particular currency are equal. There are two different theories about what governs exchange rates: one theory proposes that it is relative purchasing power between the two currencies, while the other hypothesizes that it is interest rates. The first theory, **purchasing power parity**, theorizes that exchange rates render currency denomination differences irrelevant: in a free-trade world, exchange rates make the cost of a good the same in both countries. Theoretically, if a difference in the price of the same good offered in the two countries exists, someone will see the potential to profit. They will take the opportunity, buy the good at the lower price, and offer it to buyers in the country where it commands a higher price. This process is called **arbitrage**, and those acting on price differences are called **arbitrageurs**. Theoretically, exchange rates change only when there is a change in the rates of inflation in the two countries.

Purchasing power parity is simple, and it makes sense, except that it does not seem to work well in practice. The simplest version of this theory does not take into account differences in actual costs of buying, moving the product, and reselling it, or any barriers to arbitrage (e.g., tariffs) created by the two countries. Because purchasing power parity does not explain what actually occurs in the world very well, other theories were developed. The major contender is interest rate parity.

Interest rate parity, or the **Fisher effect**, suggests that differences in *real* interest rates, and changes in those differences, are at the heart of exchange rates and their changes. In theory, exchange rates make the real returns in the two countries the same: if real rates are not the same, the potential exists to make a profit, and an arbitrageur will move in, take the profit, and drive the expected real rates of return together.[13] The mechanism that makes the rates the same is the exchange rate between the two countries. Arbitrageurs move out of the currency of the country with the lower real rate of return, buy the currency of the country offering the higher real rate of return, and thus create a demand for that currency. An increased demand for a currency puts pressure on the exchange rate, and it changes.

In reality, exchange rates are determined by a combination of such things as the differences in real interest rates, relative inflation, growth rates in available income, and perceptions about political and economic risk in the two countries.

Most exchange rates float: they can change as conditions between two countries change. A **floating exchange rate** can depreciate or appreciate, go down or up, relative to another country's currency depending on supply and demand in the market. Most industrialized nations have had floating exchange rates since the early 1970s.[14]

---

[13] Real rates are the rates after subtracting the rate of inflation.
[14] While this statement is true in theory, countries' central banks often intervene to maintain the relative exchange rates between two or more countries. This intervention is usually intended to smooth otherwise rapid exchange rate changes.

Some exchange rates are fixed, however. A **fixed exchange rate** is one where the rate of exchange is set relative to some other currency—often the U.S. dollar. For example, Argentina and over 30 other countries have, or have had, a currency whose value was set relative to the U.S. dollar. A country's governing body, usually its central bank, changes fixed currency relationships.[15] A decrease in the value of the currency relative to another is called a **devaluation**; an increase is a **revaluation**.

Currencies are traded. Indeed, the foreign exchange market is the largest financial market in the world. A company or individual can trade one currency for another today (**spot market**) or for some time in the future (futures or forward market).

Exchange rates are generally quoted in the home currency relative to the currency of the other country; for instance, on September 13, 1999, the spot rate for the British pound was U.S.$1.00:£0.6219. This means that you could have obtained 62 pence for a dollar, or that it cost U.S.$1.6079 to buy £1.00. To determine the exchange rate for the British pound and Japanese yen, the exchange rates for those two currencies would be used. Exchange rates for major currencies are reported in the financial press daily.

There are both **bid prices**, what a seller will pay for the currency, and **ask prices**, the price at which a seller will sell the currency, quoted for large currency transactions. Small transactions cost more than large transactions.

The futures or **forward markets** are markets in which transactions in the future can be settled today. For example, a company with a large payment to a supplier due 30 days from now could contract with a bank for the delivery of the needed currency at that time, for a price specified today. Bank **forward contracts** are arranged between the bank and its customer. The difference between the spot and the futures or forward rates depends on the volume of buyers and sellers of the particular currency for the date in the future and on the potential variability in the exchange rate. Forward contracts usually are for less than one year. The terms and conditions are arranged between the buyer of the contract and the seller.

The customer needing to make a payment or expecting to have an excess of a particular currency for a particular date in the future may also use the **futures markets**. The futures contract differs from a forward contract in that it is publicly traded and the contract is for a standardized quantity of the currency deliverable at a particular date. These contracts are similar to commodities' futures contracts and in the United States are traded on the Chicago Mercantile Exchange. On September 13, 1999, when the spot rate between the U.S. dollar and the U.K. pound was U.S.$1.00:£0.6219, the 90-day future rate was U.S.$1.00:£0.6218.[16] This latter rate reflected almost no expected change in the U.S. dollar relative to the British pound over that time period. In contrast the

---

[15] The central bank in the U.S. is the Federal Reserve Bank.
[16] Most of the currencies of major countries are freely convertible into currency of other major countries. This is not true for smaller countries with less stable currencies. In late 1999 a number of these countries were considering "dollarizing" their economies.

dollar:Japanese yen spot rate was U.S.$1.00:¥106.67 on September 13, but the 6-month futures rate was U.S.$1.00:¥101.71. This implies an expected depreciation in the dollar relative to the yen.

Most currencies are quoted relative to every other currency. This will no longer be true in the countries belonging to the European Monetary Union. For these European countries, exchange rates will all be quoted relative to the new EMU currency, the euro. The home country currencies will continue to exist until 2003, after which all members of the EMU will use euros. Until that time, the currencies are converted using a method called triangulation: each currency is translated into euros and then into the currency of the other EMU member country.

3. How Exchange Rates Affect Forecasts

When making a forecast for a company that has income or expenses from another country or countries, the analyst must make some assumptions about exchange rates at the time the cash will be transferred, not at the time the forecast is being made. For example, let's take the Tulipline Fashions, Inc. example and add some information about how and where the company does business. Tulipline uses fabric woven in another country to make some of its products. The assumption used to create the income statement shown in Exhibit 2-8 was that the cost of goods sold would be an unchanging 73 percent of sales. However, if 21.5 percent of the cost of sales was fabric from the other country, and the exchange rate went from $1:1 to $1:0.67, there would be a significant increase in the cost of purchases. As a result of the cost increases, Tulipline's need for cash would be larger. The impact on the income statement of such a cost increase is shown in Exhibit 2-20. The changes in the cash balance are shown graphically in Exhibit 2-21.

Tulipline is a very simple example of what could occur if the exchange rate changes dramatically. Managers often insure against such potentially dramatic exchange rate changes by anticipating the need for funds and hedging that need with a forward or futures contract. **Hedging** is an activity where a future price is locked in today. There are a variety of ways to hedge including the futures and forward markets as well as careful corporate financing and investment strategy. All hedging has a cost. The analyst would have to incorporate the hedging and its costs into the forecasts.

Exchange rates do change, sometimes dramatically and sometimes slowly. Exhibit 2-22 shows the exchange rate changes (in terms of the U.S. dollar) for Thailand's baht since late 1994. This country exports textiles and finished garments and might be a place from which a company such as Tulipline would import raw materials or partially finished garments. Thailand's baht, which up until mid-1997 had been very stable, became quite volatile. This country was the first in Asia to experience the currency and economic declines of later 1998, the so-called "Asian Crisis." Over this period, forecasting for a company

V. Multi-Currency Financial Statements

EXHIBIT 2-20   Tulipline Fashions, Inc.

2000 INCOME STATEMENT (in thousands)

Sales	$1,151.0	**Current COGS**	
Cost of goods sold	(929.2)	79% U.S.	$659.6
Gross profit	221.8	21% Foreign	180.6
Expenses:		Current COGS	$840.2
Selling and administrative	(161.1)	**New COGS**	
Fixed operating costs	(78.0)		
Depreciation	(6.0)	79% U.S.	$659.6
Lease and interest expense	(36.0)	21% Foreign ($180.6/.67)	269.6
Taxes	0.0	New COGS	$929.2
Net profit	$ (59.3)		

EXHIBIT 2-21   Tulipline Fashions, Inc.

CASH BALANCE WITH AND WITHOUT EXCHANGE RATE CHANGE

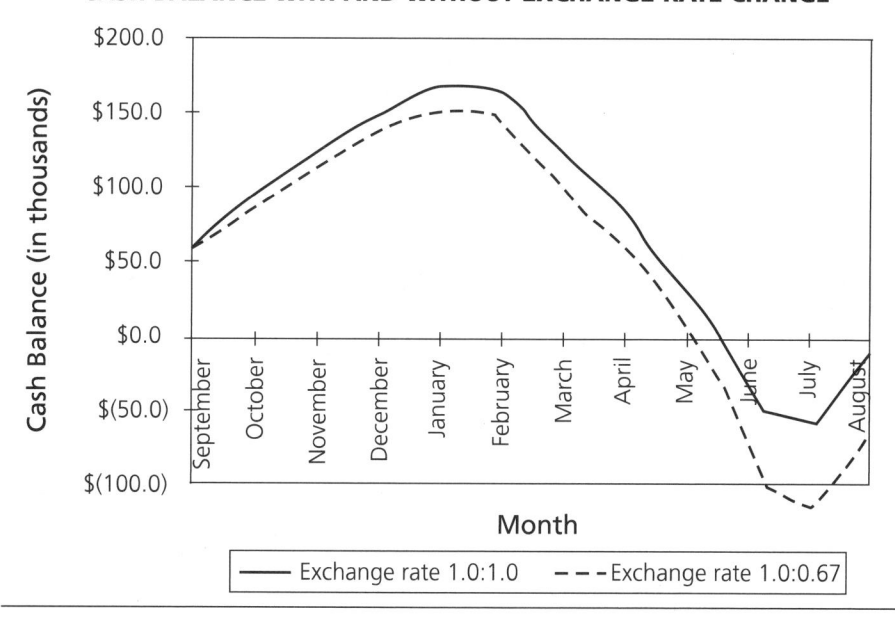

[Line chart showing Cash Balance (in thousands) by Month from September to August, comparing Exchange rate 1.0:1.0 (solid line) with Exchange rate 1.0:0.67 (dashed line). Both lines rise from ~$50 in September to peak around $150–170 in January, then decline, with the dashed line dropping below the solid line and reaching approximately −$90 in July before rising in August.]

doing business in Thailand would have presented the analyst with a serious challenge.

Thailand is classified as a developing country, and many believe that exchange rates are more volatile in developing countries with floating exchange rates. This has certainly been true since the Asian currency crisis in October

EXHIBIT 2-22 U.S. Dollar/Thai Baht Exchange Rate—1994 to September 1999

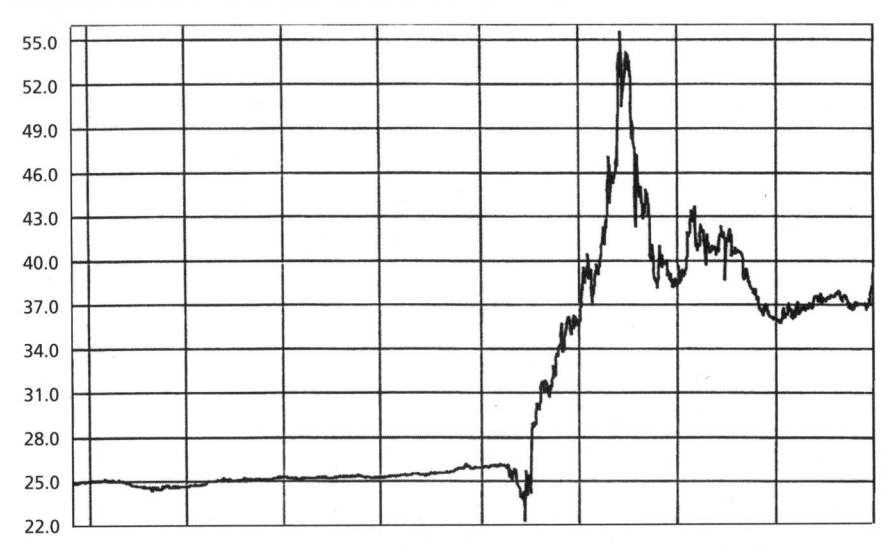

SOURCE: Bridge Information Systems, 1999.

1998. A look at the U.S. dollar exchange rates with a number of other currencies over the same period of history (Exhibit 2-23) shows that exchange rates can be volatile regardless of the level of the country's development.

For the analyst or manager, the more likely a relevant exchange rate will change, and the greater the impact that change can have on the financial viability of a company or strategy, the more effort the manager or analyst must make to understand the potential changes and to forecast them. Because this section is only a very simple introduction to exchange rates and to what makes exchange rates change over time, the competent manager will need to know much more about exchange rates, the mechanisms governing them, and methods to hedge or take advantage of changes in them.[17]

Making forecasts in highly uncertain economic and political environments is difficult. The difficulty reinforces the need for a careful understanding of the company, its industry, and the economy in which it operates. In addition to the sensitivity to exchange rate changes, the impact of inflation must be under-

---

[17] Some companies choose to insulate themselves against changes in exchange rates through certain corporate strategies. One example is to match foreign sales revenues with costs denominated in the same currency. Alternatively, the manager might choose to hedge the currency risk with forward or futures contracts. Because speculating and hedging are sophisticated activities, references for further reading are provided at the end of this chapter. Hedging is also discussed further in Chapter 7.

V. Multi-Currency Financial Statements 117

EXHIBIT 2-23 U.S. Dollar Exchange Rates—1994 to September 1999

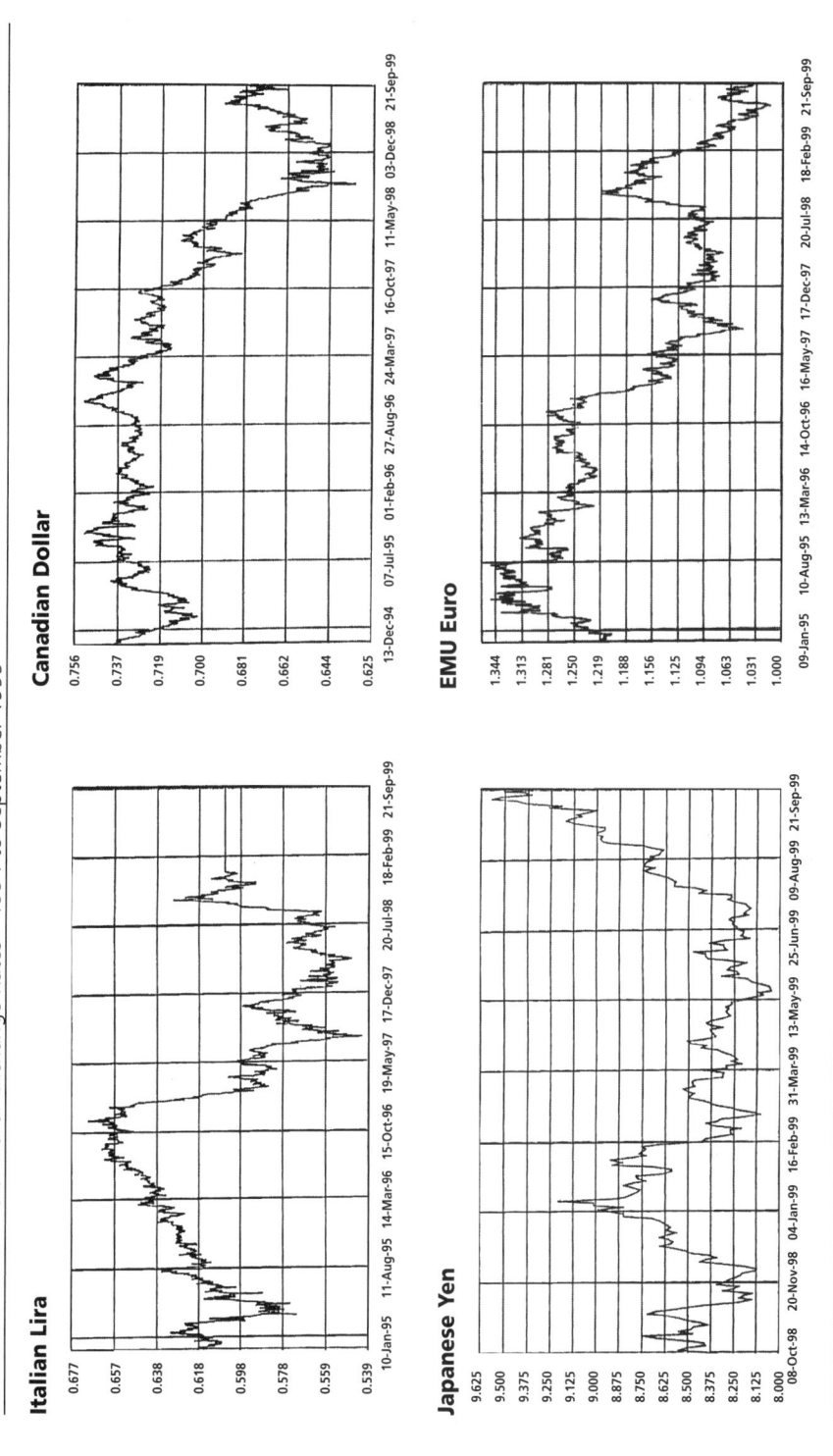

Italian Lira

Canadian Dollar

Japanese Yen

EMU Euro

SOURCE: Bridge Information Systems, 1999.

stood as clearly as possible. In volatile environments, forecasts should be changed frequently as conditions change.

Note that forecasts are not irrelevant in rapidly changing environments; management must make them more often than in stable environments. In fact, many managers contend that forecasts are more important in rapidly changing environments. Rather than despairing about forecast relevancy, we have other ways to approach uncertainty, whether that uncertainty is about the company's operations, its sales, or its environment. Sensitivity analysis, multi-scenario analysis, and simulation can help the manager deal with the dangers and opportunities, and plan for them.

VI. SUMMARY

Historical relationships can aid analysts in projecting the future performance of a company. History must be tempered, however, by the analyst's views of changes in the environment and in the company. Based on these assumptions, an analyst can estimate future cash needs using cash budgets and projected financial statements. The appropriate method depends on the needs of the company.

Projections are only as useful as the validity or reasonableness of the underlying assumptions. An important part of any forecast is testing the assumptions through sensitivity analysis. In so doing, the analyst and manager become aware of the critical assumptions and are forewarned about areas needing additional analysis and special monitoring.

One other thing must be kept in mind by those creating and using forecasts: forecasts should be constantly updated as information and conditions change. The world is not as stable as we once thought it was, and basing the future of a company on a single set of assumptions that are not kept current or tested for veracity is worse than making no forecasts at all.

SELECTED REFERENCES

For discussions of the impact of inflation on funds forecasting, see:

Seed, Allen H., III. "Measuring Financial Performance in an Inflationary Environment." *Financial Executive*, January 1982, pp. 40–50.

Vancil, Richard F. "Funds Flow Analysis During Inflation." *Financial Analysts Journal*, March–April 1976, pp. 43–56.

For a discussion of simulation, see:

Hertz, David B. "Risk-Analysis in Capital Investment." *Harvard Business Review*, September–October 1979, pp. 169–81.

For additional information on the differences between cash and accrual accounting, see:

Kroll, Yoram. "On the Differences Between Accrual Accounting Figures and Cash Flows: The Case of Working Capital." *Financial Management*, Spring 1985, pp. 75–82.

For additional discussions of forecasting financial needs, see:

Brealey, Richard A., Stewart C. Myers, and Alan Marcus. *Fundamentals of Corporate Finance*. New York: McGraw-Hill.

Brigham, Eugene F., Louis C. Gapenski, and Michael Ehrhardt. *Financial Management*. 9th ed. Fort Worth, Texas: The Dryden Press, 1999, chap. 14.

For more information on foreign exchange exposure, management, and forecasts, see:

Abuaf, Niso. "The Nature and Management of Foreign Exchange Risk." in *New Developments in International Finance*, Joel Stern and Donald Chew, Jr., eds. New York: Basil Blackwell, 1988, pp. 29–43.

Brigham, Eugene F., Louis C. Gapenski, and Michael Ehrhardt. *Financial Management*. 9th ed. Fort Worth, Texas: The Dryden Press, 1999, chap. 27.

Cornell, Bradford. "Managing Foreign Exchange Risks." in *New Developments in International Finance*, Joel Stern and Donald Chew, Jr., eds. New York: Basil Blackwell, 1988, pp. 44–59.

Damodaran, Aswath. *Corporate Finance*. New York: John Wiley & Sons, 1997, chap. 26.

Heckmann, Christine. "Don't Blame Currency Values for Strategic Errors." in *New Developments in International Finance*, Joel Stern and Donald Chew, Jr., eds. New York: Basil Blackwell, 1988, pp. 29–43.

Pringle, John. "A Look At Indirect Foreign Currency Exposure." *Journal of Applied Corporate Finance*, Fall 1995, pp. 75–81.

Pringle, John, and Robert Connolly. "The Nature and Causes of Foreign Currency Exposure." *Journal of Applied Corporate Finance*, Fall 1995, pp. 61–74.

Solnik, Bruno. *International Investments*. 4th ed. Reading, MA: Addison Wesly Longman, 1999, chap. 3.

For a discussion of taxes and corporate strategy, see:

Scholes, Myron, and Mark Wolfson. *Taxes and Business Strategy*. Englewood Cliffs, NJ: Prentice Hall, 1992.

For the original interest rate parity discussion, see:

Fisher, Irving. *The Theory of Interest: As Determined by Impatience to Spend Income and Opportunity to Invest It*. New York: Augustus M. Kelley, 1965.

STUDY QUESTIONS

1. The chief financial officer of Top Coke Company (Top C.) is meeting with two top analysts regarding working capital management. One analyst,

Charles Duncan, has suggested that a more lenient accounts receivable collection policy of 45 days would result in a sales growth of 20 percent, higher than previously forecasted for Top C. In addition, inventory turnover would increase to 600 percent and reduce bad debts to 2 percent. While management should expect operating expenses to increase 20 percent because of additional processing costs, Mr. Duncan suggests that an increase in the minimum cash balance to 20 percent of gross sales would offset any liquidity problems.

Another analyst, Ginny Fisher, counters Mr. Duncan's argument for an aggressive working capital policy. She cites, among other issues, the recession throughout the country, and notes that this strategy could help maintain operating expenses at current levels. She estimates that reducing the accounts receivable period to 30 days would stabilize the 5 percent bad debt level and still allow Top C. to grow at 10 percent. Although she states that the inventory turnover could decrease to 300 percent, a minimum cash balance of 15 percent of gross sales appears possible. Operating expenses would not change. Top C. has sufficient sources of short-term debt. The tax rate would remain at 40 percent, cost of goods sold at 40 percent of gross sales, and accounts payable at 114 days of cost of goods sold.

Of course, an argument ensues between the analysts. Mr. Duncan contends that the rest of the world where Top C. operates is not suffering from a recession. Rather, the unification of Europe and the growing purchasing power of the Chinese consumer have expanded potential and current markets. Mr. Duncan argues that Top C. should attack these markets without hesitation. The financial impact on Top C. of these two strategies is not clear.

Compute an income statement, balance sheet, net working capital ratio, and current ratio under both Mr. Duncan's and Ms. Fisher's alternatives. Compare the two alternatives.

From the financial forecasts you have created, decide which policy changes the chief financial officer should implement. The current financial statements follow.

TOP C. COMPANY
HISTORIC FINANCIAL STATEMENTS
(in thousands)
Income Statement

Sales	$ 8,600
Bad debt	(430)
Net sales	8,170
Cost of goods sold	(3,500)
Gross profit	4,670
Operating expense	(3,000)
Operating income	1,670
Taxes	(668)
Net profit	$ 1,002

	Balance Sheet		
Assets		**Liabilities and Equity**	
Cash	$1,200	Accounts payable	$1,400
Accounts receivable	850	Other short-term debt	1,500
Inventory	800	Total current liabilities	2,900
Total current assets	2,850	Long-term debt	550
		Common stock	420
Net property, plant,		Retained earnings	2,980
and equipment	4,000	Total equity	3,400
Total assets	$6,850	Total liabilities and equity	$6,850

2. In 1991 you were working for General Motors and had been assigned to study your toughest competitor, America's most successful foreign car company, Honda Motor Co., Ltd. Despite the slump in auto sales, Honda was expecting further growth in revenues. Using the financial statements for 1990 and the figures below, forecast a Honda balance sheet and income statement for 1991. In addition, to assist you in analyzing your competitor's strategic options, you should determine the change in net working capital and the current ratio for 1991. The exchange rate of the yen to the dollar for 1990 was ¥154:U.S.$1.00, but it strengthened to ¥140:U.S.$1.00 in 1991. Your assumptions were as follows:

- U.S. sales are expected to grow by 25 percent in dollar terms over the next year.
- Japanese sales are expected to grow by only 5 percent in yen terms. Cost of sales is 75 percent of total revenue.
- Research and development spending will be maintained at its current amount.
- Total operating expenses will grow 10 percent.
- Sales should be collected within 45 days.
- The company is pushing for a 60-day payables period.
- Inventory turnover is 600 percent.
- Management requires a minimum cash balance of 10 percent of sales. There will be no net changes in property, plant, and equipment. No dividends will be paid, and no long-term debt will be repaid. Funding will be in the form of short-term debt. The tax rate will remain at 40 percent.

HONDA
1990 INCOME STATEMENT
(in billions)

Net sales		
Japan		¥ 1,300
United States		2,200
Total net sales		3,500
Cost of goods sold		(2,625)
Research and development		(200)
Gross profit		675
Operating expenses		(500)
Operating profit		175
Taxes		(70)
Net profit		¥ 105

HONDA
1990 BALANCE SHEET
(in billions)

Assets		Liabilities and Equity	
Cash	¥ 250	Accounts payable	¥ 400
Accounts receivable	400	Other short-term debt	350
Inventory	475	Total current liabilities	750
Total current assets	1,125	Long-term debt	1,050
		Common stock	75
Net property, plant,		Retained earnings	750
and equipment	1,500	Total equity	825
Total assets	¥2,625	Total liabilities and equity	¥2,625

3. After reviewing your analysis, General Motors' management believes that you are slightly optimistic about your assumptions. Management expected Honda's results to be less positive, and it suggests you look into the financial statements one more time with these revised assumptions:

    - Reduce the minimum cash balance to 7 percent of sales.
    - Decrease the payables period to 45 days.
    - Increase the collection period to 60 days.

   Is the current ratio in line with the industry average of 120 percent? What are the implications of these policy changes to you as a competitor?

4. Review how your analysis would change if the ¥:$ exchange rate dropped to an unprecedented rate of ¥85:$1.00. How would such an exchange rate impact your strategy if you were Honda management? General Motors' management?

5. Mary Turnbull, of Mary's Ski Chalet, is attempting to plan a monthly cash budget for the coming year but is having difficulty determining her expected cash balance because of the seasonality of her sales. She has been able to accumulate the following data for 2001.

MARY'S SKI CHALET
SALES FORECASTS AND BALANCE SHEET BEGINNING BALANCES
(in thousands)

Projected Sales 2001				Beginning Balances 12/31/2000	
Jan.	$210	July	$ 30	Accounts receivable	$184
Feb.	175	Aug.	75	Accounts payable	173
Mar.	160	Sept.	90	Cash	65
Apr.	140	Oct.	125	Inventory	50
May	50	Nov.	165	Equity	471
June	30	Dec.	230	Plant, property, and equipment, net	345

- All collections and payments will be made on a 30-day basis.
- 25 percent of all sales will be paid for in cash.
- Cost of goods sold will be 75 percent of sales.
- Selling, general, and administrative expenses will be 19 percent of sales.
- Purchases will be 100 percent of cost of goods sold plus 8 percent of sales for a cushion against stock-outs (safety stock).
- Interest and lease expenses will be $24,000 for the year.
- Depreciation expense will be $12,000 for the year.
- Tax loss carryforwards will result in Mary's Ski Chalet paying no taxes in 2001.

Will Ms. Turnbull need additional financing to cover a monthly cash deficit?

6. Prepare a 2001 forecasted income statement and balance sheet for Ms. Turnbull using the information provided in Question 5.

7. Aries Corporation has entered a new market in early 2000 and has asked you to prepare a five-year projected balance sheet and income statement based on the following forecasts:

- Sales growth in 2000 will be the same as in 1999. In 2001, sales growth will dip to 10 percent, and then will increase 1 percent for each year thereafter.
- Negotiations with suppliers have reduced prices, resulting in an improvement in gross margin of 12 percentage points, if the payment period is decreased to 60 days. Purchases made at the higher rate and included in raw materials inventory will result in an average margin of only 10 percentage points in 2000.
- There will be no change in the percentage of sales historical relationships for operating expenses or cash balance.
- Legislation has been passed that will reduce the tax rate to 38 percent in 2002 from its current rate of 50.7 percent.
- Inventory turnover has been historically high. Management plans to increase the turnover in 2000 to 8 times and level it out in 2002 to 6 times.
- Management does not expect any change in days' sales outstanding.
- Property, plant, and equipment—net of acquisitions, disposals, and depreciation (which is included in the cost of goods sold allocation)—will be $265,000, $291,000, $323,000, $403,000, and $513,000 for 2000 through 2004, respectively.
- Any additional financing required will be short-term (notes payable) financing.

To assist in your analysis, financial statements for 1998 and 1999 are as follows:

ARIES CORPORATION
INCOME STATEMENTS
(in thousands)

	1998	1999
Sales	$ 221	$ 266
Cost of goods sold	(145)	(166)
Gross profit	76	100
Operating expenses	(38)	(35)
Operating profit	38	65
Taxes	(19)	(33)
Net income	$ 19	$ 32

ARIES CORPORATION
BALANCE SHEETS
(in thousands)

	1998	1999
Assets		
Cash	$ 22	$ 37
Accounts receivable	49	31
Inventory	47	45
Total current assets	118	113
Fixed assets	70	122
Total assets	$188	$235
Liabilities and Equity		
Notes payable	$ 0	$ 0
Accounts payable	19	34
Total current liabilities	19	34
Equity	169	201
Total liabilities and equity	$188	$235

CHAPTER 3
Managing Working Capital

Most financial managers spend a significant amount of their time dealing with immediate problems and opportunities. There is no doubt that the development of a comprehensive financial strategy in conjunction with a corporate business strategy is critical for the long-term growth of the company. However, the financial manager must ensure that the corporation can successfully cope with the present, otherwise a long-term plan has no value.

One of the major problems facing managers is the company's need for working capital. **Working capital** includes the current assets of the corporation and therefore includes inventories, accounts receivable, cash, and marketable securities. These resources are directly involved in the company's production and sales. Successful management of corporate working capital will allow managers to move their company into a prosperous future. This chapter will discuss the various working capital accounts and how they can be successfully managed.

I. THE WORKING CAPITAL CYCLE

The term **working capital cycle**, or **production-sales cycle**, refers to the ebb and flow of funds through the company in response to changes in the level of activity in manufacturing and sales. When the company decides to manufacture a product, funds are needed to purchase raw materials, pay for the production process, and maintain inventory. If the product is sold on credit, the company also requires funds to support the accounts receivable until customers ultimately pay the company for the purchased products.

The word cycle refers to the difference between the time payment is due for production expenses and the time the customer pays for the product. If the company received payment for the product at the same time it was required to pay the expenses of producing the product, there would be no working capital cycle, nor would firms have difficulty managing working capital.

This timing difference can be illustrated with the simple graph shown in Exhibit 3-1. In this highly simplified, hypothetical cycle, the raw materials are ordered on Day 0. The materials arrive and production begins. As production proceeds, workers are paid, and by Day 30, all the costs for labor and materi-

I. The Working Capital Cycle

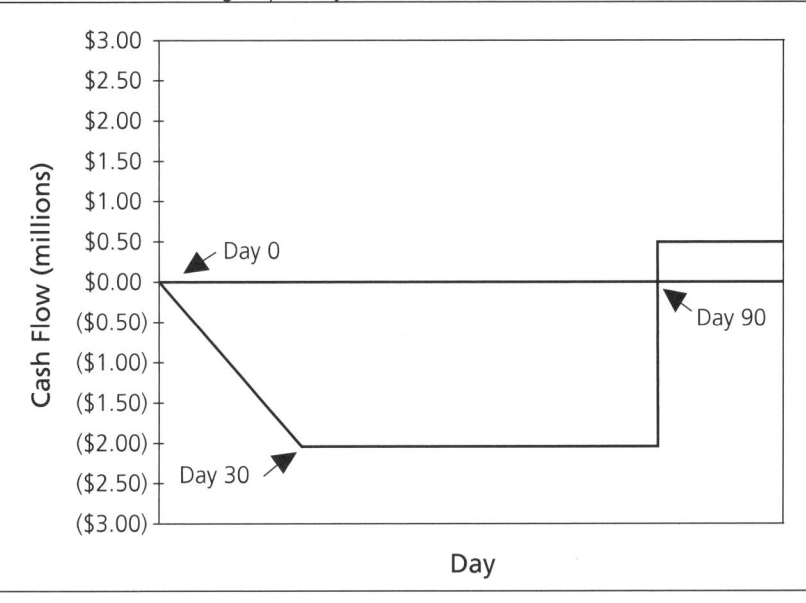

EXHIBIT 3-1 Working Capital Cycle for One Product

[Chart: Cash Flow (millions) vs. Day. Cash flow starts at $0 on Day 0, declines linearly to approximately -$2.00 by Day 30, remains flat until Day 90, then rises to about $0.50 at Day 90.]

als have been paid. The product is completed and is put into finished goods inventory on Day 60. An order is received from a customer on Day 60, and the product is sold. Payment is received from the customer on Day 90. That payment, presuming that the company has priced its product properly, covers all the costs of production plus a profit. From a cash flow standpoint, the company has made all of the cash payments for labor and raw material costs by Day 30, but it receives no cash from the customer until Day 90. Consequently, the company requires some type of financing for 90 days. In this example, the working capital cycle is a total of 90 days, or three months.

The working capital cycle length varies significantly among different kinds of companies. Two extreme examples are distilled spirits producers and grocery retailers. The distilled spirits producer typically stores the product for several years to age: there are several years between the cash outflows for production and the receipt of cash from sales to customers. The grocery retailer usually has a rapid turnover of its perishable inventory and most sales are made for cash: the working capital cycle for the bulk of its inventory is short.

The chart in Exhibit 3-1 shows the cycle for only one unit of a product. Most companies do not produce one product at a time. A grocery retailer is a good example of a company that has a variety of goods, some with short cycles, like fresh produce, others that may have a much longer shelf life, like health and beauty products. For companies like this, many products are produced and/or sold, and all are at various stages in the production-sales cycle at any given time. Thus, once a company is able to complete the start-up phase of operations successfully, it will be able to rely on a continuous flow of products through the cycle to provide funds for its needs. The company can use the cash from previous sales to pay for current production. When a company is in a stable environment with no inflation, sales growth, and changes in customer demand, these lags in the working capital cycle present little difficulty. However, it is rare to find such a working capital situation. Thus the cycle must be understood and managed.

1. The Impact of Inflation

In an inflationary environment, the cost of producing each unit increases over time. Thus, by the time the company has collected the cash from its previous sales, the production costs on subsequent units have increased. Unless the company is able to price units with sufficient profit margins, it may not be able to meet subsequent production costs with revenues from prior production.

To illustrate this problem, let's look at a simple example of a production cycle in a U.K. steel manufacturing company. The company begins with a cash balance of £450, as shown in Exhibit 3-2. This cash balance is sufficient to cover the estimated costs of manufacturing 2 tons of steel at the current price of £225 per ton. However, an unexpected outburst of inflation of 1.5 percent per month (an annualized rate of 20 percent) occurs.[1] The company sells its first ton of steel on the 120th day for £301, but it does not collect payment until 60 days later. It does not charge interest on its accounts receivable. This entire cycle is shown in Exhibit 3-2.

Note that, in spite of the fact that management initially thought it could cover its needs with its cash balance, the company must borrow to finance the production of the second ton of steel, as well as to carry the accounts receivable for the sale of the first ton. This is because the costs of production rose, while the amount held in accounts receivable once the sale was made did not. Management might choose to deal with this problem in a variety of ways, but identifying it is the first step.

This example is obviously highly simplified. Continual production and multiple products with varying working capital cycles and exposures to inflation complicate the analysis. Nevertheless, the conceptual framework for analyzing the increased working capital requirements caused by inflation is the same. The net effect of inflation is to increase the amount of working capital required by the company.

2. The Impact of Sales Growth

The effect of sales growth on working capital needs is similar to that of inflation. In the case of sales growth, the problem is not caused by an increasing

---

[1] The annualized rate of inflation is the compound rate at 1.5 percent per month, or an annual rate of 19.56 percent. A compound rate is not the simple sum of the monthly rates. To learn more about the compounding process, see Chapter 4.

EXHIBIT 3-2 Impact of Inflation on the Working Capital Cycle—Steel Manufacturer

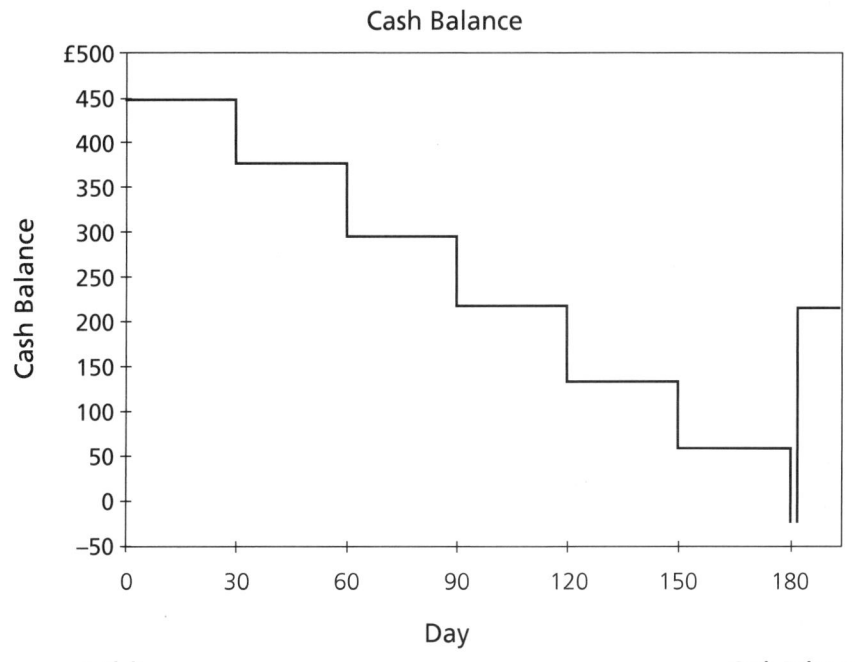

Cash Balance

Day	Activity	Cash Balance
0	Begin production of first ton.	£450
30	Complete one-third of first ton.	374
60	Complete two-thirds of first ton.	297
90	Complete production of first ton at total cost of £232.	218
90	Begin production of second ton.	218
120	Complete one-third of second ton.	138
120	Sell first ton at current price of £239.	138
150	Complete two-thirds of second ton.	57
180	Complete production of second ton at total cost of £243.	(25)
180	Receive payment for sale of first ton.	214

per-unit cost, but by an increasing number of units. Although the cost per unit may be stable, total costs increase because of the increased volume.

For example, a microcomputer producer may have been very successful in developing a market for its products. Assume that the company can produce microcomputers for a cost of $700 each. The company produces 500 computers and sells each for $800 during a particular month. The company extends credit for 30 days to buyers of the microcomputers. During the ensuing month, the demand for microcomputers is such that the company produces 600. At production costs of $700 each, the company incurs a total production cost of $420,000. However, the sales revenue collected from the previous month's sales will be only $400,000 (500 × $800). Thus, even if the company continues to charge $800 per unit, a price that allows a profit margin of 12.5 percent, the sales growth alone will result in a need for new working capital. A company in this situation will have insufficient cash inflow from collections each month to meet the expenses incurred for the production of new computers.

One way to see how important this impact may be is to calculate the net **working capital/sales ratio**. This ratio shows the dollars that need to be invested for each new dollar of sales. The higher the ratio, the more diligent management must be as the company grows. Growth demands more and more capital investment. As an example, the net working capital/sales ratios for textile manufacturers average about $0.30/$1.00 of sales, but range from 1 to 63 cents per sales dollar. The major U.S. manufacturers have working capital to sales ratios averaging 50 percent. This is a very high burden when a company is growing.[2] In our example, the microcomputer company did not misprice its products: the company's prices allowed an adequate profit margin above the costs of production. The problem stemmed from the timing differences between the payment of production expenses and the receipt of payment from sales.

This example illustrates a problem that a growing company faces. In order to grow, a company must finance that growth. A lack of adequate funding will restrict the potential growth of the company. The maximum growth rate a company can fund with its existing financing policies is termed the sustainable growth rate, as discussed in Chapter 1. Sustainable growth depends on the profitability of the company, the need for assets to support sales growth, the way the company is financed, and the company's dividend policy. In general, the more rapid the actual rate of growth, the greater the need for funds to support that growth.

3. The Impact of Variable Sales Demand

The other major factor that can cause working capital problems is a changing level of sales. Changes in sales activity are of three types:

1. **Seasonal.** Peak demand occurs during particular periods of the year. Snow-skiing equipment is one example of a seasonal product.
2. **Cyclical.** Peak demand occurs during different phases of the business cycle; for instance, the demand for building materials is cyclical.
3. **Secular.** Demand fluctuates over a long period of time. Revenues from gold are secular.

These are called cycles since they reoccur over time. Each of these cycles differs in duration but has a similar effect on the company's working capital. For simplicity's sake, we will focus on the seasonal cycle, because it is of short duration and its impact on working capital needs is easy to trace.

---

[2] For companies whose growth is declining, a high net working capital/sales ratio means the company will be awash in cash.

In a seasonal industry, the company may not have sold the completed units before it must incur the costs of producing additional units. To illustrate the problem, we will use the example of the snow-skiing equipment manufacturer. This business is highly seasonal: peak consumer demand occurs during fall and winter. The producer's peak sales period occurs in late summer and early fall, when retailers place their orders to have the equipment ready to sell during the peak snow-skiing months.

The peak sales period for the manufacturer is not, however, the peak production period. To produce skiing equipment as orders from retailers are received would be very inefficient. The manufacturer would need large production capacity, which would be idle for most of the year, and new workers would have to be hired and trained for each production season. During the peak production period the work force would be required to work overtime, and at the conclusion of the period workers would be laid off. In short, seasonal production typically is inefficient and expensive.

To avoid these problems, the ski-equipment manufacturer may produce skis all year long. During the slack sales months, in the late winter and spring, production is continued but little equipment is actually sold to retailers. The manufactured equipment is stored, and the growing inventory is used to fill sales orders as they arrive in the late summer and early fall. As inventory builds up, the company still buys and pays for the raw materials and labor needed to produce the skiing equipment.

As retailers begin to place orders in the late summer, the manufacturer ships equipment from the warehoused inventory. During this period, the manufacturer starts to draw on the finished goods inventory if orders exceed the continuing production level. However, the manufacturer still has not received payment for any of the equipment it has shipped. The retailers buy from the manufacturer on credit, with perhaps 30 or 60 days in which to pay for the equipment.[3] During this period of high but decreasing inventories, continuing production, and increasing accounts receivable, most seasonal companies experience their greatest need for working capital.

As the ski-equipment producer's selling season progresses, additional orders will be received. As these orders are filled, the large finished goods inventory is used more rapidly than it is being replenished from production. Accounts receivable increase from the credit sales, although the company does receive payment for shipments made in the late summer. By the end of the fall selling season, the company's inventory is depleted, and all of its receivables should have been collected: the company should have the cash ready to begin the next working capital cycle.

---

[3] The industry custom for payment terms varies widely. In the agricultural industry where farmers order agricultural chemicals and seed at the season's beginning and earn revenues only when crops are sold after harvest, payment terms can be at harvest's end. The working capital cycle for companies supplying to farmers on these terms can be six months or longer.

No matter how a seasonal company chooses to produce its products, there are risks. The level production company chances the obsolescence of products, or in the case of the ski company, a poor snow year. The seasonal producer must rely on a ready source of labor to tide it over during the peak demand periods. In certain industries and at certain times in the economic, weather, or fashion cycle, seasonal production is dangerous.

In any company the pattern of inflow and outflow of funds might exist for several seasonal peaks during a year, over a business cycle, or over a long-term secular trend. The working capital pattern in many businesses is determined by industry practice. When there is a choice (e.g., level versus seasonal production), the analytical techniques that will be discussed in Chapter 4 are useful in determining which approach is most attractive.

II. CASH MANAGEMENT

Because labor costs and material purchases must be paid for in cash, the critical resource in dealing with the working capital cycle is cash. Corporate managers need to ensure that sufficient cash is available to meet the obligations. This has led to the development of sophisticated, automated techniques to manage a company's cash. These techniques have three objectives: to accelerate the speed of cash receipts, decelerate the speed of cash disbursements, and maximize the return on investment of cash balances. In the 1970s and 1980s, high interest rates emphasized the importance of managing cash, while the development of computers allowed managers access to the information needed for close monitoring of cash balances.

1. Managing Receipts

The process of managing cash receipts involves collecting funds as quickly as possible and concentrating them in accounts so that the financial manager can control them.

Lockboxes. The use of lockboxes speeds the collecting, processing, depositing, and reporting of payments received through the mail. A lockbox is a special post office box to which the company's customers are instructed to mail payments. The box is checked several times daily by the processing operation, which is usually operated by a bank. Upon receipt, checks are immediately entered into the check-clearing process to be converted into funds for the company.

Electronic Funds Transfer. A faster method of collecting funds is to require that payment be made electronically rather than with a paper check. In this system, payment is made by transferring funds directly from the payer's bank account to the recipient's account. This makes the funds immediately available and also eliminates the cost of handling paper checks. For an individual, the debit card issued by a bank acts in the same way. Increasingly, banks, with their on-line services, offer to individual customers services that were once offered only to their corporate clients.

Preauthorized Checks. Preauthorized checks (PACs) are preprinted, unsigned checks. For fixed, repetitive payments, companies authorize their creditors to draw checks on their accounts. The creditor sends the PAC to the bank, which then deposits the funds into the creditor's account. This may also be done electronically.

Deposit Concentration. Because it is difficult to control funds in many different banks, most receipt management systems provide for transferring funds electronically into one or more large accounts. Central accounts can be more closely managed.

Note that all these systems can be used within a country and between parties in two different countries. When a payment must cross borders, the primary criterion is that the currencies of the two countries involved be freely convertible; that is, the currencies can be readily exchanged for each other at a known exchange rate. If the currencies are not freely convertible, the problem is somewhat more complex. International banks have specific expertise in dealing with payments across borders.

2. Managing Disbursements

The goal in managing disbursements is to delay payments so that funds can be used by the company as long as possible.

Managed Balance Account. A managed balance account is a special checking account that has a zero balance. As checks are presented to this account, a negative balance is created. Funds are then automatically transferred from a master account to bring the account back to zero or another predetermined balance. In this way, all funds are centralized and no idle balances remain in the disbursing account.

Controlled Disbursement System. The purpose of this system is to maximize the time it takes for checks to clear a company's account. By making payments through geographically remote banks, the clearing time, also called float, is increased. The purpose is to postpone the date when the company must provide funds to cover checks and to either allow funds to remain in interest-earning assets or reduce the need to borrow.

3. Investing Cash Balances

By carefully managing cash accounts, a financial manager can minimize the cash the corporation must maintain. This increases the amount of funds available to invest or reduces the need to raise additional capital. By maximizing the amount of funds available to invest in productive or working assets, the manager is operating efficiently.

Despite the efforts to control and predict disbursements, there may be unforeseen disbursements or slower than expected receipts. Therefore, companies typically maintain a positive cash balance for transaction liquidity. Having idle cash is unproductive. Good managers maximize the return on these fund balances by investing them in the money market or by using a line of credit to cover a temporary imbalance.

The **money markets** match borrowers and lenders of short-term funds. Although technically money-market instruments can have a maturity of up to one year, most have shorter maturities, some overnight. Money-market instruments are considered to be "near cash" because the market is quite liquid (has many buyers and sellers) and the borrowers generally are institutions with high credit ratings.

Money-market instruments in the United States include Treasury bills (short-term notes issued by the U.S. government), commercial paper (short-term notes issued by corporations), and certificates of deposit (short-term notes issued by banks). Although the returns from these short-term investments may be relatively low in comparison with longer-term, less liquid investments, the returns are superior to idle cash balances.

The short-term investment opportunities may be quite different in other countries. For instance, in smaller economies, the shorter-term market may be arranged only through banks. Very short-term investments may exist exclusively through borrowing and lending between corporations. In countries where domestic currency values are volatile, there may be instruments issued by the government or banks that are denominated in a more stable currency—for instance, U.S. dollars.

While the particular instruments available for short-term investments or to finance a company's short-term needs vary from country to country, one additional major, organized money market exists: the **Eurobond market**. Eurobond borrowing can be in one of several widely tradable currencies. However, much of the borrowing and lending is done in U.S. dollars, even though the market is outside the United States. A company can borrow or lend in this market from overnight up to one year. One can also borrow and lend for more than one year, a subject we will discuss in Chapter 6. Because the lending is done in dollars, the interest rates paid for Eurodollar deposits and charged on loans are similar to those of similar transactions in the United States.[4]

In order to invest in these instruments, the financial manager must know how much cash is available to invest. Cash management systems are designed to provide daily, or even more frequent, information about the amount of funds that can be invested. In many cases, investments must be made for periods as short as overnight to maximize the return available from cash balances.

---

[4] This also can be done in other currencies, such as the Japanese yen.

In times of low interest rates and economic stability, cash by itself is not a productive asset. In such times, and in such countries, managers need to make sure that their companies have minimized the cash that is maintained in the company and that all available resources have been invested in assets being used to produce the company's products. The cash balance should be maintained at the level needed for the operations of the business alone.

Not all environments are stable or have low interest rates, however. In some circumstances, the most productive asset the company has is its cash. In situations where the company's management can lend at rates that generate higher returns than those that could be earned in the company's product market, management will want to adopt policies that maximize the cash at its command and invest it in the money market or the longer term, capital markets.

Opportunities to invest cash in the capital and money markets became evident to many managers around the world in the 1980s. For many companies, the returns they made on their financial transactions exceeded those earned on selling their products. In some cases, financial profits compensated for product/market losses. Periods of above-normal inflation often provide such opportunities. Terra Blanca, a company we looked at in Chapter 2, is an example of such a company.

III. MANAGING OTHER WORKING CAPITAL REQUIREMENTS

Just as a company's cash must be managed, so must other working capital investments. The general rule is to minimize working capital investments while still providing the resources required to produce quality products.

1. Accounts Receivable

Its competitive environment to a large extent, determines the size of a company's accounts receivable. The company often has little control over the magnitude of its credit sales. If competitors are selling goods on credit, the company may be forced to follow that practice to remain competitive. In that case, the only method of reducing accounts receivable is to ensure that credit collections are prompt. If goods or services are sold on 30-day terms, management should vigorously attempt to ensure that payment is received within the 30-day period. Any extension represents a non-interest-bearing loan by the producer to the customer. Some companies charge their customers overdue account penalties or interest to encourage timely payment or to compensate for inflation. Other companies offer an incentive, such as a discount, for early payment.

A method of monitoring accounts receivable based on the due date is called **accounts receivable aging**. In this process, receivables are categorized according to the number of days they are overdue. For example, they might be categorized as 30, 60, and 90 days overdue. Collection efforts can then focus on those accounts that are most overdue. The intent is to minimize the number of accounts that are not collected punctually. Because of the costs associated with the financing of a company's working capital needs, any unnecessary increases in accounts receivable caused by lax collection of overdue accounts must be recognized as an extraneous expense for the company.

In an environment in which a company can independently determine its accounts receivable policy, the critical factor is the relationship between sales and the credit policy. By reducing the financing offered to buyers, a company may be eliminating potential customers. Thus, accounts receivable may be reduced, but only at the cost of reducing total revenues. In such an environment, credit policy should be considered a marketing tool, and the cost of the resulting accounts receivable should be considered a cost of marketing the company's products.

On the other hand, extending more credit to customers may have the effect of reducing the inventory the company must keep. With easier credit terms, buyers may purchase more goods, thereby assuming some of the costs of inventory maintenance from the manufacturer. However, while the company's inventory would decline, its accounts receivable would increase.

An increased volume of credit sales has two other effects. First, it exposes the company to additional risk of uncollectible accounts. The potential cost of unpaid accounts (bad debts) must be weighed against the profits resulting from new sales generated by the easier credit terms. Second, the company extending the credit must have adequate capital to finance its customers' purchases. As you already know, and we will discuss in later chapters, money has a cost. Whether the company borrows to extend credit, or diverts resources from other uses, there is a cost.

2. Inventories

Like accounts receivable, inventory is directly related to sales volume.[5] While maintaining too much inventory is expensive, it will have no impact on sales volume. However, too little inventory may cause stock-outs, and may result in lost sales. Maintenance of an appropriate inventory level is so significant that sophisticated inventory models, including those based on neural networks and fuzzy logic, are used in inventory planning. The aim of these models is to determine the relationship between inventory levels and sales levels so that the company can have the optimum production and inventory levels.

During the 1980s, many managers reevaluated the size of the inventory their companies maintained. One reason for this reevaluation was high interest rates: the cost of financing additional current assets was high. A second reason for reevaluating inventory positions was the method introduced by Japanese companies called "just-in-time" inventory management. This method places the burden for inventory maintenance on the suppliers and

---

[5] That is without a change in the system for managing inventory and/or inventory contents.

forces both buyers and sellers to institute new inventory management procedures. In effect, this inventory method minimizes the inventory kept on hand: shipments of materials and/or goods arrive just as they are needed for production or sales. While this has the effect of reducing inventories, it does present the danger of stock-outs, not having enough inventory, particularly in cases where a supplier falters.[6]

Where inventory is kept, at the supplier or customer, depends upon the nature of the inventory and the balance of power between the supplier and customer. Both supplier- and customer-based inventory systems, like "just-in-time" inventory or more traditional systems, have their risks. "Just-in-time" systems place the responsibility for inventory storage, planning, and shipping on the supplier. This system places the risk of stock-outs, a lack of inventory, on the customer, but obsolescence and warehousing costs and risks on the supplier. When inventory is kept at the customer, the risks are reversed. The choice of inventory system depends in part upon the kind of goods being sold, the geographic proximity of supplier and customer, the relative power of the supplier and customer, and the risks the managements are willing to take.

In sum, from the standpoint of reducing the need for working capital, the company should attempt to reduce its investment in accounts receivable and inventories. However, the company risks the loss of sales if these accounts are reduced inordinately. The managerial task is to ascertain the appropriate level for cash, accounts receivable, and inventory.

IV. FINANCING WORKING CAPITAL

Having determined the minimum level of working capital needed to carry out the production and sales cycle, the manager must then select the most appropriate method of financing it. Not surprisingly, an important consideration is the cost of various sources of financing.

The most significant source of self-funding is a company's profits. If the competitive environment allows, the company may be able to price its products so that profits are sufficient to fund its working capital needs. For example, in an inflationary environment, the company might attempt to increase its prices in excess of the inflation rate in order to finance the working capital needs caused by inflating production costs. The company's ability to adjust its prices in this manner naturally depends on the competitive situation and the economic and political environment in which it operates. In a restrained political environment, above-average price increases may create excessive scrutiny and the potential for price freezes or other industry controls by the govern-

---

[6] This problem was apparent as suppliers suffered disruptions due to the major earthquake in the port and production center of Kobe, Japan, in the spring of 1995. Computer chip scarcity was expected after the September 1999 earthquake in Taiwan, the biggest source of computer chips in the world.

ment.[7] In a highly competitive environment, the company may not have much latitude in its pricing and will need to turn to other sources.

One of the most readily available external sources of funds is the company's suppliers, through the credit terms they allow. Unfortunately, there is a limit to supplier-supplied credit: the company's suppliers may refuse to ship materials needed for production, and such refusals might force the company to stop production. This is usually the last course of action a supplier will take, however, because it results in the loss of a customer.

More often, suppliers encourage prompt payment by providing an incentive. For example, the supplier may offer the purchaser a discount from the sales price if the payment is made within a specified time period. For example, suppliers may indicate payment terms of 2/10, net 30. This means that, if the purchaser pays within 10 days, a discount of 2 percent from the sales price is allowed, otherwise, the full sales price is due in 30 days. If the purchaser decides to wait 30 days to pay rather than paying within 10 days and taking the 2 percent discount, the cost of holding the funds for the additional 20 days is 43.5 percent on a compounded annualized basis.[8] Even if the purchaser decides to pay after 60 days rather than the 30 days specified by the terms of the sale, the effective cost is 5.1 percent for the 50 days. These figures suggest that, when a supplier offers a discount, stretching the payables period is an expensive source of funds unless payment is delayed for a long time.

In countries where tax authorities collect taxes as the profits are earned, another creditor or source of credit financing is the government. Note, however, that while some government taxing authorities may allow a temporary deferral of taxes, nonpayment of taxes is a punishable offense, thus limiting the usefulness of this source of funds.

A typically less expensive source of short-term financing is bank debt. A standard borrowing arrangement for creditworthy companies is a **line of credit** with a bank. This is an agreement that the bank will lend up to a specified amount during a specified period of time. The borrower can borrow, or draw down, against the credit line as the need arises. In situations where the borrower may not be considered a good credit risk, the bank may extend a **secured line of credit**. In this case, the bank has a claim on specific assets of the company—usually the accounts receivable and inventory—if the borrowed

---

[7] Those reading this book who live and work exclusively in the United States may not recall any period of price freezes or price-induced government scrutiny, but both occurred in the 1970s—price freezes during the Nixon administration and price scrutiny of the oil industry during several periods of rapid price increases or lagging price decreases. Current discussion regulating prescription drug prices may result in some form of price controls. For many readers who live in different economic and political environments, price scrutiny and price freezes are common, particularly in politically sensitive or highly visible companies or industries.

[8] If the discount is not taken, and the bill is paid on the due date in 30 days, the customer has paid 2 percent for the use of the funds for 20 days—an annualized compound rate of 43.5 percent. Compounding is explained in Chapter 4.

funds are not repaid as agreed. A standard practice is for secured lines not to exceed some portion of the value of receivables and inventory.

Some companies have found it advantageous to sell their accounts receivable to a financial institution. This process is called **factoring**. The company receives immediate payment for the receivables and does not have to wait until accounts are collected to have funds available. The factoring company buys the receivables at a discount from their stated, or face, value, so the company incurs a cost in selling its receivables. The advantage of factoring is that it reduces the firm's need for working capital. In addition, for a somewhat higher discount, the receivables may be sold without recourse. This means that if an account is not collectible, the financial institution, rather than the company, absorbs the loss.[9]

Companies considered to be good credit risks have developed direct access to short-term financial markets without using commercial banks as intermediaries. These high-quality companies can issue short-term notes, called **commercial paper**, at interest rates slightly below the rates banks would have charged. Other companies, such as insurance companies, are large purchasers of commercial paper. Companies are using increasingly sophisticated and innovative methods of raising short-term funds. The objective is to obtain funds at the lowest cost.

Another method of financing for companies that have accounts is called **securitization**. Securitization has been used primarily by companies with financial assets, such as the financing subsidiaries of large corporations and financial institutions. In general, these companies bundle a number of receivables into a package that is then sold like a security in the capital markets, hence the name securitization. The first assets that were securitized in this way were mortgages. Others, such as credit card receivables, have also been securitized.

Our focus on financing for working capital needs has, in this chapter, been short-term sources. Short-term sources generally are considered appropriate because the need is short-lived. For this reason, a company's **net working capital** is defined as current assets minus current liabilities. While a current asset (that is, a particular credit sale or product in inventory) may be short-lived, the inventory or accounts receivable balance sheet accounts are not short-lived; they are a permanent part of the assets of the company. Thus, many believe that a more appropriate way of financing working capital investments is through a more permanent, long-term form of financing. This notion of using permanent financing for working capital is especially attractive when working capital increases are secular.

If a company chooses to use short-term, temporary financing for permanent or long-lived increases in working capital, there are risks to the strategy. The

---

[9] Factors frequently assume the credit checking function for the company's new and existing customers.

risk comes when a short-term source must be renewed. At that time, the company is exposing itself to interest rate changes and the possibility that funds will not be available when needed. Financing with longer, more permanent sources of financing may be a more appropriate strategy, even though they can be more costly. These sources will be discussed in Chapters 6 and 7.

V. SUMMARY

Through the normal course of business operations, companies require current assets. These assets—inventories, accounts receivable, and cash—are needed to allow the company to create and sell its products. However, because of the timing differences between the cash outflows for creating the products and the cash inflows from the sale of products, companies usually require some financing for these working capital needs.

Because of the magnitude of the amounts required for working capital, skillful managers of working capital can make a significant impact on a company's profitability. Such steps as shortening the working capital cycle or eliminating unneeded assets can reduce the need for cash. In assessing working capital needs, managers must balance reducing working capital and reducing sales and profits. Having achieved an appropriate working capital level, management's remaining responsibility is to finance working capital by taking cost and funds availability into consideration.

SELECTED REFERENCES

For a discussion of cash management and cash management systems, see:

Brealey, Richard A., and Stewart C. Myers. *Principles of Corporate Finance*. 4th ed. New York: McGraw-Hill, 1991, chap. 31.

Brigham, Eugene F., Louis C. Gapenski, and Michael Ehrhardt. *Financial Management*. 9th ed. Fort Worth, Texas: The Dryden Press, 1999, chaps. 22 and 23.

Kamath, Ravindra R., Shahriar Khaksari, Heidi Hylton Meier, and John Winklepleck. "Management of Excess Cash: Practices and Developments." *Financial Management*, Autumn 1985, pp. 70–77.

Ross, Stephen A., Randolph W. Westerfield, and Jeffrey F. Jaffe. *Corporate Finance*. 4th ed. Homewood, Ill.: Richard D. Irwin, 1996, chap. 27.

For a discussion of accounts receivable management, see:

Brealey, Richard A., and Stewart C. Myers. *Principles of Corporate Finance*. 4th ed. New York: McGraw-Hill, 1991, chap. 30.

Brigham, Eugene F., Louis C. Gapenski, and Michael Ehrhardt. *Financial Management*. 9th ed. Fort Worth, Texas: The Dryden Press, 1999, chap. 23.

Gentry, James A., and Jesus M. DeLa Garza. "A Generalized Model for Monitoring Accounts Receivable." *Financial Management*, Winter 1985, pp. 28–38.

Halloran, John A., and Howard P. Lanser. "The Credit Policy Decision in an Inflationary Environment." *Financial Management*, Winter 1981, pp. 31–38.

Mian, Sherzad, and Clifford W. Smith, Jr. "Extending Trade Credit and Financing Receivables." *Journal of Applied Corporate Finance*, Spring 1994, pp. 75–84.

Ross, Stephen A., Randolph W. Westerfield, and Jeffrey F. Jaffe. *Corporate Finance*. 4th ed. Homewood, Ill.: Richard D. Irwin, 1996, chaps. 27 and 28.

For information on inventory management, see:

Brigham, Eugene F., Louis C. Gapenski, and Michael Ehrhardt. *Financial Management*. 9th ed. Fort Worth, Texas: The Dryden Press, 1999, chap. 21.

Damodoran, Aswath. *Corporate Finance*. New York: John Wiley & Sons, 1997, chap. 14.

For more on working capital management in an international company, see:

Shapiro, Alan C. *Multinational Financial Management*. 6th ed. New York: John Wiley & Sons, 1999, chaps. 12 and 13.

STUDY QUESTIONS

1. Chateau Royale International is anticipating explosive sales growth in 2001. As the company's account manager at Bank & Trust, you are concerned about the amount of short-term borrowing that will be required under current working capital policies. Forecast a balance sheet and income statement for 2001, as well as the change in net working capital and the current ratio, to assist management in understanding the effects of this increase in sales volume. Financial statements for 2000, followed by your assumptions, are given below.

CHATEAU ROYALE INTERNATIONAL
2000 INCOME STATEMENT
(in billions of units of currency)

Sales	375,000
Cost of goods sold	(276,150)
Gross profit	98,850
Operating expenses	(75,000)
Depreciation	(5,100)
Operating profit	18,750
Taxes	(7,500)
Net profit	11,250

CHATEAU ROYALE INTERNATIONAL
2000 BALANCE SHEET
(in billions of units of currency)

Cash	75,000	Accounts payable	23,116
Accounts receivable	46,233	Short-term debt	51,867
Inventory	93,750		
Current assets	214,983	Current liabilities	74,983
		Long-term debt	125,000
Net property, plant,		Common stock	100,000
and equipment	115,000	Retained earnings	30,000
		Total liabilities and	
Total assets	329,983	owners' equity	329,983

Based on your knowledge of the company and the industry, you have made the following assumptions:
- Sales will increase 60 percent. Cost of goods sold will be 75 percent of sales. Operating expenses will grow 10 percent.
- Depreciation will be 8,000.
- For this analysis, common stock and long-term debt will remain constant from 2000 onwards.
- Receivables will be outstanding 45 days.
- Purchases equal the cost of goods sold. Payables payment period will be 30 days.
- Inventory turnover will be 3 times.
- Management requires a minimum cash balance of 20 percent of sales.
- There are no purchases or disposals of property, plant, or equipment.
- The tax rate will be 34 percent.
- No dividends will be issued in 2001.
- Additional funding will be in the form of short-term debt.
- Cash will be 20 percent of sales.

2. After reviewing your analysis, Chateau Royale management suggests the following working capital policy changes:
   - Reduce minimum cash balance to 15 percent of sales.
   - Increase payables payment period to 45 days.
   - Increase inventory turnover to 400 percent.

   Recompute the balance sheet and net working capital to reflect these changes. Is the current ratio in line with the industry average of 320 percent? What are the implications of these policy changes?

3. Cindy Brittain, chief financial officer of Kurz Corporation, located in Edmonton, Ontario, Canada, is meeting with her two top analysts regarding management of working capital. Tony Triano has suggested that a more

lenient accounts receivable collection policy would result in higher sales. He has estimated that, by increasing the receivables collection period to 60 days, sales would be 50 percent higher than the original forecast, inventory turnover will increase to 700 percent, and bad debt will be only 2 percent of net sales. Furthermore, an increase in the minimum cash balance to 20 percent of net sales will offset any liquidity problems.

Jim Dine, however, has advised against an aggressive working capital policy citing, among other issues, the expectation of slower economic growth. He has estimated that, by reducing the receivables collection period to 30 days, there will be no bad debt expense and sales growth will still be as originally forecast at 20 percent. Although inventory turnover will decrease to 500 percent, the minimum cash balance can be reduced to 15 percent of net sales.

All additional financing will be in the form of short-term debt. The tax rate will remain at 35 percent, cost of goods sold at 75 percent of gross sales, accounts payable at 29.7 days, and operating expenses will be constant.

a. Compute an income statement, balance sheet, net working capital, and current ratio under each alternative. To assist in your analysis, the financial statements, without the strategy change, are provided.
b. Which policy changes should Ms. Brittain implement?

KURZ CORPORATION
FORECASTED INCOME STATEMENT
(in thousands of Canadian dollars)

Sales	CD$ 505,000
Bad debts	(5,000)
Net sales	500,000
Cost of goods sold	(375,000)
Gross profit	125,000
Operating expense	(90,900)
Operating profit	34,100
Taxes	(11,935)
Net profit	CD$ 22,165

KURZ CORPORATION
BALANCE SHEET
(in thousands of Canadian dollars)

Cash	CD$ 90,000	Accounts payable	CD$ 30,822
Accounts receivable	61,644	Short-term debt	86,322
Inventory	62,500	Current liabilities	117,144
Current assets	214,144	Long-term debt	110,000
Net property, plant, and equipment	130,000	Common stock	75,000
		Retained earnings	42,000
Total assets	CD$344,144	Total liabilities and owners' equity	CD$344,144

4. Jose Dizon, a well-known Philippine architect, has completed the design for THE CRESCENT, to be constructed at the new financial center of the Philippines, the Ortigas Center. He has invited building contractors to bid for the work, and Pablo Lucas has won the bid for 45 million pesos (P). In the contract, Mr. Dizon agreed to pay Mr. Lucas P4.5 million at the beginning of construction, 20 percent of the total contract fee for every additional 25 percent of the job completed, and the final 10 percent 90 days after construction and a successful inspection is completed. Construction is expected to last one year, beginning January 2001. To start the project Mr. Lucas expects to have P1 million in cash on hand at the beginning of January 2001.

Develop a monthly cash budget for 2001 for Mr. Lucas assuming:

- Cement is now scarce because of a boom in the construction industry. As a result, it will have to be imported from Taiwan. Every other month, 33,750 bags will be needed at a cost of U.S.$3.60 per bag. A letter of credit will be used to finance the cement purchases from the Taiwanese supplier. The letter of credit will be opened with a bank one month prior to a shipment. The full value of the letter of credit must be deposited in the bank at the time the letter is obtained. The first shipment will arrive in February 2001, and the last in August 2001. The exchange rate in January 2001 is expected to be P28:U.S.$1, but it is expected to rise to P30:U.S.$1 as early as February.
- Granite tiles to be used for the building exterior must be imported from Italy. The order must be placed in May, and a letter of credit in U.S. dollars must be opened at that time. The total cost is expected to be P5 million.
- Beginning in March and ending in December 2001, 40 molded plastic window frames will be imported from Germany per month. Each window unit will cost $100. The supplier requires a letter of credit.
- Two elevators will be ordered from Korea's Goldstar in February, at a cost of U.S.$10,000 each. Goldstar requires a letter of credit in its favor when the order is placed.
- A generator will be ordered in January. Because the producer, Caterpillar Co., has a locally operated sales office, the payment can be made in local currency. Mr. Lucas expects the generator to be delivered in April and installed and paid for in May. The cost of the generator is P2 million.
- Bathroom fixtures will be imported from Italy. A total of 130 pieces are needed at an expected cost of U.S.$150 per piece. The fixtures will take 2 months to be delivered and are needed one month before the project is completed. A letter of credit will be used to facilitate this purchase.
- Employed on the job will be 200 people with an average monthly salary and benefits of P1,875.
- Overhead expenses are expected to be P10,000 per month.

- Mr. Lucas expects to complete the job in four equal portions in May, August, October, and December.
- No taxes will be paid until 2002.

Mr. Lucas has a revolving credit line with the United Coconut Planters' Bank. The bank has asked him to provide a forecast of the amount of funds he will need and the timing of those needs during THE CRESCENT project. As his financial analyst, you are expected to provide the detailed forecasts for Mr. Lucas to take to the bank.

CHAPTER 4
Valuation 1: Capital Budgeting

Forecasting the future is one of the most important and challenging tasks a manager faces. The task of making forecasts for the future and then turning them into financial forecasts forces the manager or analyst to think in detail about what might happen, and turn both the detailed and ambiguous forecasts into their financial details. In Chapter 2 we discussed some simple methods of forecasting future financing needs. Most of the techniques used the history of the business to create forecasts for the future. These forecasts are useful for examining the financial effects of corporate strategy and policy. However, each forecast assumes that a specific strategy has been decided on and will be undertaken. What we did not discuss in Chapter 2 was how managers choose among different alternative investments and strategies. In this chapter, we will examine the process by which managers allocate capital among different courses of action. Because we are allocating a usually scarce resource, capital, this process of forecasting future performance and making investment decisions is called **capital budgeting**.

Capital investments can be spontaneous or long-term. In Chapter 3, we discussed the increases and decreases in current assets that can occur in businesses where sales are seasonal, cyclical, or growing. Most of these changes could be called **spontaneous** since they do not occur as a consequence of managers' actions but are, instead, the normal result of changing sales levels. For instance, during a cyclical upturn, a manufacturer that makes sales on credit will need funds for both increased inventories and larger accounts receivable. Both of these increases are investments, even though they are spontaneous.

An investment is an outlay of funds on which management expects a return. The return comes, of course, from the profit on the expected sales increase. Spontaneous investments often have short-term benefits and usually involve transient changes in working capital (inventory or accounts receivable) rather than capital investments. Typically, a **capital investment** is thought of as having potential benefits extending over a longer period of time, usually more than one year. It includes such things as permanent additions to working capital (such as an increase in accounts receivable as a result of a change in the company's credit policy); the purchase of land, buildings, or equipment to expand capacity; and the costs associated with an advertising campaign or a research and development program. Because capital investments are often irreversible, or the redeployment of assets comes only at considerable loss of time, money, and managerial effort, capital investments are evaluated more formally and intensely than are spontaneous investments.

In most firms, the capital budgeting process consists of five steps:

1. Generating and gathering investment ideas.
2. Analyzing the costs and benefits of proposed investments:
   a. Forecasting costs and benefits for each investment.
   b. Evaluating the costs and benefits.
3. Ranking the relative attractiveness of each proposed investment and choosing among investment alternatives.
4. Implementing the investments chosen.
5. Evaluating the implemented investments.

Of course, these five steps are continuously repeated in any company. Because financial analysts are most involved in estimating and evaluating the costs and benefits and choosing among the alternative investments, we will concentrate on steps 2 and 3 in this chapter.

I. COST-BENEFIT ANALYSIS OF PROPOSED INVESTMENTS

The goal of investing is to create value for the owners of the firm. An investment creates value for its owners when the expected returns from the investment exceed its costs. In economic terms, we say that the **marginal** or **incremental benefits**—the benefits derived solely from the investment—must exceed the **marginal** or **incremental costs**. There are several hidden difficulties with this concept. First, the very word incremental implies there is another entity or alternative. Thus, we must ask, incremental to what? The second difficulty is in choosing how to measure the costs and benefits.

In estimating the value of an investment, we care about only the costs and benefits that would not have occurred if the company had not undertaken this particular project. To estimate the investment's benefits and costs, the analyst forecasts the cash flows associated with the investment at the time they will be received or disbursed as measured by the receipt and disbursement of cash.[1] Many companies use the accrual method of accounting: sales are recorded when an order is shipped, and obligations are recorded when incurred. Accrual accounting can trick the investment analyst. For instance, the investment may be charged with a portion of the ongoing expenses of the firm—the overhead.[2] This is an accounting allocation of costs, not a marginal or incremental cost associated with the investment itself. Thus, if this investment neither increases

---
[1] As we discussed with cash budgeting in Chapter 2.
[2] Overhead usually consists of charges for such things as cleaning services, accounting, and so forth.

nor decreases overhead expenses, then overhead is not a cost or benefit for the purposes of the investment analysis. Only incremental, new expenses or benefits are relevant in the analysis of new investments. The real benefit derived is the receipt or disbursement of cash that comes solely as a result of this investment, and it is cash that concerns the investment analyst.

1. Cash Benefits

Four sources of cash benefits or receipts may be derived from an investment:

1. Cost reductions when a more efficient process is substituted for a less efficient one.
2. Cash received as a result of increased sales.
3. Cash received when replaced equipment is sold.
4. Cash expected to be received from the salvage value or sale of the plant or equipment at the end of its useful life.

To illustrate these benefits we will describe the analysis done by a shipping company management that was considering an investment in a sail-assisted tanker. Management was analyzing whether to replace one of its diesel-fueled, ocean-going tankers with a tanker that had auxiliary metal sails to take advantage of the wind. The firm might benefit from this investment in several ways. First, the sail-assisted ship would use less fuel and thus be less expensive to operate than the diesel-powered vessel. This cost reduction would lower the operating costs for every year the ship would be in operation. Furthermore, because the new ship has a larger cargo space, the tonnage carried by the ship would exceed that carried by the old tanker, resulting in increased yearly revenues. In addition to the benefits from reduced operating expenses and increased sales, the company would sell the old diesel-powered ship for cash and gain favorable tax treatment as a result of the sale. Finally, at the end of its useful life, the salvage value of the sail-assisted ship and any favorable tax effects would also be benefits.

The sail-assisted tanker, like most investments, offers a variety of benefits at various times throughout its useful life. The analyst's task is to identify all the benefits (and costs) and their magnitude and timing.

2. Cash Payments

The cash payments (costs) associated with any investment fall into three categories:

1. The initial capital cost of the investment.
2. Added capital costs over the life of the investment, including capital improvements made to plant or equipment during the life of the project.
3. Operating costs.

I. Cost-Benefit Analysis of Proposed Investments

Capital costs include the initial price of making an investment (e.g., buying equipment) as well as any subsequent major outlays of cash required to extend the life of the project or equipment. In our tanker example, capital costs include the costs of obtaining the new ship, the subsequent major engine replacements, and other major repairs needed to extend the life of the vessel. Operating costs are the recurring, annual cash outlays that are required once the investment becomes part of the company's operations. Finally, by purchasing the tanker, the company will have to cover such annual operating costs as wages, fuel, taxes, and maintenance that exceed those that would have been spent with the old tanker.

Any cash already expended on the investment, such as research to develop the new tanker's sails, is not a relevant cost in this investment analysis. Instead, this type of expense is considered a **sunk cost**: it represents a past outlay of funds that has no bearing on the present decision. The manager's concern is not to recover sunk or irreversible costs but to create value from subsequent new investments. In other words, any investment being considered must have a positive marginal return.

The company, as a result of making an investment, will also incur tax benefits and costs. Unfortunately, the exact effect tax laws will have over the life of a given project may not be known at the time an investment is made. If current tax laws are expected to continue in effect during the life of the project, the impact of taxes on the costs and benefits can be forecasted with relative ease. However, tax codes change, sometimes dramatically and quickly. For instance, during the years 1981–1991 there were three major changes in the U.S. tax code that affected the tax treatment of capital investments. From 1981 to 1986, the Accelerated Cost Recovery System (ACRS) was in use. In 1986, a new tax code was enacted that lowered tax rates, removed the investment tax credit, and lengthened depreciation schedules.[3] In 1991, the code was further adjusted and called the Modified Accelerated Cost Recovery System (MACRS).[4]

---

[3] Under the tax law adopted in 1986, assets were assigned to different depreciable categories depending on their expected life. Personal property was divided into six different categories (expected lives of 3, 5, 7, 10, 15, and 20 years), and real property (real estate, not including land) was divided into two groups (expected lives of 27.5 and 31.5 years).

Capital costs in the 3-year to 10-year classes were depreciated using an accelerated depreciation called the double-declining-balance method, with a switch to the straight-line method permitted near the end of the life. The switch was allowed in order to optimize deductions. Costs in the 15- and 20-year categories were depreciated using a 150 percent declining-balance rate, switching later to the straight-line rate. Real estate, on the other hand, had to be depreciated using the straight-line method.

For taxes in 1999, the rules were a little simpler. Buildings were depreciated for 39 years starting in the month in which they were put in service, property like computers and the bundled software could be written off over 5 years, with half the depreciation in the first and sixth years, and assets such as office furnishings depreciated over 7 years. Unbundled software was considered to have a 3-year life.

[4] The first year was considered a half year and depreciation is 20 percent, half that under ACRS. In the following five years, the rates were 32.00, 19.20, 11.52, 11.52, and 5.76 percent, respectively.

The straight-line and double-declining-balance methods of depreciation were most used under the 1980 U.S. tax codes and are widely used in other countries. With **straight-line depreciation**, the annual depreciation is calculated by simply dividing the investment cost by the allowed depreciable life. For example, if a company purchases a piece of equipment for $150,000 that has a depreciable life of five years, the annual depreciation expense is $30,000:

$$\text{Annual depreciation expense} = \frac{\text{Cost of asset}}{\text{Depreciable life}}$$

$$= \frac{\$150{,}000}{5 \text{ years}}$$

$$= \$30{,}000$$

Double-declining-balance depreciation allows a higher deduction from taxes in earlier years than does straight-line depreciation. This method is a little more difficult to calculate. To calculate double-declining-balance depreciation, we double the straight-line rate of depreciation and multiply it by the undepreciated investment value. Note, the first year is considered a half year.

For our example the straight-line rate of depreciation is 20 percent, based on a five-year life. Thus, the first year's depreciation using the double-declining-balance method would be twice 20 percent for a total of 40 percent. Since we take depreciation for only half the year, the depreciation expense is half of the total.

Double-declining-balance for the first year's depreciation:

$$= [(0.20 \times 2) \times \$150{,}000]/2$$
$$= \$30{,}000$$

Double-declining-balance for the second year's depreciation:

$$= (0.20 \times 2) \times \$120{,}000$$
$$= \$48{,}000$$

This depreciation expense is much higher than the amount that would be expensed during the second year using the straight-line method. This results in lower taxes than under straight-line depreciation. Because depreciation is higher and taxes lower, a method like this is called **accelerated depreciation**. Note, the total depreciation over the life of the investment is the same under both methods, only the timing of the depreciation expense differs. At some times, and in some countries, the double-declining-balance rate is simply double the straight-line depreciation, and the first year is considered a full year.

Exhibit 4-1 shows the differences in depreciation using three methods: straight-line depreciation; ACRS, the method under the tax code in force from 1981; and double-declining-balance and MACRS, the method under the 1999

EXHIBIT 4-1 Depreciation Expense Using Three Methods of Depreciation

Year	Straight-Line	ACRS*	Double-Declining-Balance MACRS[†]	Double-Declining-Balance Traditional[‡]
1	$ 30,000	$ 22,500	$ 30,000	$ 30,000
2	30,000	33,000	48,000	48,000
3	30,000	31,500	28,800	28,800
4	30,000	31,500	17,280	17,280
5	30,000	31,500	17,280	12,960
6	0	0	8,640	12,960
Total	$150,000	$150,000	$150,000	$150,000

* Most machinery and equipment was depreciated over five years under U.S. ACRS rules. For those five years, depreciation was 15, 22, 21, 21, and 21 percent, respectively. An investment tax credit was allowed in the first year, generally amounting to 8 percent of the investment's cost, and the marginal tax rate was 48 percent.

† This is the 1999 tax code framework. The first year is considered to be a half year, regardless of the actual length of time the asset is owned during the year. The depreciation rates for the six periods are 20.00, 32.00, 19.20, 11.52, 11.52, and 5.76 percent, respectively.

‡ This is simply double the straight-line depreciation rate with a switch to straight-line depreciation when it is advantageous. In this case the switch occurs in the fourth year. At the beginning of Year 5 there is a balance remaining of $25,920 to be depreciated equally over the remaining two years.

U.S. tax code revision.[5] By comparing the depreciation expense allowed under the two recent U.S. tax codes to straight-line depreciation, a method favored by many corporations for their public reporting, you can see how the depreciation method chosen can affect the company's reported profitability. Because depreciation expense is much larger in the early years under the double-declining-balance method, the company's taxes will be lower during those years and its cash flow larger. It is because of this that accelerated depreciation methods are believed to encourage investment in capital projects.

There is a dark side of accelerated methods: they decrease profits. Thus, most U.S. companies do not use accelerated methods of depreciation for their financial reports, in spite of the fact that accelerated methods are used to calculate tax payments. This difference in tax and reporting methods results in financial statements that do not accurately reflect the taxes that were paid in any given year. Over time, of course, the two are equal.

Because a tax code and its effect on a project's costs and benefits are sources of uncertainty, potential changes and their impact should be assessed. Some

---

[5] In addition to changes in the method of depreciation, the U.S. 1991 tax code stipulated a lower maximum tax rate for corporations of 34 percent (the ACRS marginal rate was 48 percent). For corporations with taxable incomes of less than $75,000, the rate dropped to 25 percent, and below $50,000 the rate was 15 percent. Investment tax credits, amounting to 8 to 10 percent under ACRS, were abolished.

changes in a tax code can be anticipated; others cannot. In fact, the nature of the changes and their impact can be quite unexpected.

This uncertainty is only one of many that face the analyst in making forecasts. Later in the chapter we will describe methods for incorporating uncertainty into the analysis. To identify and estimate the costs and benefits associated with any investment, the analyst will call on experts in marketing, engineering, accounting, operations, and the economy to provide needed forecasts.

Before we conclude this section on costs and benefits, note that we have not dealt with one kind of costs and benefits—those associated with financing. It is important to determine both the value created from an investment and the value that comes from the way that investment is financed. In this chapter we discuss only the evaluation of an investment from the point of view of the owners of the corporation, without considering subcontracting any of the owners' financing responsibility. Therefore, no costs or benefits associated with financing the investment are included in the analysis. The issue of financing, since it is a complex topic, is left to Chapters 6 and 7. In Chapter 6 we will discuss how shareholders, or managers on their behalf, decide to subcontract some of the financing of the company to other capital providers, principally lenders. In Chapter 7 we discuss what tools can be used to determine the proportion of financing that should be subcontracted to lenders and whether value can be created or destroyed through judicious leverage. In that chapter we show how financing costs (particularly interest payments and principal repayments) and financing benefits (primarily, new loan receipts) can be included in the analysis of an investment.

II. EVALUATING INCREMENTAL COSTS AND BENEFITS

Once costs and benefits have been itemized, the analyst's major task is to determine the marginal or incremental effect the investment will have on the firm as a whole. To evaluate incremental costs and benefits, many analysts group investment proposals into categories that help them examine each proposal in terms of its relationship to the firm's business as a whole.

The most useful scheme is to group projects according to the degree of independence of their costs and benefits from the costs and benefits of the company and its other investments and projects. **Independent investments** are projects that can be accepted or rejected regardless of the action taken on any other investment, now or later. **Mutually exclusive investments** are projects that preclude one another: once one project is accepted, the others become unavailable or inappropriate. Mutually exclusive projects often are designed to solve the same problem or to serve the same function. For example, managers often must choose among alternate means of adding plant capacity, or among advertising programs, or between two new product lines.

II. Evaluating Incremental Costs and Benefits

There are two types of mutually exclusive and independent investments—**replacements** and investments in **new products and processes**. Replacement investments are made to modernize an existing process or to revitalize an old product line. Because estimating the net effect on the company of replacing a process or product can be especially difficult, analysts often place these investments in a separate category. They are, however, just an especially troublesome type of mutually exclusive or independent investment. To understand the process of evaluation, we will analyze two mutually exclusive investments, keeping in mind that independent investments would be evaluated using the same tools.

The management of Betty's Better Big Boys, one of the largest franchisers of fast foods in the West, is considering two investment proposals. Betty's Better Big Boys sells a variety of sandwiches, drinks, and other fast foods through its 500 restaurants. Management has capitalized on the public's health concerns by offering whole-grain sandwich buns, sandwich wraps, toppings such as tomatoes and sprouts, french fries with potato skins, and tofu shakes, as well as regular fare. Betty's Better Big Boys managers are considering either of two investments—opening their restaurants for breakfast or adding salad, sushi, and pasta bars to their existing lunch and dinner menus. Because of the management effort needed to implement either project, management considers these investments mutually exclusive: it may choose one or the other, but not both.

1. Mutually Exclusive Investments: The Breakfast Proposal

Betty's Better Big Boys restaurants currently are open from 11 A.M. to 11 P.M. Because many of Betty's competitors have begun to serve breakfast, Betty's managers are considering opening from 6:30 to 11 A.M. to serve breakfast. They believe Betty's Better Big Boys has an edge over its competition because it pioneered the "healthy hamburger" concept. They would emphasize tasty and nutritious breakfast offerings, as well as more traditional Southern breakfast items such as biscuits and gravy, sausage and ham biscuits, fried apples, and grits.

The same buildings and equipment could be used for serving breakfast, although the longer serving hours would increase overhead expenses. There would be added costs for ingredients, salaries of managers and employees, and advertising the new items and hours. Together, incremental overhead and operating expenses for all 500 restaurants are expected to total $14.25 million per year. In addition, since breakfast would be a new product, management is planning an extensive employee-training program. The program, to be completed before the company starts offering breakfast in July, would cost $1.75 million. New inventory would total $1,800 per restaurant, and all remaining inventory would be fully recovered at the end of the project in five years.[6] Betty's

---

[6] Little or no inventory would remain at the end of the project's life. All perishable and nonperishable goods would have been used and not replaced, thus reducing inventory to zero.

Better Big Boys expects to benefit from an estimated $15 million increase in sales per year to be made from the breakfast service.

The estimated costs and benefits of this project are detailed in Exhibit 4-2. Since management expects no inflation, costs and benefits are shown in real dollars. Costs and benefits are forecast for five years because management believes that the equipment used in each restaurant will last only five years.

Exhibit 4-2 is a typical presentation of the analysis of a capital investment. The first part looks like an income statement forecast, but the second part, below the net profit entry, does not. Recall that this forecast is for cash costs and benefits. Then why is a noncash charge, such as depreciation, included in the top half of the exhibit? This is because depreciation reduces taxable income and thus taxes, and taxes are paid in cash.[7] In the second section the noncash charges are added back, leaving only its impact on taxes.

You will also recall that these cash flows belong to the shareholders, because we are assuming that only its owners finance the company.[8] Thus there

EXHIBIT 4-2 Betty's Better Big Boys' Breakfast Proposal

MARGINAL COSTS AND BENEFITS (thousands of real dollars)

	Period					
	0	1	2	3	4	5
Income Statement Changes						
Sales	0	$15,000	$15,000	$15,000	$15,000	$15,000
Operating expenses	0	(14,250)	(14,250)	(14,250)	(14,250)	(14,250)
Training costs	$(1,750)					
Depreciation	0	0	0	0	0	0
Profit before taxes	(1,750)	750	750	750	750	750
Taxes*	595	(255)	(255)	(255)	(255)	(255)
Net profit	(1,155)	495	495	495	495	495
Noncash Charges						
Depreciation		0	0	0	0	0
Capital Investments						
Property, plant, and equipment	0	0	0	0	0	0
Inventory	(900)	0	0	0	0	900
Residual net cash flow	$(2,055)	$ 495	$ 495	$ 495	$ 495	$ 1,395

* Positive taxes are a tax reduction in the rest of the business due to the training expenses in the year prior to start up. This benefit occurs only if the company has profits in other parts of its business.

---

[7] Some analysts choose to put in an item called tax impact of depreciation, forgoing the deduction on the income statement and addition in the cash flow section of depreciation. They are equivalent methods. The explicitness of this approach avoids expository problems.

[8] Financial subcontracting occurs when shareholders' funds are supplemented from sources such as lenders.

II. Evaluating Incremental Costs and Benefits

are no provisions for interest payments, principal payments, or new loans in the cash flows. Because these cash flows belong to the shareholders alone, and shareholders have the residual claim on the company's cash flows, we call them **residual cash flows**. We will show in Chapters 6 and 7 how financial subcontracting changes an analysis.

The second set of adjustments shown to the income in Exhibit 4-2 are capital investments—cash payments for property, plant, and equipment or for working capital. Property, plant, and various items of equipment are not expensed, and thus do not affect taxes, at the time they are purchased. Instead, plant and equipment are expensed over the period allowed by the tax code. This annual capital investment expense is called depreciation. Property is put on the balance sheet at its purchase price and neither depreciated nor revalued.

Working capital investments—increases in inventory, accounts receivable, or needed cash—are also included. These are considered to be investments just as real as investments in a piece of equipment, and thus are shown as cash investments when they are made. Until these investments are recovered by the company at its discretion, they remain a part of the firm's invested capital.[9]

2. Mutually Exclusive Investments: Salad, Sushi, and Pasta Bar Proposal

As an alternative to adding breakfast, managers at Betty's Better Big Boys are considering adding an all-you-can-eat salad, sushi, and pasta bar to their existing lunch and dinner menus starting in July. They have already spent $600,000 in developing the salad, sushi, and pasta bar concept in limited test marketing. To introduce the product into all of their restaurants, they estimate that personnel would have to be trained at a cost of $832 per restaurant and that display cases would have to be bought and installed at $2,800 per bar. The managers expect that the display cases would be scrapped in five years and that the value of the scrap would be offset by disposal costs. Incremental (marginal) operating expenses include the cost of ingredients, additional refrigeration, and the salary of one additional employee per restaurant to stock the salad, sushi, and pasta bar. On the basis of test market results, the marketing department estimates sales of salad, sushi, and pasta at $15 million per year and operating expenses at $13.934 million. New inventories would be $1,800 per restaurant.

The different effects these two proposals would have on Betty's Better Big Boys illustrate the usefulness of categorizing investments as independent or mutually exclusive. Managers consider the two proposed investments to be mutually exclusive because they do not believe that they could adequately oversee both projects at the same time. The breakfast option would be independent of Betty's existing business because it would extend the existing

---

[9] Working capital investments, like inventory and accounts receivable, are long-term assets, even though the constituents of the accounts change. This was described in Chapter 3.

product line. The salad, sushi, and pasta bar, however, would be a partial replacement since it would affect existing sales of sandwich meals at lunch and dinner. In fact, the marketing staff estimate that half of the salad, sushi, and pasta bar's sales would come from customers who would otherwise have purchased sandwiches and french fries. Thus, while total salad, sushi, and pasta sales would be $15 million, incremental sales would be only half, $7.5 million per year.

The salad, sushi, and pasta bar's status as a partial replacement would be responsible not only for lower net cash receipts but also for lower incremental overhead and operating expenses than the breakfast project. Unlike the breakfast option, it would add less to current overhead and operating expenses because it would be offered during existing hours and primarily manned by existing employees. If the analyst did not realize that the salad, sushi, and pasta bar option would be a replacement investment, he or she might erroneously include two inappropriate items. First, the analyst might include a portion of the costs of buildings and equipment as part of its incremental costs. These are not incremental since the company currently has the buildings and equipment. A second error would be to include its total sales of $15 million as a benefit, rather than the $7.5 million incremental sales. The net cash flow for the salad, sushi, and pasta bar is the net profit plus any noncash charges that were deducted from profit before taxes for the purpose of calculating taxes, minus the new costs for the salad bar equipment and inventory.

Details of this evaluation of the net benefits of the project appear in Exhibit 4-3. Note that the $600,000 in expenses incurred in developing and test-marketing the salad, sushi, and pasta bar concept are not included. They are sunk costs: cash already spent and not relevant in making this decision.

Now that the incremental costs and benefits for the two projects have been estimated, Betty's management must decide whether to accept one or the other of the plans or reject both projects and seek a different opportunity. To make these decisions, the managers need a method for measuring the relative value of the two proposals. Without some measure of an investment's value, the choice becomes a question of preference and power.

III. CHOOSING AMONG INVESTMENTS

The relative attractiveness or value of investments may be ranked in a number of different ways. Each of these methods has advantages and disadvantages.

1. Simple Valuation Methods

Benefit/Cost Ratio. The easiest way to compare two investments is to compare their benefit/cost ratios. If the benefits of an investment exceed the costs—if the benefit/cost ratio is greater than 1.0—the project is deemed acceptable using this measure. To choose among acceptable investments, managers select

III. Choosing Among Investments   157

EXHIBIT 4-3 Betty's Better Big Boys' Salad, Sushi, and Pasta Bar Proposal

MARGINAL COSTS AND BENEFITS (thousands of real dollars)

	\<td colspan=7>Period
	0	1	2	3	4	5	6
Income Statement Changes							
Sales		$7,500	$7,500	$7,500	$7,500	$7,500	0
Operating expenses		(6,967)	(6,967)	(6,967)	(6,967)	(6,967)	0
Training costs	$ (416)						
Depreciation*	—	(280)	(448)	(269)	(161)	(161)	$(81)
Profit before taxes	(416)	253	85	264	372	372	(81)
Taxes[‡]	141	(86)	(29)	(90)	(127)	(127)	28
Net profit	(275)	167	56	174	245	245	(53)
Noncash Charges							
Depreciation		280	448	269	161	161	81
Capital Investments							
Property, plant, and equipment	(1,400)						
New inventory	(900)	—	—	—	—	900	—
Residual net cash flow	$(2,575)	$ 447	$ 504	$ 443	$ 406	$1,306	$ 28

* Depreciation based on the 1999 U.S. tax code rules.
[‡] Positive taxes that result from the expense of training are a tax reduction. This tax reduction is a benefit only if the company has profits from other businesses and these losses can offset the profits and lower the company's total taxes.

the project with the highest benefit/cost ratio. For Betty's Better Big Boys' proposed investment in breakfast, the benefit/cost ratio is calculated as follows. This analysis uses the residual net cash flow figures in Exhibit 4-2.

$$\text{Benefit/cost ratio} = \frac{\text{Benefits}}{\text{Investment}}$$

$$= \frac{\$495 + \$495 + \$495 + \$495 + \$1{,}395}{\$2{,}055}$$

$$= \frac{\$3{,}375}{\$2{,}055}$$

$$= 1.64$$

A comparable analysis of figures in Exhibit 4-3 for the salad, sushi, and pasta bar yields a ratio of 1.22 ($3,134/$2,575). The benefit/cost ratio at best is a blunt tool for determining the attractiveness of a project, and is a poor measure of relative attractiveness.

Average Payback Period. Average payback period or just average payback is similar to the benefit/cost ratio. Quite simply, average payback is used to measure the number of years before the annual benefits of the project are equal to its initial cost. For the breakfast proposal, the average payback period is calculated as follows:

$$\text{Average payback} = \frac{\text{Investment}}{\text{Average yearly benefit}}$$

$$= \frac{\$2{,}055}{\$675}$$

$$= 3.04 \text{ years}$$

A similar analysis of the salad, sushi, and pasta bar proposal yields an average payback of 4.1 years, using five years to average the yearly benefits.[10]

The average payback period is fraught with problems. First, it does not take into account the fact that the cash flows occur at different times over a five-year period. The timing of the cash flows is important. For instance, two projects, one paying all the benefits in the first year, the other paying all the benefits in the final year, would have identical average payback periods. Clearly management would prefer the investment with the earlier benefits. This measure does not take this into account.

Payback Period. The payback period is similar to the average payback period calculation, except that the actual yearly benefits, rather than the average benefits, are used to calculate the payback period. This method is widely used.

---

[10] In this exhibit we use five years of benefits since the depreciation shield that occurs in the sixth year is a convention under MACRS. The sixth year has no other benefits from the project.

Exhibit 4-4 shows the payback calculation for the breakfast option: the payback equals 4.05 years where the remaining investment in the fourth year takes 0.05 ($75/$1,395) years to recover. For the salad, sushi, and pasta bar, the payback is 4.6 years.

Whether a payback of 4.05 years is adequate for the breakfast option is a decision for Betty's management. To use the measure, managers typically set a limit on the length of the payback period they will accept and reject those investments with longer paybacks. To choose among several projects with acceptable payback periods, managers select the project with the fastest payback period.

Payback period is a better measure than the cost/benefit ratio or the average payback. It can be useful as a quick approximation of a project's relative attractiveness. The best use may be to indicate whether a firm can recover an investment's costs in time to make another planned investment. This is particularly useful when there are rapid changes in products, technology, or the political and economic environment. The problem with the payback method is that it ignores all benefits that are received after the payback date, thus arbitrarily excluding potentially attractive investments with longer lives.

Let's look at an example to illustrate this problem. Vast Resources, Inc. (VR) has two projects in which it can invest the $1.5 million it has available. VR management uses a payback criterion of three years and will not accept a project that fails to meet this standard.

Exhibit 4-5 presents data for the two projects. On the basis of this data, management has chosen to invest in Project A and reject Project B. Do you agree with this choice? Under most circumstances, Project B should be the preferred investment. The situation where Project A is preferred is when VR needs the $1.5 million by the second year for another investment or to pay an obligation. Project B eventually provides a much larger cash flow and should be the most attractive project to management.

The VR example points out obvious problems that can occur when using payback. Similar problems exist using benefit/cost analysis and the average payback. None of these methods take the timing of cash flows into account.

EXHIBIT 4-4 Betty's Better Big Boys' Payback Calculation for Breakfast Option (in thousands)

Period	Investment	Cash Flow	Remaining Investment
0	$2,055		$ 2,055
1		$ 495	1,560
2		495	1,065
3		495	570
4		495	75
5		1,395	(1,320)

EXHIBIT 4-5 Vast Resources, Inc.

ALTERNATIVE INVESTMENTS (in millions)	Project A	Project B
Cost	$1.5	$1.5
Residual cash flows:		
Year 1	$1.6	0.0
2	0.0	0.0
3	0.0	0.0
4	0.0	0.0
5	0.0	$8.0
Payback	0.94 years	4.19 years
Benefit/cost ratio	107%	533%

The benefit/cost ratio treats cash received at all points in time as equivalent. This does not reflect the reality of investor preferences: we know that investors prefer cash received sooner to equivalent amounts received later. While the payback method attempts to take investors' preferences for early cash flows into account, it fails to take into consideration cash flows beyond the payback period. We know later cash flows are not irrelevant to investors, particularly if they are large. Thus, none of these methods that evaluate investments solely on the size or speed of their returns adequately incorporate the investor's **time value of money**, the return the investor would expect to earn on a riskless investment.

2. Dealing with the Timing of Cash Flows: Discounting Techniques

There are a number of methods that do explicitly take into account the timing of an investment's cash flows. These methods are important because investors want to be rewarded for waiting for future returns. Thus we need a method for evaluating investments that will take into account the time value of money and will compensate investors for any temporary lack of liquidity by promising increased returns for more distant cash flows.

We have a very straightforward way of determining the value of later cash flows. It is called **future value**. Exhibit 4-6 illustrates this method. You can see the value of the investment at the beginning of each year and the interest that would be paid on the investment at a rate of 5 percent. The interest in each year is added to the beginning investment to determine the investment on which interest will be paid for the following year. In the exhibit you see that the value of $6.27 million invested at an annual rate of 5 percent is a little over $8 million at the end of five years. This is the sum that the investor will have if all the annual earnings are reinvested at a compounding rate of 5 percent.

Exhibit 4-6 shows the interest for each year. Adding interest to the beginning investment value across each of the five years gives us the total amount

EXHIBIT 4-6 Future Value of an Investment at a 5 Percent Annual Rate of Return

	Year				
	1	2	3	4	5
Investment, beginning of year	$6,270,000	$6,583,500	$6,912,675	$7,258,309	$7,621,224
Interest (@ 5%)	313,500	329,175	345,634	362,915	381,061
Investment, end of year	$6,583,500	$6,912,675	$7,258,309	$7,621,224	$8,002,285

that we would expect to receive in five years. While this example shows a straightforward analysis, the task becomes much more cumbersome when dealing with a more complex situation.

There is a much easier way to calculate the future value of a sum invested today. To take a shortcut, first we need to create a factor that can be used as a beginning investment multiplier. We call this factor the **future value factor**.

$$\text{Future value factor} = (1 + R)^n$$

where
R = The rate of return
n = The number of periods, usually years[11]

The process for creating this future value factor for an investment made for five years at a 5 percent compound rate of return is:[12]

$$\begin{aligned}\text{Future value factor} &= (1 + R)^n \\ &= (1 + .05)^5 \\ &= (1.05)^5 \\ &= 1.27628156\end{aligned}$$

To calculate the future value of a cash flow (CF), use the following formula.

$$\text{Future value} = (1 + R)^n \times (CF)$$

Using this future value factor to solve the problem in Exhibit 4-6, we find the same answer, $8,002,285. However, the process to obtain this solution was much easier.

$$\begin{aligned}\text{Future value} &= (1 + R)^n \times (CF) \\ &= (1 + .05)^5 \times \$6,270,000 \\ &= 1.27628156 \times \$6,270,000 \\ &= \$8,002,285\end{aligned}$$

---

[11] Actually we can do this for periods of any length. We simply use the interest rate for a period of that length.

[12] To calculate the future value factor without the exponential function, simply multiply (1 + R) by itself n number of times. For our example, Future value factor = [(1 + .05) × (1 + .05) × (1 + .05) × (1 + .05) × (1 + .05)] = 1.27628156.

The process we just went through is called **compounding**.

We can use an adaptation of the compound value process to determine what a future cash flow would be worth today. Today's worth, or value, is called **present value**, or **discounted present value**. The process of **discounting** is simply the inverse of compounding.

$$\text{Present value factor} = \frac{1.00}{(1 + R)^n}$$

$$= \frac{1.00}{(1.05)^5}$$

$$= \frac{1.00}{1.27628}$$

$$= 0.7835$$

The 0.7835 figure means that a dollar received five years from now is worth 78.35 percent of its future value, or $0.78, today. To calculate the value of more than $1.00 received five years in the future, multiply cash flow received by the present value factor. For instance, the present value of $8 million received in five years is $6.27 million ($8.0 million × 0.7835). To calculate the present value of a series of cash flows, discount each to the present value and sum their present values. The present value of a dollar received in each of the next five years is shown in Exhibit 4-7.

There is a shortcut to this present value process when the future cash flows are identical. A series of identical cash flows received over time is called an **annuity**. To create a future value factor for an annuity, we simply add the future value factors for each of the years the annuity will be earned.

$$\text{Future value of annuity} = \text{Sum future value factors}_n$$

For an annuity of $1.00 received for five years compounding at 5 percent, the future value annuity factor would be as follows:

$$\text{Future value of annuity factor} = (1 + .05)^1 + (1 + .05)^2 + (1 + .05)^3 +$$
$$(1 + .05)^4 + (1 + .05)^5$$
$$= 1.0500 + 1.10250 + 1.15763 + 1.21551 + 1.27628$$
$$= 5.80$$

EXHIBIT 4-7 Present Value of Cash Flows

	Period				
	1	2	3	4	5
Cash flow	$1.00	$1.00	$1.00	$1.00	$1.00
Present value (@ 5%)	0.952381	0.907029	0.863838	0.822702	0.783526
Total present value	$4.3295				

Note: Rounding of present or future value factors may cause small discrepancies in the results.

III. Choosing Among Investments

Once again, to use this, multiply the annuity factor times the sum to be received. For instance, if you win a lottery of $1 million per year for five years, you will have $6.15 million. If you have a choice of taking the $1 million per year or a sum of $3.5 million, use the present value annuity factor to decide which is better.

$$\text{Present value factor} = \sum \frac{1.00}{(1 + R)^n}$$

For the four-year, 5 percent problem the factor is:

$$\text{Present value of annuity factor} = \frac{1.00}{1.05} + \frac{1.00}{1.10} + \frac{1.00}{1.16} + \frac{1.00}{1.22} + \frac{1.00}{1.28}$$
$$= 4.32$$

This makes the present value of the lottery worth $4.32 million. In this case, you should not take the lump sum of $3.5 million.

Fortunately, one does not have to go through the laborious process of calculating compound value factors. Lists of factors are available on web sites. Moreover, all but the simplest modern calculators perform compounding and discounting functions quite painlessly, thus generally rendering the direct use of discount factors an unnecessary step.

Present Value Payback. The most simplistic use of discounting is an adaptation of payback called the present value payback. To calculate a present value payback, discount each residual net cash flow to its equivalent present value. These discounted present values are summed until the total equals the amount of the original investment. Exhibit 4-8 provides the data needed to calculate the discounted payback for the breakfast project. Using 5 percent as the discount rate, the discounted payback value of this project is 4.27 years. The

EXHIBIT 4-8 Breakfast Proposal

PRESENT VALUE PAYBACK (in thousands)

Year	Residual Net Cash Flow	Present Value Cash Flow		Remaining Investment
0	$(2,055)	$(2,055)/(1.05)^0 =$	$(2,055.00)	$2,055.00
1	495	$495/(1.05)^1 =$	471.43	1,583.57
2	495	$495/(1.05)^2 =$	448.98	1,134.59
3	495	$495/(1.05)^3 =$	427.60	706.99
4	495	$495/(1.05)^4 =$	407.23	299.76
5	1,395	$1,395/(1.05)^5 =$	1,093.02	

The total present value payback is 4.27 years. The 0.27 is calculated as follows:

$$\frac{\$299.76}{\$1,093.02} = 0.274$$

salad, sushi, and pasta bar project's discounted payback is 4.95 years, using five years as the project life.

While including the time value of money, the discounted payback still ignores cash flows beyond the payback period. This is a particularly critical fault when projects with large future returns, such as new products, are being considered. It is neither necessary nor appropriate to discriminate arbitrarily against projects with returns in the more distant future. Better methods should, and do, exist to take into account those critical future cash flows.

Net present value and internal rate of return are two frequently used discounting techniques that take all cash flows into consideration. Either method provides a better measure of value than do the simpler ranking methods.

Net Present Value. The **present value** calculates today's lump sum value of all current and future benefits. The **net present value** is the present value of the benefits less the present value of all current and future costs. The net present value can also be described as the present value of the net worth an investment will contribute to a company by the end of its useful life. This is a particularly useful way to think about net present value if you are an owner or shareholder.

Net present value (NPV) is calculated using a discount rate. The discount rate is used to adjust each year's returns according to the time between it and the date the decision would be implemented, usually the time of the initial investment. The discount rate is better known as the investors' **required rate of return**. A discount rate has a variety of names, including **hurdle rate**. Hurdle rate is used to signify that the project must exceed or "jump over" the hurdle. Net present value is calculated as follows:

$$NPV = \left(\frac{NCF_1}{(1+R)^1} + \frac{NCF_2}{(1+R)^2} + \ldots + \frac{NCF_n}{(1+R)^n}\right) - I$$

Where:
NCF = The net cash flow per year (cash flow benefits minus cash flow costs)
R = Annual discount rate
$1, 2, \ldots, n$ = Years from the date of original investment
I = Amount of initial investment

While the discounting and compounding processes were described in terms of annual rates of return and years, any period can be used. For instance, shorter periods are useful when cash flows vary over the year. This can be especially true in development projects and in inflationary environments. The analyst using different periods must, however, make sure that the rate of return, the discount rate, is appropriate for a period equivalent to the length of the periods being used in the cash flows. For instance, if the analyst is evaluating the project over quarters, the rate of return would be a quarterly rate of return. In our example, the annual 5 percent rate of return would be equivalent to a 1.23 percent quarterly rate. This latter rate would be used to discount or compound quarterly cash flows. Rates of return are discussed in Chapters 6 and 7 in more detail.

For Betty's Better Big Boys, the net present value of the breakfast option using 5 percent as an annual discount rate is calculated as follows:

$$NPV = \frac{\$495,000}{(1+.05)^1} + \frac{\$495,000}{(1+.05)^2} + \frac{\$495,000}{(1+.05)^3} + \frac{\$495,000}{(1+.05)^4} + \frac{\$1,395,000}{(1+.05)^5} - \$2,055,000$$

$$= \$793,265$$

The NPV of $793,265 is the present value of the net worth the breakfast project will contribute to Betty's by the end of the investment's five-year life. The NPV of the salad, sushi, and pasta bar project is $71,199 at a 5 percent discount rate. Clearly the breakfast option is superior.

The NPV approach offers a logical method of evaluating investments. The process is quite simple when a calculator with a net present value function or a computer spreadsheet is used. It takes into account the timing of cash flows by placing a higher value on those received immediately than on those to be received in the future. Once the timing of cash flows has been taken into account, acceptable investments are those with net present values *equal to or greater than zero*.[13]

Present Value Index. Some managers prefer to use the profitability or present value index (PVI) rather than net present value. The PVI is simply an adaptation of the benefit/cost ratio:

$$\text{Present value index} = \frac{\text{Present value of net benefits}}{\text{Present value of investment costs}}$$

Calculating the present value index is simple and straightforward. Using the breakfast option as an example, and the 5 percent discount rate, the index is calculated as follows:

$$PVI = \left(\frac{\$495,000}{(1+.05)^1} + \frac{\$495,000}{(1+.05)^2} + \frac{\$495,000}{(1+.05)^3} + \frac{\$495,000}{(1+.05)^4} + \frac{\$1,395,000}{(1+.05)^5} \right) / \$2,055,000$$

$$= \frac{\$2,848,265}{\$2,055,000}$$

$$= 1.39 \text{ or } 139 \text{ percent}$$

---

[13] Some people require that the NPV be greater than zero. However, if we have an appropriate discount rate, it includes the time value of money and compensates the investor for the risk being taken. Thus the discount rate adequately compensates the investor: value is neither created nor destroyed. An NPV greater than zero signifies that value is being created. Creating value is the objective, but it is difficult to obtain.

For the salad, sushi, and pasta bar project the PVI is 1.02.

Internal Rate of Return. A second discounted cash flow technique is internal rate of return (IRR). The IRR is used to measure the average rate of return that will be earned over the life of the project. To calculate the IRR, the same formula for calculating net present value is used. To calculate the IRR, we set the net present value equal to zero and solve for R, the discount rate.

Solving for R is somewhat more difficult than solving for NPV. To solve for R we must use a trial-and-error method, or a computer or financial calculator must do so. To begin the process we choose an arbitrary discount rate, say 5 percent, and calculate the NPV. If the resulting NPV is positive, a higher discount rate is next selected, and the NPV is recalculated. We continue choosing discount rates until we find the discount rate that yields an NPV of zero. For the Betty's Better Big Boys' breakfast project, the IRR is obviously larger than 5 percent since, at that rate, the NPV is $793,265. Note that at a discount rate of zero the net present value is the simple sum of the undiscounted cash flows.

It is useful to keep track of this trial-and-error analysis. We could do so in a table listing the NPVs at various discount rates. However, this is where a graph is much better, as you can see looking at Exhibit 4-9. This exhibit, also called a **net present value profile**, graphs the results of this trial-and-error approach for both Betty's projects. As you can see, the IRR for the breakfast project is 15.9

EXHIBIT 4-9 Net Present Value Profile

SALAD, SUSHI, AND PASTA BAR AND BREAKFAST OPTIONS

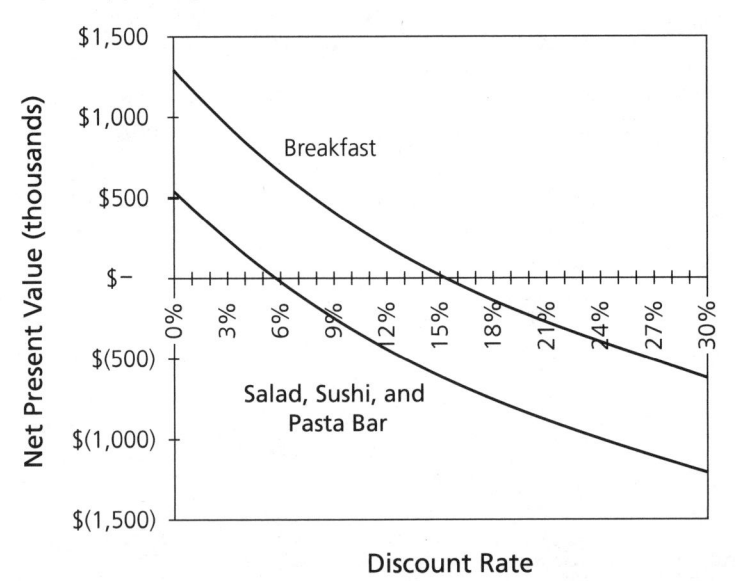

percent. For the salad, sushi, and pasta bar project the IRR is 5.8 percent. As you can see from the graph, at all discount rates the breakfast project provides a higher NPV than does the salad bar project.

While management would certainly prefer the breakfast option in choosing between the two, how do they know if either is acceptable: will it maintain or create value for shareholders? An acceptable IRR for a project is a return that equals or exceeds the investors' required rate of return. Here we have used 5 percent as the required return for these investments. Thus both projects would be acceptable, but the breakfast option is best.

Investors are accustomed to using rates of return in analyzing potential investments. This is the attraction of IRR. However, while the IRR method is purported to be equivalent to the net present value method, there are some situations in which it can produce more than one IRR. This can occur when:

- Investments are of different sizes.
- The timing of the cash flows is different for each project under consideration.
- Negative and positive net cash flows alternate over the life of the project.

When one or more of these things is true, the internal rate of return can give results that are misleading and/or difficult to interpret. The analysis of the sail-assisted tanker project presents just such a situation.

In evaluating the sail-assisted tanker project, we noted there would be significant investments at several points over the useful life of the tanker: positive and negative cash flows alternate over the life of the project. At the beginning of the project the tanker will be purchased. Later, extensive engine overhauls will be needed. Thus its net cash flows will be negative in the first year and when the vessel is overhauled in the future. During the intervening years, cash flows will be positive as the company operates the tanker. As a result of alternating negative and positive net cash flows, several different discount rates exist that make the NPV equal to zero. Exhibit 4-10 shows the net present value profile for the sail-assisted tanker project. There are IRRs of both 8.1 and 21.0 percent: the NPV is zero at both discount rates. Does this mean that for companies using discount rates below 8.1 and above 21 percent, the project is acceptable? Yes, it does. Furthermore, if the required rate of return is between 8.1 and 21 percent, the investment should be rejected.

Unfortunately, most computer models and calculators are designed to solve for one IRR. The analyst may erroneously believe he or she has the complete information necessary to analyze and make a decision about the investment. Thus it is very helpful to use the net present value profiles. These graphs provide more complete data, and let managers avoid making decisions on the IRR alone.

The net present value will tell management or the investor if the investment will maintain or create value at the required rate of return. Thus it provides an unambiguous choice, while the IRR may not. For these and other reasons, the net present value technique is the preferred approach.

EXHIBIT 4-10   Net Present Value Profile

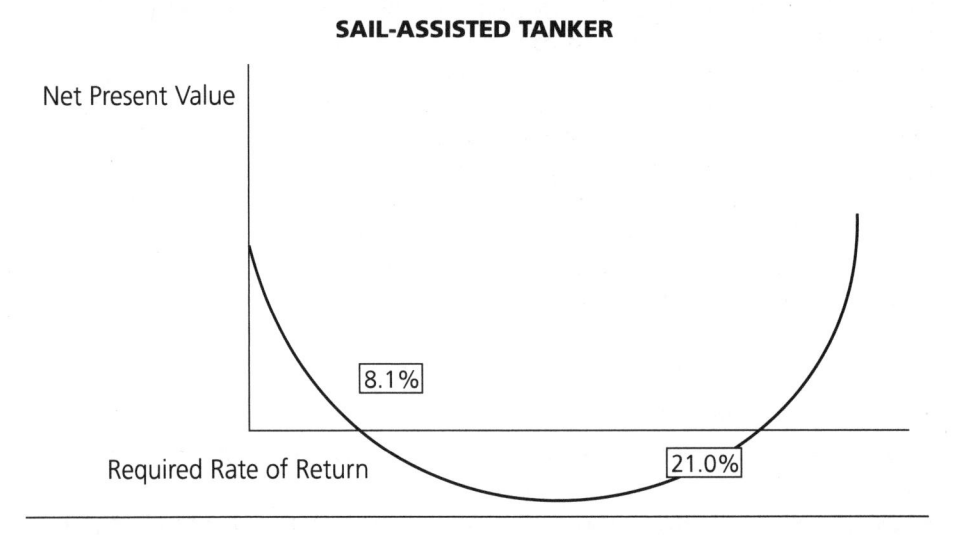

SAIL-ASSISTED TANKER

[Graph showing Net Present Value curve versus Required Rate of Return, with values 8.1% and 21.0% marked where the curve crosses zero]

We have summarized in Exhibit 4-11 the results of using six ranking methods for Betty's two projects. The benefit/cost ratio and payback period take into account the size of the residual cash flows, but not their timing. The net present value and internal rate of return take into account both the size and

EXHIBIT 4-11   Value of Breakfast Versus Salad, Sushi, and Pasta Bar Option (dollars in thousands)

Method	Breakfast	Salad	Decision Rule
Benefit/cost ratio	1.64	1.22	B/C ≥ 1.0
Average payback period	3.04 years	4.10 years	Average payback ≥ management minimum
Payback period	4.05 years	4.60 years	Payback period ≥ management minimum
Present value payback	4.27 years	4.95 years	PV payback ≥ management minimum
Net present value at discount rate of:			
5%	$793.27	$71.20	NPV ≥ 0
10%	$380.27	$(313.02)	
Present value index, at discount rate of 5%	1.39 or 139%	1.02 or 102%	PVI ≥ 1.0
Internal rate of return	15.9%	5.8%	IRR ≥ hurdle rate

timing of the residual cash flows, although for the reasons described, the net present value is superior. Fortunately for Betty's Better Big Boys, all our methods indicate that the breakfast option is more attractive.

3. Ranking Projects

So far, we have assumed that if an investment creates value it should be accepted—the company can and should invest in all attractive projects. In a company with more projects than resources, projects must be ranked from highest to lowest in value, with management choosing the investments with the highest relative values.

Net present value is the best ranking method: it provides a ranking that is consistent with the goal of value creation. For Betty's Better Big Boys' management, does this mean that the breakfast proposal is the one it should choose? Maybe, but the breakfast proposal is riskier: customers may not come to breakfast. The salad, sushi, and pasta bar seems less risky since it merely supplements the present sale of sandwiches, a product line and meal in which the restaurants are firmly established. So should management choose the investment that creates less value because it is less risky? Since risk is obviously an issue we should include it in our analysis.

IV. ASSESSING AND INCORPORATING RISK

1. Defining Risk

First we need a definition of risk. For capital investments the risk is that our residual cash flow forecasts might be wrong, that we might have a higher or lower than expected return.[14] Investors, in addition to preferring large, rapid returns, also prefer certain returns: they do not like to take risks unless rewarded to do so. To induce the typical risk-averse investor to invest in risky projects, that investor must anticipate higher returns. The higher the risk, the larger the return premium required to compensate for that risk.

Of all the problems facing the investment analyst, risk is the most troublesome. In spite of the fact that many have sought the best method to define and analyze risk, so far there is no ideal method for incorporating risk into the measurement of an investment's value. There are methods investors and managers use. While none is flawless, we will discuss several and describe how they are used and the problems associated with each.

In most analyses of corporate investments, we assume that there is no change from the risk we know. Explicitly, management assumes that the risk of the investment is identical to that of the company as a whole: the cash flows for

---

[14] There are a number of sources of risk, but all result in either wrong or highly variable forecasts. We will discuss what can be done about both kinds of risk later in this chapter.

the project are as predictable as those from the firm's current business. Once that assumption is made, management can use the firm's average required return as a discount rate for any new investment prospect.[15] But this is rarely the situation.

2. Changing the Discount Rate

What if the risk of the investment is higher or lower than the corporate average risk? In this situation, many managers increase or decrease the corporate required rate of return to compensate for the difference. The rate that includes the risk differential is no longer called the corporate required rate of return, it is called a hurdle rate. As the hurdle rate increases—that is, as investors require greater returns as compensation for greater risks—the net present value of an investment diminishes. You can see the dramatic impact of increasing hurdle rates if you look at the net present value profile in Exhibit 4-9. When the discount rate is 5 percent, the breakfast and salad, sushi, and pasta bar options provide net present values of $793,260 and $71,200, respectively. If a discount rate of 10 percent is used, the net present values diminish dramatically to $380,270 and a loss of $313,019. However, no matter what rate is used, the breakfast proposal is better for Betty's shareholders.

These calculations assume that the risks of Betty's two projects are equal. On the contrary, management believes that opening for breakfast is more risky than adding salad, sushi, and pasta bars. New employees must be hired, a new advertising campaign must be undertaken, new food items will be offered, and a large unrecoverable investment in training is required. The fact is that Betty's Better Big Boys' managers are concerned that their forecasts of potential sales and costs of the breakfast option could be wrong. Salad, sushi, and pasta bars, on the other hand, add little to the risk of the firm. The initial investment is small and a portion of it is recoverable, training costs are low, and few additional employees must be hired. The two projects have different levels of risk, and how can these differences be included in the comparison?

So far, neither academics nor business practitioners have answered this question very well, although many techniques are currently being used. One approach is to present the problem of risk directly to the managers. Using the firm's required rate of return as a discount rate, managers can determine for themselves whether the net present value compensates for the risk of the project. For instance, the net present value of the breakfast option at a discount rate of 10 percent is greater by $693,289 than that of the salad, sushi, and pasta bar alternative. Is this amount adequate, in the managers' view, to compensate for the differences in risk between the two investments? It is up to them to decide.

---

[15] We will discuss how this return, often called the cost of capital, is estimated in Chapters 6 and 7.

3. Risk Categories by Investment Type

This approach is not scientific and managers often prefer a more structured method. Another approach is to modify the discount rate according to the apparent risk of the investment. For example, new products may be considered to have greater risks than the risk of the firm as a whole. Consequently, management will set a higher hurdle rate for new products than the firm's marginal cost of capital. A scheme, such as the one shown in Exhibit 4-12, is used by many firms to categorize investments.

Managers who use a scheme like this believe that investments in cost reductions are less risky than their firm's average risk and that new products are more risky. Using this scheme, Betty's management might discount the salad, sushi, and pasta bars' cash flows at a rate of 5 percent, but since breakfast is a new product and is considered riskier its cash flows might be discounted at an even higher rate, for instance, 10 percent. Doing this, the NPV for the breakfast proposal is $380,270. This still exceeds the $71,200 NPV for the less risky salad bar.

While some variety of this risk-adjustment scheme is often used, it has two flaws. First, it leads to predictable results: discounted at higher rates the new products are less attractive, whereas cost-reduction projects are usually acceptable.[16] This may or may not be appropriate for the specific firm or investment. Second, it is difficult to determine the appropriate changes to make to the discount rate: should the differences between "risky" and "less risky" projects be 5 or 10 percent, or more or less? These two problems make finding a better method for dealing with risk very important.

Managers with a number of divisions or lines of business have attempted to adapt their corporate discount rates for the specific risks of the division or product line. Because the required rate of return for a division is not available, a number of methods are used to estimate the appropriate discount rate. Most

EXHIBIT 4-12 Risk Categories for Investment Analysis

Investment Category	Risk Level	Hurdle Rate
Cost reduction	Less than firm's average risk	Lower than firm's required rate of return
Plant expansion	Average risk	Marginal average required rate of return
New products	Higher than average risk	Higher rate than required rate of return

---

[16] In fact, if management wants to encourage the "riskier" projects, such as new products, to build the company's future, this scheme effectively cuts off those opportunistic growth projects, or forces managers who champion them to adapt the numbers to get them accepted.

often the rate is calculated by using information about a number of publicly traded proxy firms—firms with similar characteristics. These proxy methods are imprecise, but are better than using a single rate for businesses and investments that have very different levels of risk.[17]

4. Danger of Raising Discount Rates: New Products and New Processes

Companies face real risks when introducing new products or processes. When new products are introduced to customers, management does not know if the customers will accept the product, or if they do, how enthusiastically. Such things as test markets, focus groups, product sampling, and advertising are designed to increase the trial rate of customers, and thus the size of the market for the product. But will those strategies work? Will the consumers buy the product? How many? Will the competition emulate the product, or even introduce a more attractive alternative? These are real risks that face management when introducing a new product. Because of this, management often raises the discount rate for new products. The same occurs for new technologies where management is not certain of the technology or its impact on the workforce or process.

Should management raise the discount rate for these high-risk investments? Maybe, but maybe not. The question management must ask itself is, Will the risk persist over the life of the investment, or is it a short-term phenomena? Will we know with much greater certainty what the cash flows for this investment will be after the initial shakeout period?

Often the high levels of uncertainty last only a short period of time: the product is introduced and either the customers buy it or not; the new process is put in place and it either works as expected or not. Once the initial period of uncertainty is over, management knows much better what to expect. This does not mean that the returns will be good, they could be bad. What management has is much greater certainty about the outcome.

Is raising a discount rate, a rate that impacts the cash flows over the whole life of the project, the best way to deal with this temporary risk? No. The discount rate should reflect the risk over the life of the project, not just the short term. It should reflect the risks that come from changes in the basic assumptions about the economy. There are better ways to deal with these company-specific, shorter term, shakeout period risks. Scenario analysis is one approach and contingent claims another. Both of these will be discussed in the following sections.

5. Cash Flow Manipulation to Incorporate Risk

Instead of changing the discount rate, some managers and analysts manipulate the cash flows to account for risk. The most simplistic method of revising the

---

[17] This will be discussed in Chapter 6.

cash flows for risk is commonly called "conservative" forecasting. To do this managers of Betty's might decide to use a conservative forecast for breakfast sales, lower than their best estimate, and a conservative forecast for costs, higher than their best estimate. This is not an unusual approach. However, a conservative forecast is one that typically overestimates costs and underestimates revenues, even if in management's best judgment that is not what is likely to happen. The conservative forecast does not reflect a set of likely circumstances, and it often has very little likelihood of actually occurring. Rather than being conservative, such a forecast is wrong. "Conservative" estimates paint an inaccurate picture of the real potential of the project. While such conservatism is broadly practiced, the good analyst will seek the most accurate forecasts and analyze risk using a different method.

There are two other ways to include management's uncertainty into our analysis. Both of these methods are based on forecasting multiple scenarios—several probable outcomes for costs and benefits for an investment. Each scenario should be based on a realistic forecast of what might happen to the investment under different economic, competitive, or technological futures.

6. Multi-Scenario Analysis

In the simple use of multiple scenario analysis, an analyst forecasts just three alternative outcomes—optimistic, pessimistic, and most likely—for each of the project's costs and benefits.[18] The forecasts made for the breakfast project (shown in Exhibit 4-2) were management's most likely estimates. However, the managers were quite uncertain about what would occur if they opened their restaurants for breakfast. If sales from the new breakfast menu exceeded the most likely estimate of $15 million, the operating costs as a percentage of sales might be expected to be slightly lower, since some costs (for instance, maintenance) would not increase with sales. Likewise, if sales were lower than expected, operating costs would not decrease as fast as sales and the net profit might be lower. Exhibit 4-13 provides the annual residual cash flows for the breakfast proposal's optimistic, most likely, and pessimistic scenarios. The net present value for each scenario is given at the bottom of the exhibit. Obviously, the investment cost of $2.055 million remains the same regardless of the success of the project.[19]

If the pessimistic scenario materializes, the company will experience a loss from offering breakfast. Furthermore, the net present value of the breakfast project is negative: the costs exceed the benefits. Using a higher discount rate

---

[18] This a different use of the three-scenario forecast that we first used in Chapter 2.
[19] A reminder that these scenarios should not be based on the worst (or best) outcomes possible for every cost and benefit. Such a forecast is usually possible but quite improbable. Possible but not probable forecasts give managers very little information on which to base decisions. Therefore, in making these forecasts, the analyst must take care that all three sets of forecasts are probable, not just possible.

EXHIBIT 4-13   Betty's Better Big Boys' Breakfast Proposal

ANNUAL RESIDUAL CASH FLOWS (in thousands of real dollars)

	Pessimistic	Most Likely	Optimistic
Incremental sales	$ 3,300	$ 15,000	$ 26,000
Operating expenses*	(3,168)	(14,250)	(24,440)
Depreciation	0	0	0
Pretax profit	132	750	1,560
Taxes (34%)	(45)	(255)	(530)
Profit after taxes	87	495	1,030
Noncash charges	0	0	0
Residual net cash flow[†]	$ 87	$ 495	$ 1,030
Net present value (@ 5%)	$ (982)	$ 793	$ 3,110

* Operating expenses are projected by management to decline as sales increase. Management expects them to be 96, 95, and 94 percent of sales, respectively.
† This assumes that each year's cash flows follow the pattern shown in Exhibit 4-2.

---

reduces the net present value further. However, if customers find the new breakfast menu appealing, the project could be quite a boon to Betty's and its shareholders: the net present value would be very attractive. What should management do, given these three different potential outcomes?

To decide whether to proceed with the breakfast proposal, management must decide on the likelihood of the pessimistic scenario occurring and whether the most likely and optimistic scenarios are attractive enough, that is, create enough value, to offset this danger.

Most managers who use this three-scenario analysis approach implicitly assume that each scenario is equally likely, and they use the information to decide whether the company could afford the pessimistic scenario. When creating the scenarios, managers do not need to believe that each of the outcomes is equally likely to occur. Using the breakfast proposal as an example, the management of Betty's might think it most likely, based on the experience of other fast-food restaurants in introducing a breakfast menu, that the breakfast proposal will have sales of $15 million as predicted in Exhibit 4-2. While $15 million is a good estimate of the expected sales, there is a reasonable chance that the innovative menu Betty's management is planning will be very successful and little chance it will fail. Thus the three outcomes would not be equally likely. In addition, management may see more than three probable scenarios. Instead of only three scenarios, the analyst might estimate five or more scenarios and the probability that each might occur. In Exhibit 4-14, the Betty's Better Big Boys' analyst has estimated five alternative outcomes for the breakfast proposal and the likelihood that each will occur.

To put the forecasts into perspective, the analyst weights the net present value for each scenario by the probability that it will occur to obtain what is

EXHIBIT 4-14 Probabilistic Analysis

BREAKFAST PROPOSAL (in thousands of real dollars)

Scenario	Probability	Net Present Value	Weighted Value
1	15%	$ (977)	$(147)
2	20	(102)	(20)
3	30	793	238
4	20	2,100	420
5	15	3,105	466
Expected value =			$ 957

called an **expected value**—the probability-weighted net present value.[20] Exhibit 4-14 provides the result of such an analysis. While the net present value of $957,000 is not one that the analyst explicitly forecasted, it represents a sort of average expected for the project.[21]

In a more complex investment analysis, where there are numerous costs and benefits for which an analyst could assess probabilities, computer-assisted analysis, especially simulation, provides a good means for analyzing complex data and estimating the expected value and the possible up- and downsides in the net present value.[22]

One word of caution in the use of multiple scenario, expected value analysis: this method depends on the company engaging in a number of projects at the same time, or over time. If only one project is undertaken, only one outcome can occur: no other projects exist to average the results. In order for the expected value to represent the average net present value that the company will receive from its projects, the company must analyze and make a number of investments: it must have a portfolio of investments.[23] In a portfolio the return the company earns will be the weighted average of all the returns from the investments. However, the risk of the investments is offset, particularly if the investments are not all concentrated in one product, process, market, and/or technology.[24]

Probabilistic analysis can yield rich information for a knowledgeable user, but holds dangers for the naive. For managers, analysts, and investors, much of the value of forecasting and multi-scenario analysis comes from the insight gained during the modeling process.

---

[20] To calculate the expected value, multiply each outcome by its probability and sum the products.
[21] The analyst also could compute a standard deviation to obtain a measure of risk.
[22] One way to measure the potential variation of the net present value is the standard deviation.
[23] For a single investment there is just one outcome. For a group of projects with different outcomes, the company receives the average.
[24] This is the basis of portfolio theory, the basics of which will be described in the context of a securities portfolio in Chapter 6. The theory and mathematics are rich, and sources for greater understanding of these portfolio concepts are listed at the end of the chapter.

Simulation analysis is used by an increasing number of companies. Managers find that the discipline of deciding what might occur for each of the various costs and benefits keeps their assumptions reasonable and makes the analysis even more useful. Although this technique is time-consuming and requires a computer, the increasing use of microcomputers has made multiple scenario simulation and analysis more accessible and useful for managers.

7. Upside Risk Analysis— Contingent Claims Analysis

All forms of risk analysis that we have described in this chapter treat risk as a negative attribute: as risk increases so must the investors' required rate of return; decreases in risk reduce the required return. Virtually all investments have upsides and downsides. Virtually none are immune to changes in customers' requirements, competitive pressures, and economic change. All these investments have the possibility that their cash flows, and thus their value, could be higher or lower. The usual approaches to risk analysis require that roughly equivalent upside and downside cash flow potentials exist.[25] In some cases, management can avoid some or most of the downside—the negative cash flows—by doing such things as purchasing insurance, test marketing, or arranging a partnership with another company. Eliminating the downside typically has a cost, however, and managers will want to be certain that the cost is appropriate.

How does a manager or analyst evaluate an investment where the potential losses have been reduced or eliminated?[26] Some analysts have adapted option-pricing techniques to value the investment with these characteristics. The method developed for use in valuing options in the securities markets has real potential for analyzing certain kinds of capital investments. Those investments are called contingent claims or options. A **contingent claim**, or **option**, is the right to further invest later in a set of assets at a particular price, or the right to abandon the investment at a point in the future.

In the capital markets, standardized contingent claims, called calls and puts, are available and traded. A traded **call option** gives the option holder the right to buy a stock or index at a particular price up until some specified date in the future. A **put option** allows the holder to sell a stock or index at a preset price up to a date in the future. Using the option is called **exercising**. There are some calls and puts that are only exercisable at a particular time. These are called **European options**. Those that can be exercised for a period of time are called **American options**.

---

[25] To be specific, a normal distribution of outcomes.

[26] One way that losses can be reduced in a project that is not developing as it was forecasted is to stop investing and abandon the project.

What is the advantage to having a contingent claim, or option, rather than making the investment in the first place? First, the cost for this claim is much smaller than the cost of making the full investment. Second, the investor can choose to exercise the claim on the investment or not: if the investor chooses not to exercise the claim, the only cost is the initial cost of the option. Thus, for a small price, the investor has the right, but not the obligation, to make the investment.

To demonstrate this, let's use an example. Consider the following: Strike-It-Rich Oil Co. has just heard that the government is going to sell drilling rights in the interior of the country, in a remote jungle area. From satellite maps, the area appears to have the necessary conditions for oil, so Strike-It-Rich management is interested. If it buys the right to drill in the area, management can decide later, or after more exploration, whether to make the investment in complete exploration and development of oil wells. The cost of the drilling right is small, the cost of developing wells is large, but Strike-It-Rich does not have to drill.

The typical discounted cash flow analysis that we have used in this chapter would discount all the costs associated with this investment and all the benefits that might accrue. Those costs would include exploration, drilling, and transporting the oil, as well as the benefit of the sales price for the oil. Yet, at this point, management is not even sure that it is going to drill: Strike-It-Rich management can stop investing at any point and walk away from the project. Thus there is a limit to the losses, and it is up to management's discretion whether to invest or not. Discounted cash flow has a very hard time dealing with this sort of dynamic, if/then sort of possibility that is coupled with an investment. This is dynamic decision making, and this sort of decision making is not taken into account in a traditional discounted cash flow.

Discounted cash flow analysis is static: the outcomes are presumed to be without management discretion once the investment is made. However, contingent claims or options analysis is dynamic, and thus more realistic. One of the critical differences is that a static technique like NPV does not adequately consider the risk of projects that have **embedded options**, options to be exercised later at the discretion of management. When the investor has an option, high potential variability is attractive: it increases the possibility of reaping the rewards from the investment. NPV analysis treats variability as risk, assigns it a cost, and discounts the higher risk (more variable) cash flows at higher rates than the rate at which it discounts more certain cash flows. The result is that NPV analysis often unduly penalizes the value of investments that have contingent claims embedded in them. In a dynamic world, they should not be penalized but sought.

Option-pricing techniques are one form of capital investment analysis that allows us to value dynamic projects where decisions about what will happen can be made later. Since these techniques are rather new in their application to capital investment analysis, a detailed description of how they are implemented is not included in this chapter. Rather, this information is in an appendix to this chapter. Whether you have a fleeting or in-depth knowledge of this type of analysis, the forward-thinking analyst should know that discounted cash flow analysis deals with both limited-loss and later investment-in-growth projects very poorly, and that option-pricing methods lend themselves well to analyzing such problems. Thus, analysts and managers who are faced with analyzing investments that have such characteristics should read further. References for more about option-pricing methods and a brief description of their use can be found in Appendix 4A.

None of the widely available risk-adjustment methods is completely satisfactory. Therefore, while new methods for incorporating risk into capital investment decision making are being developed or learned, some managers assign different hurdle rates to divisions or strategic business units that are exposed to different levels of risk. Other managers attempt to quantify risk differences for each individual investment. Still others use statistical techniques, such as probabilistic simulation analysis, to estimate directly the riskiness of investments. To date, risk is the most difficult problem in assessing value.

V. OTHER CONSIDERATIONS IN CREATING VALUE

Not all investments are as complex or as risky as our Betty's examples. Some are simple replacements of old, antiquated, or technologically inferior equipment. Analysis of one of these replacement investments will allow us to examine the impact of such things as different methods of depreciation and taxes on an investment's cash flows and its value.

1. The Impact of Taxes and Depreciation on Value

Depreciation and taxes can have a major impact on the value of an investment. Most managers and investors would tell you not to take an investment where the only real value comes from avoiding taxes. To make sure we understand where the value comes from, we need to understand how to analyze and value these cash flows. Let's turn to Betty's Better Big Boys once again. Management is considering a replacement investment—microwave ovens.

Currently, each of Betty's restaurants uses conventional electric ovens to heat some foods. Such ovens are large, take an average of 10 minutes to heat the food and, because they warm up slowly, must be kept hot whether they are being used or not.

Microwave ovens have been proposed to replace these ovens. They are small, cook much more rapidly and, because the method of heating and cooking is totally different, need only be turned on when actually in use. Thus the primary savings would be in the expense for electricity.

Management has made the following estimates of the costs and benefits associated with each new oven.

1. Microwave ovens can be purchased, fully installed, for $630 by July.
2. The old ovens can be sold to a used-equipment dealer for their book value of $25 each.
3. While annual usage and costs of electricity vary from restaurant to restaurant, the average cost per year per oven has been $300. The new ovens would use about one-third the electricity, for a cost of $100 per oven per year.
4. The new ovens are expected to be fully useful for five years. After that time the ovens will be obsolete or in need of substantial repair. Management believes the ovens would have no salvage value at the end of the fifth year. Management would depreciate the new ovens over six years, according to the 1999 tax code.

This is a very straightforward problem. As you can see in Exhibit 4-15, reduced costs are treated the same as increased income. The IRR that results from this analysis is 13.5 percent and the NPV (at a 10 percent discount rate) is $54.5 per oven, seemingly a reasonable investment opportunity.[27]

However, there are changes within management's discretion that can increase the value of the investment. As an example, under certain tax codes management could have elected to use another rapid method of depreciation or straight-line depreciation. Different tax codes use different accelerated methods. Let's examine the effect of using other depreciation methods on the value of the microwave oven investment.

The impact of using different depreciation methods on the cash flows and net present value of the microwave oven are shown in Exhibit 4-16. The double-declining-balance method yields the largest increase in the project's value.

At first glance, this may seem like numerical black magic, but it is, in fact, a real change in the value of the investment to the company. While the same total depreciation is taken, the amount taken in each year is different. Thus the timing of the taxes paid by the firm is different. Since the discounting process deems earlier cash flows to be more valuable, and since accelerated depreciation methods result in larger, earlier cash flows, the method of depreciation chosen by or allowed to management can create value. As shown in Exhibit 4-16, the present values under each tax code are different. Accelerated depreciation methods result in higher values, and the double-declining-balance method has the highest net present value.

This analysis of the differences in the way the tax law treats depreciation illustrates the impact external factors can have on the operations and decisions of the company. With the tax shield having a significant impact on the attractiveness of a project, the analyst should always be informed of not only current tax regulations but pending legislation as well. Keeping abreast of the

---

[27] An analysis for ovens for all 500 restaurants would yield the same IRR of 13.5 percent, but an NPV of $27,250 (500 × $54.5).

EXHIBIT 4-15 Betty's Better Big Boys' Microwave Oven Investment Analysis—Per Oven

	\ Period	0	1	2	3	4	5	6
Income Statement Changes								
Revenues			0	0	0	0	0	0
Electricity cost:								
Old oven			$ 300.0	$ 300.0	$ 300.0	$ 300.0	$ 300.0	
New oven			100.0	100.0	100.0	100.0	100.0	—
Electricity cost decrease			200.0	200.0	200.0	200.0	200.0	—
Depreciation:								
Old depreciation			—	—	—	—	—	
New depreciation			121.0	193.6	116.2	69.7	69.7	$ 34.8
Depreciation increase			121.0	193.6	116.2	69.7	69.7	34.8
Change in pretax profits			79.0	6.4	83.8	130.3	130.3	(34.8)
Taxes (@ 34%)*			(26.9)	(2.2)	(28.5)	(44.3)	(44.3)	11.8
Profit after taxes			52.1	4.2	55.3	86.0	86.0	(23.0)
Noncash Charges								
Depreciation increase			121.0	193.6	116.2	69.7	69.7	34.8
Asset Changes								
Property, plant, and equipment:								
Microwave oven		$ (630.0)						
Old oven salvage value		25.0						
Net cash flow		$ (605.0)	$ 173.1	$ 197.8	$ 171.5	$ 155.7	$ 155.7	$ 11.8

Net present value at 10% = $54.37
Internal rate of return = 13.5%

* Negative taxes are a tax credit against earnings in another portion of the company's business.

V. Other Considerations in Creating Value   **181**

EXHIBIT 4-16 Yearly Depreciation Charge

DIFFERENT DEPRECIATION METHODS FOR THE MICROWAVE OVEN INVESTMENT (in thousands)

Cash Flows	1	2	3	4	5	6
Straight line*	$121.0	121.0	121.0	121.0	121.0	0
Double-declining-balance[†]	242.0	145.2	87.1	65.3	65.3	0
Sum-of-years' digits[‡]	201.7	161.3	121.0	80.7	40.3	0
U.S. ACRS[§]	90.8	133.1	127.1	127.1	127.1	0
MACRS/1999 U.S. tax code[§§]	121.0	193.6	116.2	69.7	69.7	34.8

Net Present Value (@ 10%)	
Straight line	$ 51.3
Double-declining-balance	62.2
Sum-of-years' digits	61.2
U.S. ACRS	49.6
MACRS/1999 U.S. tax code	54.4

Internal Rate of Return	
Straight line	13.3%
Double-declining-balance	14.2%
Sum-of-years' digits	14.1%
U.S. ACRS	13.1%
MACRS/1999 U.S. tax code	13.5%

* The depreciation rate is calculated by dividing 100 percent by the number of years. In this case, the depreciation rate is 100/5 = 20 percent per year. To determine yearly depreciation, multiply the purchase price, minus the salvage value, by the depreciation rate.
† Double the straight-line depreciation rate is multiplied by the fully depreciated value of the asset. A switch to straight-line depreciation occurs when it is larger.
‡ To calculate the sum-of-the-years' digits factor:
   a) Sum the numbers of the years, in this case 5 + 4 + 3 + 2 + 1 = 15.
   b) For each year, divide the number of remaining years by the summed years. In this case, the depreciation factor for the first year is 5/15 or 0.33.
   c) Multiply the depreciable value by this factor.
§ Five-year U.S. ACRS rates are 15 percent the first year, 22 percent the second year, and 21 percent the remaining three years.
§§ MACRS depreciates at the following rates: 20, 32, 19.2, 11.52, 11.52, and 5.76 percent, for years one through six, respectively.

economic, social, and political environment is essential for the analyst in order to analyze managerial decisions properly.

2. Including Investment-Size Considerations

We have looked at three investments Betty's Better Big Boys could make—the breakfast service; the salad, sushi, and pasta bar; and installing microwave ovens. Each has a different net present value. While the breakfast option appears to be the best choice, we have failed to take note of one other thing: Betty's investments will require different amounts of capital. Thus, if we simply compare the net present values of the three alternatives, we have ignored the invested capital. As an example, all 500 microwave ovens require a net investment of only $302,500 while the breakfast proposal requires $2.055 million, a difference of $1.752 million. That means if management chose the microwave investment it would have $1.75 million in funds to use for another investment. Thus if we simply compare net present values, or any other measure of relative return for that matter, we could make a bad decision. In essence, by failing to take into account the investment of all the capital, we would be comparing different corporate strategies.

Must managers have an intended use for the extra capital in order to compare the projects? No. They can examine the value the added investment would create for the owners. To do this, the analyst must first determine the differences in the initial costs and the annual residual cash flows of each of the two investments. A simple method is to subtract the annual residual cash flows of the smaller investment from those of the larger investment. Exhibit 4-17

EXHIBIT 4-17 Betty's Better Big Boys Residual Net Cash Flows

	TWO ALTERNATIVES		
	(1) Breakfast Option	(2) 500 Microwave Ovens	(1) – (2) Difference
Net investment	$ 2,055,000	$ 302,500*	$ 1,752,500
Annual net cash flows			
0	$(2,055,000)	$(302,500)	$(1,752,500)
1	495,000	86,550	408,450
2	495,000	98,900	396,100
3	495,000	85,750	409,250
4	495,000	77,850	417,150
5	1,395,000	77,850	1,317,150
6	0	5,900	(5,900)
NPV (at 10%)	$ 380,269	$ 27,184	$ 353,084
IRR	15.9%	13.5%	16.2%

* This is the net present value per oven from Exhibit 4-15 times 500 ovens, one for each restaurant.

shows the results of this analysis of differences between the breakfast and microwave oven options for Betty's Better Big Boys. By looking at the last column in the exhibit, you can see that the breakfast option would require an additional investment of $1.75 million beyond that required for installing microwave ovens in all the restaurants.

What does Betty's get for its investment? To determine the benefit, we can discount the differences between the two sets of cash flows. The discounted value is $353,084, as shown in column 3 of Exhibit 4-17, a significant contribution to the shareholders' value. This is the incremental present value from investing $1.75 million more in the breakfast proposal than what is invested in the microwave ovens. Of course, Betty's management will want to compare this present value with the present values generated by other investments that it might make with the incremental $1.75 million. However, whatever use it might have for the capital, the exhibit clearly shows that the return would have to be more than 16.2 percent (the incremental IRR) to render any other use equal to the breakfast investment. Management would likely conclude that the incremental return on the added investment in the breakfast option is attractive.[28]

3. Incorporating Expected Inflation

Inflation can have a neutral, positive, or negative effect on the value of an investment, depending on whether managers can pass on their costs in the form of prompt price increases. If cost increases can be passed on immediately and fully, the relative value of the project will remain the same regardless of the level of inflation. If there is a lag between the time the company's costs increase and the time when it can raise prices, however, inflation can have a very negative effect on the value of a project. Of course, if management can raise prices more than inflation, or has cash that it can invest, the company can prosper from inflation.[29]

Inflation can have yet other effects. Revenues themselves may rise or fall depending on the rate of inflation. For instance, if more people eat breakfast at fast-food restaurants than at traditional restaurants when inflation and prices rise, Betty's Better Big Boys may find that its revenues rise in both real terms (more customers are eating breakfast) and in nominal terms (prices rise to account for the increased costs of producing the same number of breakfasts).

The effects of these increases should be well understood by the manager. Up to now, all the cash flows Betty's management forecasted for its investments were in real terms; they did not include inflation. Exhibit 4-18 provides a forecast for the salad, sushi, and pasta bar proposal that Betty's Better Big Boys' management is considering, with 10 percent inflation. In this example

---

[28] If Betty's Better Big Boys had a number of investments of different sizes, the comparisons made in Exhibit 4-17 would have to be repeated for each pair of investments.

[29] Terra Blanca, an example used in Chapter 2, showed such inflation-related gains.

EXHIBIT 4-18 Betty's Salad, Sushi, and Pasta Bar Proposal

MARGINAL COSTS AND BENEFITS WITH ANNUAL INFLATION OF 10% (thousands of dollars)

				Period			
	0	1	2	3	4	5	6
Income Statement Changes							
Sales		$ 8,250	$ 9,075	$ 9,983	$ 10,981	$ 12,079	
Operating expenses		(7,663)	(8,430)	(9,273)	(10,200)	(11,220)	
Training costs	$ (416)						
Depreciation		(280)	(448)	(269)	(161)	(161)	$ (81)
Profit before taxes	(416)	307	197	441	620	698	(81)
Taxes	141	(104)	(67)	(150)	(210)	(237)	28
Net profit	$ (275)	$ 203	$ 130	$ 291	$ 410	$ 461	$ (53)
Noncash Charges							
Depreciation		280	448	269	161	161	81
Capital Investments							
Property, plant, and equipment	(1,400)						
New inventory	(900)					1,449*	
Residual net cash flow	$ (2,575)	$ 483	$ 578	$ 560	$ 571	$ 2,071	$ 28
Net present value @ 5%	$1,006.4						
Net present value @ 10%	$454.2						

*We have grown the inventory value with inflation. Had we not done so the inventory value in year 5 would have been $900, and each NPV would have been lower $430.0 at 5 percent, and 340.9 at 10 percent. The impact of inflation on inventory value is a critical factor. Note, depreciation is calculated on the initial equipment cost unadjusted for inflation.

there is no real increase in revenues and unit sales remain the same; the only increases arise from the expected inflation. Inflation alone decreases the net present value (at a discount rate of 10 percent) from a negative $313,019 to a positive $454.2.

Before you conclude that inflation has increased the value of this project, remember that we discounted these cash flows at 10 percent, the same rate we used on the cash flows before we introduced inflation. Investors do not ignore inflation. If the required return for this project was 10 percent before inflation, investors certainly will expect a higher return once they include inflation. Using a more appropriate discount rate of 20 percent results in an NPV of $330,005.[30] Obviously, inflation's effect on value in this case is negative, not positive.[31] Critical to this return is the inventory value in year 5. If it does not appreciate with inflation, the NPV at 20 percent is $109,374.

You might have noted depreciation did not change at all in Exhibit 4-18, especially if you compared the cash flows with those shown in Exhibit 4-3. This is because, in many countries, depreciation schedules for capitalized property are calculated on the basis of historical cost, and companies are not allowed to revalue assets to incorporate inflation-driven changes. As a result of this situation, as the rate of inflation increases, depreciation does not change, and neither do the taxes that are deferred by the depreciation tax shield. Thus the investment is less valuable. Appendix 4B describes this inflation drag, which is one of the insidious costs of inflation. In some countries, particularly those with high rates of inflation that have persisted for some time, companies are allowed to increase the book value of fixed assets to keep pace with inflation. As the book value rises, the depreciation increases too, keeping pace with inflation.[32] For companies operating in these environments, profits actually increase at a rate comparable to that of inflation.

VI. SUMMARY

Good investments are critical to the future of a company. The analyst's job is to gather and analyze the relevant information and present it in a way that allows managers to make informed decisions. Analysts have three major problems in assessing potential investments. First, the appropriate cash costs and benefits must be determined. That process, as we have suggested, can be difficult, particularly when evaluating replacement investments or when operating in an inflationary environment. The analyst's second problem is to evaluate the relative attractiveness of the investment's net marginal benefits. This book sug-

---

[30] We will discuss the impact of inflation on discount rates in Chapter 6.
[31] Ten percent required rate of return and 10 percent for expected inflation is a fair estimate of the combined required return.
[32] It depends upon the index used to calculate the inflation adjustment. The adjustment usually is statutory and often lags the actual increases in inflation.

gests that the NPV method is the most appropriate technique to use in measuring this value.[33] Third, the particularly vexing problem of incorporating risk into the evaluation of any investment must be dealt with. If all of the investments are of a risk similar to that of the firm, an appropriate method is to use the firm's marginal required return as a hurdle rate. If the investment is more or less risky than the firm, the analyst may leave it to the managers to decide subjectively whether the return is adequate to compensate for the risk. Some managers find the information from multiple scenario or simulation analysis to be useful in making their decisions; others prefer to adjust the required return to compensate for risk. While understanding and incorporating risk into an analysis is one of the most difficult things that faces investors, ignoring it is not a sensible approach. Determining the investments a company makes is challenging and critical.

SELECTED REFERENCES

For comprehensive reviews of the capital budgeting process, see:

Bierman, Harold, Jr., and Seymour Smidt. *The Capital Budgeting Decision*. 7th ed. New York: Macmillan, 1988.

Levy, Haim, and Marshall Sarnat. *Capital Investment and Financial Decisions*. Englewood Cliffs, NJ: Prentice Hall International, 1990.

Shapiro, Alan. "Corporate Strategy and the Capital Budgeting Decision." *Midland Corporate Finance Journal*, Spring 1985, pp. 22–36.

For an analysis of the capital budgeting and planning process in one firm, see:

Bower, Joseph. *Managing the Resource Allocation Process: A Study of Corporate Planning and Investments*. Homewood, Ill.: Richard D. Irwin, 1970.

For descriptions of various approaches to risk analysis, see:

Bodie, Zvi, and Robert Merton. *Finance*. Upper Saddle River, NJ: Prentice Hall, 2000, chap. 10.

Bower, Richard S., and J. M. Jenks. "Divisional Screening Rates." *Financial Management*, Autumn 1975, pp. 42–49.

Damodoran, Aswath. *Corporate Finance*. New York: John Wiley & Sons, 1997, chaps. 10 and 11.

Hertz, David B. "Risk Analysis in Capital Investment." *Harvard Business Review*, September–October 1979, pp. 169–81.

Weston, J. Fred. "Investment Decisions Using the Capital Asset Pricing Model." *Financial Management*, Spring 1973, pp. 25–33.

---

[33] Augmented by contingent claims analysis when appropriate.

For information on the effects of inflation on capital budgeting analysis, see:

Bodie, Zvi, and Robert Merton. *Finance*. Upper Saddle River, NJ: Prentice Hall, 2000, chap. 4.

Rappaport, Alfred, and Robert A. Taggart, Jr. "Evaluation of Capital Expenditure Proposals Under Inflation." *Financial Management*, Spring 1982, pp. 5–13.

For more on international capital budgeting, see:

Shapiro, Alan C. *Multinational Financial Management*. 6th ed. New York: John Wiley & Sons, 1999, chap. 21.

Shapiro, Alan C. "International Capital Budgeting." in *New Developments in International Finance*, Joel Stern and Donald Chew, Jr., eds. New York: Basil Blackwell, 1988, pp. 165–180.

For information on capital budgeting in general, see:

Aggarwal, Raj. *Capital Budgeting Under Uncertainty*. Englewood Cliffs, NJ: Prentice Hall, 1993.

Brealey, Richard A., and Stewart C. Myers. *Principles of Corporate Finance*. 5th ed. New York: McGraw-Hill, 1996, chaps. 5 and 9–12.

Brigham, Eugene F., Louis C. Gapenski, and Michael Ehrhardt. *Financial Management*. 9th ed. Fort Worth, Texas: The Dryden Press, 1999, chaps. 11 and 12.

Damodoran, Aswath. *Corporate Finance*. New York: John Wiley & Sons, 1997, chaps. 7–9.

Levy, Haim, and Marshall Sarnat. *Capital Investment and Financial Decisions*. 4th ed. Englewood Cliffs, NJ: Prentice Hall, 1990.

Ross, Stephen A., Randolph W. Westerfield, and Jeffrey F. Jaffe. *Corporate Finance*. 4th ed. Homewood, Ill.: Richard D. Irwin, 1996, chaps. 3, 4, 6, 7, and 8.

For information on discounting, see:

Bodie, Zvi, and Robert Merton. *Finance*. Upper Saddle River, NJ: Prentice Hall, 2000, chap. 4.

Brealey, Richard A., and Stewart C. Myers. *Principles of Corporate Finance*. 5th ed. New York: McGraw-Hill, 1996, chaps. 2 and 3.

Brigham, Eugene F., Louis C. Gapenski, and Michael Ehrhardt. *Financial Management*. 9th ed. Fort Worth, Texas: The Dryden Press, 1999, chap. 7.

STUDY QUESTIONS

1. In December 1996, Metalwerks' management was considering the development of a new assembly line. The necessary machinery was estimated to

cost 1.4 million deutsche marks. The tax code would allow the equipment to be depreciated in 20 years, its useful life, using the double-declining-balance method of depreciation with a switch to straight-line depreciation when advantageous. Management estimated that the costs associated with owning and running the machinery (gas, minor repairs, etc.) would be constant over time and total DM260,000 over its 20-year estimated life. Twenty people would be required to work the assembly line. These would be new employees, each earning an average of DM24,000 a year in salary and benefits. Sales from the new assembly line were estimated to total DM1.625 million a year, with raw materials representing 37 percent of that amount. No other costs specific to the project were anticipated. Metalwerks had a 34 percent tax rate and a required payback period of four years on all new projects. Should the company develop the assembly line? What is the project's benefit/cost ratio?

2. BELLA LUNA of Italy is considering an investment that will cost 200,000 lira initially. The new equipment is estimated to have a useful life of five years but will require an additional investment of 60,000 lira in the second year for specialized equipment. The initial investment will be depreciated under the tax code for five years. The second investment will meet the guidelines for the three-year class. Sales specific to the project are forecasted at 120,000 lira in year one, increasing 15 percent a year to year five. Necessary raw materials, labor, etc., are estimated at 39 percent of sales.

The tax code allows the following depreciation schedules.

Year	5-Year Schedule	3-Year Schedule
1	15%	26%
2	22	32
3	21	42
4	21	
5	21	

a. Compute the project's net present value using a 10 percent discount rate and a 45 percent tax rate.
b. What is the major factor creating the project's net present value?

3. Cloud Frame Company operates in an environment where capital is scarce. Management is trying to decide between the two capital projects described below. Evaluate each of the projects on the basis of their payback period, benefit/cost ratio, and net present value. Which project would you recommend Cloud Frame Company undertake? Why?

Project 1: Expand existing production by acquiring new machinery costing Libra 800,000 and having a productive life of 10 years:

- Incremental sales = Libra 500,000 a year
- Cost of goods sold = 49 percent of sales
- Advertising = Libra 50,000 a year
- Depreciation computed using double-declining-balance for 10 years

Project 2: Expand product line by undertaking a project estimated to cost Libra 600,000 for production facilities, depreciable using double-declining-balance for its 10-year life, and Libra 200,000 for production training for employees. Cloud Frame management has already funded Libra 100,000 worth of market research, which documented the product's sales potential. Cloud Frame management hopes to recoup this outlay through further sales.

- Sales in year 1 are estimated to be Libra 350,000, increasing 10 percent a year in years 2–4, 15 percent a year in years 5–7, and 10 percent a year in years 8–10
- Cost of goods sold is projected at 50 percent of sales
- Advertising is to be 25 percent of sales for the first three years and to level off at Libra 100,000 thereafter

Cloud Frame has a 34 percent tax rate and uses a 10 percent discount rate to evaluate all projects. There is a 10 percent tax credit on production facility investments applicable to this investment.

APPENDIX 4A
Real Options and Capital Investing[1]

In Chapter 4 we discussed net present value analysis. We forecasted our best estimate of the future cash flows from the investment, and discounted them at a rate that reflected the risk of the investment. We defined risk as the possibility that our cash flows could be wrong, and varied the discount rate according to the risk. Discounted cash flow analysis has one big flaw: we assume that once management makes the investment, nothing can be changed. It's a kind of "what will be, will be" analysis, and it's not a good reflection of what can really happen. After the initial investment has been made, management can decide that the prospects are so good more should be invested, or that they overestimated what could happen and should "cut the losses" and abandon or scale back the investment. Management can influence the final outcome from an investment. The traditional NPV approach does not account for changes management might make later, but it should.

Net present value analysis is a fine method for analyzing investment opportunities when, once the investment is made, no action can be taken to change the outcome. NPV evaluates a **static decision**: a decision where the outcome cannot be altered. If, however, a manager has future discretion and the opportunities, the analysis is of a **dynamic decision**. Generally, for dynamic decisions it is not appropriate to use net present value analysis.

Options for action are all around us. Every time we use the phrase "if . . . then," we are talking about a **contingency**, an optional choice, something we can do if something else happens. For managers making investments, there are a number of different kinds of options that can exist:

1. To acquire or use something that currently has little or no value, but could if conditions change. These are called **investment options**.
2. To increase the investment or commitment to an investment or strategy, if it is attractive to do so. These options usually offer the opportunity to grow, and are called **growth** or **production options**.
3. To abandon a project or strategy in the future if it is not proceeding as desired. These are called **abandonment** or **bailout options**.

---
[1] This appendix benefitted greatly from the fine work of Asst. Professor Diane Lander, Babson College, MA.

Appendix 4A Real Options and Capital Investing

An investment project can have both static and dynamic features. Some things about an investment may be unchanging and unchangeable once the investment is made. Other features are optional. In some cases these options are a natural part of the investment; in other situations management designs future choices into the investment. Because the option or options often are bundled together with an investment project, these options generally are called **embedded options**.[2] An example will make this clear.

The RAPTOR Group needs a new plant to build its products. The primary reason that it needs to expand is to manufacture a new product developed by the Mesozo Division. The new product was the brainchild of their hot new designer, but it is so revolutionary the marketing staff is not sure just how many the company will sell. Management has secured a contract for production for the first three years. If the market is as large as the Mesozo Division head has forecasted, the company will need a large plant with special technology for the product, called the X Design. If, however, most customers decide to stay with the old technology, the company's sales after three years will not grow.

Management has been presented with two possible ways to satisfy X Design's production needs: build a small plant that can be expanded in three years or build a large plant now. The smaller plant plus the later expansion would cost more than the large plant, but the smaller plant would allow management to test the market's acceptance of the revolutionary new product before expanding the plant. However, if the market does not develop, management would continue to produce for their one customer of the X Design, but sales would not grow and management would not add to the small plant. If management chooses the larger and more sophisticated plant and the market does not develop, the company would have a large, expensive, partially used plant that would be hard to use for another purpose. The option available with the smaller plant is to expand later. There is no option embedded in the larger plant investment. Management believes that the more flexible two-stage construction is better, but before making a decision management needs to know the value of each of these alternatives.

In this appendix we will show how net present value analysis is not up to the task of valuing the small plant with later expansion.[3] Through an example it will be clear that using net present value to compare the two alternatives is not appropriate. We will present an explicit approach to value this real option. But first we must set the groundwork and look at options where they are valued most frequently, in the capital markets.

---

[2] In this appendix, we limit ourselves to real options such as options to invest, disinvest, or grow. The company also can use options in its financing activities.

[3] We will not discuss the use of financial options to craft the risk characteristics of financial investments and strategies here. This use of financial options, also called financial engineering, is discussed in Chapter 7.

I. FINANCIAL OPTIONS

While options exist all around us, the formal valuation of options has been more highly developed in the capital markets where standard option contracts are used. Because of the magnitude of the markets for financial options, standard approaches have been developed to deal with them. These methods also can be used for the real options that accompany capital budgeting decisions.[4]

There are options on a variety of financial instruments that are designed to suit the insurer or the owner. There are two basic kinds of **financial options**: calls and puts. **Call options** give the owner the right, but not the obligation, to buy a specific asset (the **underlying** asset) at a specific price (the **strike price**) at, on, or before a specific time (the **maturity** or **exercise date**). Options that can be exercised from the date of purchase to expiration are called **American**. Options that can only be exercised on a specific date are called **European** options. Embedded options can be either American or European. **Put options** allow the owner to sell a specific asset, at a specific price, on or before a specific time. In essence a put option is the reverse of a call option.

In the capital markets both put and call options are publicly traded. However, not all financial securities have puts or calls or both. Options that are freely traded are listed on an organized exchange, such as the Chicago Board Options Exchange (CBOE).

Financial options allow the investor to take later action. For instance, a call option on a specific common stock allows an investor to acquire a particular number of shares of the stock at a later date at the specified price. Exhibit 4A-1 shows the call prices listed for Philip Morris shares on August 14th. The last date on which the call can be used, the date it expires, is listed in the third column. As you can see there are a variety of options with different expiration dates. The second column is the strike or exercise price, the price for which the stock can be acquired. You will note that for Philip Morris options the exercise prices are near the stock price of $90. The calls at the various strike prices allow the owner of the call to purchase shares or sell the option to someone who wants the shares at the strike price. However, the owner of the call does not have to buy the shares now. They can wait, conserving their capital, in the hope that the actual share price will rise and a profit will be earned.[5] The value of the call as the stock price rises depends upon the difference between the stock price and the stock price at which the option can be exercised.[6] Notice that Philip

---

[4] In this appendix we will use the most general of the option-valuation methods, the binomial model. Other models, most notably the Black-Scholes option-pricing model, do not allow us to examine as carefully or to consider changes as dynamically as the binomial option-pricing approach.

[5] The owner of the call does not actually have to buy the stock to make money. Since the option price reflects the rise in prices, the option can be sold to realize the gain. Furthermore, if the option has not expired, it is more profitable to sell the option than to exercise it.

[6] If the stock price is below the exercise price, the value of the call option is zero, even though the price is not. The price reflects investor expectations.

EXHIBIT 4A-1 Options on Philip Morris Stock—August 14

Option	Strike Price	Expiration*	Call	Put	Option	Strike Price	Expiration	Call	Put
90	80	Sept	11.00	1.00	90	100	Sept	0.06	9.50
		Dec	12.75	2.63			Dec	1.00	11.25
		Sept	7.25	2.25			Mar	3.25	N.Av.
		Dec	9.38	4.25			Aug	4.38	N.Av.
		Mar	N.Av.	5.75		105	Sept	0.44	4.88
	90	Aug	1.56	1.38			Dec	2.13	16.50
		Sept	4.25	4.25			Mar	3.50	N.Av.
		Dec	7.25	6.63		110	Aug	0.06	20.00
		Aug	0.25	4.63			Sept	0.25	N.Av.
	95	Sept	2.06	7.25			Dec	1.25	N.Av.
		Dec	4.63	9.06			Mar	2.50	20.06
		Mar	6.50	10.13		115	Aug	0.06	N.Av.
		Aug	0.06	9.50			Sept	1.00	N.Av.
							Dec	1.25	N.Av.

N.Av. means that there are no options at this price.
* There is an actual day of expiration.

Morris call prices at exercise prices below $90 are rather high. These are called in-the-money options: the exercise price is below the current stock price.

Put options allow the owner to sell shares at the strike price on or before the put expiration date. Put options become more valuable as the strike price rises above the actual price. Put option prices are in the last column.

To understand the true value of options, let's look at what can happen to the value of a put and call option at the moment of expiration.

The value of a stock is its current market price. That price could be much higher or lower later, for instance, next March for the Philip Morris example. This is because many things can happen to the company, its competitors, and the economy between August and March. The more time that exists between the time the option is purchased and the maturity date, the more that can happen to the stock price.

The value of an option is the difference between the exercise price of the option and the market price of the stock.[7] In other words, the call-option holder gains from share price increases. However, if the exercise price is above the stock price, the option value is zero, even though the option price is greater than zero. The call option holder has limited the downside. The total cost to the holder of the call is the price that was paid for the option. The put option has value when the exercise price is above the stock's market price: the put-option

---

[7] The option is worth nothing when it is at maturity and the stock price is lower than the exercise price.

holder can sell shares having a lower market price at the higher strike or exercise price.

Thinking about these options, we can see that the option price depends upon five things.

1. *The price of the underlying asset.* If the price rises, the value of a call (put) option rises (falls). If the price declines, the value of a call (put) option falls (rises). The lowest value of the option is zero.
2. *The exercise price.* Holding the price of the asset constant, the higher (lower) the exercise price, the lower (higher) the value of the call (put).
3. *The time until the option expires.* The longer the remaining life of the option, the greater is its price. As we said before, the longer the time to expiration, the greater chance things can happen, and there is, therefore, a greater possibility that the option will have value.[8]
4. *The variability of the returns of the underlying investment.* The more variable the price of the underlying asset, the greater the possibility that the price will change and that the option can be profitably exercised.
5. *The current market interest rate.* The higher the rate, the more valuable the option. This is because in owning the option rather than the underlying investment, we have avoided investing the full value of the underlying investment, and we invest in the option alone. Since the option has a lower price and the underlying investment a much larger price, we defer making the investment and can invest the difference. Thus the higher the interest rate, the more we earn on this investment. This is the reverse of net present value analysis where the higher the discount rate, the less valuable the investment. Exhibit 4A-2 summarizes the NPV/option differences.

There are five things that we know about the price of an option on a stock.

1. The option price is never greater than the stock price.
2. The option price cannot drop below zero.

EXHIBIT 4A-2 American Call Price Changes from Changes in Critical Variables

Change in Critical Variables	Option Price Impact	
	Call	Put
Stock price	Positive	Negative
Exercise price	Negative	Positive
Volatility of stock price	Positive	Positive
Time to expiration	Positive	Positive
Risk-free rate	Positive	Negative

---

[8] For European options all the actions are the same, except the time to expiration. With these options, this impact has outcomes that cannot be easily classified as positive or negative.

3. The option price is never below the value that could be earned if the option were exercised immediately.
4. The option price, less the present value of the price paid for the option, will approach the stock price when there is a large stock price increase.[9]
5. Because an option has a small price relative to the stock, the option's price volatility is higher than the underlying stock's price volatility. The higher the price of the stock and option, the lower the option's volatility. The lower the price of the stock and option, the higher the volatility. Thus the risk of an option is always higher than that of the stock, but it changes and the change depends upon the relationship between the stock price and the exercise price.

These factors are used in different ways in options and net present value analysis, thus they have a very different impact on the value of a capital investment. The major differences are shown in Exhibit 4A-3.

Financial options often come in bundles. There may be several puts and/or calls contained in one instrument. These combinations of options are usually called synthetic securities. We will discuss these briefly in Chapter 7.

Options on such things as common stocks are called **financial options**; options embedded in corporate investment decisions are called **real options**. In this chapter, we take what we know about financial market options and apply it to corporate investment options.

II. REAL OPTIONS

Real options allow managers to increase their potential returns while limiting their potential losses. In the past, many managers, not having the proper tools to value real options, called these strategic or intangible investments. They intuitively knew that these real options had a value, but net present value analy-

EXHIBIT 4A-3 Impacts on Option and Net Present Values from Changes in Critical Variables[10]

Variable	Option Value	Net Present Value
Risk-free rate rises	Increases value*	Decreases value
Variability of outcomes increases	Increases value	Decreases value
Life of investment lengthens	Increases value*	Decreases value

* For a put the impact may be different.

---

[9] This is different for European options.
[10] There are some exceptions to this simplistic scheme, but in general the impact shown in this chart is accurate.

sis did not allow a value to be placed on them. Thus managers would argue on strategic grounds for an investment with a negative net present value. Purists would say that anything could be valued using net present value techniques while realists knew that net present value analysis did not provide a complete valuation. Let us return to the plant expansion example to see what the valuation differences might be between net present value and an option valuation method. RAPTOR can build a new plant now for $10.0 million. The analysis of this alternative is shown in Exhibit 4A-4.

The net present value of investing in the larger plant today is $12.5 million. The net present value of building a smaller plant now for $8 million and waiting to build the remainder (at a cost of $5 million in three years) is $11.5 mil-

EXHIBIT 4A-4   NPV Analysis

RAPTOR LARGE PLANT EXPANSION WITH 5% TERMINAL GROWTH

	0	1	2	3
Sales		$ 7,962,400	$ 9,395,632	$11,086,846
Variable costs		(3,821,952)	(4,509,903)	(5,321,686)
Depreciation		(1,000)	(1,000)	(1,000)
Fixed costs		(5,000)	(5,000)	(5,000)
EBIT		4,134,448	4,879,729	5,759,160
Taxes (@ 40%)		(1,653,779)	(1,951,891)	(2,303,664)
Operating profit		2,480,669	2,927,838	3,455,496
Depreciation		1,000	1,000	1,000
Operating cash flow		2,481,669	2,928,838	3,456,496
Change in plant	$(10,000,000)			
Terminal value*				26,588,430
Net cash flow	(10,000,000)	$ 2,481,669	$ 2,928,838	$30,044,926
Net present value @ 18%	$ 12,492,824			

Assumptions
Operating characteristics:
Year 1:
   Sales volume (units)   592,000
   Sales price per unit $13.45
Variable cost per unit   48.00%
Fixed costs $5,000
Depreciation $1,000
Sales growth rate   18.0%
   Required rate of return   18.0%
   Risk-free rate of return   7.0%
Terminal value growth rate   5.0%
Marginal tax rate   40.0%
Initial cost $10,000,000

* Terminal value calculated using the perpetuity for a growing cash flow. Thus the terminal value is $26,588,430 in year 3 [$3,456,496/(0.18 − 0.05)].

lion, as shown in Exhibit 4A-5. Since the large plant investment has the larger NPV, RAPTOR management would choose to build the larger plant now, rather than the two-phase plan.

In spite of the higher net present value from building the larger plant today, there is a value to being able to wait before deciding to build the rest of the plant. The value comes from being able to expand *if and only if* the market materializes. Since management is not sure the market will materialize, this option is interesting and potentially valuable.

Our analysis in Exhibit 4A-5 presumed that the company would proceed with the plant expansion whether or not the new market develops. What is it worth to management to be able to wait until they have more information about the market before deciding to build the second phase of the plant? To understand the value of this flexibility, we must look at what will happen if the added capacity is not needed in the third year.

Whether management chooses to build the smaller or large plant, sales for the first three years do not change. However, if the product does not meet expectations no new customers will buy from RAPTOR and the sales will not grow after the third year. If management has built the large plant, they will have overbuilt for its needs. If it has built the smaller plant, no expansion would be undertaken. Exhibit A4-6 shows the analysis of the wait-and-see strategy if terminal sales growth is zero and management decides not to expand the plant. The net present value is almost $10 million.

Management is not certain what market demand will be. Depending upon the growth, the cash flows from the third year onwards could be much higher

EXHIBIT 4A-5 Net Present Value of Wait-and-See Plant Expansion—Expand Year 3

	5% TERMINAL GROWTH			
	0	1	2	3
Sales		$ 7,962,400	$ 9,395,632	$11,086,846
Variable costs		(3,821,952)	(4,509,903)	(5,321,686)
Depreciation		(800)	(800)	(1,300)
Fixed costs		(5,000)	(5,000)	(5,000)
EBIT		4,134,648	4,884,374	5,758,860
Taxes (@ 40%)		(1,653,859)	(1,953,750)	(2,303,544)
Operating profit		2,480,789	2,930,624	3,455,316
Depreciation		800	800	1,300
Operating cash flow		2,481,589	2,931,424	3,456,616
Change in plant	$ (8,000,000)			(5,000,000)
Terminal value*				26,579,354
Net cash flow	(8,000,000)	$ 2,481,589	$ 2,931,424	$25,035,970
Net present value @ 18%	$11,446,009			

* Terminal value is calculated using the perpetuity for a growing cash flow. Thus the terminal value is [$3,456,616/(0.18 − 0.05)] or $26,579,354.
Note: Depreciation in year 3 reflects the depreciation from the initial plant and its expansion.

EXHIBIT 4A-6 Cash Flows and NPV of Wait-and-See Strategy—Don't Expand Year 3

NO GROWTH BEYOND YEAR 3

	0	1	2	3
Sales		$ 7,962,400	$ 9,395,632	$11,086,846
Variable costs		(3,821,952)	(4,509,903)	(5,321,686)
Depreciation		(800)	(800)	(800)
Fixed costs		(5,000)	(5,000)	(5,000)
EBIT		4,134,648	4,879,929	5,760,960
Taxes		(1,653,859)	(1,951,972)	(2,304,384)
Operating profit		2,480,789	2,927,957	3,456,576
Depreciation		800	800	800
Operating cash flow		2,481,589	2,928,757	3,457,376
New plant	$ (8,000,000)			
Terminal value*				19,207,644
Net cash flow	(8,000,000)	$ 2,481,589	$ 2,928,757	$22,665,020
Net present value	$10,001,060			

*Terminal value is calculated as a perpetuity with no growth and a discount rate of 18 percent.

or lower than our expected value of 5 percent. This growth rate impacts the terminal value, and thus the NPV. Exhibit 4A-7 summarizes the present and terminal values with different assumptions about terminal growth.

If the growth is zero, management does not have to build the added plant. However, if the growth is 8 percent, the added terminal value from being able to build the plant is $15.4 million and management would build the plant. If the growth were only 2 percent, management would gain only $2,400,345. Since the plant costs $5 million, the added terminal value would not cover the cost of building the plant.[11]

EXHIBIT 4A-7 Present and Terminal Values of Wait-and-See Strategy

DIFFERENT RATES OF GROWTH WITH NO NEW PLANT IN YEAR 3

Terminal Rate of Growth	Present Value	Terminal Value
0%	$10,001,060	$19,207,644
2	11,462,356	21,608,600
5	14,497,355	26,595,200
8	19,353,353	34,573,760

---

[11] By the way, the difference between the zero growth scenario and the expected value of 5 percent growth is $7,385,675. The expected value is the mean of the outcomes, or in terms we used in Chapter 4, it is the most likely outcome. This is a probability-weighted outcome, not an explicit scenario.

The only trouble with this analysis is that at the time the investment is made, management does not know what sales growth will be after the third year. How can it decide about the plant when it just does not know what will happen? In the past when managers believed that the option to build later had a value they could either assert that the option had a value, construct numbers to fit their beliefs, or use their persuasive abilities. Now they can put a value on the option using option-pricing techniques.

We already know most of what we need to know to figure this option.

- The value of the ability to grow at 5 percent after year 3 is $7,387,556: the difference between the terminal values at zero and 5 percent.
- The annual discount rate is 18 percent per year, or 64.3032 percent for the three-year period.[12]
- The present value of the difference between the terminal values at zero and 5 percent is $4,496,294.
- The risk free rate is 7 percent per year, or 22.5043 for the three-year period.

The only thing that we do not know is what the chances are that the growth will be 8 or 2 percent. We know that the probability-weighted upside change in terminal value plus the probability-weighted downside change in terminal value must be equal to $4,496,294, the differences in present value at zero and 5 percent. From this we can determine the probabilities. Exhibit 4A-8 shows the calculations.

Now we can calculate the value of the option. Exhibit 4A-9 shows the binomial option-pricing framework that we use for this problem.

Notice several things about this exhibit. First, we describe the outcomes in terms of what management might do. If the downside occurs, management could spend $5 million to get $2.4 million, but it does not make economic sense to do so. Thus they would forgo the $2.4 million benefit and the $5 million cost, and get nothing more than originally expected: the terminal value without any growth. If the upside occurs, management is faced with the same possibilities,

EXHIBIT 4A-8 Expected Value of Terminal Values

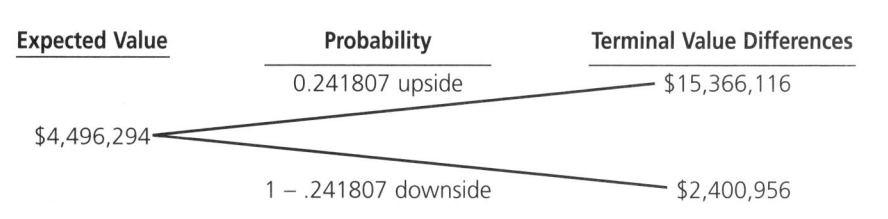

Expected Value	Probability	Terminal Value Differences
	0.241807 upside	$15,366,116
$4,496,294		
	1 − .241807 downside	$2,400,956

Note: Discount probability weighted terminal value at the risk-free rate for one three-year period.

---

[12] Actually, we are treating the three years as if it is one 3-year period. Thus the discount rate is 64.3032 percent $(1.18)^3$.

EXHIBIT 4A-9 Option Value Using Binomial Option Pricing

Present Value @ 22.5043%	Probability	Outcomes
$2,046,131	0.241807	Max {0, $15,366,116 − $5,000,000}
	1 − .241807	Max {0, $2,400,956 − $5,000,000}

do nothing and get no added terminal value, or get $15.4 million at a cost of $5 million. The present value is the value of the probability-weighted present value of each of the logical outcomes. In fact, the downside is zero. The present value of the upside terminal value is the value of the options to wait-and-see before building the plant expansion.[13]

Now what should management do? If the value of the small plant plus the option is greater than building the large plant today, they should invest in the small plant. The value of the first phase of the small plant with no growth after the third year plus the option is $12,047,191 as shown in Exhibit 4A-10. The value of the large plant, shown in Exhibit 4A-10 is $12,492,824. Management should, on economic terms, be almost indifferent between the two alternatives. However, the large plant has an advantage so management should build the large plant now.

III. CONCLUSION

This is the briefest of introductions to the basics of embedded or real options. As you can see, this is a powerful, realistic analysis that is and should be gain-

EXHIBIT 4A-10 Present Value of Large Plant and Small Plant Plus Option[14]

	Net Present Values
Asset in Place—Small Plant	$10,001,060
Option	2,046,131
Total Small Plant	$12,047,191
Large Plant	$12,492,824

---

[13] Notice we are using the risk-free rate of return for discounting. This is because option valuation depends upon a concept called the riskless hedge. For more about this see the references at the end of the chapter.

[14] Note, using the Black-Scholes method, a formulaic method, results in a similar outcome.

ing widespread acceptance. The mathematics of the methodology, particularly some of the shortcut methods like the widely used Black-Scholes option-pricing model, can be daunting. However, using the binomial method can be relatively straightforward, portray decisions as they are likely to be taken by management, and incorporate into the valuation of an investment the likely courses of action. More and more corporate managers are recognizing that net present value analysis depends upon static, unchanging, outcomes—outcomes that are unlikely even at the outset of an investment. Managers already knew that many investments held options to abandon, expand, or grow, and those that didn't could be adapted to do so. What they did not know was a method for analyzing the options. Analyzing and valuing embedded options is a skill analysts must gain. Creating the options and understanding their value is the job of good managers.

SELECTED REFERENCES

On options in general, see:

Brealey, Richard A., and Stewart C. Myers. *Principles of Corporate Finance*. 5th ed. New York: McGraw-Hill, 1996, chap. 20.

Brigham, Eugene F., Louis C. Gapenski, and Michael Ehrhardt. *Financial Management*. 9th ed. Fort Worth, Texas: The Dryden Press, 1999, chap. 24.

Bodie, Zvi, and Robert Merton. *Finance*. Upper Saddle River, NJ: Prentice Hall, 2000, chap. 15.

Cox, John, and Mark Rubinstein. *Options Markets*. Englewood Cliffs, NJ: Prentice-Hall, 1985.

Damodaran, Aswath. *Corporate Finance*. New York: John Wiley & Sons, 1997, chap. 27.

Ross, Stephen A., Randolph W. Westerfield, and Bradford D. Jordon. *Fundamentals of Corporate Finance*. 3rd ed. Homewood, Ill.: Irwin, 1995, chap. 23.

Stoll, Hans, and Robert Whaley. *Futures and Options*. Cincinnati, OH: South-Western Publishing, 1993.

Thomsell, Michael. *Getting Started in Options*. 3rd ed. New York: John Wiley & Sons, 1997.

On real options, see:

Amran, Martha, and Nalin Kulantilaka. *Real Options: Managing Strategic Investment in an Uncertain World*. Cambridge, MA: Harvard Business School Publishing, 1998.

Brealey, Richard A., and Stewart C. Myers. *Principles of Corporate Finance*. 5th ed. New York: McGraw-Hill, 1996, chap. 21.

Brennan, Michael, and Lenos Trigeorgious, eds. *Project Flexibility, Agency and Product Market Competition: New Developments in the Theory and Application of Real Options Analysis*. Oxford University Press, 1999.

Brigham, Eugene F., Louis C. Gapenski, and Michael Ehrhardt. *Financial Management*. 9th ed. Fort Worth, Texas: The Dryden Press, 1999, chap. 13.

Bodie, Zvi, and Robert Merton. *Finance*. Upper Saddle River, NJ: Prentice Hall, 2000, chap. 15.

Damodoran, Aswath. *Corporate Finance*. New York: John Wiley & Sons, 1997, chap. 27.

Dixit, Avinash K., and Robert S. Pindyck. "The Options Approach to Capital Investment." Boston, MA: *Harvard Business Review*, May–June 1995.

Leuhrman, Timothy A. "Capital Projects as Real Options: An Introduction." Boston, MA: *Harvard Business School Case Series*, 1994.

Ross, Stephen A., Randolph W. Westerfield, and Jeffrey F. Jaffe. *Corporate Finance*. 4th ed. Homewood, Ill.: Richard D. Irwin, 1996, chap. 7.

Trigeorgious, Lenos. *Real Options: Managerial Flexibility and Strategic Resource Allocation*. Cambridge, MA: MIT Press, 1996.

APPENDIX 4B
Tax Codes and Depreciation in Highly Inflationary Environments

Tax codes in highly inflationary environments often have a feature that an analyst must incorporate into an investment analysis: assets are revalued, usually every year. Companies are allowed to revalue their assets to compensate for the erosive effects of inflation. For many analysts, especially stock analysts dealing with companies in many different countries, this asset revaluation presents a special challenge. This is the reason that the EBITDA ratio, described in Chapter 1, is so useful in cross-border analysis.

An example will serve to make clear why asset revaluation occurs and how the revalued asset depreciation expense will be quite different from that calculated when using a historically based asset value. Exhibit 4B-1 shows the depreciation that a company can expense in a country with 35 percent inflation, a rate reached by many countries each year. Since this exhibit would be very large if all the data were included, we show only 3 of the 10 years.

Exhibit 4B-1 shows the impact on a company's financial statements of asset revaluation. From this exhibit you can see that the tax shield does not rise to offset the changes in the value of the currency over time. Perhaps the most

EXHIBIT 4B-1   Inflationary Impact on Financial Performance: Depreciation With and Without Asset Revaluation—Inflation 35 Percent per Year (in units of currency)

Asset Value Based on Historical Cost

	Year 1	Year 5	Year 10
Net asset value (beginning of year)	$500,000	$300,000	$50,000
Depreciation	(50,000)	(50,000)	(50,000)
Asset value (end of year)	450,000	250,000	0
Profit before depreciation	100,000	332,151	1,489,375
Depreciation	(50,000)	(50,000)	(50,000)
Profit before taxes	50,000	282,151	1,439,375
Taxes (32%)	(16,000)	(90,288)	(460,600)
Profit after taxes	34,000	191,863	978,775
Cumulative profit after taxes	34,000	506,898	3,372,131
Cumulative taxes	16,000	238,540	1,586,885
Cash flow*	84,000	241,863	1,028,775
Cumulative cash flow	$ 84,000	$756,898	$3,872,131

(continued)

EXHIBIT 4B-1 *(continued)*

Asset Value Based on Inflated Asset Value

	Year 1	Year 5	Year 10
Net asset value (beginning of year)	$500,000	$1,220,703	$3,725,295
Depreciation	(50,000)	(122,070)	(372,529)
Inflated asset value (end of year)	675,000	1,647,950	5,029,148
Asset value less depreciation (end of year)	625,000	1,525,880	4,656,619
Profit before depreciation	100,000	332,151	1,489,375
Depreciation	(50,000)	(122,070)	(372,529)
Profit before taxes	50,000	210,081	1,116,846
Taxes (32%)	(16,000)	(67,226)	(357,391)
Profit after taxes	34,000	142,855	759,455
Cumulative profit after taxes	34,000	397,860	2,581,534
Cumulative taxes	16,000	187,228	1,214,838
Cash flow*	84,000	264,925	1,131,984
Cumulative cash flow	$ 84,000	$ 808,211	$4,244,177

* For simplicity, cash flow is simply profit after taxes plus depreciation.

important item, the cumulative cash flow, is higher when assets are revalued to keep pace with inflation. The differences in profits and cash flows under the two scenarios are shown most clearly in the graph in Exhibit 4B-2.

What should be clear from this very brief example is that an analyst or manager working in or analyzing a company from an environment with high inflation must be aware of what the accounting rule can do to the company and its asset-investment plans.

EXHIBIT 4B-2 Annual Profits and Cash Flows with Two Different Methods of Accounting for Inflation

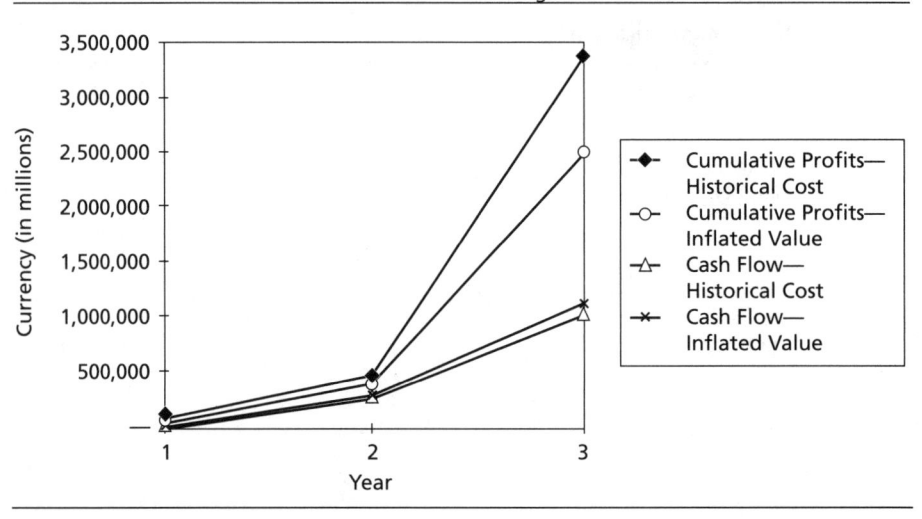

CHAPTER 5
Valuation 2: Acquisitions and Divestitures

Merger activity in the United States by domestic and nondomestic firms burgeoned during the late 1960s and the 1980s. In the early part of the 1990s, as shown in Exhibit 5-1, merger activity dropped precipitously, and did so for non-U.S. firms as well as U.S. firms. One might have expected that U.S. companies, on the trail of global business partners, would have taken their acquisition activity outside the United States. The decline in worldwide merger activity may well have been the result of a backlash to the merger boom of the 1980s and the recession that was spreading around the world. In addition, acquisitions by Japanese companies in the United States declined in the early 1990s because of the recession and the steep decline of the Japanese stock market that reduced Japanese investor liquidity. Merger activity revived again in 1993, expanding further in 1994, and reaching boom proportions in 1997,

EXHIBIT 5-1 Acquisitions of U.S. Companies by U.S. and Non-U.S. Companies

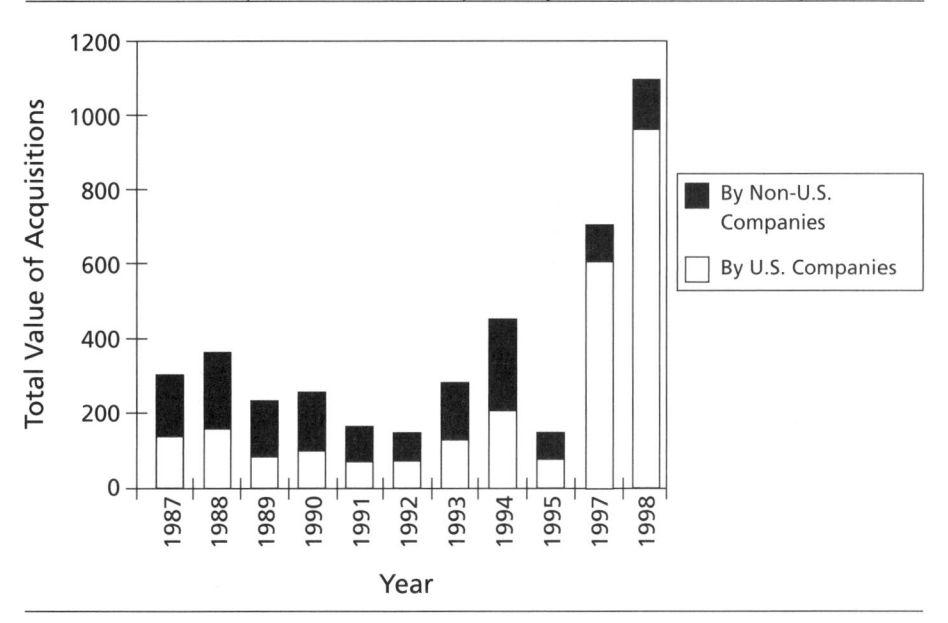

SOURCE FOR DATA: "1998 M&A Profile," *Mergers and Acquisitions*, March/April 1999, p. 42.

1998, and continued into 2000. Much of the renewal in mergers can be attributed to the rebound of the U.S. economy and increases in stock market valuations.[1] Exhibit 5-2 shows the acquisition activity of U.S. companies outside the United States and Exhibit 5-3 shows that U.S. companies acquiring other U.S. companies dominated the acquisition activity in the United States.

While foreign acquisition in the United States was not the main source of the merger increase, there had been a serious increase in merger activity outside the United States, as shown in Exhibit 5-4. Moreover, in Europe, with its restructuring toward monetary union and economic integration, activity grew rapidly, particularly toward the end of the decade. While the number of deals increased, it was the size of the mergers that had increased even more rapidly. This data is depicted in Exhibit 5-5 (page 208). You will note that the size of the mergers both in Europe and outside the United States increased. This was true in the United States as well. This merger boom was called, by *Mergers and Acquisition*, the bimonthly reporting of mergers and acquisitions, a "juggernaut" as it broke all records. In 1998 the total value of deals was over $1 trillion.

By early 2000 three things were clear. First, there was an increasing number of strategic mergers to expand or enhance business globally. Second, there had been a very large increase in intra-European mergers, including mergers

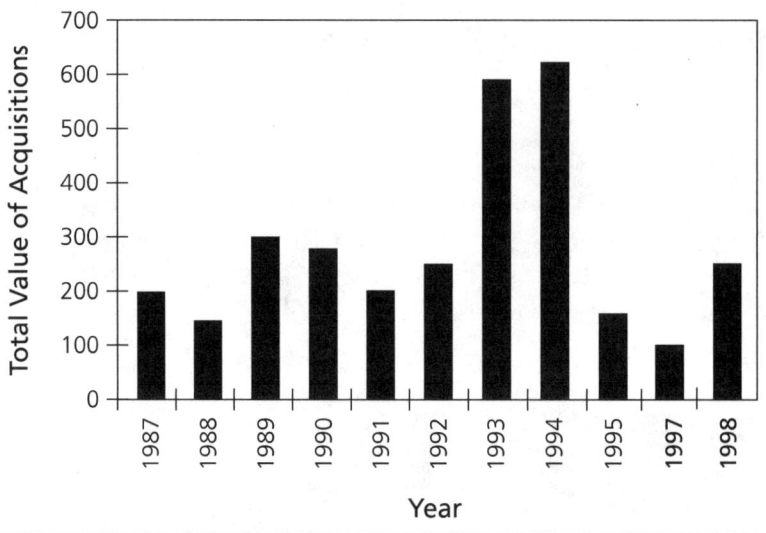

EXHIBIT 5-2 Acquisitions of Non-U.S. Companies by U.S. Companies

SOURCE FOR DATA: "1998 M&A Profile," *Mergers and Acquisitions*, March/April 1999, p. 42.

---

[1] Perhaps much of the decline in activity in 1995 may have been due to stock market valuations in the United States. The growth in the number and size of deals in the late 1990s is related to high market valuations and the relative price of an acquisition when it is made with the acquirer's stock.

Chapter 5   Valuation 2: Acquisitions and Divestitures   **207**

EXHIBIT 5-3   Acquisitions of U.S. Companies by Origin of Acquirer

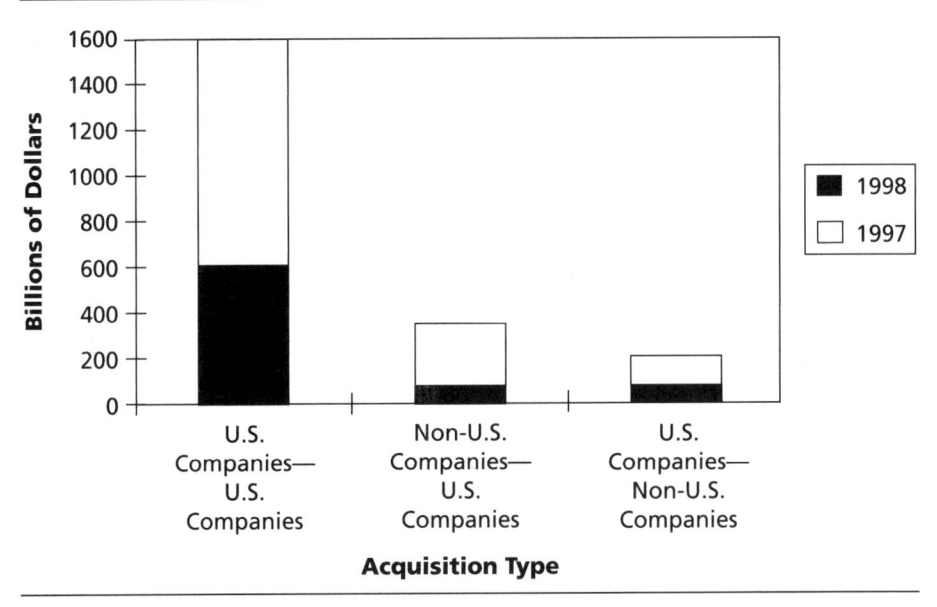

SOURCE FOR DATA: "1998 M&A Profile," *Mergers and Acquisitions*, March/April 1999, p. 42.

EXHIBIT 5-4   Merger Activity Outside the United States

SOURCE FOR DATA: "Cross-Border M&A," *Mergers and Acquisitions*, March/April 1999, p. 56.

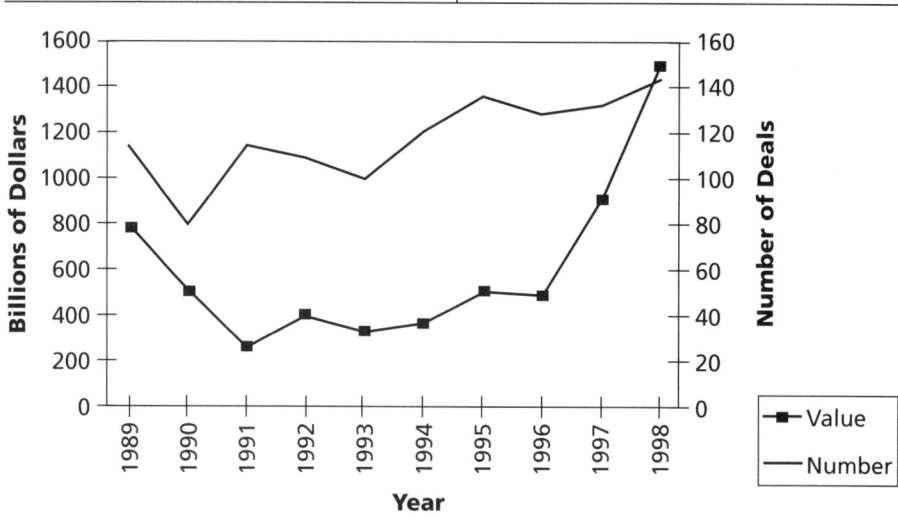

EXHIBIT 5-5 Cross Border Deals in Europe

SOURCE FOR DATA: "A Vintage Year for European M&A," *Mergers and Acquisitions*, March/April 1999, p. 16.

involving Eastern European companies. Third, companies that facilitated mergers, investment bankers in particular, had begun expanding their Japanese operations, in advance of what they believed would be a serious period of restructuring and mergers in Japan.

In addition to the volume of mergers in the late 1990s another change was due to occur at the end of 2000. Until year-end 2000 U.S. companies could choose to use either the pooling or purchase method to account for a merger. In the **pooling** method companies combine their assets and earnings. This method does not seriously impact earnings of the acquiring company, and thus, it was believed, the merger would not impact stock price. The acquirer used its stock to acquire. Thus the shareholders got a tax-free transaction.

The purchase method of accounting for a merger already is used in most of the rest of the world. In the **purchase** method one party to the merger must be identified as the purchaser. Anything that the purchaser pays for the acquired company above its net asset value is called goodwill, placed on the purchaser's balance sheet, and written off in the future. This reduces future earnings, but usually does not reduce taxes: it is not a tax-deductible expense in most countries.

Some attribute the increase in U.S. mergers to the change to a purchase-only method in the United States in 2000. However much the purchase method may impact future earnings, many believe that investors are aware and take into account the impact the merger will have on the earnings: they see through a pooling to the impact as if the company had been purchased. Thus a change from pooling to purchase should not negatively impact the shareholders' analysis of an otherwise good merger, even in the United States.

Chapter 5 Valuation 2: Acquisitions and Divestitures

Managers engaged in merger activity have given a number of reasons for making acquisitions. They report mergers are attractive to:

1. Lower financing costs.
2. Diversify and thus reduce risk.
3. Increase the earnings per share of the acquiring firm.
4. Use excess funds.
5. Provide needed funds.
6. Purchase an undervalued company.
7. Take advantage of economies of scale or size.
8. Enter a business or market.
9. Acquire technology or research.
10. Gain market share or presence.

Experts believe that the late 1990s boom was a consequence of companies and their managements acquiring the resources to succeed in global competition, the last three reasons on our list. This appears particularly true for Internet mergers.

These are a variety of reasons for an acquisition or merger. However, all these reasons can be reduced to one: to create value for the acquiring company's shareholders. This creation of value comes only as the result of synergy between the merging firms. Synergy comes from combining unused capacity in one company with a need for that capacity in another. Value for an acquiring firm's shareholders can be the result of paying less for the targeted company than it is worth. However, real synergy may come from combining or better using such things as plant capacity, sales forces, distribution systems, equity or debt-market access, brand presence, or management talent. Synergy could also come from the willingness of one company's owners to take risk, combined with another's too-conservative approach. Acting on potential synergies can result in the creation of value, the goal of shareholders.

Creating value is a familiar goal, one that was discussed in relation to capital investment decisions in Chapter 4. The goal is the same with the sale or purchase of businesses. Although a business is usually larger than the typical capital investment, the acquired firm, division, or line of business must still generate an adequate return for the acquiring company's shareholders. Thus the tools used in Chapter 4 apply here. An acquisition is just like any other corporate investment. If capital budgeting and acquisition analysis is the same, why do we devote another chapter to its discussion?

There are five reasons:

1. Since acquisitions usually require large investments, companies frequently have a separate staff of acquisition analysts.
2. Merger analysts often borrow the analytical tools of stock analysts, using them instead of or as a supplement to traditional valuation (capital investment) techniques and criteria. The stock analyst's approach is used because many acquisitions are made by purchasing the stock of the

acquired firm with cash or securities of the acquiring firm. Because stock often is used or exchanged in the transaction, stock analysis techniques appear appropriate.
3. Acquisitions are a separate topic because the real benefits of an acquisition can be difficult to identify and awkward to evaluate, since the costs and benefits are unusually influenced by tax and accounting issues.
4. Companies often rely on outside advisers, such as investment bankers or business brokers, to identify, analyze, and value potential acquisitions or divestitures. These outside analysts may use special language to describe their analysis and special tools to value a business. Managers who are acquiring or divesting a business should be aware of the basic valuation concepts and how experts use and interpret them.
5. The acquisition decision is an excellent example of the way a manager can create or destroy value for a company's owners.

Analyzing a corporate strategy—whether the investment is in property, plant, or equipment; a line of business; or a whole company—requires valuation tools. The only real differences between capital budgeting and corporate valuation lie in the scope and availability of the data needed to create estimated cash flows and discount rates. Because acquisitions and divestitures are large, are strategically important, and seem to require special analytical approaches, we consider their analysis as a separate topic in valuation.[2]

The capital investment framework presented in Chapter 4 can be used to determine whether a potential acquisition will create value for the acquiring firm's owners. This chapter will describe and recommend the present value analysis of cash flows as a method for valuing and pricing a business. It also will discuss some of the other valuation techniques currently used by analysts. Note that while an acquisition is the primary focus, a divestiture is the same transaction seen through the seller's eyes, and the approach to the analysis is the same.

Acquisitions are done to create value. There are two ways in which value can be created in making an investment. First, finding unusual benefits that accrue from the investment itself can create value. Second, value can come from the way the investment is financed. Because these sources of value are quite distinct, the analysis of these sources should also be distinct. In Chapter 4 we discussed the methods for valuing an investment, but we did not consider whether special forms of financing might enhance or detract from the value. In this chapter we will follow the same process, saving the discussion of how a company should finance itself and how that financing might affect the value of capital investments, including mergers, for Chapter 7. In the appendix to Chapter 7 we will discuss leveraged mergers, also called leveraged buyouts.

---

[2] In the past, the words *merger* and *acquisition* were used to denote different forms of corporate combinations. In general, the word *merger* now is used to designate the physical combining of companies after acquisition is complete.

Before we begin to look at how capital budgeting tools are adapted to value businesses, a word of warning: the combination of poor analysis, misuse of tools, and overenthusiasm among buyers creates a dangerous situation. Buyers can let their enthusiasm for a merger cloud the analysis of the potential costs and benefits of the merger. When enthusiasm overwhelms judgment, management can overvalue the benefits and misjudge the costs. In this chapter you will see that when management pays too much for an acquisition, the acquiring company's shareholders' value is reduced. Shareholders recognize that enthusiasm often impacts their value in an acquisition. That is why in the United States the stock price of an acquirer is often negatively affected by the announcement of a pending merger, whereas the shareholders of the company being acquired often find positive and significant returns from their shares.[3]

Now, armed with our knowledge about basic valuation techniques gained in Chapter 4, we are ready to value lines of business, divisions, or whole companies.

I. PRESENT VALUE ANALYSIS OF CASH FLOWS

There are two steps in valuing an acquisition:

1. Identify the value of the equity of the company to be acquired (NPV_A).
2. Identify the present values of the synergies that may result as the acquired firm's business is joined with that of the acquirer (NPV_S).

The marginal value of the acquisition depends both on the value of the company to be acquired and on the value of the **synergies**, the value that only comes as a result of the combination:[4]

$$\text{Acquisition value} = NPV_A + NPV_S$$

What follows is an example demonstrating the analysis of an acquisition using these two steps.

1. Calculating the Value of an Acquisition Without Synergy

The management of Lifelike Cabinets Co., a manufacturer of kitchen cabinets, has identified another company that is an interesting acquisition, Tract Co.

---

[3] A major consulting firm, McKinsey and Company, verified this stock market impact in a study it conducted of 200 acquisitions made by the largest U.S. public corporations in the late 1970s and early 1980s. McKinsey found that 70 percent of the acquirers failed to earn the required return on their investments. Few, it found, added value for the acquiring company's shareholders. In fact, many mergers during the period studied provided returns below those of very low-risk U.S. Treasury securities. This result is disheartening, and continues to exist today. Because of findings like these, it is critical that the analyst evaluating the purchase of another business do so with great care, and for management to temper its enthusiasm with solid analysis.

[4] The concept of marginal value was discussed in Chapter 4.

Tract Co. is a printer, binder, and distributor of books for little-known religious organizations whose beliefs are based on early Greek mythology. Since the demand for Tract's books has been level for years and is not expected to rise, the current cash flow for Tract is expected to continue without change into the foreseeable future. Management expects Tract's 2001 sales to be $10.3 million, operating expenses to be 92 percent of sales, depreciation to be $50,000, equipment purchases to be $50,000, and taxes to be 34 percent of income before taxes. Net income is expected to total $510,840. Income and costs are not expected to grow, and there is a widely held view that there will be no inflation. Using these assumptions, management has produced the forecasted income and residual cash flow forecast shown in Exhibit 5-6.[5]

Note that in Exhibit 5-6 we have only one year of cash flows. Is that all that Lifelike will get from Tract? No. We need to forecast all the cash flows Lifelike management expects to get from Tract in the future. Usually that would be years and years of forecasts. However, since Tract's cash flows are expected to be the same for every year in the future, we can use the shortcut—the perpetuity method of valuation.[6]

To use the perpetuity method of valuation divide the annual cash flow by the discount rate.

$$NPV_A = \frac{NCF_A}{R_{eA}}$$

EXHIBIT 5-6 Tract Co.

2001 INCOME AND RESIDUAL CASH FLOW FORECAST (in thousands)

	2001
Sales	$10,300.00
Operating expenses	(9,476.00)
Depreciation	(50.00)
Income before taxes	774.00
Taxes	(263.16)
Income after taxes	510.84
Depreciation	50.00
Change in property, plant, and equipment	(50.00)
Annual residual cash flow	510.84
Terminal value	—
Residual cash flow	$ 510.84

---

[5] Residual cash flow is the cash flow that is available after the company has paid all its suppliers. For this example we are assuming that the whole company is financed by its shareholders, thus there are no interest payments. How to include financing into these decisions is discussed in the Chapter 7 appendix.

[6] This is the same perpetuity method we described in Chapter 4.

where
R_{eA} = Investors' required return on equity for a company
NCF_A = Yearly residual net cash flow for a company
NPV_A = Net present value of equity cash flows for a company

Tract management expects no growth of its cash flows into the future and it estimates that its investors require a return of 13.8 percent.[7] Because the residual cash flow will remain the same every year in perpetuity, or at least for a very long time, the value of Tract is:

$$NPV_T = \frac{NCF_T}{R_{eT}}$$
$$= \frac{\$510{,}840}{0.138}$$
$$= \$3{,}701{,}739$$

The present value of Tract's future cash flows is $3.7 million. The perpetuity method gives us a valuation that is identical to one that would be calculated by discounting every year's cash flows, but it is a lot easier and quicker.[8] The method comes with a warning, however: use the perpetuity method only if unchanging cash flows will last a very long time. In a situation where the cash flows are expected to be level for a few years and then end or grow, we cannot use the perpetuity method of valuation.[9]

Whether Lifelike should acquire Tract depends upon the price Lifelike pays for the company. If Lifelike pays a fair price for Tract, there will be no expected benefit or loss to the owners of either firm. At a price of $3.7 million, Lifelike shareholders pay what Tract is worth and Tract shareholders get what their company is worth. Both sets of shareholders should be satisfied: neither is better off than they were before the acquisition. If by skillful negotiation Lifelike management can acquire Tract for less than $3.7 million, Lifelike's owners will gain value and the Tract investors will lose value. A simple formula can be used to show the important relationship between price and value:

$$NRC_A = Price_A - NPV_A$$

where
NRC_A = The net real cost to acquire a company
$Price_A$ = The purchase price of a company
NPV_A = The present value of a company

---

[7] Chapter 6 discusses how to calculate a discount rate. In this chapter we use the management-determined rate.
[8] If you are not certain that the two methods are equivalent, try it yourself.
[9] Actually there are adaptations of the perpetuity method to value companies with various stages of growth. Most were developed to ease the tedium of analysis before the widespread use of computer spreadsheets.

If Lifelike management pays $3.7 million for Tract, the value created for Lifelike's owners will be zero.

$$NRC_T = \$3.7 - \$3.7$$
$$= \$0 \text{ million}$$

If Lifelike management pays more than $3.7 million, Lifelike's owners lose value: the present value is below zero. As shown below, if the price were $4.0 million the expected cost would be $300,000.

$$NRC_T = \$4.0 - \$3.7$$
$$= \$0.3 \text{ million, or } \$300,000$$

Lifelike's shareholders' cost is a gain to the shareholders of Tract. If Lifelike's management manages to skillfully negotiate a price below $3.7 million, its shareholders would gain from the acquisition. This example makes it clear that both value and price are important in a merger, and the two are not the same.

2. Calculating the Marginal Benefit of an Acquisition with Synergy

Our calculations thus far have assumed that the acquisition offers no new benefits, also called **synergies**. What if the combined companies were expected to have cash flows in excess of those the two companies would have had without each other? This increase in cash flows might come from a variety of synergies. For example, if Tract were operating at full capacity with a large backlog of orders for its products and Lifelike had an empty manufacturing facility that could be used with no change to produce products for Tract's customers, the combination of Tract's unfilled need and Lifelike's excess capacity would produce new benefits, or synergies. Synergies clearly have a value, but they can be hard to forecast. Synergies can be estimated directly or indirectly.

Direct Forecasts of Synergies. To use the direct method, management would forecast the cash flows associated with the synergies and discount them. To do this for Tract, it would need to estimate the increase in Tract's sales, the marginal costs incurred in using Lifelike's plant, and any other new costs associated with producing, selling, and delivering the additional pamphlets. In the case of the Tract acquisition, Lifelike management estimated that revenues from the sales of the new booklets would be $350,000 per year, and new expenses, expenses not already being incurred by either company, would be $85,000, including the taxes on incremental net income. Since Tract had equipment that was not being used and the skilled workers with the time to install it, there would be no need for new equipment. Tract management was quite certain that all the new products could be sold, but it did not expect sales to grow. Since management believed that these sales were more certain than

I. Present Value Analysis of Cash Flows

Tract's regular business, management estimated investors' required return for these cash flows of 13 percent, lower than the discount rate used to value the company as a whole. Assuming that the synergies will last for a very long time we can use the perpetuity method of valuation. The present value of the synergies is just over $2 million.

$$\begin{aligned} NPV_S &= \text{Cash flows}_s / R_{es} \\ &= (\text{Benefits} - \text{Costs})/R_{es} \\ &= \frac{\$350{,}000 - \$85{,}000}{0.13} \\ &= \$2{,}038{,}462 \end{aligned}$$

Once the synergies are valued they are added to Lifelike management's estimate of Tract's value without synergies, making the total value of Tract plus the synergies $5.7 million. This means, taking the synergies into account, Lifelike management could offer up to $5.7 million for Tract without losing value for its shareholders. However, Tract's shareholders would gain all the synergy value. At a price of $4.7 million, the buyer and seller share the synergies equally, and at a price of $3.7 million, Tract's owners are not paid for their contribution to the synergies. The graph in Exhibit 5-7 shows the relative positions of the two sets of owners at a variety of prices if there are no synergies.[10] As you can see, the price that is paid is critical in determining whether the acquirer creates value for its owners.

This direct valuation of synergies focuses management on forecasting what can be achieved. For those who find estimating the value of synergies difficult, there is the indirect method.

Indirect Method of Synergy Forecasting. The indirect valuation of synergies is a three-step process: first, estimate the present values of Lifelike and Tract operating alone; second, estimate the value of the combined firms after the merger; third, subtract the two. The difference between the two cash flow forecasts is the synergies.[11] For our example the result is shown in Exhibit 5-8. As you can see, the synergies are worth $2.0 million, the same amount we calculated directly. Of course, whether the Tract shareholders, or those from Lifelike, will actually receive the value of the synergies depends upon the purchase price.

The analysis of the Lifelike-Tract merger and its synergies was deceptively straightforward. Projecting the costs and benefits of the synergies of the combined companies is subject to even greater forecasting error than is forecasting

---

[10] If the synergies are taken into account, the two lines cross at $4.7 million.
[11] Many companies forecast the with-synergies cash flows. However, these cash flows are often the only ones valued. When the synergies are positive, forecasting and valuing only these cash flows can lead to overpayment by the acquirer.

EXHIBIT 5-7 Value to Owners of Tract and Lifelike at Different Purchase Prices for Tract—Without Synergies

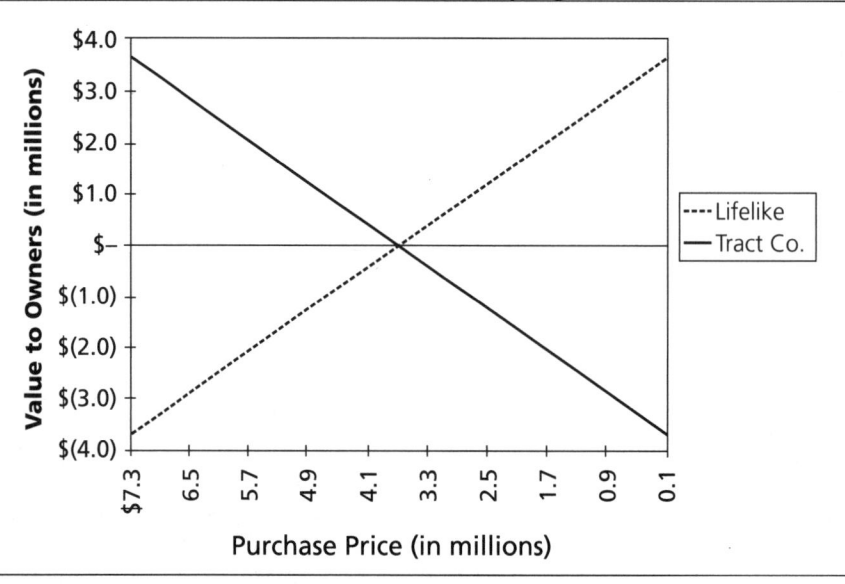

[Chart: Value to Owners (in millions) vs Purchase Price (in millions), showing Lifelike (dashed) and Tract Co. (solid) lines crossing near $4.0 million purchase price. X-axis values: $7.3, 6.5, 5.7, 4.9, 4.1, 3.3, 2.5, 1.7, 0.9, 0.1. Y-axis ranges from $(4.0) to $4.0.]

the cash flows for the original entities. For example, management believed that Tract might benefit by using Lifelike's excess capacity. However, the benefits of using that space could depend on such factors as the availability of local labor, the suitability of the space, and unpredictable conversion costs. The benefits could be quite different from those originally forecasted. Most acquisitions provide far greater forecasting ambiguity than does our example, and most managers hot on the trail of an acquisition overestimate the benefits and underestimate the costs of merging the companies.

Risk and Synergies. Thus far most of the discussion has been about cash flow forecasting. However, risk and the impact of an acquisition on risk also must be estimates, and this is difficult. In the Lifelike-Tract example, the analyst's life was made simple by assuming that the business risk of the new firm was the average of the firms' risks prior to acquisition plus the risk associated

EXHIBIT 5-8 Net Present Value of Combined Firms with Synergies

	Lifelike	Tract Co.	Combined Companies
Residual net cash flow per year	$600,000	$510,840	$1.376 million
Investors' required return	12.0%	13.8%	12.8%
Net present value	$5.00 million	$3.70 million	$10.75 million

with the synergies. This simplifying assumption rarely holds true in practice. For example, joining a cyclical to a countercyclical firm can greatly reduce the risk of the combined firm, all other factors being equal, but joining two firms with the same cycle would not have the risk-reducing effect.[12]

3. The Value of Redundant Assets

In the example of Tract, Lifelike management valued its cash flows. Tract used all its assets to produce the cash flows, and all its assets were dedicated to the publishing business. What if Tract had assets that it did not use in the publishing business, the business that Lifelike wanted to own? For instance, what if Tract owned a large, undeveloped piece of land for which it had no need, or had a cash account far in excess of that required for its publishing business? How should these be included in a valuation?

Redundant assets, assets not needed to support the business, should be valued independently of the business-related cash flows. To value these assets, segment any cash flows associated with the redundant asset and value them independently. Once again, an example will demonstrate the problem.

Suppose Tract has a piece of property purchased years ago, but never used. On this property Tract pays property taxes, but earns no income. While the property is reported on the balance sheet at its original cost, and the property taxes are recorded on the income statement, Tract management knows that it will never use the property. Unless the property has no resale value, Lifelike management can value the property at the value for which it could be sold and reduce property tax payments on the income statement. Thus Tract has more value to Lifelike: the income is higher and the value of the land is an added benefit. In net present value terms, the company is worth the net present value of the tax-adjusted cash flows plus the sale value of the property.

To include redundant assets in a valuation, you must be certain that the:

- Asset is truly redundant and can be eliminated.
- Asset can be valued and the value realized.
- Cash inflows or outflows associated with the asset are removed from the net present value analysis.
- Value of the asset is added to the net present value of the ongoing business.

There are a wide variety of redundant assets. Such things as excessively large cash accounts and real property are the most obvious.[13] To value the redundant asset, any of the tools discussed in the chapter may be appropriate depending upon the nature of the asset.

---

[12] In Chapter 6 there is a discussion of the portfolio effect.
[13] Excess cash typically is invested in marketable securities. The cash is valuable, and its total value can be added to the net present value if, and only if, any of the interest earned on the marketable securities is deducted from the cash flows before the net present value is calculated.

4. Calculating the Marginal Benefit of an Acquisition with Growth

Both analyses of Tract assumed that the company was anticipating no growth in its future cash flows. However, forecasts by industry experts suggest that growth in splinter religions is expected to increase from 2000 until well into the new millennium. Management believes that this means that Tract will experience growth in the sales of its products: growth in sales could be as high as 10 percent for the next five years, before it drops to zero. Management knows that the current equipment will not be adequate to sustain this growth, and added investments will be necessary. Management must consider both the cash flows that might result from the change, as well as dealing with the following questions.

1. What will be the value of the deal including the growth?
2. What should be the least Lifelike should pay to acquire Tract?
3. What should be the most Lifelike should pay to acquire Tract?

The analysis shown in Exhibit 5-9 was prepared by management, based on the assumption that Tract's sales will grow at a rate of 10 percent to 2005, and will not grow thereafter.[14] The present value of this growing Tract is just over $4.6 million.[15] The present value exceeds that calculated with no growth. The value would be even greater if management could grow without investing in the new assets needed to support the growth.

To value Tract, Lifelike's analyst forecasted the cash flows for six years. The first five years were growing at 10 percent, but after that the millennium-induced growth would stop. Once Tract's growth stops, the perpetuity method can be used to value the cash flows that are expected in the ensuing years. Thus, in this case, the perpetuity method is used to value the cash flows for 2006 onward.

The calculation for the perpetuity value for 2006 and onward is shown at the bottom of Exhibit 5-9. This value, $6.09 million, is added to the cash flow of $840.6 thousand forecasted to be received in 2006. This value is also called the terminal value. The sum of these two cash flows in 2006, $6.9 million, is discounted back to its present value, the value at the beginning of 2001. This present value plus the sum of the present values for 2001–06 are the value of a growing Tract Co.

5. Terminal Value

Terminal value is a curious concept. In general, it means the value of an investment at the time the investment is liquidated. In valuing a business, how-

---

[14] However, in this case we simplified what is usually a more complex analysis by forecasting that the capital investments will equal the depreciation, and there will be no other investments, even with the growth.

[15] The analysis shown is the same sort we used in Chapter 4 to value capital investments.

I. **Present Value Analysis of Cash Flows**   219

EXHIBIT 5-9 Tract Co.

INCOME AND RESIDUAL CASH FLOW WITH GROWTH (in thousands)

	2001	2002	2003	2004	2005	2006
Sales	$ 11,330.0	$ 12,463.0	$ 13,709.3	$ 15,080.2	$ 16,588.3	$ 16,588.3
Operating expenses	(10,423.6)	(11,466.0)	(12,612.6)	(13,873.8)	(15,261.2)	(15,261.2)
Gross income	906.4	997.0	1,096.7	1,206.4	1,327.1	1,327.1
Depreciation:						
Original	(50.0)	(50.0)	(50.0)	(50.0)	(50.0)	(50.0)
Growth-induced	(0.5)	(1.1)	(1.7)	(2.3)	(3.1)	(3.4)
Income before taxes	855.9	945.9	1,045.0	1,154.1	1,274.0	1,273.7
Taxes	(291.0)	(321.6)	(355.3)	(392.4)	(433.2)	(433.1)
Income after taxes	564.9	624.3	689.7	761.7	840.8	840.6
Depreciation:						
Original	50.0	50.0	50.0	50.0	50.0	50.0
Growth-induced	0.5	1.1	1.7	2.3	3.1	3.4
Change in property, plant, and equipment:						
Original	(50.0)	(50.0)	(50.0)	(50.0)	(50.0)	(50.0)
Growth-induced	(5.0)	(5.5)	(6.1)	(6.7)	(7.3)	(3.4)
Working capital change	(206.0)	(226.6)	(249.3)	(274.2)	(301.6)	—
Annual cash flow	354.4	393.3	436.0	483.1	535.0	840.6
Terminal value**						6,091.3
Residual cash flow	$ 354.4	$ 393.3	$ 436.0	$ 483.1	$ 535.0	$ 6,927.2

Net present value @ 13.8% = $4,668.7

Assumptions
Working capital is 20% of the change in sales.
** Terminal value is the perpetuity value of the annual residual cash flow in 2002 at a discount rate of 13.8% [$840.6/(0.138 − 0.0]. The growth is zero from 2006 onwards. Thus we assume further capital investments equal depreciation.

ever, the terminal value usually means the present value of an investment's cash flows from some point in the future onwards. That point should be when the cash flows are not expected to change. The perpetuity method also may be used when the cash flows are expected to grow at a constant, low rate for a very long time.[16] The perpetuity with growth model is called a **constant growth perpetuity**.

Suppose you were making an investment in a company that was expected to return $100 forever, and the required return for its level of risk was 10 percent. What would it be worth, what price would be fair for this investment? Using the perpetuity approach, your answer would be as follows:

$$\text{Present value perpetuity} = \frac{\text{Annual cash flow}}{\text{Investors' required rate of return}}$$

$$= \frac{\$100}{0.10}$$

$$= \$1,000$$

Suppose someone told you that you could have an investment that, while otherwise identical to the first investment, would provide $100 plus 3 percent every year. What would this investment be worth? To value this growing perpetuity we will use an adaptation of the perpetuity shortcut that is called a constant growth perpetuity valuation:[17]

$$\text{Constant growth present value} = \frac{\text{Annual cash flow} \times \left(1 + \frac{\text{Growth in residual cash flows}}{\text{cash flows}}\right)}{\text{Investors' required rate of return} - \text{Growth in residual cash flows}}$$

$$= \frac{\$100 \times (1 + 0.03)}{0.10 - 0.03}$$

$$= \$1,471$$

The question of when an analyst can use one of the perpetuity shortcuts is one that is widely debated. Analysts often use this shortcut to value cash flows long before the cash flows have either stopped growing or are growing at a slow but steady rate. This is generally because the analyst's fear of forecasting overcomes common sense: they just do not know what the cash flows are likely to be, so why not use a shortcut? Fear, however, is not a good reason to use a shortcut, especially when it can lead to significant errors in value.[18] One gen-

---

[16] At a high rate of growth into perpetuity, the company would eventually be unrealistically enormous. Thus, when high growth is expected for some time, the cash flows must be forecasted annually until the abnormal growth is exhausted.

[17] This is also called the Gordon Model when used with dividends. It is named after Myron Gordon, who devised it.

[18] The more important reason not to use this shortcut inappropriately is because the information and insight gained from doing the detailed analysis is glossed over, buried, and provides neither insight nor information.

eral rule about when a shortcut can be used can be developed from the concept of sustainable growth rate described in Chapter 1: when the expected growth rate of the company into the future is equal or very close to its long-term sustainable rate of growth, the analyst can use a perpetuity shortcut.

A bit later in this chapter we will discuss the use of price/earnings ratios in valuation. As you read this section, keep in mind that P/E multiples are frequently used as a way to estimate a terminal value. You will see both the benefits, ease, and the danger—it buries assumptions into a single number.

6. Inflation and Growth

Inflation is a factor that affects the value of a company, and it is an important one. It affects both the cash flows and the discount rate—sometimes in unexpected ways. In the appendix to Chapter 1, we discussed the impact of inflation on depreciation. When the tax code requires that assets be depreciated at their historical cost, depreciation does not keep up with inflation: depreciation is calculated based on a currency whose value has changed. In Chapter 2 we looked at an example of the problems that one can encounter in making a forecast in a highly inflationary environment. Clearly, inflation affects cash flows and discount rates, and those impact value.

Exhibit 5-10 shows cash flow forecasts for Tract with 10 percent inflation from 2001 to 2006. Compare the depreciation shown in Exhibit 5-10 with the depreciation when there was real growth of 10 percent (Exhibit 5-9). You can see that the depreciation is lower and the taxes are higher under inflation.[19] This is the so-called depreciation penalty of inflation.

Inflation has another impact on the value of a company. It increases the investors' required rate of return.[20] A higher discount rate reduces the value of any given set of cash flows, as you can see by looking at the net present values shown in Exhibits 5-9 and 5-10. The higher discount rate better reflects the rate that investors would require in a world with 10 percent inflation. The twin impacts of inflation on cash flows and on the investors' required rate of return point out a critical element in valuation: the forecasts for the discount rate and the cash flows must both rest on the same assumptions for the future.

Thus far we have not discussed how the acquisition will be financed. We will postpone that discussion until Chapter 7, and confine ourselves to the valuation of a company from the shareholders' perspective alone. Financing of an acquisition is a critical decision. We need to discuss financing in more detail before we discuss the acquisition financing decision and its implications on valuation.

---

[19] Note, we assumed that Tract operates in a country where the tax code does not allow for the revaluation of assets due to inflation. This revaluation of assets due to inflation is described in the appendix to Chapter 1.

[20] This is because investors do not want to lose money in real terms, as you will learn in Chapter 6.

EXHIBIT 5-10 Tract Co.

CASH FLOW WITH NO REAL GROWTH AND 10% INFLATION FOR FIVE YEARS AND NO INFLATION OR GROWTH THEREAFTER (in thousands)

	2001	2002	2003	2004	2005	2006
Sales	$ 11,330.0	$ 12,463.0	$ 13,709.3	$ 15,080.2	$ 16,588.3	$ 16,588.3
Operating expenses	(10,423.6)	(11,466.0)	(12,612.6)	(13,873.8)	(15,261.2)	(15,261.2)
Gross income	906.4	997.0	1,096.7	1,206.4	1,327.1	1,327.1
Depreciation:						
Original*	(50.0)	(50.0)	(50.0)	(50.0)	(50.0)	(50.0)
Growth-induced	—	—	—	—	—	—
Income before taxes	856.4	947.0	1,046.7	1,156.4	1,277.1	1,277.1
Taxes	(291.2)	(322.0)	(355.9)	(393.2)	(434.2)	(434.2)
Income after taxes	565.2	625.0	690.8	763.2	842.9	842.9
Depreciation:						
Original	50.0	50.0	50.0	50.0	50.0	50.0
Growth-induced	—	—	—	—	—	—
Change in property, plant, and equipment:						
Original	(50.0)	(50.0)	(50.0)	(50.0)	(50.0)	(50.0)
Growth-induced	—	—	—	—	—	—
Working capital change	(206.0)	(226.6)	(249.3)	(274.2)	(301.6)	—
Annual cash flow	359.2	398.4	441.5	489.0	541.3	842.9
Terminal value**						6,107.9
Residual cash flow	$ 359.2	$ 398.4	$ 441.5	$ 489.0	$ 541.3	$ 6,950.8

Net present value at 13.8% = $4,698
Net present value at 23.8%* = $3,108

* Assets are not revalued for inflation.
** Since there is no inflation from 2006 onwards, and Tract is not expected to grow, the perpetuity value is $842.9/(0.138 − 0.0), whether the discount rate is 23.8 or 13.8 percent.

II. VALUATION USING MARKET MULTIPLES

Some analysts discount earnings rather than cash flows. We have not done that so far. First, earnings do not reflect the real earning power of the company. You will note that while some analysts discount earnings rather than cash flows, that is not done here: earnings reflect the impact of accounting rules on the timing of expenses and revenues. If the tax authorities allowed companies to recognize revenues when customers paid for their orders and costs when the company paid for its purchases, earnings and cash flows would be identical. Since few, if any, tax authorities allow this, cash flow reflects when the company receives cash.

In some circumstances earnings and cash flow are the same. This can occur with slow-growing, mature companies. Under no circumstances should the earnings of a company be discounted to estimate the value of a business, only the cash flows. Earnings are useful for perspective and communication, however.

1. Earnings Multiples

Most of us would like an easier way to estimate the value of a company: making assumptions and cash flows is laborious. To avoid elaborate projections of cash flows, risks, and required rates of return, some analysts use the relationship between a firm's projected earnings and its stock price to value a company.[21] From this ratio, the analyst estimates the price per share for the business to be acquired as follows:

$$\text{Price per share} = \text{EPS} \times \text{P/E}$$

where
  EPS = Earnings per share
  P/E = The firm's estimated price/earnings ratio after acquisition

The price for the whole company would be:

$$\text{Price} = \text{Earnings} \times \text{P/E}$$

where earnings are equal to annual net income.

Companies with publicly traded stock already have a P/E. That P/E reflects the relationship between the earnings per share and the current market price, the markets' assessment of the company's value. So how can you use the P/E multiple to value a company when the P/E itself is created from the mar-

---

[21] In Chapter 1 we discussed the P/E ratio:

$$\text{Price/Earnings} = \frac{\text{Market price per share}}{\text{Earnings per share}}$$

kets' assessment of the company's value? There are a variety of companies for which there is no P/E or where the current P/E cannot be used. These are companies:

1. With no publicly traded stock.
2. Where the expectations for the future are quite different from current circumstances:
   a. An acquisition or merger is expected to create synergies.
   b. The acquisition is expected to change the structure of the company.
   c. The company is over- or undervalued in the stock market.

For the company with no publicly traded stock, analysts either use a discounted cash flow or create an estimated P/E for valuation. Let's look at our Tract/Lifelike example.

Suppose that Lifelike's management expected Tract's earnings for the next 12 months to be $510,840.[22] With 100,000 shares of stock outstanding, expected earnings per share would be $5.11. Tract is not publicly traded. Thus it has no P/E ratio to use as a starting point for the valuation. To overcome this lack of information management must estimate the appropriate P/E for its valuation. As usual, management will turn to other sources of information about the appropriate P/E to use, a proxy for the actual P/E. For a proxy it might use the average P/E for a group of similar, but publicly traded companies, assuming that companies in the same industry will command the same P/E. It might use as a proxy the P/E of the most similar company it can find.

Proxies are tricky and should be used with care. The price/earnings multiples of comparable stocks in the same industry can be very different. The P/Es for companies in Tract's industry are shown in Exhibit 5-11.

Using the industry average P/E of 11.4 to value Tract, the estimated value per share would be as follows (see next page).

EXHIBIT 5-11 Selected Publishing Companies' Average Annual P/E Ratios

	1999	2000
Banly	6	7
Brown Inc.	8	4
C.C.&H.	8	6
Delfin	6	7
Grants Industries	19	28
Hightower	24	21
John Howard	11	12
McDougal	8	6
Average	**11.3**	**11.4**

---

[22] As shown in Exhibit 5-6.

II. Valuation Using Market Multiples

$$\begin{aligned}\text{Value} &= \text{Earnings} \times \text{P/E} \\ &= \$510{,}840 \times 11.4 \\ &= \$5{,}823{,}576\end{aligned}$$

On a per-share basis it would be:

$$\begin{aligned}\text{Value} &= \text{EPS} \times \text{P/E} \\ &= \$5.11 \times 11.4 \\ &= \$58.25\end{aligned}$$

This is higher than any of the present values we calculated for Tract using the cash flow method.

The fact that we found Tract's value using the cash flow and the earnings methods to be quite different is typical. There can be a number of reasons why the valuations are different. The most important cause for valuation differences is the difference between the proxy companies and the company being valued. While Tract is in the same industry, it is not like most of the companies in Exhibit 5-11: it is not publicly traded, sells different products and to different customers, and has had virtually no growth in the recent past.

In addition to the fact that the universe of competitors listed in Exhibit 5-11 is not reflective of the character of Tract, several of the proxy companies have P/Es that are much higher than that which Tract might command if it were publicly traded.[23] In this situation, the analyst may choose to exclude one or more of the companies on the list, thus creating a group believed to be more reflective of the situation being valued.

When the list of publicly traded companies does not closely resemble the company being valued, the analyst must seek other companies for comparison, or adapt the proxy P/E average.[24] For instance, the analyst might choose to use the company's most similar competitor, or the P/E implied from the purchase prices of recent acquisitions of similar companies.

The price/earnings method requires an estimate that is difficult to make no matter how we might choose to proxy a P/E. There are other reasons why using the P/E ratio is tricky. First, to use it we must assume that recent earnings represent the real earning power of the firm. In the past, the reported earnings of U.S. corporations have become less and less representative of the

---

[23] If the analyst knew more about why Grants Industries and Hightower P/Es were so high, or why Brown Inc. had a P/E of only 4 in 2000, they might choose to exclude them as noncomparable. Others might be candidates for exclusion based on their lack of comparability on the basis of such things as company size or major lines of business.

[24] Perhaps the most important difference between Tract and the list of publishers is company size: Tract is quite small while the publicly traded companies on the list are large. A knowledgeable analyst would know that smaller companies typically have lower P/E ratios when compared to their larger competitors. Thus the analyst might reduce the proxy P/E to account for the difference in size.

companies' economic earnings. Changes in accounting methods for such items as retiree health benefits and management discretion in realizing revenues and earnings, have made the reported earnings of many U.S. corporations resemble only vaguely the firms' real earning power. As for the veracity of earnings of companies in other countries, they vary greatly.

Second, the P/E method assumes that the price/earnings ratio is a reliable indicator of value. While the current P/E of a publicly traded firm reflects its shareholders' present estimates of its future as an independent company, it is just the relationship between the market price of the company's stock and its earnings.[25] It does not reflect the potential synergies that might result from a merger.[26] To estimate the value of synergies using the earnings-valuation approach, the analyst must forecast the new earnings after the merger and forecast the P/E ratio as if the merger were known to investors. The current P/E reflects prospects without a merger, and a P/E reflecting the potential for a merger is difficult to estimate. If the acquisition is expected to create value, the analyst is justified in using a higher estimate. The problem is that no simple method exists for making this estimate.[27]

There are still other assumptions behind the earnings-valuation method. While it appears an easy and straightforward valuation approach, it is neither. The NPV method, on the other hand, assumes that any acquisition with a positive marginal value will increase the value of the acquiring company and that the increased value will eventually be reflected in the market price of its stock. The logic behind the NPV method is clear and powerful.

While we dismiss the P/E multiple method as the sole approach to valuing an acquisition, it can be very useful in putting the net present value analysis into a capital market perspective. For instance, we can compare the P/E *implied* by a present value analysis to a P/E estimated using the earnings analysis. In Exhibit 5-6 we determined the 2001 earnings and cash flows, and in Exhibit 5-9 we determined the present value. Exhibit 5-12 summarizes the information.

The **implied price/earnings ratio** is equal to the net present value per share divided by the earnings per share.[28]

---

[25] Actually, stock analysts may choose to use the current 12 months, the trailing 12 months, the last fiscal or calendar year, or an estimate of the future earnings in calculating the P/E ratio, as we discussed in Chapter 1. When using published P/E ratios, the analyst should know how the ratio is calculated.

[26] In addition, P/Es of growing firms depend heavily upon future expectations. The P/E can be temporarily, and perhaps unrealistically, high. The was certainly the case in late 1999 and early 2000 with the Internet stocks. In addition, healthy cyclical companies have high P/Es when they are at their cyclical lows for earnings, and low P/Es when their earnings are at their best.

[27] In an earlier section about terminal values, we noted that P/E ratios are used to estimate the terminal value. In the discussion of P/Es and their use in valuation, it should be clear that forecasting a P/E to use far into the future is virtually impossible and holds no details about the assumptions being made by the analyst.

[28] Of course this does not need to be done on a per-share basis; the total figures can be used to the same end.

EXHIBIT 5-12 Tract Co.

VALUATION INFORMATION

Cash flow per year	$510,840
Earnings per year	$510,840
Discount rate	13.8%
Net present value with 10 percent growth for five years (Exhibit 5-9)	$4.7 million
Number of shares	100,000

$$\text{Implied P/E} = \frac{\text{PV/Share}}{\text{Earnings/Share}}$$

$$= \frac{\$4{,}668{,}689/100{,}000}{\$510{,}840/100{,}000}$$

$$= \frac{\$46.69}{\$5.11}$$

$$= 9.1 \text{ times}$$

The implied P/E is lower than the average P/E for the companies shown in Exhibit 5-11, so should we use a higher P/E? Why is the implied P/E only 9.1? There are several possible reasons for the difference between what we found for Tract and what we found for others in the publishing business: (1) the predicted cash flows and their underlying growth may be less than what the market is forecasting, (2) the predicted risk incorporated in the required rate of return may be higher than the market's prediction, (3) there may be an error in the inflation forecasts, or (4) the P/E of Tract could be lower than that of others in the industry because of its size, markets, products, or prospects. A good analyst would return to the analysis to determine which cause is likely, and adjust the analysis or conclusions where needed. As for Tract, the implied P/E is lower because the expected growth is lower than that expected for the industry over the long run due to its concentration in the religious publishing business. Thus a lower P/E seems justified.

To use the P/E for valuing a whole company has serious problems, but what about using it for estimating the terminal value? In the analysis of Tract's value once growth had slowed, we used the perpetuity valuation method. Some analysts choose to use a multiple of terminal year earnings to calculate the terminal value. Interesting, but doing so has the same problems as valuing the whole company, and one more: we have to forecast what the company or industry P/E will be at some point in the future. This really adds a degree of fragility to the forecast.

2. Other Multiples for Valuation

Price/earnings ratios depend upon both the company's earning and earnings prospects, and the capital markets' optimism. Over time the average P/Es for the market change. At times of robust economic prospects or market enthusiasm, P/E ratios, as well as other multiples like the market/book value and price/cash flow or sales, may be quite high. This indicates that investors feel confidence and are willing to take risk. Such was the case in 1999 and early 2000, particularly among many companies with Internet-related businesses. Exhibit 5-13 shows this quite dramatically.

This can be a very short-term phenomena, and to forecast it would have been quite difficult. In fact, if you were in the middle of 1999, could you forecast that multiples would be lower or higher in five years, and the magnitude of the change, and how these changes would impact various industries, not just the market as a whole? Very tough indeed.

Managers, corporate and investment analysts, and investment managers frequently use multiples in their valuations. Often they are used as a shorthand by those who fully know industries and companies or for cross-border comparisons (EBITDA). There are industry-specific multiples that have been developed to represent value—for instance, multiples of revenue per subscriber line for cable companies. For those companies with no earnings—for instance, Internet companies—analysts use multiples of revenues.

In their simplicity using P/Es and other price multiples avoids the detail and explicitness of the cash flow forecasts. While multiples can be useful in describing valuations and communicating, taking such shortcuts for valuation results in a loss of critical information for good decisions and complete valuation. This is a particularly important loss when the investment is significant. No manager can afford to lose information, know less than they can, or lack information about how the forecasts and the valuation might be impacted by changes in the company, the industry, and the economy. Cash flow forecasting forces us to look at the details. Big investments deserve this careful attention.

III. OTHER VALUATION TECHNIQUES

Acquisition analysts use several other valuation techniques. Each is used in valuing the company or estimating a terminal value. However, these methods

EXHIBIT 5-13 Standard and Poor's 500 Market Multiples[29]

	Standard and Poor's 500			1999 Technology Stocks
	1999	5-Year Average	Difference	
Price/earnings	32.6	23.7	8.9	166.1
Market/book value	6.1	2.9	3.2	61.3
Price/sales	2.9	2.1	0.8	64.9
Price/cash flow	20.7	16.2	4.5	132.1

---

[29] The data in this exhibit is in multiples, not percentages. You may choose to use multiples or percentages; we use both in this book.

III. Other Valuation Techniques

are best used as supplements to the present value analysis, not as substitutes for it.

1. Book Value

To use the book value to value a company or to calculate a terminal value, the analyst multiplies the book value of the equity of the company, the net assets minus liabilities, by a market/book value ratio. The ratio might come from any one of the sources we discussed in the section on P/E multiples. Using market/book value multiples as a valuation technique is quite basic and lacks any but the most simplistic reasons for its use. In addition to the problem with using any multiple, book value has its own peculiar problem: book value is a poor estimate of economic value. There are several reasons for this. Book value:

1. Depends on the accounting practices of a firm. It is usually only a vague approximation of the real economic value of the company's equity.
2. Ignores intangible assets. Intangibles—copyrights, trademarks, patents, franchise licenses, and contracts—protect a company's right to market its goods and services and thus have value. If the book value of the assets is less than the present value of the cash flows of the firm, intangible assets may account for the discrepancy.
3. Ignores liabilities not reflected on the balance sheet. These liabilities may be such things as lawsuits pending against the company for off balance sheet financing, or employee retirement benefits that are not reported on the balance sheet.
4. Ignores the price appreciation of real assets. Since assets are valued on the balance sheet at their depreciated costs, some assets may be valued far below even their liquidation value. Assets such as land, precious metals, and mineral reserves are prone to valuation discrepancies.

Particularly with privately or closely held firms, owners may believe that book value is the least they should receive when selling the company. When this is true, book value provides a floor below which a successful offer is unlikely to go. However, it is not always a floor value: book value may overstate the value of the company.[30] Since it is thought to provide a floor for valuation, you should be aware of it in contemplating the price at which a merger offer might succeed.

2. Liquidation Value

Liquidation value is the cash value the acquirer would receive if the assets of the acquired firm were sold. This method of valuation is useful if the acquirer intends to sell the assets of the acquired firm, as often happens when the target

---

[30] Overstating occurs when management has invested and still holds, at book value, assets that are obsolete, worthless, or worth less than their original, depreciated cost.

company has assets the acquirer may not want or need.[31] It may also be used to aid in determining the fair book value of under- or overvalued assets. Analysts sometimes use liquidation value as a floor price for an acquisition. If liquidation value exceeds the present value, the company is worth more if its assets are sold. Liquidation value can also be used as a terminal value in valuing a company when its products or services have a finite life. This valuation method might be useful, for instance, in valuing the patent protection on prescription drugs.[32]

3. Replacement Cost

Replacement cost is a measure of the cost of replacing the assets of the potential acquisition. While some analysts use it to set a ceiling price on the acquisition, replacement cost estimates can be difficult to make. There are times when this form of analysis has been of special interest. If the cost of acquiring assets by buying a whole company is less than buying the assets themselves, then replacement cost is a valuable approach. This has happened at various times with such things as oil reserves, brand franchises, mineral rights, and manufacturing facilities.

4. Market Value

The market value of the firm's stock is often a good starting point in estimating an acquisition's price. If the stock is publicly traded, its market value is simply the market price per share times the number of shares. The reason market value is only a starting point should be clear from the present value analysis we performed for Tract and Lifelike. If the acquisition is expected to increase value for the shareholders of one or both firms, this increase in value is unlikely to be reflected in the public price of the common stock of either firm.[33] Thus, if there are synergies and value will be created from those synergies, the current market prices underestimate the present value of the merging firms. Still, the market price of the stock is a benchmark from which the analyst can begin.[34]

Under a certain set of circumstances, all these values should be the same. Liquidation value should reflect what a buyer is willing to pay for the earning

---

[31] This can also be used by stock analysts considering the potential for an acquisition and the value of the deal if pieces of the acquired company are sold. This kind of analysis might be called a "the parts are greater than the whole" analysis.

[32] This and other methods are used to value companies in a sum-of-the-parts valuation. Such a valuation is performed when the acquirer expects or is expected to sell off assets, divisions, or lines of business.

[33] Of course, the expectation of increased value may be reflected in the price once the merger becomes public knowledge.

[34] For an investment manager, companies where the stock price is less than the intrinsic value are stocks to buy. Managers who seek undervalued securities often are called value managers. They seek stocks where the intrinsic/market value is greater than 1.0, and as high as possible. They also look for a *catalyst*: an event or action that will allow the market price to reach the intrinsic value.

power of the firm's assets. Thus a liquidation value, if it can be obtained, should be close to the value estimated using present value analysis. Likewise, book value, if it truly reflects the economic value (the earning power of the assets), will be similar.[35] Only because of estimation errors, accounting conventions, inflation's impact, or value creation or destruction are the values different.

5. Dividend Discount Valuation

Dividend discount models are among the earliest methods for discounting in finance, and are commonly used by investment analysts and managers. Closely akin to discounted cash flow and earnings models, they concentrate on only what the investor actually receives in cash payments, or dividends, and when it is received.

$$\text{Value} = \sum \frac{DPS_n}{(1 + R_e)^n}$$

where
Σ = The sum
DPS = Future dividends per share
R_e = Required return on equity
n = The period, usually a year

The perpetuity version of the dividend discount model is:

$$\text{Value} = \frac{DPS (1 + g)}{R_e - g}$$

In this case the g is the expected growth rate in the future dividends, not growth in earnings or cash flow. Once again we will use an example to show how this model is used to determine the intrinsic value of the equity of a company, in this case a share of stock.

We will use a company that pays dividends and is well known in the United States and around the world: Kellogg, a producer of ready-to-eat cereals and other convenient breakfast foods, like Lender's Bagels. The company has paid dividends for years. For the year ending August 1999 the dividend was $0.93. Dividend growth has been fairly regular: over the past five years the dividends have been $0.70, $0.75, $0.87, $0.90, and $0.93, an average growth rate of about 6 percent per year.

Since the dividend growth is relatively steady the perpetuity model can be used for valuation. The required return that we will use for the discount rate is

---

[35] When the earning power of the asset is greater than the book value, management has created value.

8.66 percent. This rate reflects the fact that Kellogg is in a steady, relatively low-risk business.[36]

$$\text{Value} = \frac{\text{DPS}(1+g)}{K_e - g}$$

$$= \frac{\$0.93 \times (1 + 0.06)}{0.0866 - 0.06}$$

$$= \$37.06$$

The stock price at the time of the data was $37.00. Thus our model did a good job of valuing Kellogg, with some rounding errors to account for the difference between the model's value and the stock price at the time.

6. Relationship between Earnings, Cash Flow, and Dividend Discount Models of Valuation

We now have discussed three kinds of valuation models. Each discounts a different thing, cash flows, earnings, or dividends. How are these models related? Will the dividend and cash flow discount models find the same value for a company and its stock? The answer is yes—if you are discounting information about the same company.

Look at the chart in Exhibit 5-14. This shows one company's cash flow, earnings, and dividends at various stages of its life cycle. As a company first begins, cash flows are negative, as are earnings. The company is making investments into its brand franchise, equipment, inventory, and so forth. At this stage the company cannot and does not pay a dividend. As the company produces its products, markets them, and gains success, its cash flows and earnings go from negative to positive, and are growing. As we saw in Chapter 1, such growth still requires investments, and paying a dividend, at least as the company grows rather rapidly, is not feasible. Finally, the company is mature. In sustainable growth terms, the rate of growth and the sustainable rate of growth are close, and the company no longer needs to build its investment base. It can pay a dividend. Thus over the company's life the cash flows and dividends are different and grow at different rates: early cash flow growth is positive and high, while dividend growth is zero. Later dividend growth is high, and cash flow growth is low. Finally, the rates of growth of the two are quite similar. So long as the data used reflects the position of the company in its life cycle, the dividend and cash flow discount models will result in the same valuations. So should you use earnings, dividends, or cash flow in your valuation?

The dividend discount model requires that you describe the dividend policy of the company, the cash flow model does not.[37] The earnings model relies

---

[36] Required return on equity is discussed in Chapter 6.
[37] Remember that earlier we discussed the earnings model and the way earnings can be managed. Both the cash flow and dividend models discount cash either in the form of dividends or cash flow, the dividends plus cash retained on the shareholders' behalf. The earnings model does not.

EXHIBIT 5-14 Life Cycle of a Company's Earnings, Cash Flow, and Dividends

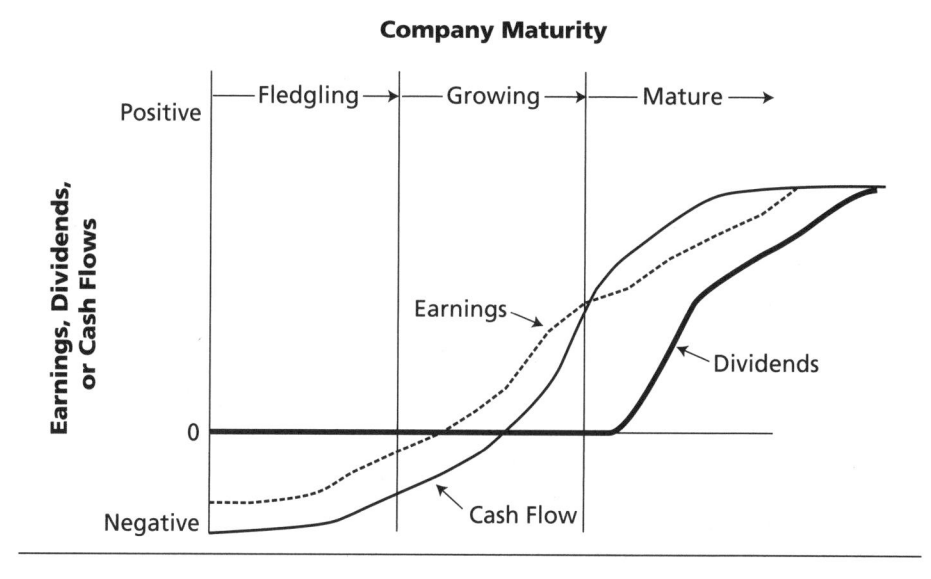

on tax-adjusted data. The cash flow model requires that the company invest all retained funds, funds that we discount, at the required rate of return. These invested funds are used for future dividends. All three models require assumptions about what the company will do. The cash flow model does not require assumptions about when and what the company will pay in dividends, and thus allows the analyst to forecast that the company should continually reinvest on the shareholders' behalf. It deals with companies that pay no dividend more easily and it is explicit. For those reasons, and others, the cash flow model is superior.[38]

7. Cross-Border Acquisitions

The increase in cross-border and non-U.S. merger activity in the later half of the 1990s has been extraordinary. In its increase it has posed for the analyst all the problems that we discussed in other chapters and then some. The problems that must be addressed in these mergers are:

- *In what currency should the company be valued?* In Chapter 2 we discussed forecasting in multiple currencies. The same rules apply to the analysis of a merger, with one special consideration. When using the dividend discount model an analyst must forecast when the dividend will be paid, and what the relevant exchange rate will be at the time of transfer.

---

[38] Many analysts, especially stock analysts, use a discounted cash flow to verify valuations based on P/E, MV/BV, or EBITDA multiples.

- *Do local customs dictate the use of special analysis?* In some countries special analytical customs exist. For instance, in countries with a large number of closely held companies, a measure like book value may be an important consideration.
- *Are the financial statements reliable indicators of the company's past performance?* There are two primary considerations in dealing with this problem: do the accounting rules allow for transparency, and has the economy been sufficiently stable that the information has meaning? If the accounting masks what has actually occurred or the economy has had a recent outburst of inflation, the historic information may be relatively meaningless.
- *Is there capital market information on which to rest forecasts or obtain proxies?* In many countries the capital markets are either very small or represent a narrow spectrum of the companies operating in the country.[39] When valuing an acquisition in such an economy, proxies and information from other countries may be adapted.
- *Is the company considered a part of its domestic industry or a part of the global industry?* Companies operating as a part of the global industry, for instance telecommunications companies, may be valued on the basis of their expanded industry, rather than as a purely domestic company. Larger companies in a global industry tend to be valued higher than smaller, domestic-industry players.

These are only a few of the considerations in valuing a potential merger from or in another country.

IV. SUMMARY

There is only one purpose in making an acquisition. That purpose is to create value for the owners. Value can be created through increased returns or reduced risk. In general, an increase in value comes from increased capacity being matched with a need for that resource—a matching that cannot occur unless the two firms merge. The analyst's task is to estimate the effect of a merger on a firm's return and risk characteristics. Since projected earnings are, at best, only a vague indication of real earning power of the company, the analyst should project cash flows with and without the benefits of the merger, and discount them to determine the value. Other valuation techniques, such as earnings analysis, should be used merely to corroborate the present value analysis.

SELECTED REFERENCES

For methods of analyzing a merger and/or stock, see:

Bodie, Zvi, Alex Kane, and Alan Marcus. *Investments.* 4th ed. Boston, MA: Irwin/McGraw-Hill, 1999, chaps. 18 and 19.

---

[39] For instance, in Canada a large number of companies are natural resource-based.

Bodie, Zvi, and Robert Merton. *Finance*. Upper Saddle River, NJ: Prentice Hall, 2000, chap. 17.

Brealey, Richard A., and Stewart C. Myers. *Principles of Corporate Finance*. 5th ed. New York: McGraw-Hill, 1996, chap. 33.

Brealey, Richard A., and Stewart C. Myers. "A Framework for Evaluating Mergers." In *Modern Developments in Financial Management*. New York: Frederick A. Praeger, 1976.

Brigham, Eugene F., Louis C. Gapenski, and Michael Ehrhardt. *Financial Management*. 9th ed. Fort Worth, Texas: The Dryden Press, 1999, chap. 26.

Damodaran, Aswath. *Corporate Finance*. New York: John Wiley & Sons, 1997, chap. 25.

Damodaran, Aswath. *Damodaran on Valuation*. New York: John Wiley & Sons, 1994.

Hall, Alvin. *Getting Started in Stocks*. 3rd ed. New York: John Wiley & Sons, 1997.

Hooke, Jeffrey. *Security Analysis on Wall Street*. New York: John Wiley & Sons, 1998.

Klein, Peter. *Getting Started in Security Analysis*. New York: John Wiley & Sons, 1998.

Myers, Stewart C. "The Evaluation of an Acquisition Target." *Midland Corporate Finance Journal*, Winter 1983, pp. 39–46.

Ross, Stephen A., Randolph W. Westerfield, and Jeffrey F. Jaffe. *Corporate Finance*. 4th ed. Homewood, Ill.: Richard D. Irwin, 1996, chap. 29.

Salter, Malcolm S., and Wolf A. Weinhold. *Diversification Through Acquisition*. New York: Free Press, 1979, part II.

Shrives, Ronald E., and Mary M. Pashley. "Evidence on Association between Mergers and Capital Structure." *Financial Management*, Autumn 1984, pp. 39–48.

Weston, J. Fred, Kwang S. Chung, and Susan E. Hoag. *Mergers, Restructuring and Corporate Control*. Englewood Cliffs, NJ: Prentice Hall, 1990.

For more on shareholder value creation, see:

Finegan, Patrick T. "Maximizing Shareholder Value at the Private Company." *Journal of Applied Corporate Finance*, Spring 1991, pp. 30–45.

For more on estimating divisional required returns, see:

Fuller, Russell, and H. Kerr. "Estimating the Divisional Cost of Capital: An Analysis of the Pure Play Technique." *Journal of Finance*, December 1981, pp. 997–1009.

Gup, Benton E., and Samuel W. Norwood, III. "Divisional Cost of Capital: A Practical Approach." *Financial Management*, Spring 1982, pp. 20–24.

Harrington, Diana R. "Stock Prices, Beta, and Strategic Planning." *Harvard Business Review*, May/June 1985, pp. 157–164.

Harris, Robert S., Thomas J. O'Brien, and Doug Wakeman. "Divisional Cost-of-Capital Estimation for Multi-Industry Firms." *Financial Management*, Summer 1989, pp. 74–84.

For studies on the relative values of mergers, see:

Cusatis, Patrick, James Miles, and J. Randall Wooridge. "Some New Evidence That Spinoffs Create Value." *Journal of Applied Corporate Finance*, Summer 1994, pp. 100–107.

Mueller, D. C. "The Effects of Conglomerate Mergers: A Survey of the Empirical Evidence." *Journal of Banking and Finance*, December 1977, pp. 315–48.

Rappaport, Alfred. "What We Know and Don't Know About Mergers." *Midland Corporate Finance Journal*, Winter 1983, pp. 63–67.

Rumelt, Richard. *Strategy, Structure and Economic Performance*. Boston: Harvard Business School Press, 1986.

STUDY QUESTIONS

1. Magnus Corporation and Carr Company both operate in the same industry, and although neither is experiencing any rapid growth, both provide a steady stream of earnings. Magnus's management is encouraging the acquisition of Carr because of its excess plant capacity, which it hopes to use. Carr Company has 50,000 shares of common stock outstanding, which are selling at about $6.00 per share. Other data are shown in the following table.

	Magnus Corporation	Carr Company	Combined Entity
Profit after taxes	$48,000	$30,000	$92,000
Residual net cash flow/year	$60,000	$40,000	$120,000
Required return on equity	12.50%	11.25%	12.00%

CARR COMPANY BALANCE SHEET

Assets		Liabilities and Owners' Equity	
Current assets	$273,000	Current liabilities	$134,500
Net PP&E	215,000	Long-term liabilities	111,000
Other	55,000	Owners' equity	297,500
Total assets	$543,000	Total liabilities and owners' equity	$543,000

Compute the maximum price the management (for the shareholders) of the Magnus Corporation should be willing to pay to acquire Carr Company, and the minimum price Carr's management should accept for its shareholders.

2. Smythe Instrument Company wishes to acquire Robinson Research Lab through a merger. Both companies are Canadian and operate exclusively in Ontario Province. Smythe Instrument expects to gain operating efficiencies from the merger through distribution economies, advertising, manufacturing, and purchasing.

   The required rates of return for Smythe and Robinson are 16.2 percent and 14.5 percent, respectively. Neither company has any long-term debt outstanding. The effective required rate of return after the merger is estimated to be 15.5 percent. The projected real growth rate for each of the firms is 4 percent per year, and management expects that growth rate to continue when the two companies are merged. All revenues and costs are expected to keep pace with inflation of 4 percent annually. The current net cash flow per year is Canadian $6.45 million for Smythe and Canadian $2.20 million for Robinson. Based on management's analysis of the synergies for the combined company, the combined net cash flow would have been Canadian $10.92 million if the two had been combined for the past year.

   Calculate the price Smythe Instrument should offer to acquire Robinson Research and the price above which Robinson should accept the merger offer.

3. Action Corporation makes cardboard boxes for a wide range of clients. The industry is experiencing a severe slowdown in terms of sales. Several substitute products are threatening to win over Action's major clients. In spite of the fact that entry into the industry is relatively cheap, fixed costs account for a large percentage of the total expenses. Thus volume is important, and there is pressure on margins.

   In late 2000, a large packaging company that wanted to add a cardboard box manufacturer to its portfolio of companies approached Action.

   Mr. Santiago, CFO at Action, was concerned about the price he should expect for this acquisition and wondered how best to maximize the return to Action's owners.

   Action was rated by Moody's rating service as a moderate risk. Mr. Santiago believed that Action's owners would demand at least an 11.2 percent return on their investment. Sales in 2000 were $250 million and were expected to grow at 5 percent annually until 2007, and 3 percent thereafter; cost of sales is 75 percent of sales; and selling, general, and administrative expenses are 10 percent of sales. Taxes are 34 percent. Depreciation is at $7 million per year and not expected to change, and PP&E and working capital investments total $7 million per year. The company has no debt. In the past, Action paid dividends of 10 percent of net income, and the return on the investment was about 3.4 percent. At what price should Mr. Santiago sell to provide the owners a fair return?

4. Mr. Santiago assumed the company that was interested in acquiring Action was a U.S. company. Thus the cash flows and valuation were in U.S. dollars. How would Mr. Santiago change the analysis if he discovered the potential acquirer was Mexican? Be explicit about what would change in each step of the valuation process.

CHAPTER 6
The Required Rate of Return on Equity

Valuation is one of the most important topics in finance. Whether valuing an investment in a new product, process or technology, or a company or its stock, valuation requires that the analyst know about the investment, its prospects, and how changes in competition, technology, and the economy will affect the value. The analyst also must know how to go about assigning a value to the future.

In Chapters 4 and 5 we looked at valuation: first capital budgeting, and then the valuation of a business. For the most part, we used the residual cash flow method of valuation. Most of what we discussed was cash flows and how to calculate and evaluate them. We did not discuss where the discount rate came from, or how to estimate it. The rate was given.[1]

In this chapter we discuss how to estimate the discount rate. Since we are not considering leverage, the cash flows belong only to the shareholders, and the rate is what they require from their investment. The return required on equity is an estimate of how investors think, process information, and determine what a fair return might be for the risk of their investment. Getting into somebody else's mind, especially when that mind is the collective mind of those in the capital markets, is a real challenge. In this chapter, we discuss how that challenge might be met, and how a discount rate that reflects the investors' required rate of return might be estimated.

I. WHAT IS A SHAREHOLDERS' REQUIRED RETURN?

Investors expect to earn a return on the funds they provide to a company—a return that compensates them for both the time that the funds are made available to the company and the risk that it will not provide the return expected. Returns on common stock come from the dividends the common shareholders receive over the life of their investment in the stock and from any gains realized by the investors on the sale of the stock that result from increases in its market price.

How do we know what equity investors expect to earn on their investment in a company? How would an analyst estimate the returns shareholders re-

---

[1] We did discuss risk-adjusting rates in Chapters 4 and 5, but not where to get the rate to be adjusted.

quire? If a single shareholder or a small group of shareholders owned the firm, the analyst could simply ask them, "What return do you expect this firm to earn on your behalf?" If the shareholder replied, "Fifteen percent would satisfy me; with that return, I would not want to buy a larger share of the firm, nor would I want to sell the ownership position I already have," the analyst would know that the shareholder's required return was 15 percent. However, companies whose stock is bought and sold in the public markets do not have such limited ownership, and it is impossible to know how shareholders would answer the return question.[2] As a result, we must find a way to estimate the return required by a large number of dispersed shareholders.

There are two categories of methods used to estimate the required return. The first category places a value on the cash the company generates for its shareholders, essentially a cash flow or fundamental approach. The second category could be called capital market estimates. Capital market methods categorize all securities into risk classes and then use the classifications to estimate the owners' required return. Note that we have been calling the return the owners' (the investors') required return. From the company's perspective, it is its cost of equity.

To understand how these models work, a basic introduction to the equity markets is useful.

II. CAPITAL MARKET BASICS

The markets for long-term funds for corporations are called **capital markets**. Capital markets differ from the money markets discussed in Chapter 3: **money market funds** are short-term investments with maturities of under one year; **capital market funds** are long-term investments with maturities exceeding one year. In addition to providing debt funds with a stated **maturity**, the date when they come due and must be fully repaid, capital markets provide equity funds that have no stated maturity.[3]

Equity capital markets exist on two levels: primary markets and secondary markets. **Primary market** transactions occur when companies issue equity to investors. Typically, these securities are sold through investment bankers, who, through their relationships with brokers, act as agents for the companies selling the instruments. The proceeds from the sales of financial instruments, minus the investment bankers' commissions, are paid to the issuing companies.[4] The primary markets are the major source of new equity capital for com-

---

[2] Even if we could ask all the shareholders what they need to earn, we could not do so simultaneously; things change over time and the answers would not be based on the same company, industry, and/or economic circumstances.

[3] We discuss debt markets more extensively in Chapter 7.

[4] The sale can be "best efforts," where the sales proceeds are delivered to the company, or on a contractual basis, where the proceeds are guaranteed. Obviously the cost of the transaction would depend upon the risk being taken by the intermediary.

panies. New equity issues by companies that have never raised equity in the public markets are called **initial public offerings**, or **IPOs**.

After the securities have been sold initially, the purchaser of the securities may then trade them in the **secondary markets**. Financial instruments may be sold individually or bundled together and then traded between individuals or institutions that may have no relationship with the original issuing company. While the company does not gain direct benefit from this trading, it is not indifferent to activities in the secondary markets. The prices of its securities may change as a result of changing prospects for the company, its industry, and the economy. The prices for secondary market trading of securities are reported in U.S. publications such as *The Wall Street Journal* and *Barron's*, in U.K. publications such as *The Financial Times*, and in the major financial or daily newspapers in other countries. In addition, there are numerous web sites where current or slightly delayed prices are available.[5]

In recent years, derivative instruments, such as options and futures contracts, have been widely traded in mature markets and in some emerging markets.[6] These instruments, which are designed to provide a means of protecting investors against price movements in the capital markets, are all secondary market instruments. They are not a source of capital for corporations.[7] Company treasurers and investment bankers have gained a real appreciation for the attractiveness of the features of some of these new instruments, however, and have included some of their characteristics into new forms of corporate securities. For those working in corporate treasury offices or in investment banks, or considering investing in synthetic or exotic securities, a careful review of the features of each security is critical.[8]

Trading in capital market instruments can take place in organized market exchanges or **over the counter (OTC)**. **Organized exchanges** such as the New York Stock Exchange (NYSE) and the American Stock Exchange (AMEX) in the United States, as well as stock exchanges around the world, allow trading only in listed securities. To achieve listed status, companies must meet specific qualifications of the exchange, including such things as the size of the company, the total market value of the publicly traded shares, and the amount of trading in the company's securities. Trading on these exchanges can be done only by members of the exchange. Members are typically brokerage companies that

---

[5] See the references at the end of the chapter.

[6] Derivative instruments are those based on another instrument. For instance, a call option on a common stock gives the owner of the option the right to buy shares at a particular price within a given time period. Put options are the right to sell. These two option types are the basic forms of derivatives. More exotic securities can be fashioned from bundles of these.

[7] For corporations, options and futures primarily are used for hedging risk and, sometimes, speculating. Some agricultural and natural resource companies do sell futures.

[8] *Synthetic securities* are those that mimic the characteristics of some other instrument or security. Exotic securities, which have a variety of features, are generally the special creation of a particular investment bank for one issuer or a group of issuers, and they are usually in vogue for a short period of time.

buy and sell securities for their customers. Increasingly, large blocks of securities can be and are traded between buyer and seller using an electronic trading system.[9] Comparable, but not identical, arrangements exist in other countries.

Unlike the exchanges, which have a specific location where trading takes place, the **over-the-counter market** consists of numerous traders located throughout a country. These traders do what is called **making a market**. That means that they buy, sell, and keep an inventory in one or several securities. Brokerage firms are market makers. In the United States, a computerized network called **NASDAQ**, sponsored by the National Association of Securities Dealers, ties these various market makers together. Many more securities are traded OTC than on the exchanges. Because listed companies tend to be larger, the average trading volume for the securities listed on the exchanges is much greater than for the OTC trades. In the late 1990s, exceptions to this exist among the technology companies. These relatively new companies, such as AOL, Amazon.com, and Microsoft, are large, but continue to trade on the NASDAQ national market. Exhibit 6-1 shows the changes in trading volume and Exhibit 6-2 shows the volume in billions of dollars. Clearly the size of the blocks and companies being traded most actively on NASDAQ has been increasing.

In the past few years a number of new trading mechanisms have evolved to allow those who have large numbers of one security, a **block**, to trade directly with a buyer or buyers; for individual investors to trade at costs close to those

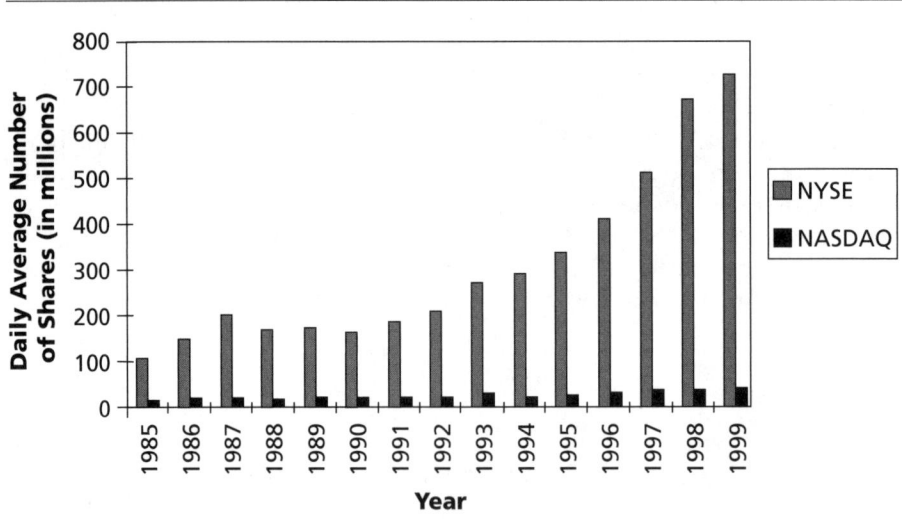

EXHIBIT 6-1 NYSE and NASDAQ Daily Average Trading Volume (millions of shares)

---

[9] Some exchanges themselves are electronic (for instance, the Singapore exchange), and in some areas (for instance, Europe) the electronic trading systems compete for trades with organized exchanges. These electronic trading networks are increasingly important.

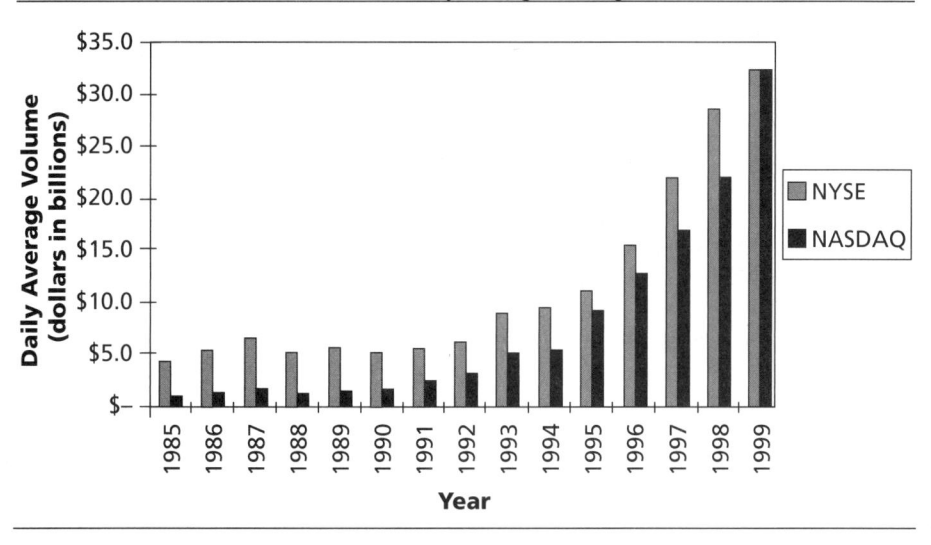

EXHIBIT 6-2 NYSE and NASDAQ Daily Average Trading Volume (billions of dollars)

of large, institutional, investors; and to trade outside the usual trading hours. The Internet provides increasingly sophisticated data and tools to make and manage investments.[10] All this has expanded the interest in investing and trading, in particular to individuals.[11] This is all secondary market activity.

While most countries have equity markets, the level of individual equity ownership varies substantially. For instance, in the United Kingdom most securities are owned by institutions. In Germany, banks own many company securities. In Japan, cross-ownership, where shares of two or more companies are owned by each other, is common. Institutional investors such as mutual funds, insurance companies, and pension funds are the largest investors in the equity markets worldwide. While many of these relationships have been stable for a long period of time, significant changes are occurring. Companies are listing their shares in more than one country or issuing bonds in more than one currency, government-run pension funds are becoming private and being invested into the capital markets, and the volatility of markets has increased.

Most countries have a small or nonexistent public bond market.[12] There are several reasons for this. First, in many countries the issuing and selling of new bonds is either directly controlled by the government or by banks. In other countries companies may issue bonds or stock into the public debt or equity market. While many restrictions exist, the increasing integration of the world's

---

[10] See the references at the end of the chapter.
[11] Some call this the democratization of the capital markets.
[12] Exceptions to this are the government bond markets for some countries and the euro market.

capital markets has led to significant increases in the volume of nondomestic securities issued in some countries, and in the number of issues that are placed simultaneously in more than one market.

In spite of the fact that equity is the fundamental core of capital for a company, equity investors often subcontract some of their financing obligations to others.[13] Most often the subcontracting is done with lenders, and the additional capital is in the form of debt. Some instruments, however, combine characteristics of debt and equity through convertible provisions. **Convertible instruments** typically allow an investor to convert a debt or preferred stock instrument into common stock at a specified conversion price and, usually, for a particular period of time.

There are two types of equity, common stock and **preferred stock**. Preferred stockholders do have a preferential position over common stockholders, hence the name preferred stock. While the company can pay dividends to common shareholders, it has no contractual obligation to do so.[14] Dividends may be paid to equity investors, but only after all obligations have been paid to bondholders. The dividend that is to be paid on preferred stock is a stated amount. Preferred stock usually provides that the preferred dividend must be paid before any dividend can be paid to the common shareholders. If the company has insufficient funds to pay the dividend, however, the dividend may be omitted without causing default. Usually any previously omitted preferred dividends must be paid before dividends can be paid to common shareholders. Preferred stock with this provision is termed cumulative preferred. Because the dividend is stated, like an interest payment, preferred stock is similar to debt. On the other hand, because the company has no obligation to pay the dividends, the preferred shareholder's return is uncertain; thus, it is also similar to equity. Preferred shareholders rarely have any voting rights.[15]

After the required preferred dividend has been paid, the common shareholders may receive any dividend that management deems appropriate and the board of directors approves. Many investors buy common stock in the expectation that the company will grow and prosper and, therefore, the stock price will increase. These increases in price come when investors revise their expectations for the company: investors increase or decrease their estimates of the company's dividend payments in the future. A change in the market price

---

[13] In publicly held companies, management, along with its advisers, makes the decision. However, shareholders' opinion about the level of debt is reflected in the pricing of the equity. It is their way of "having their say."

[14] In some cases, rather than paying dividends, the company repurchases some of its outstanding shares. This is done for one of two reasons: (1) to reduce the amount of equity outstanding or (2) to provide a tax-advantaged way for investors to receive some income by selling some of their shares.

[15] In some countries preferred stock is the primary form of stock traded in the public markets. This is particulary true where companies have close associations with a particular family or group and the control of the company is not ceded to public shareholders. This is true in countries like Brazil.

II. Capital Market Basics

of the stock is termed a **capital appreciation** if the change is positive and a **capital loss** if it is negative. In addition to owning the residual or remaining income of the company, common shareholders, unlike owners of preferred shares, elect the board of directors.[16]

Determinants of changes in stock prices are not easy to isolate. Factors that affect the general economy, such as changes in interest rates and the rate of economic growth, affect stock prices. In addition, the market price of a company's shares may be affected by a revised industry outlook as well as by changes in prospects for the specific company.

Dividends are the only source of income from equity investments.[17] Of course, if expectations change regarding future dividends, and the stock price changes, the equity holder can sell some stock and capture these revised dividend forecasts. The relative importance of the dividend or capital gain depends on how long the investor has held the shares. However, since future return is uncertain at the time the equity is purchased, investors must determine the return they require and decide if the current market price is fair, that is, if the cash flows that are expected to be generated from their investment will provide the return they want.

Having said all this, how can we use this information to ferret out the shareholders' required rate of return? To get into the shareholders' collective heads, we will take the information they give us, the stock price, and use the models from Chapters 4 and 5. When we used these models in the earlier chapters, we solved for the net present value, the **intrinsic market price**. Recall the model is:

$$\text{Intrinsic market price} = \sum \frac{RCF_n}{(1 + R_e)^n}$$

where
  RCF = Residual cash flow
  n = Period
  R_e = Required equity return

Let's think about using these formulas in a slightly different way. Let's solve for the shareholders' required return (R_e). Knowing a little algebra, you know that we can have only one unknown in any formula. Thus, if we are going to solve for R_e, we must "know" the net present value, the intrinsic market price. By making one assumption, we can substitute the current market price of the company's stock for the net present value. The assumption that we must make is that *capital markets are efficient*.

---

[16] A word of caution. Some companies have more than one class of common shares. These classes are normally labeled alphabetically and often contain different voting rights. This is particularly true in companies that were previously family owned and where the family maintains a higher proportion of the voting rights. Share classes can also exist to represent different portions of the company's assets.

[17] Companies may liquidate some or all of themselves by paying an unusual dividend, selling to another buyer, or returning the equity investors' capital.

In an **efficient market** all available information known to market participants is reflected in the current market price of a security, for instance, a company's stock. That means that the intrinsic market price (our net present value) should be the same as the market price. While a market price may change, and frequently does so, often quite dramatically, in an efficient market the price changes only when the market participants gain new information or change their attitude about the company.[18] Completely efficient markets are markets in which no one can forecast changes in stock prices, at least not at a cost that allows them to make money repeatedly. Thus the market takes all the currently available information into account in deriving this market price.

Research has shown that the capital markets are relatively efficient, especially the major markets, even though some studies conclude that the market may have some inefficiencies that an astute investor can exploit.[19] By assuming that equity markets are relatively efficient, we can use a company's current stock price as the value investors have placed on the company's future cash flows. By doing this, we have two of the formula's unknowns, and that is all we need to solve for the required rate of return.

III. CASH FLOW VALUATION MODELS

In previous chapters we discussed a variety of discounted cash flow models using cash flows, earnings, and dividends as our cash flows. Up to this point we said that the residual cash flows are the best cash flows to discount to determine the value of an investment, whether it is a company's internal investment or an investment in an acquisition. In the equity markets, however, the custom has been to look only at what the shareholders receive, the dividends. Since we are trying to emulate how investors think, and dividends are the equity market custom, that is where we will start.

1. The Dividend-Discount Method

The dividend-discount model is:

$$\text{Intrinsic market price} = \sum \frac{\text{Dividends}_n}{(1 + R_e)^n}$$

To use this model to value a company we must forecast the dividends forever, or practically for a very long time, and discount them at the shareholders' required return.

---

[18] This change can come from information about the company, the industry, the economy, or a change in investors' appetite for risk.

[19] The question of whether stock price changes can be forecasted is controversial. Most researchers conclude, however, that the markets are relatively efficient. In the late 1990s the study of "behavioral finance" has shed light on why some of the seeming inefficiencies are really the result of investors acting like humans with all of their greed and fear and herd instincts.

Let's turn to an example to show how to estimate the required return on equity using the dividend-discount model. For our example, we will use National Presto Industries, Inc., a company that manufactures pressure cookers and small electrical appliances. The company's stock is traded on the NYSE in the United States. To estimate the future dividends, we first analyze the past performance of the company to gain insight into the company and its performance and then forecast the prospects for sales of National Presto's products, its earnings, its cash flows, and dividends.[20] Exhibit 6-3 shows National Presto's historical financial performance.

As you can see from the financial statements, National Presto has had a decline in performance over the last few years, only picking up in 1998. This decline was acknowledged by shareholders whose stock price vividly showed the change in the company's performance.[21] The stock price is shown in Exhibit 6-4. The changes came as a result of a number of different factors. First, National Presto produced a group of very traditional products, and small, special-purpose kitchen appliances. In 1991, it introduced a curly french fry maker, a product that became a big seller during the holiday season. Since that time, the company has had some problems. First, it has not had another innovative and popular new product introduction like the curly french fry maker since 1991. Second, management overestimated inventory needs in 1992, and lost revenues from the closing of a munitions manufacturing plant. Third, it had problems with one of its major channels of distribution, Kmart: first it lost Kmart as a customer, then regained it just as Kmart developed its own problems. Finally, National Presto had to learn to deal with just-in-time inventory systems put in place by its major customers, including Wal-Mart. As a consequence of all these things, the company's receivables lengthened; income and returns on sales, assets, and equity declined; and sales growth rates were negative for four of the last five years. In 1999, National Presto came under quite another attack. Investors called on National Presto Industries to reduce its cash balance: valued as a redundant asset worth about $32.50 per share. Management, largely the remnants of the original founding family, had kept significant amounts of cash in preparation for a potential acquisition. By mid-1999 the stock price was in the high $30s.[22]

By mid-September of 1999, National Presto's stock price was $38.63; the total equity value was $282 million with 7.3 million shares traded. In forecasting the future dividends, there are several things to note about National Presto.

---

[20] The dividend policy typically depends upon the earnings of the company. The dividends may be a percentage of the earnings or a constantly growing sum as we saw in Chapter 1.

[21] This shows the link between performance and stock price. For some companies the link is not as obvious. That is because the future performance is expected to be dramatically different from the present performance. For National Presto, it is reasonable to expect that the recent performance is a precursor to the future.

[22] If the cash value was over $30, and the stock price was $38.63, as it was in mid-September 1999, the company's operating cash flows were worth only $8.63. While this is unlikely, investors were not very happy about National Presto's asset management.

EXHIBIT 6-3 National Presto's Historic Performance—1990–1998

	1990	1991	1992	1993	1994	1995	1996	1997	1998
Revenues (millions)	$127.00	$162.00	$128.00	$119.00	$128.00	$120.00	$106.00	$109.50	$107.10
Net income (millions)	29.00	37.00	26.00	19.00	22.00	19.00	14.70	17.00	19.70
Dividends/Share	4.15	2.70	3.80	2.55	1.90	2.15	2.00	2.00	2.00
Annual cash flow (millions)	30.30	38.00	27.10	19.80	22.60	21.50	38.30	18.80	23.70
Ratios									
Net income/Sales	22.8%	22.8%	20.3%	16.0%	17.2%	15.8%	13.9%	15.5%	18.4%
Sales/Assets	52.5%	60.9%	49.2%	42.0%	44.0%	42.1%	40.0%	40.0%	40.0%
Long-term debt/Assets	2.1%	1.9%	2.0%	1.8%	1.8%	0.0%	0.0%	0.0%	0.0%
Assets/Equity	120.4%	122.0%	83.5%	83.0%	119.8%	115.4%	120.0%	120.0%	120.0%
Dividend/Net income	105.3%	54.2%	107.6%	100.0%	65.1%	82.4%	100.0%	86.6%	74.6%
Return on equity	14.4%	16.9%	8.3%	5.5%	9.1%	7.7%	6.0%	6.8%	7.8%
Sustainable growth rate	−0.8%	7.7%	−0.9%	0.0%	3.1%	1.4%	0.0%	0.9%	2.0%
Inventory days*	97.8	78.4	105.0	110.9	100.2	120.8	89.9	91.7	82.3
Receivables days	84.5	72.5	86.6	77.7	90.7	112.4	76.8	69.0	55.6

* Calculated relative to cost of goods sold.

III. Cash Flow Valuation Models 249

EXHIBIT 6-4 National Presto Industries Stock Price 1990–mid-1999

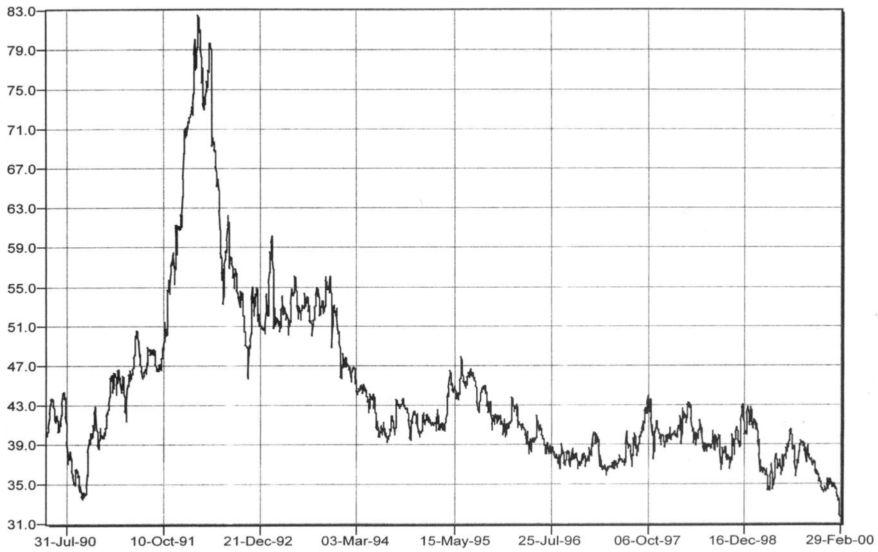

SOURCE: Bridge Information Systems.

First, the dividend rate over the years has not been level, as it is in many companies. National Presto's board has occasionally declared an extra dividend in December, depending upon the year's results. The special dividend is reflected in the rapid growth in dividends in the early 1990s that mirrored the earnings gains. However, by 1999 the dividends appeared to have returned to a more normal range. While some analysts were forecasting growth in revenues and earnings for the next few years to be higher than it had been in the past, these forecasts depended upon National Presto introducing new and attractive products. A more reasonable forecast would be that National Presto's growth would be that of a very mature company: growth in unit volume would be relatively flat, while prices would keep up with inflation. Investors might expect revenue and earnings growth over the long term to be in the 2 to 4 percent range, and thus a very long-term growth in dividends of 4 to 5 percent is within reason.

Growth rates can be a challenge. In more mature companies estimates for future growth can be found in sources such as *Value Line*. An example of what you might find there is given in Exhibit 6-5. The data is for Black & Decker, one of National Presto's main competitors. For National Presto, the analysis will be our own.

By 1999, National Presto had recovered from its weak performance in the mid-1990s. The recent concerns by investors over the size of National Presto's cash position, and the fact that its dividend had not been changed since 1996,

EXHIBIT 6-5 Black & Decker Historic and Forecasted Growth Rates

Annual Growth Rates	Historic		Forecast
	10 Years	5 Years	1996–98 to 2002–04
Revenues	4.5%	–4.0%	3.0%
Cash flow	5.0	4.5	8.0
Earnings	8.0	22.0	13.5
Dividends	0.5	3.5	7.0
Book value	2.5	3.5	NMF

NMF = No meaningful figure.

SOURCE: *Value Line*.

should encourage a dividend catch up. Thus we might expect the dividend to recover to about $2.40 in 1999. Since National Presto Industries is a mature, slow-growth company, we can use the perpetuity method of the dividend-discount model to estimate the required return on equity.

$$\text{Market price} = \frac{\text{Dividend}}{R_e - g}$$

$$\$38.63 = \frac{\$2.40 \times (1 + 0.04)}{(R_e - 0.04)}$$

Rearranged

$$R_e = \frac{\$2.50}{\$38.63} + 0.04$$

$$= 0.105 \text{ or } 10.5\%$$

National Presto's shareholders' required return on equity is 10.5 percent, at least as estimated by this model.

The dividend-discount model is in widespread use. But this widely used model has its limitations. The constant growth dividend-discount model cannot be used when:

1. The firm pays no dividends. When this situation exists, the company's revenues, earnings, cash flows, and eventual dividend policy must be forecasted to estimate the required return on equity, and the perpetuity method cannot be used.
2. The expected rate of growth is higher than the discount rate, or the rate of growth is not constant. These situations signal that the company is entering an abnormal growth phase; thus explicit, annual forecasts must

III. Cash Flow Valuation Models   251

be made for it, and the long version of the dividend-discount model used.[23]

Regardless of the fact that many companies pay no dividends, one thing is clear: it would be impossible for the dividend growth rate to exceed the cash flow discount rate over a very long time. Eventually the dividends would greatly exceed the cash flows. For some companies the disparity between the cash flow and dividend growth rates is so wide, the perpetuity versions of the valuation models cannot be used. A different model must be used. To deal with abnormal growth, you would make year-by-year forecasts and compare them to the current market price.[24]

Let's assume that we hear news about National Presto's introduction of a new line of products. This line will increase growth, and interrupt the level, low-growth forecast we would make for the company. Using the information about National Presto's prospects for future sales of these new products we could devise a scenario like the following:

1. For years 1–5, growth will come from cost cutting and higher than usual sales arising from the introduction of the new line of products.
2. For years 6–11, growth will be lower than in years 1–5, but still higher than a company could sustain for a long period of time. During this period National Presto continues to expand its new products with a series of line extensions. In addition, it is likely that dividend growth would continue as the company's growth in sales declines and its need for funds decreases. This follows the life cycle description we used in Chapter 5.
3. For years 12–15, sales, earnings, and cash flow growth slows further and dividends grow (reflecting a continuing decline in the company's need for additional capital for growth). By the end of the 15 years, the dividends, earnings, and cash flow will be virtually identical, as will their growth rates.

The historic growth rates are shown in Panel A of Exhibit 6-6. The growth rates that might result from this forecast are shown in Panel B of the exhibit. A forecast of the earnings, dividends, cash flows, and revenues based on these growth rates is shown in Exhibit 6-7.[25] Stock analysts in investment management companies frequently do this kind of forecasting.

Using the data from Exhibit 6-7 and the long version of the dividend-discount model, the required return on equity we find using this data is 10.4

---

[23] This long model is the sum of the dividends forecasted for years, discounted at the required return on equity. The dividend forecasts are explict for each year.
[24] To calculate the R_e, the internal rate of return method described in Chapter 4 is used.
[25] As with any set of forecasts, different analysts will make different forecasts. These forecasts are consistent with the history of National Presto and a forecast of successful new product introductions.

EXHIBIT 6-6 National Presto Industries, Inc.

FORECASTED GROWTH RATES IN SALES, EARNINGS, CASH FLOWS, AND DIVIDENDS

Panel A: Historic Growth Rates

Historic Growth Rates in	10 Years	5 Years
Revenues	0.0%	−4.5%
Cash flow	0.0	−7.5
Earnings	−0.5	−9.0
Dividends	5.5	7.0
Book value	3.5	2.0

Panel B: Forecasted Growth Rates

Period (years)	Sales	Earnings	Cash Flow	Dividends
1–5	14.0%	10.0%	9.5%	4.0%
6–11	7.0	5.0	4.5	4.0
12–15	3.5	2.5	2.5	2.5
16 onward	2.5	2.5	2.5	2.5

EXHIBIT 6-7 National Presto Industries, Inc.

SUMMARIZED FORECASTED FINANCIAL PERFORMANCE (dollars in millions)

	Historic			Forecasted			Terminal Year
	1997	1998	1999	2000	2005	2012	2015
Revenues	$110	$107	$125	$143	$258	$374	$425
Net income	17	20	22	24	37	49	54
Cash flow	19	22	23	26	38	48	53
Dividends/Share	2.00	2.00	2.40	2.50	3.04	3.88	4.18

percent.[26] It is identical to that from the perpetuity method because the data we used in both calculations was identical; the growth rate was 4 percent.[27] If the data from the two versions of the dividend-discount model are not identical, neither will be the results.[28]

---

[26] To estimate the owners' required return, we used the same method we used in Chapter 4 when we were estimating the internal rate of return.

[27] Note that if you try the calculation, Exhibit 6-7 only has the data for the years that are different. You need to fill in the missing years with data based on the same assumptions.

[28] Suppose National Presto management determined that it needed to slow the dividend growth for the first five years. The required return on equity would drop. Any other changes in the growth rate for short periods of time mean that we must use the longer form of the dividend-discount model, the perpetuity version will not do. However, since National Presto is mature, the shortcut perpetuity dividend-discount model is appropriate.

All our analysis is based on forecasts. Are these forecasts reasonable, and is 10.4 percent a good estimate of the shareholders' required return on equity? Let's find a way to corroborate our estimate.

2. Discounted Cash Flow Models

We based our forecasts on dividends and dividend policy. To corroborate our results let's use the discounted cash flow approach we used when we valued Tract in Chapter 5.[29] The formula we used was:

$$\text{Net present value} = \frac{RCF_1}{(1+R_e)^1} + \frac{RCF_2}{(1+R_e)^2} + \frac{RCF_3}{(1+R_e)^3} + \cdots + \frac{RCF_n}{(1+R_e)^n}$$

We also used a shortcut, a perpetuity version of the formula, when a company's residual cash flow was growing at a low, constant growth rate (g) for a long period:

$$\text{Net present value} = \frac{RCF \times (1+g)}{R_e - g}$$

Once again we substitute the market price of $38.63 for the net present value. We can estimate the required return on equity for National Presto using a long-term average of the cash flow growth rate.[30] The residual cash flow is the per-share value in 1999 ($23 million) divided by the number of shares (7.4 million). Because, in this scenario, National Presto will grow at a low, constant rate, we can use the perpetuity method to estimate the value of the company.

$$\text{Net present value (Market price)} = \frac{RCF}{R_e - g}$$

$$\text{Market price} = \frac{RCF \times (1+g)}{R_e - g}$$

$$= \frac{\$3.10 \times (1 + 0.025)}{(R_e - 0.025)}$$

$$= \$38.63$$

Rearranged:

$$R_e = \frac{\$3.17}{\$38.63} + 0.02$$

$$= 0.107 \text{ or } 10.7\%^{[31]}$$

---

[29] Depending upon our purpose, the net present value can also be called the intrinsic value or the intrinsic market price.

[30] In all these models, as the market price changes and/or company prospects, these numbers will change.

[31] If we determine the discount rate using the forecasts including new products, the required return on equity would be 10.8 percent.

This is close to the rate we found using the dividend-discount model. This is rarely the case. The dividend payout is a decision made by a company's board of directors. It may or may not follow the pattern of earnings and cash flows. As such, the forecasts for dividend policy, especially for companies without dividends, are difficult at best. The historic pattern of differences between the earnings and dividends per share can be seen in Exhibit 6-8. Since the cash flows reflect the earning power of the company, the cash flows typically provide a better forecast.

As with the dividend-discount model, if we expect changes in the company before it reaches the slow-growing, mature phase, then we should use the long form of the residual cash flow model. The data used for this model would be like that shown in Exhibits 6-6 and 6-7.

$$\text{Net present value (Market price)} = \frac{RCF_1}{(1 + R_e)^1} + \frac{RCF_2}{(1 + R_e)^2} + \frac{RCF_3}{(1 + R_e)^3} + \frac{RCF_n/(R_e - g)}{(1 + R_e)^n}$$

When dealing with common stock, analysts use a variety of approaches to estimate the terminal value, the value from year 16 onwards. One of the most common approaches is to forecast the market price at some time in the future by multiplying the forecasted earnings by an estimated price/earnings ratio. This is the value in the "terminal" year. This value is discounted. To forecast a future P/E ratio, especially 15 years from now, is very difficult and even more tenuous than forecasting the earnings themselves. Far better is the perpetuity value of the residual cash flows the company will generate from year 15 onwards. This is the method described in Chapters 4 and 5. Using this formula

EXHIBIT 6-8 National Presto Industries

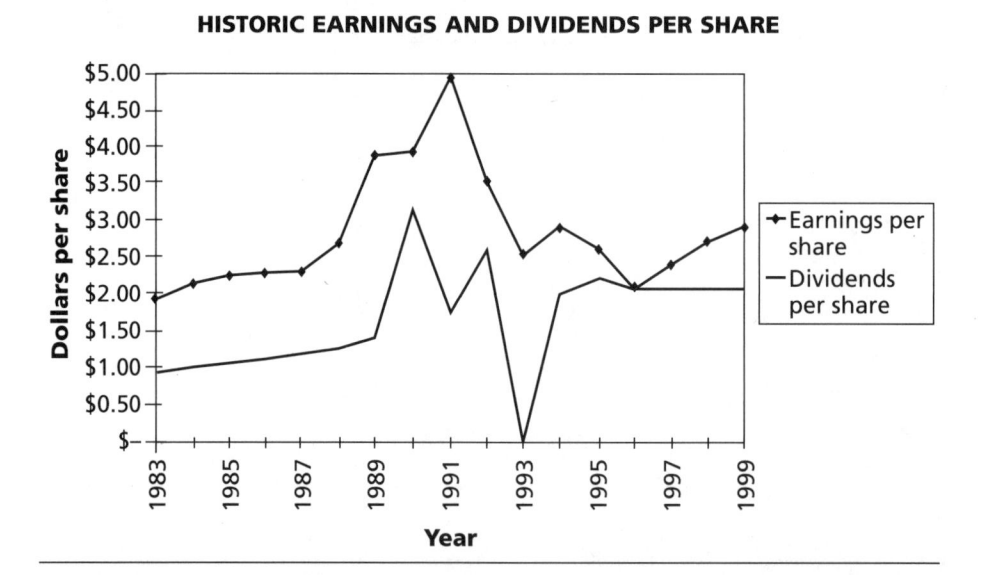

HISTORIC EARNINGS AND DIVIDENDS PER SHARE

and the 15 years of cash flows forecasted for National Presto in Exhibit 6-6, the shareholders have a 10.8 percent required return on equity.[32]

3. Implicit Required Return on Equity

In addition to the cash flow and dividend-discount models, analysts use numerous abbreviated approaches to estimate shareholders' required return—that is, the company's cost of equity. Many of the approaches rely on earnings, or the relationship between earnings and the market price, some of the same models described in Chapter 5. The most widespread method is called the **implicit required return on equity** or **implicit cost of equity**. For National Presto, the implicit required return on equity is:

$$R_e = 1/(\text{Market price/Earnings per share})$$

Or

$$= \text{Earnings per share/Market price}$$
$$= \frac{\$2.97}{\$38.63}$$
$$= 0.077 \text{ or } 7.7\%$$

The implicit cost of equity is well below the shareholders' required return estimated with the methods used thus far. The discrepancy arises because this model has no provision for any future growth. You might note that this model is similar to the others, only the company does not grow, that is, it (1) either pays out all earnings to its shareholders or (2) does not create value for its shareholders with any funds that it retains. In other words, the equation assumes that the net present value of a company's investments is zero.

Only for the most mature companies in stable and highly competitive industries would the implicit required return on equity be anything more than a rough approximation. For companies in declining industries, investors may believe that today's earnings and dividends are higher than they will be in the future. For new companies in growing markets, present earnings and dividends are less than investors expect to gain in the future. When a portion of the company's earnings will be reinvested in the firm, and these investments will create value for the owners, a simple approach to determining the required return on equity that fails to account for growth is useless.[33]

IV. CAPITAL MARKET ESTIMATIONS—RISK PREMIUM MODELS

The cash flow and dividend-discount models use cash flow and dividend forecasts and the current stock price to calculate the shareholders' required return

---

[32] To estimate the owners' required return, we used the internal rate of return method.
[33] This also holds for companies with negative growth.

on equity. These forecasts can be difficult to make. An analyst can, however, use a different approach, one that estimates the required return according to the risk of the security in comparison to other investments in the market.

The market is the great arbitrageur of risk and return. Investors, both large and small, and security traders monitor the market constantly looking for profit-making opportunities. In doing so, these market participants constantly compare the returns they are getting with the risk they are taking. We can use this same process of arraying securities by their relative levels of risk, on the understanding that riskier securities must promise higher levels of return to be attractive. This approach, called **capital market estimation**, or risk premium, assumes that investors require additional return to compensate them for added risk. This additional return is known as the **risk premium**. The concept can be expressed mathematically as:

$$R_e = R_f + R_p$$

where
  R_e = The investors' required return on equity
  R_f = The return required from a hypothetical risk-free security
  R_p = The risk premium

There are several different ways to use this simple concept to estimate the cost of equity. We will discuss two methods: the stock-bond yield spread method and the capital asset pricing model.[34]

1. The Stock-Bond Yield Spread

This simple model estimates the cost of equity by means of two key variables: (1) the firm's marginal pretax cost of debt and (2) the historical difference between the firm's costs of debt and equity. Expressed mathematically,

$$R_e = R_d + (\overset{o}{R}_e - \overset{o}{R}_d)$$

where
  R_e = The required return on equity
  R_d = The required return (pretax) on debt, for instance, the yield to maturity on the firm's bonds
  o = Indicates historical data

We will demonstrate how it is used by calculating National Presto's shareholders' required return on equity. If National Presto's historical equity/debt

---

[34] There is another risk premium model called arbitrage pricing theory. This model relies on more factors as a source of return on a security, while the capital asset pricing model uses only "the market." This is a very interesting model but much more difficult to use in practice, thus we will not feature it here. The references at the end of this chapter will help you find information on this model if you are interested.

cost difference (the spread) has been 7.5 percent and the company's marginal required return on debt is 7.3 percent, we can calculate National Presto's shareholders' required return on equity in this way:[35]

$$R_e = R_d + (\overset{o}{R}_e - \overset{o}{R}_d)$$
$$= 7.3\% + 7.5\%$$
$$= 14.8\%$$

This percentage is well above the cost of equity we calculated with the cash flow discount model. These two methods usually do not yield the same results. If they do not, the difference in results may be because the historic difference between the yields of stocks and bonds is not always constant. Panel A of Exhibit 6-9 shows annual returns on the Standard & Poor's (S&P's) 500 Index and a high-grade corporate bond index. Panel B of this exhibit shows that the differences between stock and bond returns are not as constant as the stock-bond yield spread method implies. This approach provides a quick estimate, but it should not be used unless its results are to be verified by another method.

2. The Capital Asset Pricing Model

A simple adaptation would make the simple risk premium model more universal by adding a term denoting the difference between the average risk of all securities in the market and the risk of a particular security. This new equation would be as follows:

$$R_{ej} = R_f + X_j(R_m - R_f)$$

where
- j = Term to denote a particular company's stock[36]
- X = Measure of the risk for a stock
- R_m = The return required on an asset of average risk
- R_f = The return required on a hypothetical risk-free security

This formula could also be called the **relative risk premium model**, because it contains a factor, X, to indicate the relative risk of the particular security. Notice that in this formula only X_j changes; all other factors remain constant from asset to asset.

---

[35] National Presto has no debt, but if it sought debt, it would be a very high quality credit. Thus its cost of debt would be low relative to other industrial companies. In mid-1999 Aaa rated corporate debt, the highest rated, was yielding 7.3 percent. National Presto, with its large cash position protecting any lender, would command a very low debt rate.

[36] This could be for assets other than stock. However, in this chapter we will concentrate on using it for estimating the required return on equity.

258   Chapter 6   **The Required Rate of Return on Equity**

EXHIBIT 6-9   Realized Returns on Common Stock and Corporate Bonds (1926–1998)

Panel A: Returns on U.S. Corporate Bonds and Common Stocks

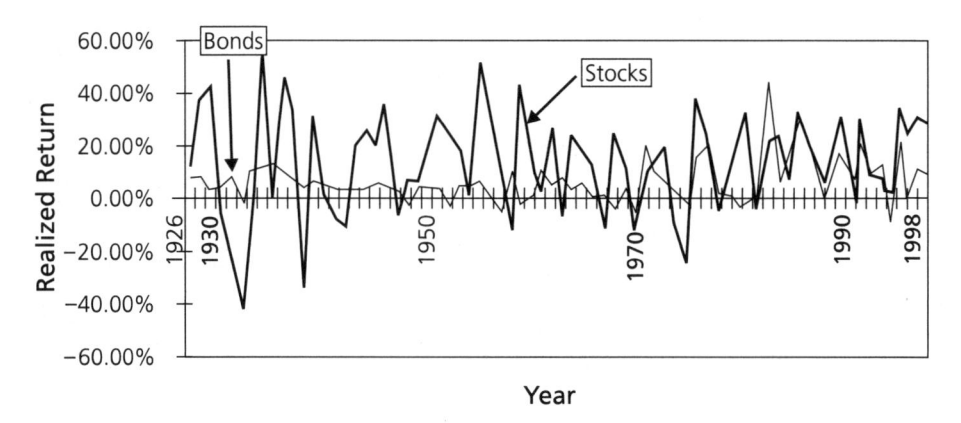

Panel B: Equity Risk Premium*

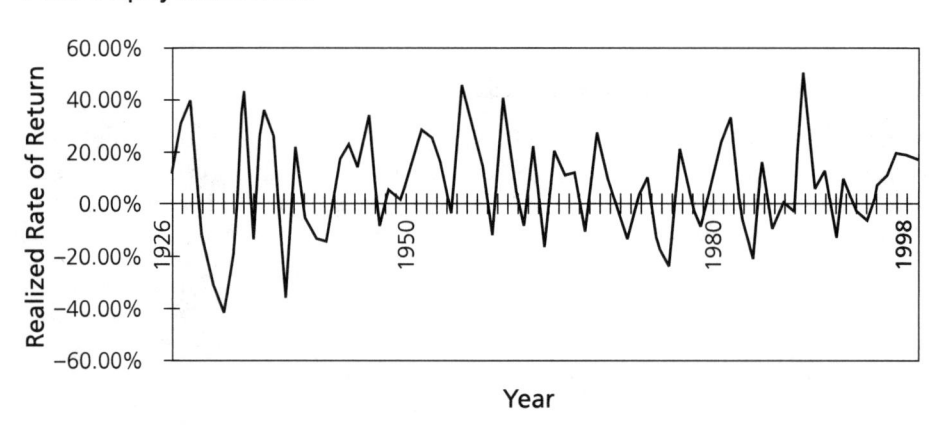

* Realized stock returns minus corporate bond returns.[37]

SOURCE: Data from Ibbotson Assoc., *Stocks, Bonds, Bills and Inflation: 1999 Yearbook.*

---

[37] We plotted the difference between the realized return for the large company stocks and corporate bonds. We could also have chosen to take the differences between the stocks and a U.S. government bond. The means and standard deviations of the two series are similar.

	Mean Realized Return	Standard Deviation
Stock – Corporate bonds	7.07%	19.69%
Stock – Government Bonds	7.49%	20.34%

The plots of the two are almost identical.

IV. Capital Market Estimations—Risk Premium Models

The capital asset pricing model (CAPM) is an adaptation of this basic relative risk premium approach. The model describes a particular relationship between risk and return. Exhibit 6-10 depicts this relationship. Since investors require a return for illiquidity, the line starts at R_f, the return required from a riskless security. The solid line represents the return required at each level of risk. This risk/return concept seems quite realistic: investors do expect greater rewards for taking greater risks, and the expected return for the common stock of any company is relative to its risk. However, in order to use this method, we must define and measure risk.

The CAPM is an attempt to make the relative risk premium model usable. In the CAPM, risk is defined as the covariance of a stock's returns with those of an asset of average risk. This definition is a bit different from the usual definition of risk as total variability. Covariance rests on a simple idea: it is not the total variability of the returns of each security that is important to the investor. Instead, what is important is how each security's variability contributes to the variability of the investor's total portfolio.[38] We could, for instance, place a security with cyclical returns (such as an automobile company's common stock) with a security whose returns are countercyclical (such as an automobile replacement parts manufacturer's common stock). Both of these stocks have risky returns. As shown in Exhibit 6-11, when the auto manufacturer is doing well, the replacement parts manufacturer is experiencing a slump. The reverse is also true: replacement parts sell when people defer new car purchases. As

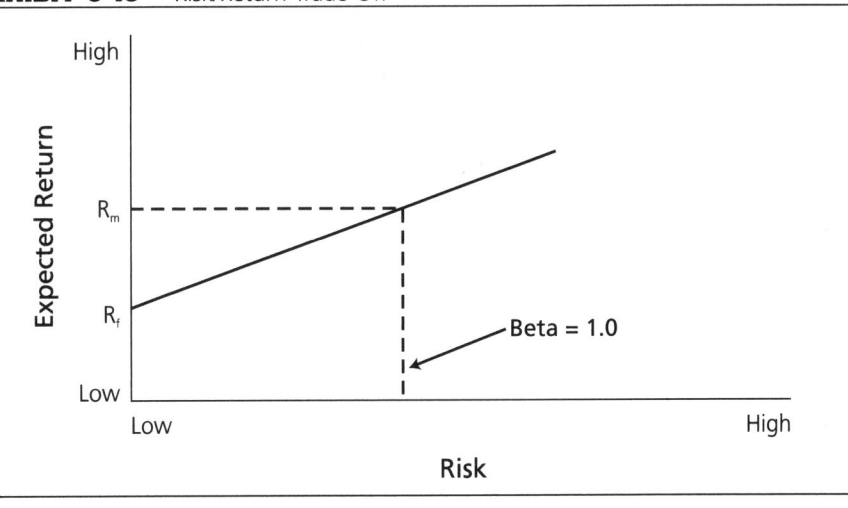

EXHIBIT 6-10 Risk/Return Trade-Off

---

[38] This is called portfolio risk, and comes from portfolio theory. Portfolio theory rests on the assumption that investors care about the risk of their portfolio, not the individual risks of the assets contained in the portfolio.

EXHIBIT 6-11 Two-Asset Portfolio Returns

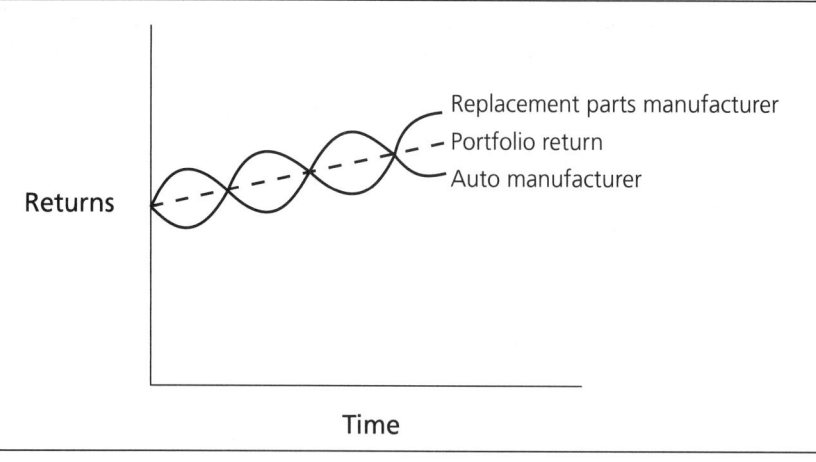

you can see, returns from the portfolio containing both stocks would be quite stable, that is, they would not be very risky according to the CAPM's definition of risk even though the returns from each are quite risky. Note our optimism about these stocks since we show the returns for both the companies growing, not diminishing, over time.

The only difference between the relative risk premium formula and the CAPM is that the CAPM defines risk as the covariability of stock returns with those of the average asset in the market. The relative risk premium model does not define risk. According to the CAPM,

$$R_{ej} = R_f + \beta_j(R_m - R_f)$$

where β_j stands for **beta**, a measure of the covariance between the total returns (dividends plus capital gains) of the asset market and those of company j's stock; all the other equation notation has been used before.

To estimate National Presto's cost of equity based on the CAPM approach, we must have estimates for the risk-free rate of return, the expected return on the average asset, and the covariability of the returns on National Presto's stock with those on the average asset, the beta. To use the CAPM, therefore, we need forecasts for R_f, R_m, and β.[39]

The Risk-Free Rate of Return. R_f stands for the risk-free rate of return. In theory, this return should entail no risk, none at all, not even the risk of a loss of purchasing power from the impact of inflation on prices. It is difficult to find

---

[39] Considerable controversy surrounds the theory and use of the CAPM. The reader should become familiar with the problems before becoming a frequent user. Since these problems are lengthy and complex, they are beyond the scope of this book.

a truly risk-free rate or even conjure one up. Thus most analysts choose a proxy that includes inflation. For investors in U.S. securities, the proxy probably would be a U.S. Treasury instrument, in particular a Treasury bond, that would be outstanding for a length of time equal to the life of the asset being evaluated.[40] Because equity securities have long lives, a longer term U.S. Treasury bond is a good choice. More precisely, since, as you can see in Exhibit 6-12, the typical U.S. Treasury yield curve has an upward slope to 7- to 10-year maturities and is rather flat thereafter, many analysts choose a U.S. Treasury bond with 7 to 10 years to maturity as an appropriate proxy.

EXHIBIT 6-12   U.S. Treasury Security Yield Curves

Panel A: The Yield Curves

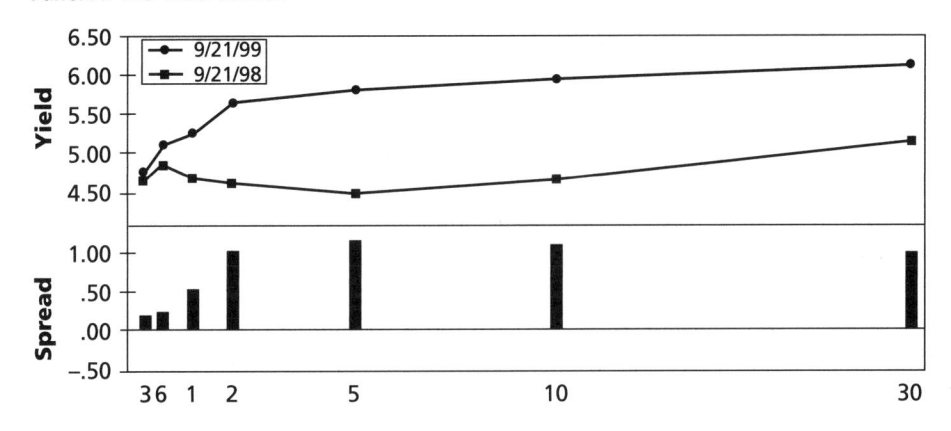

Panel B: The Yield Curve Data—September 21, 1999

Maturity	Yield
3 Months	4.784
6 Months	5.055
1 Year	5.237
2 Years	5.644
5 Years	5.809
10 Years	5.929
30 Years	6.092

SOURCE: Reprinted by permission of *Bloomberg Magazine*, June 2000.

---

[40] There are those who argue that we should use the shortest term Treasury bill here since it includes the least risk. However, in this chapter we bundle the capital markets' estimate of the return required for the lowest risk instruments we can find in the United States, Treasury instruments, with the market's estimate for inflation over the life the investment will be outstanding. Only for investments lasting 30 days or less should something like the 30-day Treasury bill rate be used as the risk-free rate.

There are a number of problems that the analyst faces in choosing and using U.S. Treasury securities as a proxy for the risk-free rate. First, rates change, and sometimes rather rapidly. You can see the kind of change that took place from September 1998 to one year later. By the way, the September 1999 yield curve had the more normal shape.

A second problem is that rates can be unusual. For example, rates might reflect high short-term inflation forecasts or unusual demand or supply imbalances. Exhibit 6-13 shows an unusual yield curve.

A U.S. Treasury bond is priced by the capital markets so that the rate will compensate the investor for the time value of money, the real rate of return, generally thought to be about 2.5 percent, and a return to compensate for U.S.-domestic inflation. Assets in other countries must return enough to compensate for the domestic inflation rate in those countries. Thus, when estimating the return required to invest in non-U.S. assets, including stock, a more appropriate risk-free proxy must be chosen.[41] Choosing the wrong proxy can make quite a difference. Exhibit 6-14 shows yield curves for the U.S. Treasury, Japanese government, and the EURO. Here you can see why there is real interest in the level of Japanese interest rates.

At the time of the data in Exhibit 6-12, a reasonable risk-free rate would have been that for the 10-year bond, a rate of 5.929 percent.[42]

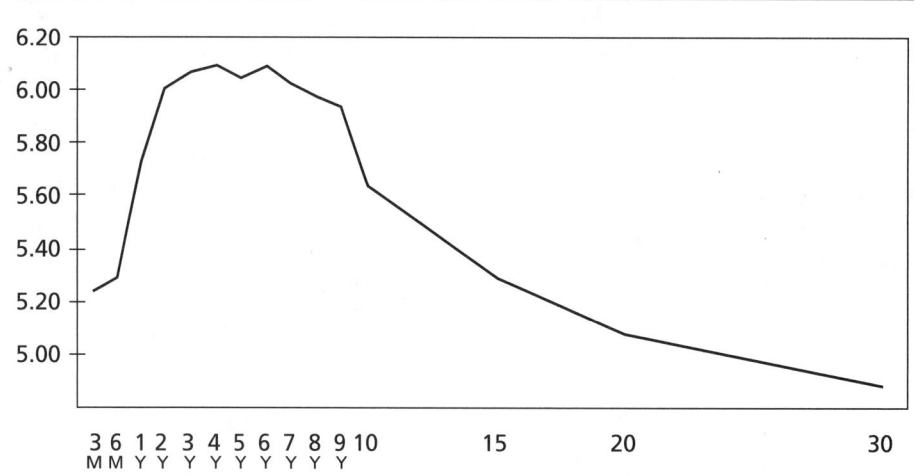

EXHIBIT 6-13 Benchmark United Kingdom Government Yield Curve

SOURCE: Reprinted by permission of *Bloomberg Magazine*, June 2000.

---

[41] Some analysts use the U.S. Treasury rate and adjust it for the inflation difference between the United States and the home country of the asset. This differential inflation method rests on the exchange rate theory discussed in Chapter 2.

[42] In 1999, the U.S. Treasury began reducing its debt at the longest maturities. This, plus the fact that the typical yield curve flattens at about 10 years, suggests that the 10-year yield is a good choice.

IV. Capital Market Estimations—Risk Premium Models 263

EXHIBIT 6-14 Government Rates, Various Countries

[Chart showing yields vs maturity (3MM, 6MM, 1Y-10Y, 15, 20, 30 years) for U.S. Treasury, Euro Benchmark Curve, and Japanese Government bonds. Yields range from -2.00 to 8.00.]

SOURCE: Reprinted by permission of *Bloomberg Magazine*, June 2000.

The Market Rate of Return. The risk-free rate is difficult to estimate and the market return is no easier. Before you stop here and decide all this is just too difficult, remember that we have the same problem whenever we make a forecast. Instead of avoidance, practice and knowledge bring skill and confidence.

The R_m in the CAPM is the expected return on an asset of average risk. Analysts have used two ways to determine the average expected return on the market average. One is a variation of the risk premium approach: the long-term historical return on the risk-free asset is subtracted from the historical return on a proxy for all assets.[43] In the United States, analysts have often used data like that shown in Exhibit 6-15 to estimate the premium. At year-end 1998, the 72-year return on the U.S. large capitalization stocks was 13.2 percent and the premium of U.S. equities above U.S. Treasury bonds was 7.5 percent.[44]

Instead of using the data from 1926 to 1998, you might choose to customize your forecast by choosing the period in the past that is most like what you would expect in the future. For instance, if we believe that the next 20 years will

---

[43] Equities are used as a proxy for the average risk asset because, if you consider all possible investments that an investor can make, equities are rather average in risk.

[44] There is considerable controversy over what is the right period of history to use as a proxy for the future. Some argue that a period longer than 40 years should be used and, because the data are easily available, they use data from 1926 to the present. Some choose to exclude the period from 1926–1950. They do so because of the market turmoil that occurred from 1929–1935 and the fact that rates were government set during the period of the Second World War. Still others choose a period of history as much like the future they foresee as possible. Finally, some argue that realized returns, however long term, are not a good proxy for expectations.

EXHIBIT 6-15 Basic Series: Summary Statistics of Annual Returns (1926–1998)[45]

Series	Geometric Mean	Arithmetic Mean	Standard Mean	Distribution
Large Company Stocks	11.2%	13.2%	20.3%	
Small Company Stocks	12.4	17.4	33.8	
Long-Term Corporate Bonds	5.8	6.1	8.6	
Long-Term Government Bonds	5.3	5.7	9.2	
Intermediate-Term Government	5.3	5.5	5.7	
U.S. Treasury Bills	3.8	3.8	3.2	
Inflation	3.1	3.2	4.5	
				−90% 0% 90%

SOURCE: *Stocks, Bonds, Bills and Inflation*® *1999 Yearbook*, ©2000 Ibbotson Associates, Inc. Based on copyrighted works by Ibbotson and Sinquefield. All rights reserved. Used with permission.

be like the last 15, we will have a market boom. Over the past 15 years, the large capitalization stocks returned 14.75 percent and the premium was 8.4 percent. The data is available to make your own calculations.

Analysts also use an estimate of the expected market premium. This estimate may come from information derived from security analysts working in money management companies whose job it is to make forecasts for individual stocks. Putting all their forecasts together produces a consensus estimate of the expected U.S. stock market return.[46]

For our analysis of the National Presto shareholders' required return, we will use the 72-year average premium of 7.5 percent.

The Risk – Beta. The beta is a measure of the asset or stock's risk relative to that of the market. We might forecast this sensitivity to changes in things that impact the market returns, such as changes in interest rates and GDP. However, our most direct approach is to go first to history to develop our forecast for beta.

---

[45] This data begins in 1926 and has not been calculated by this source to extend further into the past.

[46] The analyst forecasts and the historic returns can be quite different. For instance, in late 1991 when historic data would have shown a long-term average market return of 12.1, one group of analysts forecasted a long-term rate of return for U.S. equities of 14 percent.

IV. Capital Market Estimations—Risk Premium Models

To use history, the typical method of estimating a beta is to use a version of the simple linear regression and the monthly total rates of return for the stock and for an index like the S&P 500:

$$R_j - R_f = a_j + \beta_j(R_m - R_f) + e_j$$

where
- a = The intercept of the linear regression
- β = The slope of the line
- e = The errors that occur because the fit of the line to the data is not perfect
- j = The designated stock or portfolio

The regression for National Presto's stock is shown in Exhibit 6-16. Each dot shown on the graph represents the returns for National Presto and the Standard and Poor's 500 for one period, here a month.[47] The line is one that

EXHIBIT 6-16 National Presto and Standard & Poor's 500 Security Characteristic Line

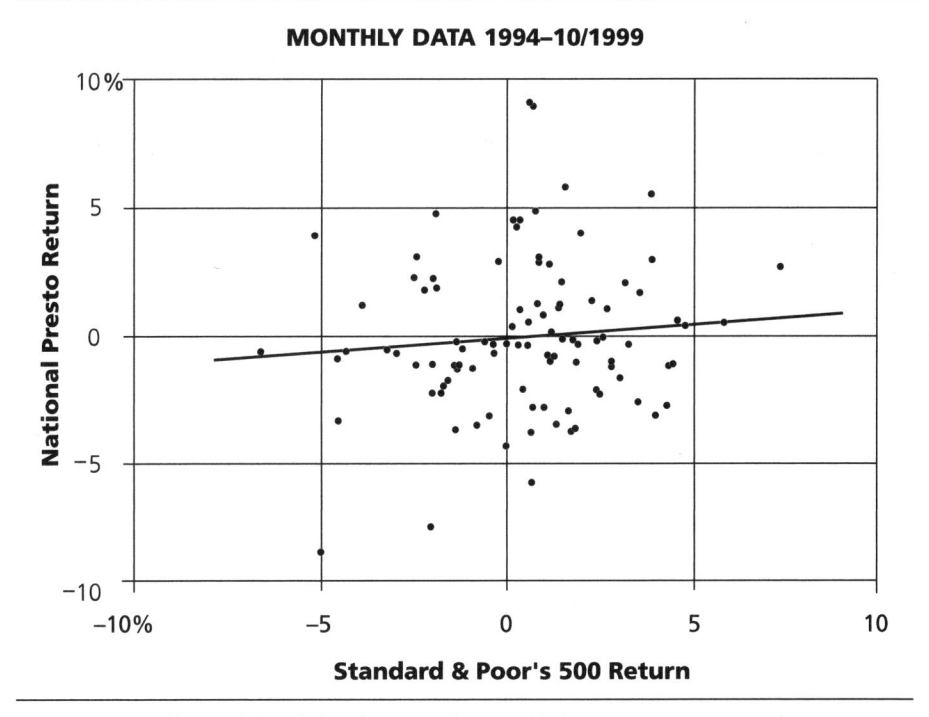

MONTHLY DATA 1994–10/1999

[Scatter plot with National Presto Return on y-axis (-10 to 10%) and Standard & Poor's 500 Return on x-axis (-10% to 10), showing regression line with slight positive slope]

SOURCE: Reprinted by permission of *Bloomberg Magazine*, June 2000.

---

[47] For those of you with such an interest, the regression statistics are shown below. For those of you seeing this for the first time, the mystery of regression can be deciphered in many of the readings listed at the end of this chapter.

Y = –0.08 + 0.44x, with an R^2 (a measure of fit) of 0.02.

minimizes the distance of the dots from the line, and is called the **security characteristic line**.[48] The beta is 0.44 from this regression. Most sources adapt betas for known problems with regression and changing risk. A beta of 0.44 is quite low.

As any financial analyst knows, however, using history as a predictor for the future is dangerous. The danger is no less here than elsewhere. Thus, even when you calculate a historical beta, it is only a guideline for what the beta might be in the future. Several companies calculate and publish betas for a number of publicly traded U.S. common equities. Standard and Poor's *Industry Survey* and Value Line's *Investment Reports* are two sources that are widely available.[49] In addition, many money management companies estimate and sell proprietary versions.

3. Using the CAPM

To demonstrate how the analyst might use the model, we will use 5.9 percent as the current yield on a 10-year U.S. Treasury bond for R_f, and 7.5 percent as the historical arithmetic return premium of equities over long-term U.S. government bonds for R_m. For the covariability, or risk, of National Presto's returns, the beta, we will use 0.60, an estimate based on the historical relationship of National Presto's returns with those of the S&P 500, adjusted by industry analysts for changes anticipated in the systematic risk of the company.[50] Using these estimates, we can calculate National Presto's required return on equity as follows:

$$R_{ej} = R_f + \beta_j(R_m - R_f)$$
$$R_{Presto} = 5.9\% + 0.60 \times (7.5\%)$$
$$= 10.4\%$$

The CAPM provides a result that is identical to those of the other methods in this case. This is not always true. For the most part, the various models will give consistent answers when the company is relatively mature, and the inputs are reasonably forecastable. Whenever you estimate a required return on equity you would be wise to use several approaches to corroborate any cost of equity estimate, and discover the sources of any serious differences. Usually, the differences stem from differences in the fundamental estimates for future growth or the company's systematic risk.

---

[48] Many beta graphs show three lines. The other two lines show one standard error, similar to the one standard deviation. The wider the lines around the center line, the less reliable is the placement of the line, and thus the beta estimate.

[49] Betas are available from sources such as those listed at the end of the chapter.

[50] Systematic risk is the risk relative to the market, not risk specific to the company. Specific risks are also called unsystematic risks.

V. OTHER CONCERNS IN DETERMINING REQUIRED RETURN ON EQUITY

1. New Equity Issues

When a firm issues new equity, it incurs additional expenses that we have not yet discussed. The firm issuing new equity must register the issue with a regulatory body such as the U.S. Securities and Exchange Commission, and the firm must rely on the advice of lawyers, accountants, and underwriters to do so. In addition to registering the stock, the underwriter usually buys the issue from the firm, thus guaranteeing its sale. The underwriter then resells the stock to the public—for a fee.[51] The average cost of these services can range from 4 to 15 percent of the equity issue, depending on the size of the company, the amount of stock to be issued, and the underwriter's confidence that the firm's stock will sell quickly.

We can demonstrate how to calculate the required return on newly issued equity. To make it, we will use the perpetuity version of the dividend-discount method. For our example, the long version makes it harder to see the impact of new issue costs. For example, if we were a small regional company with a current stock price of $15.00, paying an annual dividend of $0.40 per share and anticipating a growth of 14 percent per year, our required return on equity would be 16.7 percent. However, if the cost of issuing new stock were 8 percent, the return we would have to earn on this newly issued capital would be:

$$R_{ej} = \frac{D_1}{MP_o(1-N)} + g$$

$$R_e = \frac{\$0.40}{\$15.00(1-0.08)} + 0.14$$

$$= \frac{\$0.40}{\$13.80} + 0.14$$

$$= 0.029 + 0.14$$

$$= 0.169 \text{ or } 16.9\%$$

2. Cost of Retained Earnings

Each year a company can generate net income after taxes and dividends. This is called retained earnings, and is added to the retained earnings balance in the equity section of the balance sheet. Managers may use the new retained earnings funds to increase the firm's assets (a change in the assets) or to reduce its debt (a change in the liabilities), or the funds may be held temporarily in cash or marketable securities (an asset change). Some managers consider retained

---

[51] For a smaller fee, the underwriter may make a "best efforts" to sell the stocks or bonds. In a "best efforts" sale, the underwriter does not guarantee the sale of the securities.

earnings to be "free" funds, but that is certainly not true from the shareholders' point of view. If managers had returned the funds to the shareholders, the shareholders could have invested the funds. Thus retained earnings must generate a fair return.

In exchange for this **opportunity cost**, shareholders expect retained earnings to create value for them. Thus the return required on retained earnings is the same as the return that the manager must earn on equity investments.

3. Preferred Stock

Preferred stock presents special analytical problems because preferred stock is a cross between debt and equity. Like debt, preferred stock offers a fixed payment—fixed dividends. In bankruptcy, preferred shareholders take precedence over common shareholders. However, if preferred dividends are not paid, the firm cannot be forced into bankruptcy, as it may be if it fails to pay the interest on debt. For investors, owning preferred equity is somewhat less risky than holding common stock and more risky than being a lender. Preferred stock is also unlike debt in that the firm does not repay the investment.

Keeping these things in mind, we can calculate the return required by preferred stockholders as follows:

$$R_p = \frac{PD}{PP_o}$$

where
PD = Preferred dividend[52]
PP_o = Preferred stock price
R_p = The return required on preferred stock

This analysis of the required return by preferred shareholders is applicable only to preferred stock, not stock that is convertible into any other security. Convertible preferred stock, typically convertible into common stock, is a security that has some of the characteristics of debt and some of equity's characteristics. Therefore, a convertible security is more complex to analyze than ordinary preferred stock. Knowledge of option theory and practice is necessary. A simple introduction to options was discussed in Chapter 4 and extended in Appendix 4A.

VI. REQUIRED RETURN ON EQUITY FOR PRIVATE, NON-U.S., OR COMPANIES EXPERIENCING CHANGE

The analysis we have performed thus far was for National Presto, a U.S. company that is traded on the NYSE, the largest stock exchange in the world.

---

[52] There is no tax adjustment because preferred dividends are not a tax-deductible expense for companies in the United States and many other parts of the world. The tax deductibility is dependent upon the tax laws in the particular country where the company operates.

Considerable data are available for such companies, and there are stock analysts whose job it is to know as much about public companies as possible. Much of the writing about how to use the methods was based on the U.S. market and meant for students and practitioners in the United States. The models are equally applicable to any company, however, whether it is public or private, operates in a developed or developing country, or is stable or undergoing considerable change. The adaptations are simple, but rely on the analyst's skill:

1. *Beta.* Instead of relying on history, you must use judgment about what the beta will be: you must understand that the magnitude of the beta depends on the company's sensitivity to changes in factors that, to a greater or lesser degree, negatively or positively affect the returns from all assets worldwide.[53] Examples of such factors are inflation, worldwide industrial production growth, GDP changes, and investors' propensity to take risk. Companies that are highly sensitive to changes in these factors will have a higher than average beta. Those that are insulated from the impact of changes in these factors will have lower than average betas. Since beta is an index, the average beta is 1.0, and most betas are from 0.5 to 1.8.

2. *Market and risk-free rates of return.* For companies outside the United States returns for the market and risk-free rate must be changed from the U.S.-only rates. The nominal risk-free rate for companies operating in other countries must include the forecast for that country's inflation. The market return, the return on average assets also must be adapted for that economy. More and more we are developing a global CAPM, one that is usable for all assets, and adapted for differences in inflation and sensitivity of a domestic economy to global changes.[54] It is with non-U.S. and private companies, as well as companies undergoing significant changes, that the analyst has the biggest challenge.

To estimate the required return on equity for all companies requires ingenuity and judgment. For private and non-U.S. companies the ingenuity and judgment may be more than most analysts are used to exercising. However, with experience in estimating required return on equity, an analyst will gain skill in dealing with more varied situations where information is not available, and where an analyst's judgment is critical.

---

[53] Actually, all betas are the analysts' forecast for the future sensitivity of the company's returns to changes in those of the market. In turning to history to help us forecast, often we think that it is the only approach to estimating a beta. It is not.

[54] You might think of the local market return as a combination of the return expected on the average global asset, adapted for the sensitivity of the local market to global changes. Thus countries that are relatively insulated from changes in such things as inflation, those that have diverse economies, might be less sensitive than the average, while countries that suffer from global changes, for example, raw material/commodity exporters, might be more sensitive.

VII. SUMMARY

In this chapter we looked at what returns shareholders expect to earn on their investments. We call this return the required return on equity or the company's cost of equity. The models used to estimate what investors require are attempts to replicate the methods investors themselves are using to price an equity security. These models can be used with publicly traded companies for which there are considerable data, or they can be applied, using proxies or analogy, to companies that are privately held or are in small or developing markets.

Each of the required return on equity models we have described and used has analyst judgment as its major ingredient. If the results are approximately the same from these models, the analyst can have more confidence in his or her estimate. However, if each method results in a very different required return on equity, the analyst must think carefully about the source of the variations. The analyst's choice of data from model to model may be inconsistent; the forecasts may be optimistic or pessimistic; or the shareholders' concept of future returns may be quite different from that of the analyst. To be secure in a forecast the analyst should use more than one model and corroborate the forecasts, remembering that the purpose of all these forecasts and calculations is to capture the shareholder's expectations of future returns, not the analyst's or management's hopes and beliefs.

The required return on equity is the rate that is used to discount the cash flows to equity shareholders, the owners of the company. In many companies, however, the shareholders have chosen to share their financing obligation with others, especially with those investing in debt instruments. What happens to the company's required return when the shareholders share their rights and obligations with lenders is the subject of Chapter 7.

SELECTED REFERENCES

For information on equity markets, see:

Ball, Ray. "The Theory of Stock Market Efficiency: Accomplishments and Limitations Values." *Journal of Applied Corporate Finance*, Spring 1995, pp. 4–17.

Bodie, Zvi, Alex Kane, and Alan Marcus. *Investments.* 4th ed. Boston, MA: Irwin/McGraw-Hill, 1999, chaps. 2 and 3.

Ibbotson, Roger G., and Gary P. Brinson. *Investment Markets.* New York: McGraw-Hill, 1987, part 2.

Malkiel, Bernard. *A Random Walk Down Wall Street.* 5th ed. New York: W. W. Norton & Co., 1990.

Teweles, Richard, and Edward Bradley. *The Stock Market.* 7th ed. New York: John Wiley & Sons, 1998.

Selected References

For information about equity valuation methods, see:

Bodie, Zvi, Alex Kane, and Alan Marcus. *Investments.* 4th ed. Boston, MA: Irwin/McGraw-Hill, 1999, chaps. 18 and 19.

Bodie, Zvi, and Robert Merton. *Finance.* Upper Saddle River, NJ: Prentice Hall, 2000, chap. 9.

Brealey, Richard A., and Stewart C. Myers. *Principles of Corporate Finance.* 5th ed. New York: McGraw-Hill, 1996, chap. 4.

Brigham, Eugene F., Louis C. Gapenski, and Michael Ehrhardt. *Financial Management.* 9th ed. Fort Worth, Texas: The Dryden Press, 1999, chap. 9.

Ross, Stephen A., Randolph W. Westerfield, and Jeffrey F. Jaffe. *Corporate Finance.* 4th ed. Homewood, Ill.: Richard D. Irwin, 1996, chap. 5.

Woolridge, J. Randall. "Do Stock Prices Reflect Fundamental Values?" *Journal of Applied Corporate Finance*, Spring 1995, pp. 64–69 and 102.

For more on warrants and convertible securities, see:

Brigham, Eugene F., Louis C. Gapenski, and Michael Ehrhardt. *Financial Management.* 9th ed. Fort Worth, Texas: The Dryden Press, 1999, chap. 20.

For general information about the stock market, see:

Fogler, H. Russell, Frank Fabozzi, and Diana Harrington. *Analyzing the Stock Market.* 2nd ed. Chicago: Probus Publishing, 1988.

Levy, Haim. *Introduction to Investments.* 2nd ed. Cincinnati, OH: South-Western College Publishing, 1999.

Sharpe, William F., Gordon J. Alexander, and Jeffery V. Bailey. *Investments.* 5th ed. Englewood Cliffs, NJ: Prentice Hall, 1995.

Teweles, Richard, and Edward Bradley. *The Stock Market.* New York: John Wiley & Sons, 1998.

For those with a further interest in the capital asset pricing model and discounted cash flow methods of equity valuation, see:

Harrington, Diana R. *Modern Portfolio Theory, The Capital Asset Pricing Model and Arbitrage Pricing Theory: A Users Guide.* 2nd ed. Englewood Cliffs, NJ: Prentice Hall, 1987.

Kothari, S.P., and Jay Shanken. "In Defense of Beta." *Journal of Applied Corporate Finance*, Spring 1995, pp. 53–58.

For historical data from the stock and bond markets and information about comparable firms, see:

Arnold Bernhard & Co., Inc. *Value Line Investment Survey.*

Dun & Bradstreet, *Key Business Ratios.*

Ibbotson Associates. *Stocks, Bonds, Bills and Inflation, 1999 Yearbook.*

Robert Morris Associates, *Annual Statement Studies.*

For information on estimating the risk premium, see:

Harrington, Diana R. *Modern Portfolio Theory, The Capital Asset Pricing Model and Arbitrage Pricing Theory: A Users Guide.* 2nd ed. Englewood Cliffs, NJ: Prentice Hall, 1987.

Sharpe, William, and Katrina Sherrerd. *Quantifying the Market Risk Premium Phenomenon for Investment Decision Making.* Charlottesville, VA: Institute of Chartered Financial Analysts, 1989.

For the basics on arbitrage pricing theory, see:

Bodie, Zvi, Alex Kane, and Alan Marcus. *Investments.* 4th ed. Boston, MA: Irwin/McGraw-Hill, 1999, chap. 11.

Bodie, Zvi, and Robert Merton. *Finance.* Upper Saddle River, NJ: Prentice Hall, 2000, chap. 13.

Brigham, Eugene F., Louis C. Gapenski, and Michael Ehrhardt. *Financial Management.* 9th ed. Fort Worth, Texas: The Dryden Press, 1999, chap. 6.

Damodaran, Aswath. *Corporate Finance.* New York: John Wiley & Sons, 1997, chap. 6.

Web sites of note:

Historic interest rates from the St. Louis Federal Reserve Bank: www.stls.frb.org

International interest rates from the Federal Reserve Bank: www.bog.frb.fed.us

Interest rates and other market data: www.bloomberg.com and www.ny.frb.org

LIBOR rates can be found at www.kuhlmann.com, a site operated by Kuhlmann Commercial capital.

The following web sites are of interest to investors, and have price charts and fundamental information:

www.financialweb.com/rapidresearch

www.moneycentral.msn.com

www.wisi.com

www.bunkerco.com

www.bigcharts.com

www.thomsoninvest.net

STUDY QUESTIONS

1. Bakelite Company is a commercial bakery specializing in biscuit making that is located in rural Ohio. Recent substantial declines in grain prices have resulted in significant raw material savings. Since prices do not need to be cut, because Bakelite is already at the low-priced end of the market, cash reserves have built up well beyond historical levels. This wealth of cash spurs management, with the support of the board, to consider some capital investments they have long deferred. The various division heads have been asked to propose capital investments to Carl Borg, vice president of finance. Mr. Borg has the job of evaluating the projects and making recommendations to the board. Because it has been years since Bakelite made any significant investments, Mr. Borg is concerned about choosing the right ones. To get some advice about making these decisions, he calls an old college friend, Jane Wilson, now a finance professor at a nearby university. Professor Wilson says that, since Mr. Borg already has cash flow forecasts from the divisions, the only thing left to be done is to discount the flows at the appropriate discount rate.

   Bakelite is too small a company to be followed by investment services like *Value Line*. However, a regional investment banker has just published a brief report on the company. It includes the following information: Bakelite's beta is 1.32 and the analyst's estimate for Bakelite's nominal long-term growth in dividends is 4.9 percent, a figure with which management agrees. The company recently paid a $2.86 dividend, and its current market price in the over-the-counter market is $25. At present, U.S. Treasury 10-year bonds are yielding 8.9 percent and 90-day Treasury bills are yielding 6.5 percent. Historically, the stock market has yielded about 8.5 percent above Treasury bills and 6 percent above longer term Treasury bonds. Its taxes are 34 percent. Bakelite's balance sheet is shown below.

BAKELITE CORPORATION
(in millions)

Assets		Liabilities and Equity	
Cash	$0.2	Accounts payable	$1.4
Marketable securities	2.3	Taxes payable	0.3
Accounts receivable	1.1	Total current liabilities	1.7
Total current assets	3.6	Common stock	1.2
Net property, plant, and equipment	1.2	Retained earnings	1.9
		Total equity	3.1
Total assets	$4.8	Total liabilities and equity	$4.8

What is Bakelite's owners' required return on equity, using:
a. the dividend-discount model, where g = (1 − Payout)(Return on equity)?
b. the capital asset pricing model?

2. Kelly Services is one of the largest U.S. providers of temporary personnel for large companies. The temporary help business has been suffering from contract-building practices and the U.S. expansion: the tight labor economy has resulted in more permanent employment. In spite of this, the company's growth has been a relatively steady 4.2 percent. With U.S. Treasury 10-year bonds yielding 6.3 percent and 90-day Treasury bills yielding 3.8 percent (on average 8.9 percent below the U.S. stock market), what is Kelly's cost of equity? The company pays a $3.00 dividend per year; its stock price is $36.00; and *Value Line* reports a beta of 0.95.

3. The Grupo Mercado Tropical management was considering purchasing Hannaford Bros., a chain of U.S. grocers. The "Grupo," a Mexican company, currently owns chains of stores in Central America, Mexico, and several of the Caribbean islands. For some time it has been considering opening markets in the increasingly Hispanic northeast part of the United States. Purchasing Hannaford might be a good way to gain a foothold in this market, without having to start from scratch. Already many small bodegas were operating in many of Hannaford's areas, and local grocery chains, including Hannaford, were carrying increasing amounts of fresh and dry goods catering to this rapidly growing market. Management has asked you to review the material you already have on Hannaford (Chapter 1) and, using the information below, determine what required return on equity Grupo management should use in valuing Hannaford's cash flows.

Mexican Treasury bonds	22.5%
Mexican inflation	17.0
U.S. 10-year Treasury bonds	6.0
U.S. inflation	1.8
72-year U.S. stock market premium over U.S. Treasury bonds	7.5%
Beta:	
Grupo Mercado Tropical	1.84
Hannaford	1.02

Grupo Mercado Tropical growth rates:

Revenues	18%
Net income	21
Cash flows	23
Dividends	None

CHAPTER 7
Obtaining Outside Capital

In Chapter 6 we learned how to estimate the fair return that should be expected for an equity investment. We found that all investors require a return for:

1. *Illiquidity*: The time that money is invested and out of the investor's control.
2. *Inflation*: Losses caused by changes in the purchasing power of money.
3. *Risk*: The chance that the returns from an investment may be higher or lower than was expected.

In Chapter 6 we used the following formula to determine this required return:

Required return = Risk-free rate + Inflation premium + Risk premium

In the example we used the rate from a U.S. Treasury security as an estimate of the return required for both the time value of money and inflation for U.S. investors. As for risk, we know that investors expect more return for increased risk, and we asked capital market experts what they believed was a fair return for risk, their so-called **market price of risk**. Notice that, up to this point, we have assumed that all our investments have been financed by the owners of the company alone. However, we know that companies rarely are financed by the owners, the shareholders, alone. Many of these owners/shareholders, or the managers on their behalf, subcontract some of their financing obligations to others, especially those who prefer their investments to have predetermined repayments and want the owners to pay "rent" for the use of the money. These financing subcontractors are called **lenders**, the investment is called **principal**, and the annual rent is called **interest**. In Chapter 6 we used a variety of methods to estimate the investors' required return on equity (the company's cost of equity capital) for National Presto Industries, Inc. National Presto's balance sheets indicated that its shareholders have chosen not to subcontract their financing responsibilities to lenders. While debt has not played a role in the financing of National Presto, for most other companies the lenders provide an important portion of a company's capital, and shareholders benefit from their role.

How do shareholders, or managers on their behalf, decide if they want to use debt in financing their company? The answer is, if subcontracting increases the shareholders' value, they will subcontract to lenders. However, if it makes no difference at all in the value of the shareholders' position, then they can subcontract or not, it really does not matter. The heart of the matter is, can subcontracting to lenders create value for the shareholders? Once we answer that question, we can deal with the problem of how much debt a company should have.

Let us start with two things that we know. First, shareholders want managers to create value for them. Second, to create value, managers must make decisions that will increase the present value of the company by either reducing risk, increasing cash flow, or both. Keeping the shareholders' objectives in mind, let us see if financing the corporation with some mixture of debt and equity can actually make the company worth more than financing it without the debt.

I. THE VALUE OF LEVERAGE

To decide whether a particular capital structure can enhance shareholders' value, let's look at Greenway Corporation. Greenway currently has no debt and is located in a country where interest is *not* tax-deductible. Greenway's cash flows and their value are shown in Exhibit 7-1.

In Column 1 of Exhibit 7-1 you can see that the residual cash flow is $10.00. It is $1.00 per share. Discounted at the shareholders' required return, the company's market value, or the shareholders' value, is $66.67 million, or $6.67 per share.

Now let's see what happens when Greenway borrows enough to repurchase 10 percent of its equity. The impact of the borrowing is shown in Column 2. As you can see, if debt is not tax-deductible, the value of the company does not change—the risk and return of the company remains unchanged as debt is added.[1] However, the company's cash flows, because of the lenders' contract, belong first to the lenders: the company must pay the lenders $0.67, 10 percent on borrowed capital. Now that lenders come before shareholders, the remaining nine shareholders find themselves in a somewhat riskier situation. Thus they require a higher return now that their risk has increased. With an increase in the required return, the shareholders' total value declines to $60.0 million, but on a per-share basis it is still $6.67 per share.

Notice that the 15 percent return required for the whole company stays the same whether or not there is debt in the capital structure. To determine the required return expected for the whole company, we take the average of the returns required by capital providers. The process for calculating this average, or **weighted-average cost of capital**, for a company is as follows.[2]

---

[1] Note that we said value of the company, not the portion of the value that comes to each group. The company's value depends upon the company's cash flow and risk. The lenders' or shareholders' portion of the value depends upon cash flows and risks that have been assigned to them. Clearly their risk and return change with changes in leverage.

[2] This average is described fully in Appendix 7A.

I. The Value of Leverage

EXHIBIT 7-1 Greenway Corporation Earnings, Cash Flow, and Value—No Tax Deduction for Interest Expense (in millions, except per-share data)

	100% Equity Financed	10% Debt/Capital (Equity Cost 15.55%)
Profit before taxes	$15.00	$15.00
Taxes	(5.00)	(5.00)
Profit after taxes	10.00	10.00
Depreciation	5.00	5.00
New plant and equipment	(5.00)	(5.00)
Added working capital	0.00	0.00
Cash flow to all capital providers	$10.00	$10.00
Number of shares outstanding	10	9
Interest expense	0	$0.67
Cash flow available for shareholders	$10.00	$9.33
Book value of firm*	$66.67	$66.67
Required return on debt (interest)	10.00%	10.00%
Book value of debt	0	$6.67
Book value of equity	$66.67	$60.00
Return on book equity	15.00%	15.55%
Required return on equity	15.00%	15.55%
Future growth	0	0
Equity market value*	$66.67	$60.00
Equity market value per share	$6.67	$6.67
Company total market value†	$66.67	$66.67

* Total market value calculated using the nongrowth perpetuity method of valuation described in previous chapters:

$$\text{Value of company} = \sum \frac{\text{Residual cash flows}_n}{(\text{Required return} - \text{Residual cash flow growth})^n}$$

$$\$66.67 = \frac{\$10.00}{(0.15 - 0)}$$

† The market value of the total firm also can be calculated as the sum of the value of the equity and debt, $66.67.

$$\begin{aligned}\text{Weighted-average} \\ \text{cost of capital}\end{aligned} = \begin{aligned}&[(\text{Cost of debt} \times (1 - \text{Tax rate})) \times \text{Debt proportion}] + \\ &[\text{Cost of equity} \times \text{Proportion of equity}]\end{aligned}$$

$$= [(0.10 \times (1 - 0)) \times 0.10] + [0.1555 \times 0.90]$$

$$= 0.15 \text{ or } 15\%$$

In Exhibit 7-1 it is clear that the company itself does not change as lenders enter the picture, the only change is who gets what. The risk and return is traded among the lenders and shareholders, so their positions do change as risk increases. Recognizing this, shareholders require more for taking the increased risk as lenders increase their role. Exhibit 7-2 illustrates, more dramat-

EXHIBIT 7-2 Greenway Corporation Forecasted Earnings and Cash Flows

THREE OUTCOMES WITH AND WITHOUT LEVERAGE (dollars in millions)

	Net Income and Cash Flow		
Without Leverage	Lower	Original	Higher
Net income and cash flow to:			
All capital providers	$3.30	$10.00	$16.67
Shareholders	3.30	10.00	16.67
Book value of company	66.67	66.67	66.67
Book value of equity	66.67	66.67	66.67
Required return on debt	10.00%	10.00%	10.00%
Interest on debt	0	0	0
Book value of debt	$0.00	$0.00	$0.00
Required return on equity	15%	15%	15%
Return on book equity	4.95%	15.00%	24.75%
Market value of equity	$22.00	$66.67	$111.10
Number of shares	10	10	10
Market value of equity per share	$2.20	$6.67	$11.11
Change from original	−67%	NA	+67%
With Leverage: 10% Debt/Total Capital			
Net income and cash flow to:			
All capital providers	$3.33	$10.00	$16.67
Shareholders	$2.67	$9.33	$16.00
Book value of company	66.67	66.67	66.67
Book value of equity	60.00	60.00	60.00
Interest on debt	$0.67	$0.67	$0.67
Book value of debt	$6.67	$6.67	$6.67
Required return on equity	15.55%	15.55%	15.55%
Return on book equity	4.44%	15.55%	26.66%
Market value of equity	$17.15	$60.01	$102.88
Number of shares	9	9	9
Market value of equity per share	$1.91	$6.67	$11.43
Change from original	−71%	NA	+71%

ically, why the shareholders' return requirements increase with increased leverage. The exhibit shows the shareholders' returns (ROE) as the company's earnings change from those originally forecasted in Exhibit 7-1 to those earned under other circumstances. Without leverage, the maximum return is 24.75 percent. With only 10 percent of the company's capital from lenders, the shareholders' maximum expected return increases to 26.66 percent. When you increase the leverage more than the 10 percent, the ROE increases even further. In bad times, of course, leverage increases the downside for the shareholders. It is this range of potential outcomes that shareholders cannot know in advance. It is this that creates the risk for shareholders, and why when lenders enter the risk to shareholders increases and they require a higher return. In the case of the 10 percent debt in Exhibit 7-1, the increase is 0.55 percent.

Unless there is some way a particular form of financing either reduces the risk or increases the cash flows of the company, leverage will not change the required return, or average cost of capital, for the company. Nor will it change the company's value. At low levels of debt, lenders charge less than do equity providers because the lenders are protected by contracts, while shareholders, now in a less advantageous position, require a higher return. As debt increases the return required by each rises, but *for the company as a whole* there is no change. This is graphically seen in Exhibit 7-3.[3]

Leverage does not affect the value of the company. It does impact what portion of the cash flows belong to the lenders or shareholders. Leverage does not impact the shareholders' share value. However, there is an exception to the rule that leverage does not affect shareholders' value. The exception is when the way a company is financed changes its risk, its cash flows, or both. How could financing change a company's risk or its cash flows? How about taxes?

EXHIBIT 7-3 Greenway Corporation

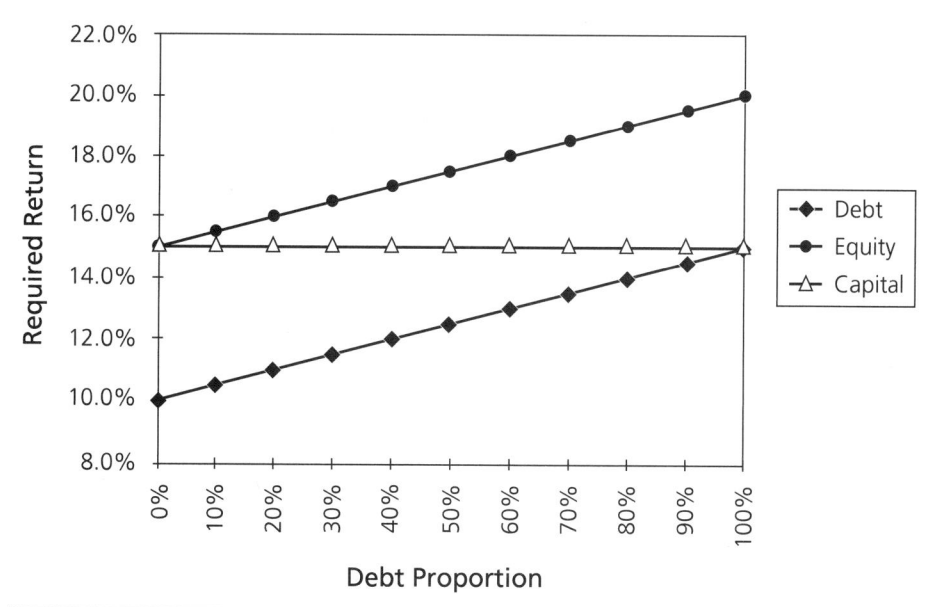

REQUIRED RETURNS ON CAPITAL IN A TAX-FREE WORLD

[3] Appendix 7A discusses a shortcut method of valuation that depends on a company's capital structure remaining constant. The method uses a weighted-average cost of capital to discount the cash flows to all capital providers. It is a quick alternative to forecasting both the operating and financing cash flows for the company in the future. It is useful, however, only under certain very narrow conditions. These conditions are outlined in the appendix.

In many countries, interest is a tax-deductible expense. Thus interest payments lower the taxes a company pays, increasing the company's cash flows with no change in risk. This makes debt more attractive to borrowers than it would otherwise be: the cost of the debt to the borrower is the lenders' required return less the taxes saved.

Company cost of debt = Lenders' required rate of return × (1 − tax rate)

For Greenway the cost of debt would be 6.6 percent.

$$\text{Company cost of debt} = 0.10 \times (1 - 0.34)$$
$$= 0.066 \text{ or } 6.6\%$$

By lowering the cost of debt, the weighted-average cost of capital for Greenway decreases. Exhibit 7-4 shows graphically the effect of taxes on the cost of capital: when interest is tax-deductible, although debt and equity costs rise as lenders finance an increasing proportion of a company, the cost of the company's capital declines.

In Exhibit 7-5 you can see the impact on Greenway's value: the more debt the company has, the more Greenway's value increases when interest is tax-deductible. If value increases with leverage, in a world where interest is tax-deductible, why don't companies finance themselves with more debt, in fact, as much as they can get?

EXHIBIT 7-4   Greenway Corporation

COSTS OF CAPITAL IN A TAXABLE WORLD WITHOUT BANKRUPTCY

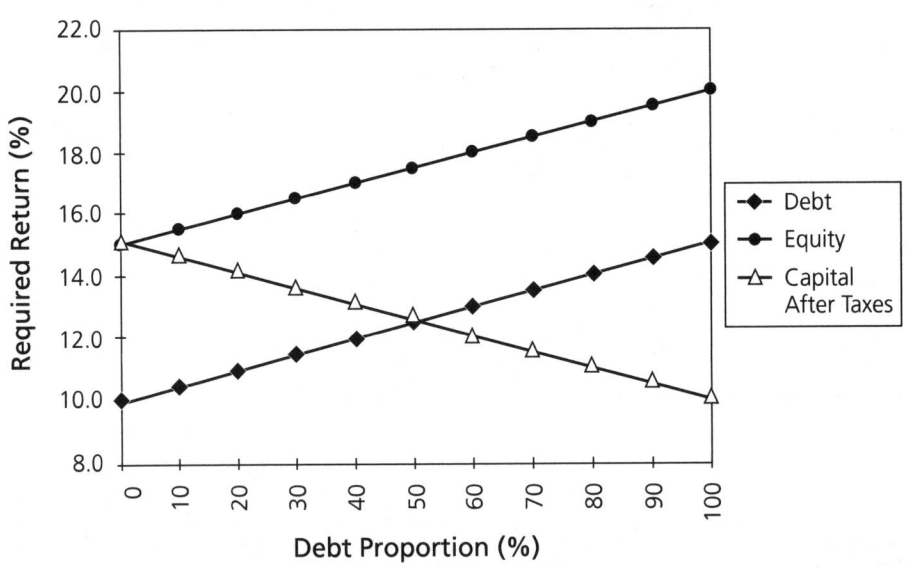

I. The Value of Leverage

EXHIBIT 7-5 Greenway Corporation Tax Effect of Capital Structure Changes on Cash Flow and Value—10 Percent Debt/Total Capital (dollars in millions except per share value)

	Interest Not Deductible	Interest Deductible
Profit before interest and taxes	$15.00	$15.00
Interest	—	(0.70)
Earnings before taxes	15.00	14.30
Taxes (@ 34%)	(5.00)	(4.86)
Profit after taxes	$10.00	$ 9.44
Depreciation	5.00	5.00
New equipment	(5.00)	(5.00)
Added working capital	—	—
Interest	(0.70)	
Cash flows to equity shareholders	$ 9.30	$ 9.44
Required return on equity	15.55%	15.55%
Weighted-average capital cost*	15.00%	14.66%
Equity market value**	$59.81	$60.71
Value per share	$6.65	$6.75
Debt value	$0.00	$6.67
Corporate value	$66.48	$67.38

* The after-tax cost of debt to the company is 10 percent if the interest is not tax-deductible and 6.67 percent if interest is tax-deductible.
** Calculated as in Exhibit 7-1 ($9.3/0.156 = $59.62). Total corporate value is equity value + debt value ($59.62 + $6.67 = $66.29). For the tax-deductible example the calculations are $9.44/0.156 = $60.51 plus the debt of $6.67 for a total of $67.18.

There is no definitive answer to why there seems to be a limit to a company's financial leverage. One of the most interesting theories is based on the concept of financial distress. Companies are **financially embarrassed** when they cannot pay the interest on the debt; they are, however, in **financial distress** when they cannot pay the interest or principal on the debt. The failure to pay its lenders can result in bankruptcy: the contract with the lender is broken and the lender, because it has a contract, can require immediate debt repayment.[4] Shareholders have no such contract, and thus cannot force the company into bankruptcy. Obviously, shareholders are not happy when a company is financially distressed, but they have no contract, only expectations. When shareholders' expectations are not met, the only things they can do are communicate with management, use their voting rights to change the board of directors, or sell their shares. If enough investors are dissatisfied the price of the shares will decline.

---

[4] For individuals this is called foreclosure or repossession.

In the case of a company with modest amounts of debt, most lenders do not worry about the possibility of bankruptcy. As the amount of debt rises, however, bankruptcy becomes more probable, and lenders begin to incorporate the expected costs of possible bankruptcy into their required return. Thus, at the point when lenders begin to be concerned about bankruptcy, they appear to add an extra charge to the cost of debt. Exhibit 7-4 showed what happened to a company's cost of capital when lenders and shareholders were not concerned about bankruptcy. However, if lenders are concerned with bankruptcy, the costs of debt and equity jump and the cost of capital starts its rise as bankruptcy becomes a concern, as shown in Exhibit 7-6.[5]

We have suggested that the lender's return increases when the probability of bankruptcy becomes real. This is only one theory that may explain a jump in the cost of capital as leverage increases. Other theories have been used to explain the phenomenon.[6] Whatever the reason, there does appear to be a point at which the weighted-average cost of capital begins to rise, and the value of the company starts to decline. The point just before this increase is where the com-

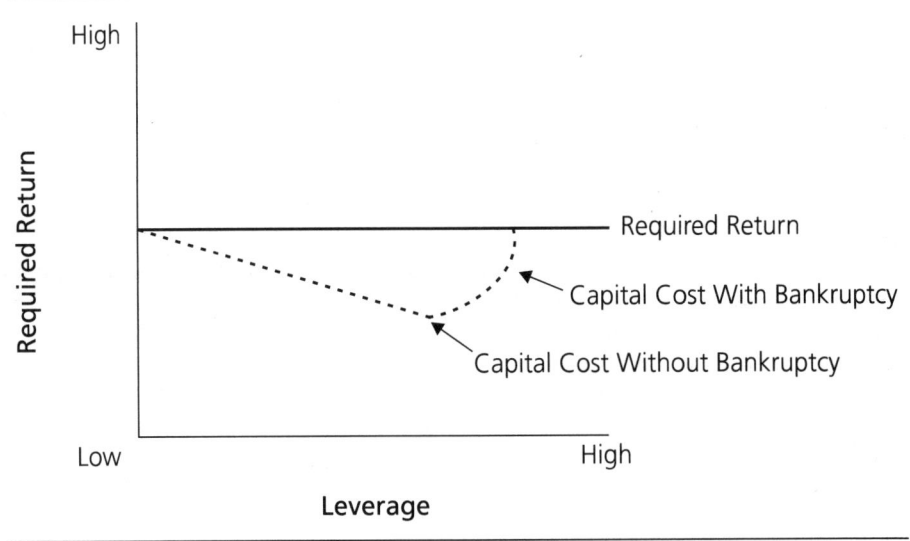

EXHIBIT 7-6 Required Return and Capital Cost With and Without Bankruptcy Considerations

---

[5] As the probability of bankruptcy increases, the "bankruptcy premium" also increases.

[6] Another possible explanation for the rise in capital costs is the impact that the company's agents have on decisions. Agents are those who work on behalf of others, but are not owners of the company. Managers and lenders are agents. Those who work for lenders, acting in their personal best interests, may become wary of lending to a company long before their employer would be: the impact of a loss on the lending agent and their job, salary, or bonus is considerable, while the impact on the lending institution may be negligible.

pany has the lowest capital cost. The capital structure at this point is called **optimal capital structure**. It is optimal because, beyond this point, as the cost of capital rises the value of the company and the shareholders' value both decline.

The manager must consider all the risks and returns in determining the appropriate mix of debt and equity. In some ways, this task is a marketing problem: the manager has several different products (the company's financial securities) and several different markets (potential investors in the company). The financial manager must match securities with investors in a way that creates the greatest value for the company. He or she does so by analyzing the potential effects of various financing alternatives on the total market value of the company. To understand the decisions that face managers as they consider the appropriate capital structure for their company, a basic understanding of debt and debt markets is important.

II. SOURCES OF DEBT FINANCING

Most companies are financed with a combination of equity and debt. Debt is different from equity in that it is contractual, typically specifying the amount to be borrowed, the interest charged for the money, and the time at which the money will be returned. The debt contract may also have some **covenants**, which are provisions that restrict the company's activities (e.g., allow no further increase in debt), or require that certain standards be met (e.g., a particular current ratio or level of net working capital). Lenders' claims appear before the shareholders' residual claim both on the balance sheet and by law.

In addition to the public markets for debt, which are similar to those for equity described in Chapter 6, capital can be raised through private placements.[7] **Public issues** are regulated by the Securities and Exchange Commission (SEC) in the United States and by similar commissions in other countries. They require the issuing company to disclose specific information about the company's business activities, the financial instrument being issued, and the use of the proceeds. Such disclosure provides the public with information that facilitates subsequent trading in the secondary market. **Private placements** are direct placements of the securities with investors such as large insurance companies. They are not registered and generally are not traded in the secondary market. However, because the issuer can negotiate directly with the investor, private placements allow more complicated and specialized financial

---

[7] The market for certain bonds can be much less liquid than markets for equity issues. This can be true even for bonds of large companies. This is because a company may have many different debt instruments (bonds), each with a different set of characteristics, and because one or a few large investors own large quantities of a particular debt instrument, making trading infrequent. This also means that since each bond has its own characteristics that depend upon the market and company conditions at the time it was issued, there may not be such a thing as a return on a company's bonds that is similar to the return on the company's stock.

arrangements between borrower and lender (or between the company and the shareholder in private equity placements) than are available in the public capital markets. Some privately placed debt has some equity characteristics.[8]

Private institutional investors such as mutual funds, insurance companies, and pension funds are the largest investors in the capital markets. Although equity markets have seen a rapid increase in individual investors, their size is still dwarfed by institutional investment. In other countries, the level of institutional ownership is quite different, and can be much higher than that in the United States.

While the two primary types of securities used by companies to raise long-term capital are debt and equity, some instruments combine the two types through "convertible" provisions. **Convertible instruments** typically allow the investor to convert debt or preferred stock into equity, usually common stock, at a specified price and usually during a particular period of time.

Long-term debt instruments are called **bonds**. A bond is a contractual debt obligation to repay a stated amount on a specified date, termed the **maturity**, and to make periodic interest, or **coupon**, payments. The stated amount is called the **principal** or **par value**. The par value is typically a standard amount in each country. For instance, in the United States the usual par value is $1,000. Specific features of the bonds issued are described in a contract called an **indenture agreement**. The stated interest or coupon payments are determined by a specified interest rate or coupon rate at the time the bond is issued. If the contractually obligated payments are not made, the bond is in default and the bondholders may have to call on, or take, some or all of the assets of the company as compensation.

For most bonds, the coupon rate is fixed for the life of the bond. Because of large fluctuations in interest rates in recent years, some bonds have been issued with variable, or floating, interest rates. For **variable-rate bonds**, the interest rate is restated at specified intervals based on a particular market index of interest rates—for example, LIBOR (the London Interbank Offer Rate) or the prime rate, the rate charged the best customers of a bank. These bonds are also called **floating-rate bonds** or **floaters**.

For fixed-coupon bonds, changes in interest rates subsequent to the date of issue affect the bond price in the secondary market but do not affect the cost to the company. If general market interest rates go up (or down), the price of the bond will go down (or up) in order to continue to provide a fair rate of return in the subsequent interest rate environment. These adjustments occur so that the bond's **yield to maturity** (return from interest plus principal repayments over the bond's life) will approximate the current market rate of interest for bonds of similar maturity, quality, and other features. Thus the price that an investor is willing to pay for a bond is a function of the par value of the bond, the

---

[8] Convertible provisions, the right to convert the debt to equity, or warrants, the right to buy some stock, may be part of the arrangement.

coupon rate, the maturity, and prevailing interest rates. The following formula is used to determine the proper secondary price of a bond. It is similar to the present value calculations discussed in Chapters 4 and 5.

$$P = \left[\sum \frac{CP_n}{(1 + R_d)^n}\right] + \frac{PAR}{(1 + R_d)^m}$$

where
- P = Market price of the bond
- CP = Periodic coupon payment (interest payment)
- R_d = Current market interest rate
- PAR = Par value of the bond
- m;n = Maturity period of the bond; the period
- Σ = Sum

If, for instance, a company had issued $2 million in bonds at 12.0 percent and the rate of interest on bonds of a similar maturity and quality rose from 12.0 to 15.7 percent, the market price of the bonds with two years remaining until maturity would drop from $2 million to under $1.9 million in order to provide a 15.7 percent yield to new purchasers:

$$P = \frac{\$240,000}{(1 + 0.157)^1} + \frac{\$240,000}{(1 + 0.157)^2} + \frac{\$2,000,000}{(1 + 0.157)^2}$$
$$= \$1,880,762$$

Conversely, if market rates dropped to, say, 10 percent, the bond price would rise to over $2 million:

$$P = \frac{\$240,000}{(1 + 0.10)^1} + \frac{\$240,000}{(1 + 0.10)^2} + \frac{\$2,000,000}{(1 + 0.10)^2}$$
$$= \$2,069,422$$

Present values (prices) of bonds with longer maturities are more affected by interest rate changes than are values of bonds with short maturities.

If the market price of a bond is known, but the effective interest rate (the yield to maturity) is not, the yield to maturity can be calculated using the same formula. The method for determining the yield to maturity is like that used in Chapter 4 for calculating the internal rate of return. A calculator is all you need to solve for yield to maturity, the R_d in the formula.

For conventional bonds, the amount the company borrows is the same as the principal or par value of the bond, net of issue costs. This statement is not true for **zero-coupon bonds**. These bonds do not require any periodic coupon payments. Instead, the par value of the bond is much larger than the amount originally borrowed (the cost of the bond to the investor). Essentially, interest is accrued during the bond's life and paid at the time the initial principal is repaid as a part of the final payment. Determining the return on these bonds is a simplification of the yield-to-maturity calculation, because there are no coupon payments. The following simplified formula would be used:

$$\text{Price} = \frac{\text{PAR}}{(1 + R_d)^m}$$

where
R_d = yield to maturity
m = the years from purchase to maturity

Using this formula, if a firm issues a zero-coupon bond today at a price of $275 per bond returning $1,000 in 10 years, the effective yield, or yield to maturity, is 13.8 percent ($275 = [1,000/(1 + R_d)^{10}]).

The 1980s saw an explosion of a relatively new version of debt. This debt was called junk bonds. There had always been a market for bonds of companies that had fallen into disfavor after their debt was issued, and whose debt-quality ratings had declined. These bonds, sometimes called fallen angels, were traded at discounts to their original issuing price.[9] **Junk debt** was, however, debt of companies that were not highly rated or of companies that were issuing unusually high levels of debt for their size or risk. The debt carried very high interest rates and was issued at a discount to its par value, thus it was called **original issue discount (OID) debt**.

Not all bonds retire the entire principal amount at the specified maturity date of the bond. Many bonds require the company to make periodic principal reductions, called a sinking fund. The purpose of a sinking fund is to reduce the risk that the borrower will not be able to repay the par amount. While the amount going into the sinking fund may be placed in a trust account to be held until the maturity date, this practice is not typical today. It is more likely that, when the sinking fund payments are due, the company will retire a portion of the issued bonds, even though they have not reached maturity. The way in which bonds are chosen to be purchased or retired before maturity is specified at the time the bonds are first issued by the company and are noted in the indenture agreement. For publicly traded bonds, commonly the company will simply purchase some of the existing bonds in the market, thus reducing the total amount of bonds outstanding.

In addition to reducing the amount of bonds outstanding to meet sinking fund requirements, companies may choose to retire the bonds before the specified maturity. This process is termed **refunding** or **calling** the bonds. Companies are especially interested in refunding when interest rates fall, since the existing bonds can be called, retired, and refinanced with lower cost debt. To protect against this possibility, many bonds have **call protection**: the bonds cannot be called for a specified period of time or may be called only if a stated

---

[9] This discount existed with no marketwide change in interest rates. Thus it was entirely due to the changed circumstances of the company.

premium is paid to the bondholders. Call provisions are specified in the indenture agreement.

As a further protection for bondholders, the bond contract or indenture may limit the company in other ways. Frequently the company will be required to maintain certain levels of assets or to limit its total amount of debt. Often these restrictions, or covenants, are specified in the form of ratios—the kind we discussed in Chapter 1. If any of the bond covenants are violated, the bond is deemed to be in technical default and is immediately due for payment. It is up to the bondholder whether the company will be forced to pay or whether the covenant will be waived or rewritten.

The general risk to the borrower is reflected in the **bond rating**. Bond ratings are important because bonds with higher potential for default (lower ratings) must have a higher coupon (that is, pay a higher interest rate) to compensate investors for the increased risk. Several organizations publish bond ratings; Moody's and Standard & Poor's (S&P) are the two most widely known in the United States. Based on these independent organizations' assessments of the general credit risk of the borrower, bonds are assigned a rating, with Aaa (Moody's) or AAA (S&P) indicating the most creditworthy bonds—those with the lowest risk of default. The ratings decrease through Aa/AA, and so on, to high-risk bonds rated Caa/CCC or below.[10] A bond's rating may be changed because of changes in the issuer's situation. A bond may be unrated.

A company may have several kinds of debt at the same time. The debt may have been issued to different lenders, at different times, and under different market conditions. The indenture agreement stipulates the differences: the amount of debt, the coupon rate of interest, payment terms, specific assets on which the lenders may call in the event of a default, the priority in which the lenders' claims will be settled, and criteria the company must meet in order to have the debt without covenant revision. Debt that holds claim to specific assets in the event of default is usually called **mortgage debt**. Debt that uses other assets such as groups of mortgages, credit card receipts, or accounts receivables is called **securitized debt**. Debt that, by contract, allows other debt precedence in the event of default is called **subordinated debt**. Different issues of debt are listed separately on a company's balance sheet. The balance sheet and the accompanying notes describe the major differences in each debt instrument. Bond guides such as S&P and Moody's in the United States provide more detail for the potential investor or company analyst.

III. DETERMINING THE COST OF DEBT

Most firms use debt to finance a portion of their assets. The proportion of debt used by U.S. firms has changed dramatically over rather short periods of time

---

[10] Bonds for countries and municipalities also have rating systems.

as shown in Exhibit 7-7.[11] In the 1990s, equity has regained favor with investors, as shown in Exhibit 7-8. Not only does the debt proportion change, so do interest rates. At a high in the early 1980s, they have, until the past year, declined. Exhibit 7-9 shows the market rates of interest on publicly traded debt of varying qualities during the last 12 years. Note that the interest rate on the best quality corporate debt is higher than that on government debt of the same maturity, and that the lower the corporate debt is rated, the higher the interest rate—the lender's required return.

Just as the reliability of the borrower affects the interest rate, so does the length of time the borrower wishes to use the principal. Exhibit 7-10 shows the market rate of interest on debt of the same quality, U.S. Treasuries, but different maturities at two points in time. The normal line is upward sloping like that shown for early September 1999. An upward slope is normal because lenders who provide capital for longer times require, quite logically, more return. At some points in time, this upward-sloping curve, the **yield curve**, does not exist. This has been particularly true in periods of high inflation. For instance, during the 1970s, the relationship between the market rate of interest and debt of different maturities was sometimes perverse. Exhibit 7-10 shows two typical yield curves and two inverse yield curves (March 1, 1981, and December 1,

EXHIBIT 7-7 Annual Growth of Capital Structure and Its Composition in the United States (nonfinancial companies)

SOURCE: Data from Federal Reserve Board of Governors Bulletin, November 1987, pp. 34–35.

---

[11] This data is difficult to obtain for more recent periods.

III. Determining the Cost of Debt

EXHIBIT 7-8 Issuance of Debt and Equity in the United States—1985–1999

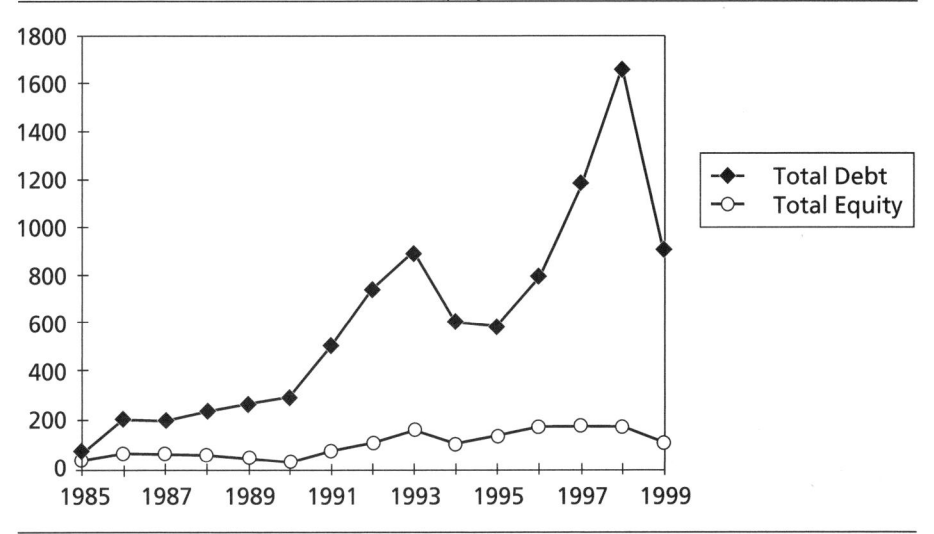

SOURCE: Data from Mathias, Edward J., *Economic and Investment Environment*, Washington, D.C.: The Carlyle Group, 1999.

EXHIBIT 7-9 U.S. Interest Rates for Debt of Different Qualities—1984–1999*

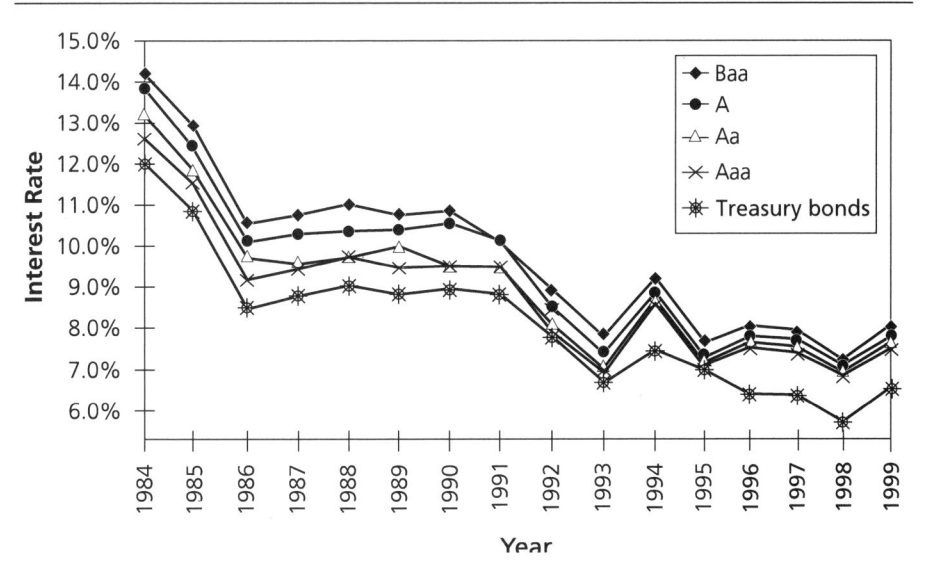

* 1999 to June

SOURCE: Data from Federal Reserve Bulletin, various issues.

EXHIBIT 7-10 Interest Rates for Debt of Different Maturities

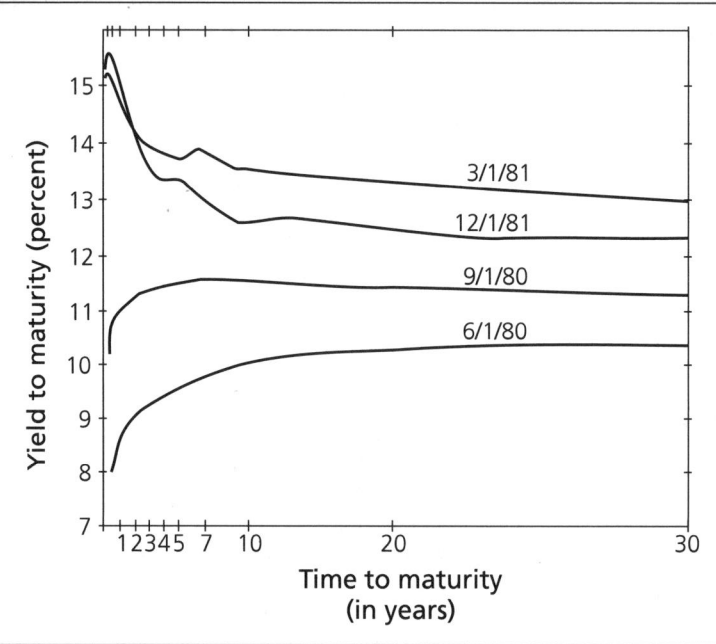

[Graph: Yield to maturity (percent) vs. Time to maturity (in years), showing curves for 3/1/81, 12/1/81, 9/1/80, and 6/1/80]

1981). The rapidity of the change, coupled with the change from a normal to an inverse yield curve, has not been repeated in the United States since that time.

In addition to interest payments, a number of special features may be required by the lender. For example, specific assets may be pledged to support the loan; the lender may require seniority over others' claims in the case of bankruptcy, or the loan may be convertible into common or preferred stock under certain conditions. Each feature offers the lender different levels of protection from risk and thus carries a somewhat different cost, which is reflected in the interest rate.

Earlier you learned that a lender's required return on debt (RR_d) is the ratio of the interest rate to the principal amount of the debt.

$$\text{Lender's required return} = \frac{\text{Interest payment}}{\text{Debt principal}}$$

However, the company's interest expense is tax-deductible, making the company's cost of debt K_d.

$$\text{Company's cost of debt} = \frac{\text{Interest payment } (1 - \text{Tax rate})}{\text{Debt principal}}$$

Let's use an example. If a company wanted to borrow $2 million, and the lender expected interest payments of $163,000 per year, the lender's required return would be 8.15 percent ($163,000/$2,000,000), but the company's cost of debt would be:

$$K_d = \frac{\text{Interest payment (1 − Tax rate)}}{\text{Debt principal}}$$

$$= \frac{\$163,000 (1 − 0.34)}{\$2,000,000}$$

$$= \frac{\$107,580}{2,000,000}$$

$$= 0.0538 \text{ or } 5.4\%$$

This formula applies whether the company issues bonds at par or at a discount. If the company issues zero-coupon bonds, however, there are no interest payments during the life of the bond, and the investor's return comes from the difference between the price paid and the principal returned at maturity. Following our example, if the company's lenders' required yield-to-maturity was 8.5 percent on zero-coupon bonds, and it wanted to borrow $2.0 million for 10 years, the principal returned at the maturity of the bonds would be $4.52 million, not $2.0 million.[12]

IV. RICHS ANALYSIS

The capital markets are complex and ever-changing. Deciding to add debt to a company's all-equity capital structure adds risk, and potential return, to the owners' position. How do a company's owners, or the managers on the owners' behalf, decide whether to subcontract some of their financing responsibilities? A convenient framework for analyzing the many different, and sometimes conflicting, forces that affect the capital structure decision is provided by the RICHS process. This acronym is used to represent five major factors that should be considered:

        R Risk
        I Income
        C Control
        H Hedging
        S Speculating

These factors are not listed in order of priority or importance; for each firm, and in different economic environments, the relative importance of the factors will differ. However, the manager should ensure that all factors have been considered.

---

[12] To determine the $4.5 million principal to be repaid, compound $2.0 million by 8.5 percent for 10 years.

The process of making the decision about a company's capital structure is not a strictly mechanical process in which computational abilities can be substituted for analysis and judgment; the manager must interpret the results of the analysis. For this reason, the RICHS analytical process can best be explained through a specific example—Greenway Corporation's decision about whether to finance a $6 million expansion in production capacity through a public equity offering or through a privately placed debt issue.

Greenway is the leading producer and marketer of sand trap graders for golf courses. The company was a market leader in both the manufacture and sale of graders until the rising value of the dollar made it economically attractive for Greenway to sell its production plants and produce the needed parts in a joint venture with a Japanese firm. Up to 2000, parts for the graders were manufactured in Japan and assembled and sold in the United States by Greenway. In late 2000 the value of the dollar declined relative to the Japanese yen and it has become economically attractive to manufacture as well as assemble the grader parts in the United States. Greenway had thus decided to buy a parts manufacturing plant, and one that is readily adaptable is available. Exhibit 7-11 shows historical and forecasted income statements and balance sheets Greenway managers made for the company, not including the new plant the company is considering purchasing. Exhibit 7-12 (page 294) shows the forecasts including the new plant investment. Greenway management also expects to pay $2.0 million in dividends per year.

To make the investment, Greenway will need a total of $6.0 million: $4.5 million to pay for plant and equipment and $1.9 million for new working capital (to be invested largely in inventory). Greenway will need the money starting in January 2001. The new plant will start operations shortly thereafter. Greenway currently has 20 percent of its $36 million of long-term capital in the form of debt issued in 2000. The coupon, or interest rate, on that debt is 9.74 percent. It is 30-year debt with no principal repayments due until 2007. Greenway can get the $6 million it needs from either debt or equity—the sale of common stock.

Greenway has 926,376 shares outstanding. The market price of the shares is $27.17 per share. To obtain the needed capital, Greenway's investment banker has said that the company can issue up to 240,000 new shares at $26.00 per share.[13] Greenway has paid its shareholders, and expects to continue to pay, $2.40 per share. This dividend represents a payout ratio of almost 100 percent. The high payout ratio reflects the wishes of the company's founder and family. They hold the single largest block of stock in the company, about 30 percent of the outstanding shares. The rest of the shares are widely held in the locale in which the company operates.

---

[13] An investment banker assists company management in designing the security to be issued, determining when the security should be issued, how much should be sold, and at what price. In addition, the investment banking company, along with others, provides marketing and distribution, also called syndication. In the United States and in other countries, firms such as Morgan Stanley, Merrill Lynch, Credit Suisse First Boston, Goldman Sachs, and Morgan Granfells provide such services.

EXHIBIT 7-11 Greenway Corporation

HISTORIC AND FORECASTED FINANCIAL STATEMENTS WITHOUT THE NEW PLANT (dollars in millions)

	Historic	Forecasted				
	2000	2001	2002	2003	2004	2005
Income Statement						
Sales	$ 32.7	$ 36.0	$ 38.5	$ 41.1	$ 44.0	$ 47.1
Manufacturing expenses	(27.0)	(29.7)	(31.8)	(33.9)	(36.3)	(38.9)
Depreciation straight line	(1.6)	(1.8)	(1.9)	(2.1)	(2.2)	(2.3)
Earnings before interest and taxes	4.1	4.5	4.8	5.1	5.5	5.9
Interest	(0.7)	(0.7)	(0.7)	(0.7)	(0.7)	(0.7)
Earnings before taxes	3.4	3.8	4.1	4.4	4.8	5.2
Taxes (@ 34%)	(1.2)	(1.3)	(1.4)	(1.5)	(1.6)	(1.8)
Net earnings	$ 2.2	$ 2.5	$ 2.7	$ 2.9	$ 3.2	$ 3.4
Cash Flow						
Depreciation	$ 1.6	$ 1.8	$ 1.9	$ 2.1	$ 2.2	$ 2.4
New property, plant, and equipment	(1.0)	(1.0)	(1.0)	(1.0)	(1.0)	(1.0)
New working capital	(0.6)	(0.8)	(0.9)	(1.1)	(1.2)	(1.4)
Residual net cash flow	$ 2.2	$ 2.5	$ 2.7	$ 2.9	$ 3.2	$ 3.4
Ratios						
EBIT/Interest	586%	643%	687%	729%	786%	843%
Cash flow/Interest	314%	357%	386%	414%	457%	486%
Balance Sheet						
Assets						
Total current assets	$ 27.7	$ 28.5	$ 29.4	$ 30.5	$ 31.7	$ 33.1
Net property, plant, and equipment	15.0	14.2	13.3	12.2	11.0	9.6
Total assets	$ 42.7	$ 42.7	$ 42.7	$ 42.7	$ 42.7	$ 42.7
Liabilities and Equity						
Total current liabilities	$ 7.2	$ 7.2	$ 7.2	$ 7.2	$ 7.2	$ 7.2
Long-term debt	7.2	7.2	7.2	7.2	7.2	7.2
Equity	28.3	28.8	29.5	30.4	31.6	33.0
Subtotal	42.7	42.3	41.6	40.7	39.8	40.2
Net financing needed	—	0.4	1.1	2.0	2.9	2.5
Total liabilities and equity	$ 42.7	$ 42.7	$ 42.7	$ 42.7	$ 42.7	$ 42.7

Greenway already has some debt. Any new debt would be subordinated to the old debt—that is, it would not have as strong a contract. The investment banker believes that Greenway would have to offer a coupon of 12 percent to attract buyers. These would be 20-year bonds, with interest and principal to fully amortize the debt beginning in 2006. To decide which is better, management will want to look at all the important factors, and determine which financing method will increase the value of the company more. First, let's look at the impact on the first factor in RICHS, risk.

EXHIBIT 7-12 Greenway Corporation

HISTORIC AND FORECASTED FINANCIAL STATEMENTS WITH THE NEW PLANT (dollars in millions)

	Historic	Forecasted				
	2000	2001	2002	2003	2004	2005
Income Statement						
Sales	$ 32.7	$ 42.4	$ 44.6	$ 47.0	$ 49.4	$ 51.9
Manufacturing expenses	(27.0)	(35.0)	(36.8)	(38.7)	(40.7)	(42.8)
Depreciation straight line	(1.6)	(2.1)	(2.2)	(2.4)	(2.5)	(2.6)
Earnings before interest and taxes	4.1	5.3	5.6	5.9	6.2	6.5
Interest	(0.7)	(0.7)	(0.7)	(0.7)	(0.7)	(0.7)
Earnings before taxes	3.4	4.6	4.9	5.2	5.5	5.8
Taxes (@ 34%)	(1.2)	(1.6)	(1.7)	(1.8)	(1.9)	(2.0)
Net earnings	$ 2.2	$ 3.0	$ 3.2	$ 3.4	$ 3.6	$ 3.8
Cash Flow						
Depreciation	$ 1.6	$ 2.1	$ 2.2	$ 2.4	$ 2.5	$ 2.6
New property, plant, and equipment	(1.0)	(5.5)	(1.0)	(1.0)	(1.0)	(1.0)
New working capital	(0.6)	(2.7)	(0.8)	(0.9)	(0.9)	(1.0)
Residual net cash flow	$ 2.2	$ (3.1)	$ 3.6	$ 3.9	$ 4.2	$ 4.4
Ratios						
EBIT/Interest	586%	757%	800%	843%	886%	929%
Cash flow/Interest	314%	–442%	514%	557%	600%	629%
Balance Sheet						
Assets						
Total current assets	$ 27.7	$ 30.4	$ 31.3	$ 32.4	$ 33.6	$ 35.0
Net property, plant, and equipment	15.0	18.4	17.1	15.8	14.3	12.8
Total assets	$ 42.7	$ 48.8	$ 48.4	$ 48.2	$ 47.9	$ 47.8
Liabilities and Equity						
Total current liabilities	$ 7.2	$ 7.2	$ 7.2	$ 7.2	$ 7.2	$ 7.2
Long-term debt	7.2	7.2	7.2	7.2	7.2	7.2
Equity	28.3	29.1	25.9	27.8	30.0	32.4
Subtotal	42.7	43.5	40.3	42.2	44.4	46.8
Net financing needed	—	5.3	8.1	6.0	3.5	(1.0)
Total liabilities and equity	$ 42.7	$ 48.8	$ 48.4	$ 48.2	$ 47.9	$ 47.8

1. Risk to Lenders

Affordability—Interest Payments. To ensure that the company can meet its debt obligations, management should determine how much cash is available to meet interest and principal payments, that is, to service the debt. The cash that will be available sets an upper limit on the amount a company should borrow. Companies that take on obligations in excess of their ability to service them readily court disaster.

In assessing how much debt a company can bear, its **debt capacity**, the manager must first forecast the company's future financial performance. While the size of the future cash flows are important, so is their variability: companies with steady, predictable cash flows can bear more debt than companies with more volatile cash flows. Because periods of cash flow shortage can impair the company's ability to service its debt, a manager will want to be sure to forecast financial performance for the company in lean times, times of cash flow shortages.

The factors that might lead to a cash shortage will be different for each business. For some companies, an unusual demand for its products, with the resulting need for cash to finance growth, might be the time when more cash, and thus greater debt financing, is needed. For other companies, an economic recession with a decline in sales might cause cash problems. Whatever the case for the particular company, the managers should examine the cash flows under the maximum likely cash shortfall in order to determine the business's ability to meet debt payments and remain solvent under adverse conditions.

There may be actions a company can take to free up cash during difficult periods. For example, during a recession, a company might postpone capital investments. If the cash shortfall is caused by rapid growth, management might decide to tighten credit terms and thus decrease accounts receivable. After evaluating the impact of all the cash-freeing alternatives, management can determine how much cash will be available to pay the company's debt obligations. The amount of debt this cash can service (pay interest and make principal payments) is the company's debt limit or debt capacity.

Management may decide to borrow less than the company's capacity. The actual debt level that management decides to attain is termed the **debt policy**. While debt capacity is limited by the ability of the company to service the debt, the debt policy is determined by management's judgment of the markets' reactions. The objective of debt policy is to maximize the market value of the company by minimizing its capital cost. Let's use Greenway to see how this might work in practice.

To measure Greenway's ability to meet its cash obligations, management could use the coverage ratios discussed in Chapter 1. These ratios focus on the relationship between the company's resources and its fixed obligations, primarily debt service. Obviously, the higher the ratio, the better the company's position in the face of bad times. As shown in Exhibit 7-11, projected earnings before interest and taxes in 2001 will cover interest, with plenty of room to spare, and will do so through 2005.

$$\text{Earnings-interest coverage} = \frac{\text{EBIT}}{\text{Interest}}$$

$$= \frac{\$4.5}{\$0.7}$$

$$= 6.43 \text{ or } 643\%$$

The coverage ratios are high regardless of whether we compare EBIT or cash flow (EBIT plus depreciation) to interest payments. Note that because Greenway does not have any principal payments until 2005, the cash flow/interest and cash flow/debt-service ratios would be identical.[14]

Interest is not the only payment Greenway management wants to make. Dividends, because of the Greenway family's policies, are a high priority. Therefore, management may want to add dividends to the payments to be covered.[15] This adjustment would reduce the EBIT coverage ratio in 2001, but to just over 100 percent, and to 132 percent four years later.

Exhibit 7-13 shows what will happen to the interest coverage if Greenway chooses either debt or equity. Because the projected cost savings are not certain, it also shows what will happen to the ratio if EBIT is only $4.5 million.[16] If the company finances its need with debt, the ratio is lower by half, but interest expense can still be covered easily. When management includes dividends, however, the contractual payment coverage ratios are just over 100 percent if new EBIT does not materialize. Even if the $5.3 million EBIT materializes, the cov-

EXHIBIT 7-13 Greenway 2001 Interest Coverage Ratios

ALTERNATIVE FINANCING SCHEMES (dollars in thousands)

	Old EBIT		New EBIT	
	Debt	Equity	Debt	Equity
EBIT	$4,500	$4,500	$5,300	$5,300
Old interest	700	700	700	700
New interest	720	0	720	0
Total interest	$1,420	$ 700	$1,420	$ 700
Interest coverage ratio (EBIT/interest)	317%	643%	373%	757%
Dividends	$2,223	$2,777	$2,223	$2,777
Dividends before taxes	$3,368	$4,208	$3,368	$4,208
Before tax contractual payments plus dividends	$4,788	$4,908	$4,788	$4,908
EBIT/contractual payments plus dividends	94%	92%	111%	108%

---

[14] The cash flow/debt-service ratio is:

$$\frac{EBIT + Depreciation - (PP\&E\ changes + Working\ capital\ changes)}{Interest + [Principal/(1 - Tax\ rate)]}$$

Note that principal payments are not tax-deductible expenses and are, therefore, adjusted to a before-tax basis.

[15] Because EBIT is a before-tax figure and dividends are an after-tax amount, the dividend must be adjusted to a pretax basis [dividends/(1 − tax rate)].

[16] This lower EBIT figure is chosen as an amount that is possible, perhaps an EBIT earned in a recent year, or an amount that could be earned if a critical customer were lost, or what is possible in a period of economic slowdown.

erage ratios leave little room for error the first year the new plant is owned and operated.

If the forecasted EBIT materializes, the company can cover its debt obligations and dividend payments. In later years, because management expects EBIT to grow, coverage ratios will improve. We can conclude that lenders will feel assured that their interest payments can be met—or can we? In 2003, EBIT covers interest more than four times. Is this enough of a cushion to comfort lenders? That depends on how volatile Greenway's EBIT might be. Lenders to companies with very volatile EBIT will want a larger cushion than lenders to companies whose EBIT are quite stable.

The most common source of risk, and thus unstable earnings, is the impact of changes in the business cycle. Cyclical expansions and contractions strain a firm's ability to service product demand, maintain proper inventories, and control its resources adequately. These strains are most vividly seen in their effects on earnings and cash flow. As economic conditions deteriorate, companies are pressed to find adequate cash flow to meet their obligations.

In addition to the problems caused by business cycles, companies face other types of risks. In some industries, strikes occur with almost the same regularity as business cycles. These disruptions cause problems not only for the companies experiencing strikes but also for its suppliers and customers. There are other unforeseeable problems, such as periodic market gluts and shortages of basic raw materials, that can affect particular industries or companies. In each of these situations, a company's ability to marshal its cash resources is critical to its ability to service debt.

Greenway's earnings and revenues have been very stable in the past. Management has been able to secure equipment orders far in advance of delivery and has not been badly hurt by previous recessions. Thus the coverage ratios should hearten lenders, if not shareholders. However, regardless of the financing method chosen, Greenway will be somewhat more risky in 2001 than it was, or than it would be without the new plant. Therefore, of the two methods, common stock financing provides better interest coverage ratio in 2001.

Note that these calculations provide only an approximation of the cash available to service obligations during an adverse cycle. Greenway may be able to generate additional cash internally through astute management of inventories, accounts payable, accounts receivable, and capital expenditures. Thus cash could increase during periods of declining sales and decline during periods of increasing sales. This strategy is, in fact, what most companies have discovered. The critical factor in the management of a company is to identify the economic situation and respond quickly to minimize any adverse impact it may have on the cash position of the company.

Affordability—Principal Repayments. Lenders are concerned not only with interest payments; they want to be certain the principal they have lent can be repaid. Since a lender's business is to make money by lending money, the lender does not want the money returned because that means the loss of interest income or creates the need to find another customer. What a lender wants is to be sure the money can be repaid. When firms are financially embarrassed, they cannot pay the interest on their debt; when they are distressed, they cannot repay the principal. To determine whether they could lose their principal, lenders often use ratios that measure the relative proportion of the company's capital they have provided. The ratio of debt to total capital is a good measure of the exposure of a lender's principal to loss.

Greenway currently has 20.3 percent of its capital in the form of debt. Exhibit 7-14 shows what will happen when Greenway adds $6 million in either debt or equity. Greenway's ratio of debt to total capital increases to 31.8 percent if it uses debt. The ratio drops to 17.4 percent if equity is raised. Increased leverage does increase the lender's risk, but does it raise it beyond a level that is acceptable?

To determine the impact of leverage and whether it is acceptable, analysts often examine what others in the same industry are doing. Exhibit 7-15 provides information on others in Greenway's industry. Producers of lawn and garden equipment obtain about one-third of their capital from lenders—more debt than Greenway will have if it raises $6 million in debt. In addition, Greenway's net EBIT/interest ratio would be above others in that industry. Based on these comparisons, if Greenway raises debt, it would still be following a conservative financing plan. However, Greenway does not really fall into the lawn and garden equipment industry. A better comparison is with producers of golf course equipment, against whom Greenway would be following a more aggressive strategy.

EXHIBIT 7-14 Greenway Corporation Debt-to-Total Capital

ALTERNATIVE FINANCING METHODS (dollars in thousands)

	Debt Financing	Equity Financing
Total capital		
Old	$35,480	$35,480
New	6,000	6,000
Total capital	$41,480	$41,480
Debt outstanding		
Old	$ 7,200	$ 7,200
New	6,000	0
Total debt	$13,200	$ 7,200
Ratios		
Debt/total long-term capital:		
Old total	20.3%	20.3%
New total	31.8%	17.4%
Debt/equity:		
Old total	25.5%	25.5%
New total	46.7%	21.0%

EXHIBIT 7-15 Industry Comparisons for Greenway Corporation

	Interest Coverage	Debt/Total Capital
Lawn and garden equipment producers		
RideRite Enterprises	310.3%	33.1%
Topflight Irrigators	253.7	34.3
General Cropharvester, Inc.	304.5	46.0
Greenway Corporation	643.0	31.8
Golf course equipment producers		
Fairway Products, Inc.	1,430.3	11.2
Greenskeepers Corporation	2,103.1	18.1
Sam Speed, Inc.	1,836.1	15.3
Greenway Corporation	643.0	31.8

Based on these comparisons, management must ask itself, "Why do golf course equipment producers have less debt and higher coverage ratios?" The likely answer is that they are more affected by economic cycles than sellers of lawn and garden equipment. Lenders have thus decided that they require more protection when making loans to them and will lend less to producers of golf equipment.

While Greenway may well be stronger and more able to handle higher levels of debt than others in its industry, following a different financing plan is likely to cause lenders to scrutinize Greenway very carefully. Therefore, we must be certain that debt financing will indeed be better than equity financing for Mr. Greenway and the rest of the shareholders. How about the shareholders? Which would they prefer? Which alternative will create more value?

2. Income

One of the obvious impacts of debt financing on shareholder value is its effect on their income—the I in RICHS. If a particular form of financing increases the riskiness of the firm, the risk could be offset by increased income. New funds are generally invested in productive assets, with the benefits from investment accruing to the lenders and shareholders. Because the debt holders' claim, although senior, is fixed, the residual benefits belong to the common shareholders. That is why management should analyze income and value from the shareholders' point of view. Such an analysis is also consistent with the concept that management should create value for the shareholders.

In determining the impact the financing decision will have on the income of shareholders, two general costs need to be considered: first, the **explicit cost of the financing**—the impact on the cash flow and earnings per share; second, the **implicit cost**—the impact on the market price of the stock.

Cash Flow Impact. To determine explicit cost, as reflected in cash flow per share, Greenway managers will estimate the effect that each financing alternative would have on the company's cash flow per share. This analysis is similar to the coverage analysis that was undertaken to estimate the impact of risk on the company. The result is shown in Exhibit 7-16.[17] The only changes in the results from those existing before financing (the first column) are caused by the alternative financing plans.

Comparing the impacts of the two alternatives indicates that the equity alternative, the issuance of common stock, lowers cash flow per share for 2001 more than the debt alternative, with and without new earnings. Although total EBIT for Greenway is expected to increase to $5.3 million from $4.5 million as the company uses its new capital, the additional shares issued dilute the impact of increased cash flow on individual shares. Each owner now holds a smaller piece of the company, although the total size of the company has increased. A reduction in cash flow per share is a common occurrence as additional common stock dilutes the benefits of stock ownership. Still, the higher the EBIT, the more attractive debt will look, because once the debt's fixed cost (interest) is covered, the residual goes to the shareholders.

There is one more thing to notice about this analysis before we use it to help Greenway management make its decision—we focused on cash flow per share, not earnings. We did this because cash flows are the basis for valuation. However, many analysts and investors are acutely aware of earnings and how earnings change. For Greenway, the earnings and cash flow are the same: depreciation offsets new investments. However, even when this is not the case, earnings are highly related to cash flows since the new working capital and PP&E investments are the same regardless of how they are financed.

The effects of different financing methods on the shareholders are often shown graphically in a chart. Exhibit 7-17 on page 302 shows what happens to the shareholders' stake as EBIT changes. This can be either a cash flow per share/EBIT or an earnings per share/EBIT chart. These charts are rather easy to create. Since the relationships are linear, only two points are necessary to plot each of the lines. Typically, analysts determine the **break-even point**—that is, the EBIT level at which the cash flow per share or EPS figures are equivalent for the financing alternatives—and one other point. For Greenway, at any EBIT level above $4.3 million, the debt alternative will provide greater cash flow and earnings per share.[18] The cash flow and earnings per share at the break-even point are $2.05, calculated by using this formula:

---

[17] You may have noted that we are doing our analysis on a per-share basis. This is because different numbers of shares will be outstanding depending on whether management chooses debt or equity financing.

[18] Remember for Greenway the cash flow and earnings are the same. This is good for our example, although it is rarely the case in practice.

EXHIBIT 7-16 Impact on Greenway's 2001 Earnings and Residual Cash Flow of Proposed Financing Schemes (in thousands except per-share data)

		Old EBIT	
			Proposed Financing	
	Before Financing	Debt	Equity
EBIT	$ 4,500	$ 4,500	$ 4,500
Old interest	(700)	(700)	(700)
New interest	0	(720)	0
Profit before taxes	3,800	3,080	3,800
Taxes	(1,292)	(1,047)	(1,292)
Profit after taxes	$ 2,508	$ 2,033	$ 2,508
Depreciation	1,800	1,800	1,800
Changes in PPE and working capital	(1,800)	(1,800)	(1,800)
Residual cash flow	$ 2,508	$ 2,033	$ 2,508
Number of shares	926	926	1,157
Residual cash flow per common share	$2.71	$2.20	$2.17
Earnings per common share	$2.71	$2.20	$2.17
Earnings dilution*	0	18.9%	20.0%

		New EBIT	
			Proposed Financing	
	Before Financing	Debt	Equity
EBIT	$ 5,300	$ 5,300	$ 5,300
Prior interest	(700)	(700)	(700)
New interest	0	(720)	0
Profit before taxes	4,600	3,880	4,600
Taxes	(1,564)	(1,319)	(1,564)
Profit after taxes	$ 3,036	$ 2,561	$ 3,036
Depreciation	2,100	2,100	2,100
Changes in PPE and working capital*	(2,100)	(2,100)	(2,100)
Residual cash flow	$ 3,036	$ 2,561	$ 3,036
Number of shares	926	926	1,157
Residual cash flow per share	$3.28	$2.77	$2.62
Earnings per common share	$3.28	$2.77	$2.62
Earnings dilution**	0	15.6%	20.0%

* We assume this equals depreciation without the new plant.
** This is the percentage decrease from the earnings before financing.

$$\frac{(EBIT - I_n - I_o)(1 - t) - P}{CS_d} = \frac{(EBIT - I_n - I_o)(1 - t) - P}{CS_e}$$

where
 EBIT = Break-even EBIT level
 I_o = Interest payments on old debt

EXHIBIT 7-17 Greenway Corporation Cash Flow/EBIT or Earnings per Share/EBIT Chart

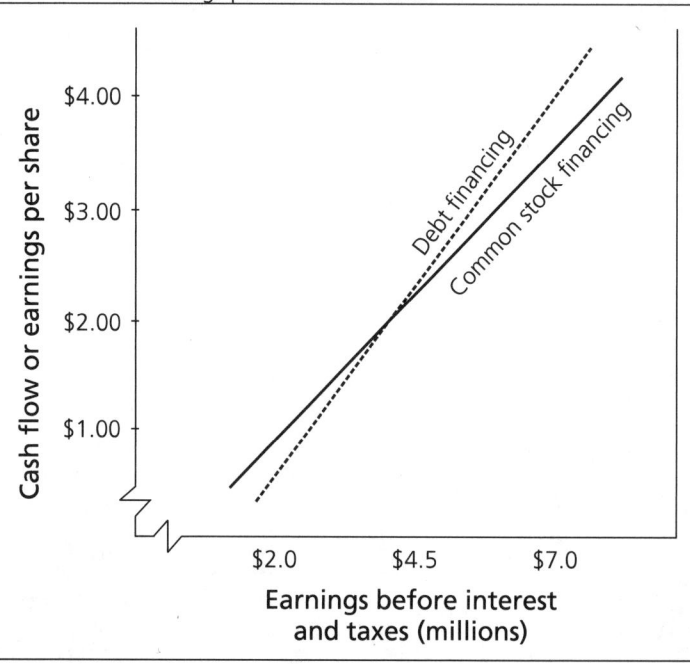

[Chart: Cash flow or earnings per share (y-axis, $1.00 to $4.00) vs. Earnings before interest and taxes (millions) (x-axis, $2.0, $4.5, $7.0). Two lines shown: "Debt financing" (dashed, steeper) and "Common stock financing" (solid), intersecting near $4.5 million EBIT.]

I_n = Interest payments on new debt
t = Tax rate
P = Preferred dividends applicable to the alternative under consideration
CS_d = The number of common shares outstanding with the debt alternative
CS_e = The number of common shares outstanding with the equity alternative

The break-even formula can be solved for the EBIT level as follows:

$$\text{EBIT} = \frac{(CS_d \times I_o) - (CS_e \times I_o) - (CS_e \times I_n)}{CS_d - CS_e} + \frac{P}{(1 - t)}$$

Although cash flow (and earnings) is higher with debt financing, in only one of the past years has Greenway surpassed the break-even levels above which debt is preferable. While debt financing does provide higher EPS for the growth rate projected, there is some danger.

The cash flow per share/EBIT chart, Exhibit 7-17, demonstrates not only the range of EBIT for which one form of financing is preferable, but it also shows the results of leverage. This is most readily apparent from the slope of the lines:

the slope of the debt financing line is greater than the slope of the equity financing line. In other words, for the same growth in EBIT, the growth in cash flow and earnings per share under debt financing exceeds that under common stock financing. This increased rate of change is the primary advantage of using leverage, or increased debt, in financing. The bigger the difference in the slopes of the two lines, the faster the rate of change and the greater the impact leverage will have on earnings and cash flow.

Although our focus has been on the benefits of leverage, below the break-even point leverage works against shareholders. When the EBIT falls below this point, the impact of the leverage will be reversed and shareholders will suffer. The same analysis can be used to study the effect of financing alternatives on dividends per share at different EBIT levels when the payout ratio is kept constant.

Risk of Increased Leverage to Shareholders. We have seen that income increases with debt. We also concluded that lenders should see that the probability of bankruptcy is not large. The question remains, how will Greenway's shareholders see the increase in risk?

Leverage certainly affects shareholders' risk. Greenway will have higher fixed costs, and while its EBIT will not be any more sensitive to changes in economic conditions after financing costs than before, earnings and cash flows will be more sensitive. These changes affect the safety of the shareholders' returns.

In Exhibit 7-2 we saw that the value of the equity rises and falls as leverage changes. Since shareholders' risk increases with added leverage, so should the shareholders' required return. Using the two models from Chapter 6, the capital asset pricing model (CAPM) and the dividend-discount model, let us look at the effect of leverage on Greenway shareholders' required return.

Think for a moment about how changes in leverage would affect the factors used in the capital asset pricing model. Only one factor in the CAPM is company specific, the beta.[19] If Greenway takes on fixed-rate debt, the beta will increase because the after-tax earnings of the company will become more volatile. The increased volatility comes from deducting a fixed charge, interest, from the potentially volatile EBIT. Currently, Greenway's beta is 1.3. Using a theory about how leverage impacts beta, we can estimate a beta at any other level of debt financing. The theoretical relationship shows increased beta with increased leverage:

$$\beta \text{ of leveraged firm} = \beta \text{ of unleveraged firm} \times \{1 + [\text{Debt}/\text{Equity} \times (1 - \text{Tax rate})]\}$$

Using this relationship, we can determine the beta under the different possible capital structures. Exhibit 7-18 shows the results. Greenway's required re-

---

[19] The nominal risk-free rate of return and market premium are common factors for all risky assets.

EXHIBIT 7-18 Greenway's Beta and Required Return on Equity—Different Debt/Equity Levels

Debt/Equity	Beta	CAPM Required Return on Equity
0.0%	1.11	14.2%
21.0	1.26	15.1
25.5	1.30	15.3
46.7	1.45	16.2
60.0	1.55	16.8

turn on equity is that shown in the last column of Exhibit 7-18. In calculating the required return, we have assumed that lenders are willing to lend $6 million to Greenway for 12 percent, the yield on a 7-year U.S. Treasury security is 7.5 percent, the market premium is 6 percent, the tax rate is 34 percent, and that the previous formula represents the relationship between capital structure and beta.

Before seeing how beta re-leveraging would affect the company's and its shareholders' value, let's double-check our CAPM estimate using the dividend-discount model:

$$\text{Shareholders' required return} = \frac{\text{Dividends}}{\text{Market price}} + \text{Growth}$$

To use this model, we need a forecast for dividend growth. Currently Greenway pays $2.40 per share in dividends. This dividend is highly related to earnings. Greenway is mature and has had few uses for its profitability inside the company, and the Greenway family has expressed a need for the money. Before the financing, earnings growth was expected to be 5.2 percent, as shown in Exhibit 7-19. With new investment, the dividend could be increased. The magnitude of the potential increase would depend upon whether management chooses to finance with debt or equity. With a 46.7 percent debt/equity ratio, shareholders might expect that management will increase dividends, perhaps at the earnings and cash flow growth rate of 6.9 percent. Using this debt-scenario information the dividend-discount model cost of equity would be:

$$\text{Shareholders' required return} = \frac{\text{Dividends}}{\text{Market price}} + \text{Growth}$$
$$= \frac{\$2.40}{\$25.50} + 0.068$$
$$= 0.162 \text{ or } 16.2\%$$

This is virtually the same as the cost of equity we calculated using the CAPM.

EXHIBIT 7-19 Greenway Corporation EBIT and Cash Flow Forecasts

	2001	2002	2003	2004	2005	Compound Rate of Growth
EBIT (millions)	$5.30	$5.58	$5.87	$6.17	$6.49	5.2%
Earnings and cash flow per share:*						
Without new financing	3.28	3.48	3.69	3.90	4.13	5.9
Debt financing	2.77	2.97	3.17	3.38	3.61	6.9
Equity financing	2.62	2.78	2.95	3.12	3.30	5.9

* See Exhibits 7-12 and 7-16 for the forecasts.

Value. We have determined and verified the shareholders' required returns. What is the value of the company to its shareholders if the $6 million is financed with debt or with equity? To discover that answer, we need to discount the residual cash flows, shown in Exhibit 7-12. Since the two different financing methods result in different shares outstanding, the best way to see the impact on the shareholders' value is on a per-share basis. Exhibit 7-19 shows the cash flow per share under the different financing scenarios. We will discount the normalized 2001 cash flows using the perpetuity method.[20] The normalized cash flows eliminate unusual or one-time charges to get a forecast of what could occur over the long-term.

The value per share if the company finances itself with debt or equity is shown in Exhibit 7-20. Clearly, given the shareholders' concern for value creation, debt financing is the preferred alternative. The per-share difference in the values is $1.52.

Debt financing increases shareholders' returns. Since the increase in income is not fully offset by increased risk, the value of Greenway increases. Thus, given our analysis, the best alternative appears to be debt financing. This

EXHIBIT 7-20 Greenway Equity Value per Share—Two Different Financing Plans

	Debt Financing	Equity Financing
Equity required return	16.2%	15.1%
Cash flow growth rate	6.9%	5.9%
2001 residual cash flow per share	$2.77	$2.62
Value per share	$29.78	$28.47

---

[20] This is Forecasted 2001 cash flow/[Equity required return − growth rate].

debt-to-total-capital ratio should not be considered too extreme by lenders: with the addition of debt, the cost of capital should decline, and shareholder value should increase. The result will be an increased price for the shareholders' stock.

3. Control

Equity Financing. In addition to diluting cash flow and earnings per share, issuing equity involves a potential loss of ownership control—the "C" in RICHS: a new issue of new common stock can expand the existing ownership and dilute voting control of the current owners of the company. Whether this dilution is important depends on the distribution of ownership of the company. For companies with a significant proportion of ownership in the hands of an individual or a small group of shareholders, where the existing owners wish to maintain a dominant voting position without buying the new stock, then an equity issue may not be appropriate. Typically, the dilution issue is critical at three levels of ownership: when the ownership block will be reduced below 100, below 50, and below 25 percent.

The problem of introducing outside owners for the first time is usually more a psychological problem than a managerial one. If the original owners can still maintain an ownership position greater than 50 percent, they are in a position to continue control of the affairs of the company. The primary change will be that outside owners now have an interest in the operations of the company and may create additional accounting, reporting, and legal requirements.

In spite of the desire to own the company, there may be compelling reasons for issuing outside equity. Not the least of these is the need to develop a market for the equity to provide for liquidity in the owners' holdings. This is particularly true with owners who are aging, and whose family members are not interested in an active role.[21] Another factor that may force a company to admit outside owners is rapid growth accompanied by capital needs that exceed the company's debt capacity or the owner's ability to provide new equity. For these or other reasons, the owner or ownership block may believe that selling equity to outsiders is necessary.

Once outside owners are involved, the original owners can maintain operating control only so long as they own 50 percent of the voting common stock. The 50 percent hurdle is a very difficult one for many owners to pass. Usually the need for outside equity must be severe before the controlling owners will relinquish their 50 percent position.

---

[21] Many canny investment bankers and investment managers predicted that there would be a wave of restructurings and public sales of previously private companies, particularly in Europe, as the post-World War II owners sought to retire. This, coupled with the changes that have come from the European Union, have resulted in a flood of mergers and restructurings in the late 1990s and early 2000s.

For publicly held companies with a widely distributed ownership position, effective control can usually be maintained with an ownership block of 20 to 25 percent. Through solicitation of proxy votes, an insider group with a significant minority position can dominate managerial decisions and control the operations of the company.[22] Because dilution of this block through the issuance of additional shares could eliminate effective control, dilution below this level is another critical point in evaluating equity control.[23]

Other than at these critical points, the dilution of control is not usually a significant issue when issuing equity. Obviously, for the company with a widely dispersed ownership and no significant ownership blocks, the control issue is moot.

Debt Financing. Although the control issue is more easily assessed when financing with equity, debt financing may also create some control issues. Lenders frequently impose restrictions on company operations in the form of debt covenants. These covenants may specify certain actions the company may or may not undertake. For example, loan covenants may require the company to maintain specific levels of working capital, to limit additional borrowings, or to limit the amount of dividends. The purpose of the covenants is to protect the lender's investment, but their effect may be to restrict the ability of owners or managers to operate the company as they believe necessary.

Jim Greenway and the Greenway family own 30 percent of the stock of Greenway Corporation. Since the rest of the shares are held by a large number of people, the Greenway family effectively controls the company. They certainly will be concerned about what happens to their control under different financing alternatives.

Greenway has 926,376 shares outstanding. If the company were to finance its needs with equity, 230,769 new shares would be sold. Jim Greenway and his family would then own:

$$\text{New proportion} = \frac{\text{Old proportion} \times \text{Old shares}}{\text{Total shares}}$$

$$= \frac{0.30 \times 926,376}{1,157,145}$$

$$= 0.24 \text{ or } 24\%$$

If even one person were to buy all the new shares, he or she would control only 20 percent of the company. The family would not lose effective control if new

---

[22] Proxy votes are the right to vote shares on behalf of the shares' owners.
[23] Companies can use equity dilution as a means of thwarting unwanted takeover bids. Through issuing new stock, the company dilutes the ownership an unfriendly suitor may have gained, thereby making the takeover more difficult. Poison pill covenants, where new stock is automatically issued upon an unfriendly takeover attempt, often are designed to create this situation.

equity were issued. Since debt financing will increase the value of the company, management should choose debt to finance the company.

4. Hedging and Speculating

Hedging and speculating, the final factors in the RICHS analysis, are actions that most of us think of in connection with the commodities or securities markets. However, while speculating is an activity that can result in a gain or a loss, hedging is really a mechanism for companies and other investors to insulate themselves from changes in prices. To make a distinction between the two, let's use an example. Elegant Edibles is a large commercial baker of sweet confections. There are four major ingredients in the products the company produces: eggs, butter, flour, and sugar. The current level of egg prices has surprised even management: they are as low as it can remember. Since Elegant Edibles uses large quantities of eggs, low egg prices mean bigger profits. Management, wanting to insulate itself from price increases in eggs later in the year, wants to hedge. To do this it can contract with an egg producer to take delivery of eggs at a predetermined price right before the Christmas baking rush. Elegant management assures itself of the cost of eggs and the egg producer knows the price it will receive for the eggs.

If you disagree with managements' assessment of egg prices, you could speculate on egg prices. To do this you would contract with the baker to deliver the eggs right before Christmas. You sign the contract expecting to fulfill your obligation by buying eggs later at a price that is lower.[24] You profit from the drop in egg prices. If it does not occur as you expected, you lose. Elegant Edibles has a guaranteed egg price, you have either a gain or loss.

Companies face a variety of risks. They can be grouped into categories:

1. Acts of God.
2. Environmental dangers.
3. Business risks having to do with a company's
   a. Products: The sources of product risk comes from uncertain and/or variable
      (i) demand and
      (ii) input costs,
   b. employees,
   c. production processes, and
   d. financing strategy.

Acts of God. These are the kinds of risks for which insurance was designed. Fires, explosions, severe storm damage, floods, and other natural disasters are in this category. The risk-adverse company insures itself, at a cost, against the full extent of these dangers. Companies may take on some of the risk by un-

---

[24] Actually a contract for egg delivery from a producer.

derinsuring or self-insuring. Self-insurers absorb the losses from these acts of God.

Environmental Dangers. In this category are the costs associated with cleaning up environmental damage caused by the company. This damage may be discovered long after the events that created the problem. In this category are oil spills, nuclear accidents, chemical dumping, and strip-mining damage. The most risk-adverse companies attempt to forestall any of these problems; others attempt to share the costly responsibility with the government.

Demand for Products. Sales are at the heart of companies, and fluctuating demand, as you saw in Chapters 2 and 3, can cause dislocations and decline for companies. There are two sources of this risk: consumers will not buy the product, or the demand fluctuates seasonally or cyclically. There are a number of risk-reducing strategies to deal with uncertain demand. With new products, companies perform market research, test markets, product sampling, and advertising to stimulate interest and demand. In addition, research and development processes are designed to keep the companies' products useful and attractive in the marketplace. For fluctuating demand, companies often add lines of business with counter-cyclical characteristics. An example of this would be a snow ski manufacturer that adds a line of water skis to its products.

Costs of Inputs. Here the manager must assess whether the company can get what it needs, and whether it can be certain of its cost. Both cause problems for managers, and to manage each, there are different strategies. To produce every product or service a company offers, the company needs raw materials and labor.

1. *Raw materials.* Just how variable input prices may be depends upon what the company produces. With our bakery example, the cost of its raw materials can fluctuate over time depending upon demand for the item and its supply. However, except in rare circumstances, the materials are available. Depending upon the risk adversity of management, flexibility of the prices of its products, and its expectations for the future prices, management may decide to self-insure, that is, take whatever prices come, or insure, that is, use futures contracts to lock in prices in the future. The risk, or you can think of it as the cost, of self-insurance is the potential increase in expenses if input prices rise. The cost of the futures contract is the price to obtain the contract. We will discuss how futures work later in this section.
2. *Labor.* Here there are two problems: supply and cost. These two are linked, and in the late 1990s concerns about rising wages in the United States were linked to a decrease in the supply of skilled workers due to the robustness of the economy. To operate a company must have workers with the skills needed to produce its products. Management uses

working conditions, benefits, recruiting strategies, and training programs as a way to reduce the risk of finding and retaining its work force. In highly variable product-demand conditions, the company hires temporary workers, may subcontract some of its work to other companies, or may move some or all of its operations to areas with more abundant supplies of labor.

Employee Actions.   Companies are liable for the actions of their employees and for their actions toward its employees. Recently there have been a series of class action suits in U.S. courts that are based on management knowing about product danger, but hiding that danger from the customers. These suits have been settled in industries such as those manufacturing carpet for airlines, breast implants, and cigarettes. Other risks from employees stem from such things as reckless driving, harassment, discrimination, and embezzlement. Formal company codes of conduct, training, mandatory drug and alcohol testing, psychological profiling, and background checks before employment are used as a defense against these risks.

Production Processes.   Here the risk comes from whether a process will work, whether the industry is subject to technological obsolescence, and/or technology leapfrogging by its competitors. The risk of an unworkable process is one that should not be dismissed. Companies have found their innovative systems for scheduling, warehousing, distributing, and manufacturing can fail to live up to their expectations or the timetable for their delivery. One example is Sperry Co. It opened a new state-of-the-art warehouse in the midwest. It took much longer for the unexpected problems with the systems to be repaired than it anticipated, and the problems almost derailed the company.

This innovative technology problem is a serious problem. Increasing competition and technology argue for the most advanced systems and processes, while concern about the efficacy urges management to proceed slowly. Prototype process and slow innovation are risk-reducing strategies. Management may not, however, want to accept the potential losses of being last or slow to innovate.

Financial Risks.   These are the risks that come from the financial transactions the company takes. These may come from choosing to finance with an inappropriate instrument, and changes in interest and foreign exchange rates.

We have discussed the impact that changes in interest and foreign exchange rates can have on a company: costs can rise and revenues can fall unexpectedly. These are dangers ripe for natural or financial hedging. To ameliorate the risk of financing with the wrong instruments, too much/little debt, or debt with the wrong features, management can buy expertise from investment or commercial bankers. They may arrange new financing, swaps, or help the company change its financial risk profile in other ways.

You can, no doubt, think of many other kinds of risks companies face. Some risks are commonplace and are relatively easy to handle, others are more complex. Facing the risks appropriately, management can reduce risks and tailor the risks to the risk-tolerance of the company. In doing so the company can:

1. increase the amount of debt it can use,
2. reduce borrowing costs,
3. avoid financial distress,
4. reduce its risk and thus the return required by its investors,
5. speed up technological innovation,
6. increase new capital investments, and
7. reduce taxes.

Before management takes action, it must assess the dangers that the company faces, and the company's risk tolerance. There are five steps in this company self-examination.

1. Identify the risks that are faced and their sources.
2. Determine whether the risk has important consequences.
3. Identify the methods that could be used to reduce the risk.
4. Determine the company's willingness to take and ability to absorb the risk.
5. Take action.

Identify the risks that are faced and their sources. In the first three chapters of this book we looked at company history. There we developed tools to assess the company's strength and resilience. In Chapter 3 we looked at the potential vulnerability to working capital changes, and in Chapters 2 and 4, forecasted the future and its impact on the company. All of this kind of analysis and more is appropriate in identifying risks.

Determine whether the risk has important consequences. Forecasting the future and the impact of potential changes is critical to this process. Management must focus on what can be affected and to what degree. In Chapter 2 we discussed using scenario analysis and probabilistic analysis to examine the impact of change on the company.

Identify the methods that could be used to reduce the risk. Here the list is limited only by imagination. The company can avoid risk, diversify or insure against it, or hedge it. There are two ways a company can hedge its risk, naturally or in the futures markets.

A **natural hedge** is one where the company itself chooses strategies to reduce its own risk. This may be liability-asset matching where the costs of the liability have the same pattern and sensitivity as the returns on the asset. Thus they offset each other. One example would be a company that has sales in a country, and produces and finances the production in that country. Another example is a company in a cyclical industry: its revenues and profits are highly variable. As a hedge, it has low financial leverage. The good natural hedge will have costs and benefits such that the result is a stable profit, or a spread.

A **futures contract** is a contract to deliver a particular quantity of a commodity at a particular time at a given price. These contracts can be on raw materials such as copper, eggs, or wheat, or financial instruments such as U.S. Treasury bills, bonds, and stock market indices. The producer or owner of the commodity can lock in the price at which it will be sold (hedged) by selling a futures contract that is large enough to cover the commodity held, such as the crop expected to be harvested. Regardless of what happens to the price between the time the future is sold and the date the commodity is to be delivered, the hedger has a guaranteed price; he or she has "hedged the risk." This also works for the consumer of the product, like Elegant Edibles.

The same futures contract can be used to speculate. For example, a speculator, believing a commodity price will decline in the future, can sell a futures contract (without owning the commodity) and, if the price declines, cover the obligation to deliver with another, less expensive futures contract. The speculator gains the difference between the price at which the first contract was sold and the price for which the covering contract was bought.

Investors who are satisfied with the current price can hedge by locking in the price and eliminating price volatility. Investors willing to bet on the upward or downward direction of prices can speculate. Corporate managers do the same thing every time they make a financing decision. Implicitly or explicitly, they bet on the direction of interest rates and stock market levels, and they either hedge or speculate. In the past, managers have used a simple rule: match the maturity of the need (e.g., new plant to be used for a long time) with that of the financing instrument (e.g., long-term debt or equity). Using this matching principle, financing decisions were made by default. While the rule is reasonable in environments where interest rates and the stock market are relatively stable, management must make a decision whether to speculate or hedge when markets are not stable. Decisions by default can be costly.

For risk-averse managers who believe interest rates are going to change, options and futures contracts can provide protection. Change is the operative word in making this decision. Changes create opportunities for speculation or hedging. Hedging provides insurance that can be bought in the futures or options markets.

Options and futures do not provide the only hedging mechanism. Indeed, even after a decision has been made the risk profile of the activity can be changed. For example, **swaps** can be used to transfer an unwanted risk to another party in trade for one that is more tolerable. For example, suppose the company chose variable rate financing and now wants fixed rate financing. Would it have to retire its debt and reissue it to make the change? Not if it can find a **counter-party**, a company wanting the reverse cash flows. Typically done through an intermediary that charges a fee for the transaction, the two parties swap the cash flows from their debt, but not the debt. These swaps are also used to modify foreign exchange exposure. References at the end of the chapter can lead you into the details of swaps.

A risk-taking manager might decide to try to capture gains from cheaper financing later. For instance, if Greenway's managers believe interest rates will fall, they might choose to finance the needed $6 million with short-term money—such as commercial paper or an existing bank line of credit—and refinance later, deliberately mismatching the lives of the asset and the liability for a short time. If the managers' bet is wrong, however, and rates go up, the speculating managers will be forced to borrow later at higher rates rather than making the expected profit.

Managers deciding to finance with equity face the same hedging-speculating dilemma. Their question is, Should we issue stock at the going price, or wait until the market rises and fewer shares need to be issued to raise the same money? Typically, managers are tempted to delay issuing new equity as long as possible because they believe that, in a growing company, earnings will steadily increase, and the stock price will follow. In that case, a stock issue should be delayed to take advantage of the impact of increased profitability on the stock price.

In considering whether to hedge or speculate, management has three primary concerns: (1) the use of long-term versus short-term financing, (2) the sequencing of financing methods over time when the company needs money continuously, and (3) how to deal with multiple-currency financing. With the increased integration of the global capital markets, other questions must be faced.

1. Should nondomestic currency obligations be matched with debt borrowed in the same currency?
2. Should the manager take advantage of perceived opportunities for reduced-rate financing?
3. Should the manager take advantage of profit-making (arbitrage) opportunities that appear to present themselves to the financing corporation?

Whenever a financing decision is made, these questions must be addressed. Forecasting interest rates and market prices is difficult, and the consequences of incorrect forecasts are especially severe in planning capital structure. If forced to raise capital in unfavorable markets, a company will bear the impact of that decision for several years. Exhibit 7-10 showed the rapidity with which short-term rates can change. Rate changes in the last 20 years have been especially severe and rapid. For most growing companies, the problem is not whether to issue debt or equity, but when to do so. Growth brings with it a continuous need for funds, and most companies find that they are unable to finance growth solely through internal sources. Recognizing that the use of external capital is inevitable, companies should seek the most opportune time to enter the markets.

The implicit and explicit speculating and hedging activities involved in financing corporations today are increasingly complex.[25] A wise manager will call on experts inside the firm and at the company's bank and investment bank to explore hedging and speculating in:

1. The general level of interest rates.
2. The level of the stock market.
3. The company's stock price.
4. The quality rating of the company's debt.
5. Multiple capital markets.

These are just a few of the difficult issues that concern present-day managers. These issues are complex, increasing, and continuously changing. Because of these uncertainties, the financing decision lends itself to the sort of multiple-scenario analysis we discussed in Chapter 4. Let's use Greenway's decision to demonstrate the process.

Suppose the treasurer of Greenway decided to issue debt to obtain the $6 million the company needs, but he believed that rates would decline in the future. The treasurer would consider three probable scenarios:

1. Interest rates do not decline and the money must be renegotiated later at the same cost.
2. Interest rates decline and the money is borrowed later at the lower rate.
3. Interest rates rise and the money is borrowed later at a higher rate.

Using the framework described earlier, the manager would find that each of the three scenarios would result in a different debt cost and different values for Greenway's shareholders. Greenway's treasurer must balance the value gained if rates decline against the value lost if rates rise. In addition, the probability that each scenario will occur must be considered. This analysis can become complex and sophisticated.

Identify the company's tolerance for risk. To a large degree this activity is a self-analysis. It may be done by looking at the company's past actions, the owners' tolerance, and any change in the risks the company will face in the future. This is done in a variety of ways. Most typical is discussions among top management and among members of the board of directors.

Take action. In the past action could be taken at a more leisurely pace. With the globalization of business, the speed of technological innovation, and the Internet, managers must assess risk, understand, hedge or accept them, and do so quickly, skillfully, and boldly.

---

[25] We also know from a number of examples that some managers who believed they were hedging were in fact speculating, or did not understand the limits of their hedging activities. Major U.S. banks and others have been involved in both unexpected activities, and in lawsuits that have resulted from these activities. The references listed at the end of the chapter provide further reading into some of these situations.

5. Greenway's Financing Decision

Now back to Greenway. On the basis of Risk, Income, Control, Hedging, and Speculating, what should Greenway management choose to finance the company's needs? Since good managers create value—they add to their shareholders' RICHS—Greenway management should borrow: value will be created for its shareholders without subjecting them to undue risks.

Greenway managers should decide to use debt. Because the company was growing slowly, management would not believe it would need much other new financing in the near future and thus should not feel the need to retain much debt capacity for future use. In addition, management was likely to believe that interest rates, lower than they had been in the recent past, were unlikely to drop much further. On the basis of the analysis, management should conclude that the shareholders would prefer debt and that the risk the added debt created was not excessive.

6. Leasing

Greenway management considered one other way to finance a part of the company's needs: it could lease new equipment for the fabrication operation in the new plant. It may seem peculiar to be discussing leasing in a chapter on financing, but leasing is a form of financing. There are some who believe that the decision management should make is whether to lease or to buy equipment. That is not the decision facing management. Management must determine whether, once it has decided to get the equipment, it should use equity or debt financing to purchase the equipment or to lease it.

Greenway's new equipment would cost $446,975 of the total $4.5 million needed for the new plant. Greenway could, of course, borrow this amount at 12 percent, but the equipment manufacturer's representative has suggested that the company might want to lease it for $76,000 a year for 10 years. To analyze the decision, we will use net present value analysis. The discount rate would be 7.92 percent (12 percent after taxes) to compare leasing to borrowing since they are both fixed cost, contractual obligations.[26] If leasing provides a lower net present value, Greenway should lease the equipment. However, if borrowing yields a superior net present value, borrowing is the way it should be financed. Remember these are NPVs of costs.

Exhibit 7-21 illustrates an analysis of the alternative financing schemes. By purchasing the equipment and borrowing the money, Greenway gets tax shields from deductions for both depreciation and interest. By leasing the equipment, Greenway benefits from the fact that lease payments are tax-deductible expenses. The total after-tax cost of the lease over its life is less than that from borrowing. However, these payments are level, and the costs from

---

[26] There is considerable disagreement about the best way to analyze the lease-borrow decision. There are references at the end of the chapter for those who want further reading.

EXHIBIT 7-21 Analysis of Borrow and Buy Versus Lease

	Borrow and Buy					Lease	
Year	Loan Payment* (1)	Interest (2)	Depreciation** (3)	Tax Shield [(2) + (3)] × 0.34	After-Tax Cash Cost (1) − (4)	Payment (5)	After-Tax Lease Cash Cost (5) × 0.66
1	$79,108	$53,637	$89,395	$48,631	$ 30,477	$76,000	$ 50,160
2	79,108	50,580	71,516	41,513	37,595	76,000	50,160
3	79,108	47,157	57,213	35,486	43,622	76,000	50,160
4	79,108	43,323	45,770	30,292	48,816	76,000	50,160
5	79,108	39,029	36,616	25,719	53,389	76,000	50,160
6	79,108	34,219	29,293	21,594	57,514	76,000	50,160
7	79,108	28,833	29,293	19,763	59,345	76,000	50,160
8	79,108	22,800	29,293	17,712	61,396	76,000	50,160
9	79,108	16,043	29,293	15,415	63,694	76,000	50,160
10	79,108	8,475	29,293	12,842	66,267	76,000	50,160
Total					$522,116		$501,600
Net present value (@ 7.92%)					$335,263		$337,796

* Actually $79,107.7, rounded for brevity.
** 10-year MACRS.

borrowing and owning the equipment are not: they start lower and rise. Thus borrowing and buying the equipment is superior to leasing since the present value of the costs is lower. In fact, the present value of the lease payments is $2,538 higher. Thus management should borrow money to buy the equipment.

V. LEVERAGE IN ACQUISITIONS

We began this long chapter by discussing whether leverage can create value for shareholders and, if so, where that value comes from. It is clear that unused debt capacity reduces shareholder value. Companies that do not fully use their debt capacity are less risky for their shareholders, but they provide lower returns. These companies also are prey for acquirers willing to take more risk and use unused debt capacity.

In Chapter 5 we discussed the valuation of acquisitions and divestitures. What we did not discuss was the value of debt capacity in making an acquisition. Leveraged buyouts are examples of acquisitions in which value is created when the acquirer permanently or temporarily increases the leverage of the target. Appendix 7B discusses the evaluation of leveraged corporate acquisitions.

VI. SUMMARY

This chapter introduced you to the markets for debt and methods for determining whether using debt capital can create value for the firm's shareholders. We determined that to create value, a company's owners (or managers on their behalf) must find debt financing that increases the company's after-tax cash flows per share or reduces the company's risk. We identified one potential source of value—the tax deductibility of interest payments. With the tax advantages of debt comes increased risk to the shareholders, however. We asked, therefore, given these opposing forces, how should management determine the best financing mix for their firm?

To investigate the decisions that had to be confronted by managers, we used the RICHS analysis, looking specifically at the risk, income, and control aspects of the financing decision, and whether management, given the financing alternatives, should hedge or speculate. To see how the RICHS analysis works in practice, we examined the decision facing Greenway management. We then used net present value to determine the best choice. However, Greenway's decision was a simple one, and each decision about financing is different. The current and future capital market conditions—coupled with the company's size, condition, and its current and future needs—require analysis, insight, and judgment. The tools discussed in this chapter help the manager confront the decisions.

SELECTED REFERENCES

For information about the effects of different financing instruments on capital costs, see:

Smith, Clifford W. "Raising Capital: Theory and Evidence." *Midland Corporate Finance Journal*, Spring 1986, pp. 6–22.

For more on capital structure and its value, see:

Brealey, Richard A., and Stewart C. Myers. *Principles of Corporate Finance*. New York: McGraw Hill, 1996, chaps. 17 and 18.

Bodie, Zvi, and Robert Merton. *Finance*. Upper Saddle River, NJ: Prentice Hall, 2000, chap. 16.

Brigham, Eugene F., Louis C. Gapenski, and Michael Ehrhardt. *Financial Management*. 9th ed. Fort Worth, Texas: The Dryden Press, 1999, chap. 16.

Damodaran, Aswath. *Corporate Finance*. New York: John Wiley & Sons, 1997, chaps. 15 and 19.

Miller, Merton H. "Leverage." *Journal of Applied Corporate Finance*, Summer 1991, pp. 6–12.

Miller, Merton H. "The Modigliani-Miller Propositions after Thirty Years." *Journal of Applied Corporate Finance*, Spring 1989, pp. 6–18.

Patrick, Steven C. "Three Pieces to the Capital Structure Puzzle: The Cases of Alco Standard, Comdisco, and Revco." *Journal of Applied Corporate Finance*, Winter 1995, pp. 53–61.

Ross, Stephen A., Randolph W. Westerfield, and Jeffrey F. Jaffe. *Corporate Finance*. 4th ed. Homewood, IL: Richard D. Irwin, 1996, chaps. 15–16.

Shapiro, Alan C. "Guidelines for Long-Term Corporate Financing Strategy." *Midland Corporate Finance Journal*, Winter 1986, pp. 6–19.

For more on the characteristics of debt and debt markets, see:

Brealey, Richard A., and Stewart C. Myers. *Principles of Corporate Finance*. New York: McGraw Hill, 1996, chaps. 23 and 24.

Bodie, Zvi, and Robert Merton. *Finance*. Upper Saddle River, NJ: Prentice Hall, 2000, chap. 8.

Bodie, Zvi, Alex Kane, and Alan Marcus. *Investments*. 4th ed. Boston, MA: Irwin/McGraw-Hill, 1999, chaps. 1–3, 14, and 15.

Brigham, Eugene F., Louis C. Gapenski, and Michael Ehrhardt. *Financial Management*. 9th ed. Fort Worth, Texas: The Dryden Press, 1999, chap. 8.

Damodaran, Aswath. *Corporate Finance*. New York: John Wiley & Sons, 1997, chap. 4.

Fabozzi, Frank J., and T. Dessa Fabozzi. *Bond Markets, Analysis and Strategies*. Englewood Cliffs, NJ: Prentice Hall, 1989.

Ross, Stephen A., Randolph W. Westerfield, and Jeffrey F. Jaffe. *Corporate Finance*. 4th ed. Homewood, IL: Richard D. Irwin, 1996, chaps. 14 and 20.

For more on financing strategy, see:

Barclay, Michael, J., Clifford W. Smith, and Ross L. Watts. "The Determinants of Corporate Leverage and Dividend Policies." *Journal of Applied Corporate Finance*, Winter 1995, pp. 4–19.

Brealey, Richard A., and Stewart C. Myers. *Principles of Corporate Finance*. New York: McGraw Hill, 1996, chap. 19.

Shapiro, Alan C. *Multinational Financial Management*. 5th ed. Needham Heights, Mass.: Allyn & Bacon, 1996, chap. 20.

For more on finance theory and financial practice, see:

Myers, Stewart C. "Finance Theory and Finance Strategy." *Midland Corporate Finance Journal*, Spring 1987, pp. 6–13.

Wruck, Karen Hopper. "Financial Policy as a Catalyst for Organizational Change: Sealed Air Corporation's Leveraged Special Dividend." *Journal of Applied Corporate Finance*, Winter 1995, pp. 20–37.

For more on financing corporate growth, see:

Cornell, Bradford, and Alan C. Shapiro. "Financing Corporate Growth." *Journal of Applied Corporate Finance*, Summer 1988, pp. 6–22.

For more on leasing, see:

Bayless, Mark E., and J. David Diltz. "An Empirical Study of the Debt Displacement Effects of Leasing." *Financial Management*, Winter 1986, pp. 53–60.

Brealey, Richard A., and Stewart C. Myers. *Principles of Corporate Finance*. New York: McGraw Hill, 1996, chap. 26.

Brick, Evan E., William Fung, and Marti Subrahmanyam. "Leasing and Financial Intermediation: Comparative Tax Advantages." *Financial Management*, Spring 1987, pp. 55–59.

Brigham, Eugene F., Louis C. Gapenski, and Michael Ehrhardt. *Financial Management*. 9th ed. Fort Worth, Texas: The Dryden Press, 1999, chap. 19.

Damodaran, Aswath. *Corporate Finance*. New York: John Wiley & Sons, 1997, chap. 13.

Ross, Stephen A., Randolph W. Westerfield, and Jeffrey F. Jaffe. *Corporate Finance*. 4th ed. Homewood, IL: Richard D. Irwin, 1996, chap. 23.

Schall, L. "The Evaluation of Lease Finance Options." *Midland Corporate Finance Journal*, Spring 1985, pp. 48–65.

For more on international capital structure issues, see:

Jacque, Laurent, and Gabriel Hawawini. "Myths and Realities of the Global Capital Markets." *Journal of Applied Corporate Finance*, Fall 1995, pp. 81–94.

Shapiro, Alan C. *Multinational Financial Management*. 6th ed. New York: John Wiley & Sons, 1999, chaps. 6, 15, and 16.

For more on risk and financial engineering, see:

Bodie, Zvi, and Robert Merton. *Finance*. Upper Saddle River, NJ: Prentice Hall, 2000, chaps. 10 and 11.

Brigham, Eugene F., Louis C. Gapenski, and Michael Ehrhardt. *Financial Management*. 9th ed. Fort Worth, Texas: The Dryden Press, 1999, chap. 24.

Damodoran, Aswath. *Corporate Finance*. New York: John Wiley & Sons, 1997, chap. 29.

Mason, Scott, Robert Merton, Andre Perold, and Peter Tufano. *Cases in Financial Engineering*. Englewood Cliffs, NJ: Prentice Hall, 1995.

Web sites of interest:

Options quotes from the Chicago Board of Options Exchange: www.cboe.com

Futures data from the Chicago Board of Trade: www.cbot.com

Historic interest rates from the St. Louis Federal Reserve Bank: www.stls.frb.org

International interest rates from the Federal Reserve Bank's site: www.frb.fed.us

For a good site to get answers to financial questions: www.financialweb.com

STUDY QUESTIONS

1. Management at Zumar, Inc., a chain of gourmet food stores located primarily in New York, was planning to expand its main store in Manhattan. By expanding, Zumar could add an imported beer and wine section. Management believed this $15 million addition would increase sales by 20 percent, to $120 million, in the next year, 2001. The new EBIT sales would be the same as Zumar had on its current product lines, 13 percent, and once the new beer and wine lines were established, management expected overall growth to go back to its traditional 2 percent. Taxes were expected to be 34 percent. Zumar currently had $40 million in 7 percent coupon long-term debt. While principal payments on this debt were $2.8 million per year, management expected to keep debt at this level and thus borrowed whenever principal payments were due. In addition to the debt, Zumar had 2 million shares of stock outstanding, with a par value of $2. The current balance sheet for the company follows.

ZUMAR, INC.
2000 BALANCE SHEET
(in millions)

Assets	
Cash	$ 54
Long-term assets	80
Total assets	$ 134
Liabilities and Equity	
Current liabilities	$ 40
Long-term debt	40
Common stock ($2 par)	4
Retained earnings	50
Total debt and equity	94
Total liabilities and equity	$ 134

To finance the $15 million needed for expansion, management had two alternatives:
a. Borrowing $15 million of 10-year, 10 percent coupon debt with annual principal payments beginning after 5 years.
b. Issuing equity of 750,000 common shares, netting, after issue costs, $20 per share.

Prepare an EPS-EBIT table and chart using the existing and proposed levels of EBIT. What is the break-even EBIT? How do you interpret these data?

2. Zumar management currently had a policy of increasing dividends about 5 percent per year. In 2000 the dividend per share was $0.75. Analyze and compare the present dividend coverage with that likely under both debt and equity financing schemes at the projected level of sales.

3. Which of the two financing schemes is expected to create more value for Zumar's shareholders assuming that:
   a. there will be no changes in net working capital, and corporate expenditures will be equal to depreciation? (These aspects are typical of a low-growth company.)
   b. the required return on equity is 16.9 percent if the expansion is financed with debt, and 15.4 percent if the expansion is financed by equity?

4. Zumar management believed the beer/wine business would bring the company enough notoriety that it could start a web site ordering system within a year. Which financing scheme would allow the company financial capacity to further expand into this web-based business?

APPENDIX 7A
The Weighted-Average Cost of Capital and Free Cash Flow Valuation

Throughout this book, our perspective has been that of the company's owners.[1] Even when we were discussing how to finance the company, we took the owners' point of view: we treated the introduction of debt into a company's capital structure as a subcontracting of the owners' financing obligation to those with different needs, like lenders.

We took this same perspective when we valued capital investments, acquisitions, and financing schemes, using residual cash flows as the basis for our valuations. Since residual cash flows belong to the shareholders, we discounted them at the owners' required return on equity. When we considered how the investments might be financed, we incorporated the costs of debt into our residual cash flows: we subtracted interest payments from the income statement. To take the principal into account we added new principal to the cash flows when we got new debt financing, and subtracted it when debt was paid off. An example of such residual cash flows for Tai Chin, a financially leveraged company, are shown in Exhibit 7A-1. To create this exhibit, we used the following assumptions:

- Sales and costs are expected to grow at 11 percent for five years before they level off to a growth rate of 7 percent. The residual cash flow terminal growth rate will be 8 percent.
- The company currently has $7 million in debt and is in a stable market where debt levels often exceed its current 70 percent level.
- Management expects to continue providing 30 percent of the company's capital from owners.

In this exhibit, all the costs and benefits are included, all providers are paid, and all debts are considered. The only beneficiaries of the net cash flows can be the shareholders. To value these cash flows, we discount the cash flows by the required return of equity holders, 20 percent. The value of the shareholder's equity is $3 million.

This process is rather straightforward and, now that you have seen it throughout this book, you may think redundant. However redundant it is, it is

---

[1] Or management working on behalf of the owners.

EXHIBIT 7A-1 Tai Chin, Inc.

RESIDUAL CASH FLOW FORECAST AND VALUATION
(in thousands of units of currency)

	2000	2001	2002	2003	2004
Revenues	10,000	11,100	12,321	13,676	15,181
Operating expenses	(6,420)	(7,126)	(7,910)	(8,780)	(9,746)
Operating income	3,580	3,974	4,411	4,896	5,435
Depreciation	(1,600)	(1,776)	(1,971)	(2,188)	(2,429)
Interest*	(980)	(1,088)	(1,207)	(1,340)	(1,488)
Earnings before taxes	1,000	1,110	1,233	1,368	1,518
Taxes	(400)	(444)	(493)	(547)	(607)
Net income	600	666	740	821	911
Depreciation	1,600	1,776	1,971	2,188	2,429
Capital expenditures	(2,689)	(2,985)	(3,314)	(3,679)	(3,479)
Changes in					
Working capital	(11)	(12)	(13)	(14)	(13)
Debt principal*	770	855	949	1,053	744
Annual residual cash flows	270	300	333	369	592
Terminal value**					5,328
Residual cash flows	270	300	333	369	5,920

Net present value (@ 20%) = 3,183

* Since revenues grow at 11 percent with a constant capital structure with 30 percent debt, there will be annual increases in debt. Interest payments reflect these changes.
** In 2001, growth in equity will slow to about 8 percent per year. Thus, the value of the cash flows from 2001 onwards is 5,328 [592 × 1.08/(0.2 − 0.08)]. Note, since growth continues, depreciation does not fully offset capital expenditures.

still a laborious process. There is a shortcut, and one that works the case companies in Tai Chin's circumstances: the capital structure is unchanging; and the required returns on debt and equity and the tax rate are expected to stay the same over time. For situations where these three things are true, we can use a shortcut that includes the cost of the debt into the discount rate and assumes that when debt is repaid, it is replaced with an equal amount of debt at the same cost. The debt-free cash flows are called the **free cash flows** and the discount rate is called the weighted-average cost of capital.

I. FREE CASH FLOWS

In our valuations thus far we have included both the costs of debt and changes in debt principal in the cash flows. The resulting cash flows, called the **residual cash flows**, belong only to the company's owners. In this short-cut approach we do not include any debt related cash flows into the cash flows, and the resulting net cash flows are called **free cash flows**. These cash flows belong to both lenders and shareholders—to all capital providers. To contrast the residual and free cash flows, compare Exhibit 7A-1 with Exhibit 7A-2. The difference between the two exhibits is the treatment of capital flows. In Exhibit 7A-1 the interest expense and principal payments appear in the residual cash flows alone. The free cash flows shown in Exhibit 7A-2 belongs to both shareholders and lenders. Lest you forget, to use the free cash flow method for valuation, the company must have:

- The same costs of debt and equity over time,
- The capital structure, and
- Tax rate must remain the same.[2]

When this is true, we can value the cash flows at the weighted-average cost of the company's capital.

EXHIBIT 7A-2   Tai Chin, Inc.

FREE CASH FLOW FORECAST AND VALUATION
(in thousands of units of currency)

	2000	2001	2002	2003	2004
Revenues	10,000	11,100	12,321	13,676	15,181
Operating expenses	(6,420)	(7,126)	(7,910)	(8,780)	(9,746)
Operating income	3,580	3,974	4,411	4,896	5,435
Depreciation	(1,600)	(1,776)	(1,971)	(2,188)	(2,429)
Earnings before taxes	1,980	2,198	2,440	2,708	3,006
Taxes	(792)	(879)	(976)	(1,083)	(1,202)
Net income	1,188	1,319	1,464	1,625	1,804
Depreciation	1,600	1,776	1,971	2,188	2,429
Capital expenditures	(2,689)	(2,985)	(3,314)	(3,679)	(3,479)
Changes in working capital	(11)	(12)	(13)	(14)	(13)
Annual free cash flow	88	98	108	120	741
Terminal value*					16,518
Free cash flows		88	98	108	120	17,259
Net present value of free cash flows (@ 11.8%)   10,192

* In 2001 growth will slow to about 7 percent per year. Thus, the value of the cash flows from 2001 onwards is 16,518 (741 × (1 + 0.07))/(0.118 − 0.07). Because of growth, depreciation does not offset PPE.

---

[2]   This means that the proportions of debt and equity are unchanging.

II. CALCULATING THE WEIGHTED-AVERAGE COST OF CAPITAL

The discount rate used in this method includes both the company's cost of equity and debt. It is the weighted-average cost of all the sources of capital. To calculate it multiply the costs of debt and equity by their respective portions in the company's expected capital structure.

$$R_{WACC} = [(R_d \times (1 - \text{Tax rate})) \times D/V] + [R_e \times E/V]$$

where
- R_{WACC} = Weighted-average cost of capital (WACC)
- D = Amount of debt expected in the firm's capital structure
- E = Amount of equity expected in the firm's capital structure
- V = D + E, the value of the firm's capital
- R_d = Marginal required return on debt
- R_e = Marginal required return on equity

Because the cost of debt to the company is partially offset by the tax effect, that effect must be taken into account. To see how this is done, let's calculate the WACC for Tai Chin.

Let us look at Tai Chin. Lenders making new loans to Tai Chin say that they would require a return of 14 percent. Using the methods described in Chapter 6, Tai Chin analysts have determined that the equity holders require a return of 20 percent for their investment in the company. Management's target debt/total capital ratio is 40 percent debt. Management does not expect the company's current tax rate of 40 percent to change. Using these assumptions, Tai Chin's weighted-average cost of capital is 11.88 percent:

$$R_{WACC} = [(0.14 \times (1 - 0.40)) \times 0.7] + [0.20 \times 0.30]$$
$$= 0.1188 \text{ or } 11.88\%$$

To estimate the weighted-average cost of capital we used four things:

1. the marginal required return on debt,
2. the marginal required return on equity,
3. the marginal tax rate, and
4. the marginal proportions in the capital structure.

Let us look at each one in turn.

1. Marginal Required Return on Debt

In this short-cut analysis of new investments, we use the WACC as the discount rate. New investments is the key word. Since it is the future we are considering, everything, the free cash flows and required rates of return, must be those that will occur in the future. This means that any rates we use, including the required return on debt, must take into account the potential risk of the investment and expected market conditions. Thus we cannot use the cost of old debt, the **embedded cost**, the price the company has paid on debt that it borrowed in the past.[3] Instead, we will use the **marginal cost of debt**, the cost if the company borrowed today.

How do we find a marginal cost of debt for the company? If the company is in the process of borrowing, the marginal cost of debt is obvious, it is the rate at which lenders say they will lend. If the company is not borrowing, then we have to estimate what new debt would cost. One estimate could come from the yield-to-maturity. The yield-to-maturity is the yield on the company's outstanding debt.

When debt is first issued, unless it is junk, its coupon (the interest rate on the face value) is appropriate for the market conditions: if rates are 10 percent for Aaa corporate bonds, an Aaa-rated company's debt would cost 10 percent. However, conditions change, and investors change their required return for Aaa debt, and the price of the bond will change to reflect this new reality: the price will decline to yield a higher rate or increase to yield a lower rate. The change will be reflected in the bond's yield on this new price, or the **yield-to-maturity**.[4] The formula for this is in Chapter 7.

Many companies issue different kinds of debt at different times: some debt may be placed with banks or insurance companies, and other debt may be sold to the public. Each kind of debt will have different features. The differences in such things as maturity, coupon, and security will result in different interest rates, even if it were all issued at the same time. The marginal cost of debt will be the weighted average of the costs of all the company's debt.

The marginal debt cost is an average of the costs of several kinds of debt used by the company. Most analysts exclude short-term (current) debt from the calculation primarily because it will be repaid within one year. Analysts have reconsidered the exclusion of short-term debt because it has become an important source of funds for many firms, either because the borrowers use it as a stopgap financing source while they wait for long-term rates to drop or because lenders prefer it in order to monitor the borrower or to frequently revise rates. The best rule for an analyst to follow in dealing with short-term debt is to exclude it if it is being used to supply temporary needs (such as seasonal inventory buildup) but include it and its cost if the short-term funds represent permanent financing for the firm's assets.

---

[3] Analysts mistakenly take the interest payments from the income statement and divide that number by the total debt principal from the balance sheet. This is cost that debt, borrowed in the past under different conditions, cost. It is not appropriate to use this figure to evaluate future opportunities.

[4] If there is no publicly traded debt, the analyst might use the yield-to-maturity on the debt of a comparable company or companies as a proxy. The yield-to-maturity is the rate of return that equates interest and principal payments to the current market price of the debt.

II. Calculating the Weighted-Average Cost of Capital

If the company has no traded debt, then what proxy could be used? In a case where individuals or institutions that do not trade hold the company's debt, we will use an analogy or proxy process. In this case we must determine what bond rating the company might command if it had publicly traded debt, and use the current rate on debt of that quality. These rates are available in the financial press and from many web sites.

2. Cost of Equity

In Chapter 6 we discussed at length methods for estimating required return on equity, the cost of equity. For Tai Chin we would use a model like the CAPM to calculate the marginal required return on equity. The return on equity would be 20 percent.

3. Tax Rate

The tax rate is important in determining the company's after-tax cost of debt. Since this is a forward-looking analysis, we are interested only in the marginal tax rate, not the company's historic rate. For a cursory analysis we typically use the statutory rate, the rate required by law. However, that rate can change, and any expected changes should be incorporated into the analysis. For a large investment or acquisition, the actual expected tax consequences should be built into the analysis, and, because of the changes over time, the WACC method should not be used for valuation in those circumstances.[5]

4. Debt and Equity Proportion

While calculating the amounts of debt and equity used to finance a company might appear to be quite simple, it is, like most of the analyst's jobs, not completely straightforward. The capital structure we want to use in calculating the weighted-average cost of capital is what investors *believe* the structure will be in the future. This may or may not be the proportions currently held by the company.[6]

Just as rates change in the marketplace, so do the values of the securities. The value of debt, for instance, declines as rates rise. The market value of stock rises as the company prospers.[7] Because this is so, the book value of the debt and equity usually do not reflect their true value. Thus many analysts use the

---

[5] In fact, the WACC method can be used with changing capital structure, tax rates or capital costs. However, the tediousness of adjusting the WACC each year for the changes suggests that either the residual cash flow valuation or the adjusted present value, described in Appendix 7B, is more appropriate.

[6] The current proportions on the balance sheet represent the cumulative impact of all past financing.

[7] Given no change in marketwide required returns, the risk-free and market rates of return in the CAPM will remain the same.

market-value capital structure, the value of the capital structure in current capital market terms. For the value of equity the analyst would take the current market price per share times the number of shares; for debt, the principal value at current market yields. This can result in a very different capital structure than the book value structure. It is really a proxy for what is the theoretical objective, the target structure.

Many analysts use the book value or market value capital structure in the WACC, even though this may or may not represent the proportions that management will use in the future. Some analysts estimate the company's marginal or "target" capital structure—that structure wherein sufficient capital is raised to finance all value-creating investments. They use this target capital structure presuming that is the capital structure that investors expect the company to use.[8] For some companies, the target capital structure is one at which the cost of capital is at its minimum. For other firms, the marginal capital structure reflects decisions to keep the leverage within a certain range. However the marginal capital structure is determined, it is a challenging task since it is the financing proportions that are anticipated by lenders and shareholders, not what the company currently holds.[9]

For simplicity, we assumed that Tai Chin's current book value capital structure was the same as its market value and target capital structures. The **book value capital structure** is the percentage of debt and equity currently financing the assets of the firm. It can be calculated directly from the balance sheet. The **market value capital structure** is calculated by taking the current market values of the company's debt and equity and recalculating the same percentages. In Tai Chin's book and market value, and target capital structures, 30 percent of the capital was equity and 70 percent was debt.

We made the Tai Chin example especially easy by assuming that the book, the market value, and management's target capital structures were all the same. If they were not, we might use the current market value to provide a clue to investors' expectations, we might turn to statements made by management about its future intentions, or we might examine the financing activities of similar companies to gain insight about their practices.[10] In spite of the vagueness of the marginal capital structure, and our love of facts and ease, it is not ap-

---

[8] Since lenders and shareholders "price" their securities with company and market conditions in mind, plus a view to their relative positions as capital providers, this target structure is the appropriate choice. Unfortunately, targets are not observable.

[9] When companies make investment decisions, they may be raising no outside capital: they may have sufficient resources to make the investment. Even a company in need of capital usually does not simultaneously issue debt and equity securities just to fit its target capital structure. Rather, the firm would issue first one and then the other, depending on market prices and available investors in the capital markets. Over time, however, the firm would issue sufficient debt and equity to achieve its targeted capital structure.

[10] While many firms use their book value structure as the target, analysts are concerned with the market value of the marginal capital raised. If the target is the same as the book value capital structure, the market value of the capital raised will be in the same proportions as the book value, regardless of the market value of the capital already in use by the firm.

propriate to use either book value or market value capital structures in the calculation of WACC if they differ from the target expected for the funds being raised.

III. WHEN TO USE FREE CASH FLOW VALUATION

Because they believe using the free cash flow valuation and the WACC frees them from having to determine the explicit debt-service schedule associated with any investment, many people choose to use the free cash flow valuation exclusively. However, the WACC includes an *implicit* forecast of the capital structure and costs. We believe *explicit* forecasts are superior to error-prone shortcuts, and thus suggest that the residual cash flow valuation method is superior. Using the free cash flow method of valuation exclusively is a mistake.[11]

The free cash flow valuation is an acceptable shortcut under certain circumstances. Those circumstances are when the company's capital structure, costs of debt and equity, and the tax rate are not expected to change. If they are expected to change, then the residual cash flow method is much better.[12]

There is a rational use of the WACC—to value small investments that a company frequently makes, where managers find the time and effort needed to make explicit forecasts of the financing arrangements prohibitive. While it eases the pain of valuing the myriad of small investments companies make, the result of using this shortcut in this way is to discount some investments at a rate that is too low and others at a rate that is too high. In an effort to deal with the problem and still use the free cash flow valuation, managers have adapted discount rates for risk—grouping investments into so-called risk classes. We showed such a risk class scheme in Chapter 4. In spite of its ease, except for the small projects a company evaluates, one would do better to avoid such arbitrary hurdle rates. The residual cash flow valuation is explicit. The magnitude of the potential errors when using free cash flows can be significant. These errors can be seen in such valuations as those done in leveraged acquisitions. Appendix 7B describes such valuations.

Before we conclude, let us value Tai Chin using the free cash flow method and the WACC. Return to Exhibit 7A-2 and you will see the free cash flow valuation of Tai Chin. These are the debt-free cash flows discounted at Tai Chin's WACC of 11.8 percent. The value of Tai Chin is $10,000, $7,000 higher than the value we calculated using the residual cash flows and the cost of equity in

---

[11] The analyst could, of course, change both the costs of debt and/or equity or their proportions in the WACC calculation. However, if the analyst is making explicit forecasts of costs and capital structure changes, they can be incorporated directly into the residual cash flows. In many ways the WACC is an artifact of a time when analysts' tools were pencil and paper, not a calculator or computer.

[12] For financial structure implications for the value of the company, the adjusted present value method described in Appendix 7B is very useful.

Exhibit 7A-1. How can Tai Chin be worth $10,000 and $3,000 at the same time? Does the change in method actually change the value? If not, which method is right?

In spite of the fact that the value of the company from Exhibits 7A-1 and 7A-2 do not appear to be equal, they are. The free cash flow valuation values the total company to lenders and shareholders; the residual cash flow valuation belongs to the equity shareholders alone. Thus to obtain the value of the company to its shareholders using the free cash flow method, the value of Tai Chin's debt must be deducted from the free cash flow value. For Tai Chin, the free cash flow value is $10,000, and the debt value is $7,000. The resulting value of the equity is $3,000. This is identical to the residual cash flow valuation except for a slight rounding error.

For the two valuations to be the same, both must use all the same assumptions.[13] If the cash flows are the same, the only difference in the two methods is where the costs of debt are incorporated. In the residual cash flow method we incorporated debt activity into the cash flows; in the free cash flow method they were incorporated in the discount rate.

One thing that may bother you in looking at these calculations is taxes. In the residual cash flows, interest is a tax-deductible expense. In the free cash flows, the interest expense and its impact on taxes is taken into account in the discount rate. As for the new debt inflows or the repayment of debt, the free cash flow method assumes that any debt repayments would be offset by new debt. Remember, in the typical use of this method capital structure does not change in the WACC.

IV. SUMMARY

The free cash flow method of valuation is a very useful shortcut when the company's capital structure, financing costs, and tax rate are unchanging into the future. In spite of its ease, in estimating the weighted-average cost of marginal capital, the analyst's judgment is required again and again. The costs of debt and equity and the marginal capital structure all are needed to calculate a WACC. We must try to estimate what investors expect from owning a share of our company, what lenders will require, and how the company is expected to raise capital. While we have several approaches that will help the analyst make these estimates, each must be used thoughtfully. Furthermore, as conditions in the world and domestic economies change, the capital markets react, and investors' expectations change—sometimes quite rapidly. When these changes occur, the firm itself may change: new projects may be announced, and old pro-

---

[13] There is one other way we have valued a company, the dividend-discount model. If we did this for Tai Chin, since it is based on the same assumptions about the company, we will obtain the same valuation.

jects may succeed or fail. Once again, investors' and lenders' expectations will change, and so will their required returns. The analyst not only must estimate elusive figures, but must do so at the same time that figures are changing. Skill and judgment take the financial analyst's job beyond the mechanical and the routine, making it a continual challenge.

SELECTED REFERENCES

For more on estimating and using the weighted-average cost of capital, see references in Chapter 7 and:

Ehrhardt, Michael C. *The Search for Value: Measuring the Company's Cost of Capital.* Boston, Mass.: Harvard Business School Press, 1994.

For more on the weighted-average cost of capital in an international context, see:

Cooper, Ian, and Evi Kaplanis. "Home Bias in Equity Portfolios and the Cost of Capital For Multinational Firms." *Journal of Applied Corporate Finance*, Fall 1995, pp. 95–102.

Shapiro, Alan C. *Multinational Financial Management.* Needham Heights, Mass.: Allyn & Bacon, 1989, chap. 18.

Stulz, Rene. "Globalization of Capital Markets and the Cost of Capital: The Case of Nestle." *Journal of Applied Corporate Finance*, Fall 1995, pp. 30–38.

STUDY QUESTIONS

1. Bakelite Company, located in rural Ohio, is a commercial bakery specializing in biscuit making. Recent substantial declines in grain prices have resulted in significant raw material savings. Because prices do not need to be cut—Bakelite is already at the low-priced end of the market—its cash reserves have built up well beyond historical levels. This wealth of cash spurs management, with the support of the board, to consider some capital investments it has long deferred. The various division heads are asked to propose capital investments to Carl Borg, vice president of finance. Mr. Borg has the job of evaluating the projects and making recommendations to the board. Because it has been years since Bakelite made any significant investments, Mr. Borg is concerned about choosing the right ones. To get some advice about making these decisions, he calls an old college friend, Jane Wilson, now a finance professor at a nearby university. Professor Wilson says that, because Mr. Borg already has cash flow forecasts from the divisions, the only thing left is to discount the flows at the relevant cost of capital.

    Mr. Borg is well aware that the company's bonds were rated B when they were issued several years earlier. The coupon rate was 17.3 percent. At present, two insurance companies hold all the bonds, so they do not trade. The current yield on newly issued B-rated bonds is 14.5 percent.

Appendix 7A The Weighted-Average Cost of Capital

Bakelite is too small a company to be followed by investment services such as Value Line. It pays a $3 dividend, and its current market price in the over-the-counter market is $25. However, a regional investment banker has just published a brief report on the company. It includes a beta of 1.32, and the analyst's estimates for Bakelite's nominal long-term growth of 4.9 percent, a figure with which management agrees. At present, U.S. Treasury 7-year bonds are yielding 8.9 percent, and 90-day Treasury bills yield 6.5 percent. Historically, the stock market has yielded about 8.5 percent above Treasury bills and 6 percent above longer term bonds. Bakelite's balance sheet is as follows:

BAKELITE CORPORATION
(in millions)

Assets		Liabilities and Equity	
Cash	$0.2	Accounts payable	$0.8
Marketable securities	2.3	Taxes payable	0.3
Accounts receivable	1.1	Total current liabilities	1.1
Total current assets	3.6	Long-term debt	1.3
Net property, plant,		Common stock	0.5
and equipment	1.2	Retained earnings	1.9
Total assets	$4.8	Total equity	2.4
		Total liabilities and equity	$4.8

Mr. Borg believes that Bakelite's current capital structure represents the mix the company will continue to use. Its taxes are 34 percent. What is Bakelite's weighted-average cost of capital?

2. Select Company is in the process of developing a discount rate to evaluate capital projects that have been proposed for the following year. The company, with net income of $504,000 in 2000, has been growing steadily, with both sales and earnings increasing at about 5.7 percent per year. The firm's return on equity has also been fairly constant at about 7.7 percent per year. Without any change in the company's strategy, these trends are expected to continue into the future. At the end of 2000, Select Company had an A bond rating. Debt on the balance sheet had been issued at an average rate of 10 percent. Long-term A-rated bonds are currently being sold at 9.6 percent. Select's stock is selling for $6.90, 300,000 shares are outstanding, and the company consistently pays out 24 percent of earnings in dividends. Because of its growth and performance, Select's beta is estimated at 1.10.

Based on the following data, compute the company's marginal weighted-average cost of capital, using:
a. The dividend discount model, where $g = (1 - \text{Payout})(\text{ROE})$.

b. The capital asset pricing model (six-month Treasury bills are selling for approximately 6.2 percent; U.S. Treasury 7-year bonds are selling for 8.1 percent; the long-term market premium is 3.6 percent).
c. The Select Company 2000 and 2001 projected equities and liabilities as shown below.

	2000	2001
Current liabilities	$1,227.7	$1,421.5
Long-term debt	2,261.5	2,487.7
Common stock par value	1,500.0	1,500.0
Retained earnings	2,700.0	3,120.0
Long-term debt and equity	6,461.5	7,107.7

APPENDIX 7B
Adjusted Present Value: The Case of the Leveraged Acquisition

Leveraged acquisitions in the United States in the 1980s came to be called leveraged buyouts. Leveraged acquisitions, or leveraged buyouts, are acquisitions in which the form of the financing has the potential of significantly affecting the value of the company being bought. These highly leveraged acquisitions might be made by a management group buying its publicly held company and making it private, often in conjunction with an investment partnership. They may be made by an individual or company, with the object of holding, dismantling, or selling the target firm.

In general, those making these acquisitions used substantial amounts of debt to acquire a company, with the expectation of repaying the debt from the acquired company's future cash flows or from the proceeds of selling assets the acquired company owned. In the earliest part of the highly leveraged takeover binge in the United States in the 1980s, attractive candidates had several or all of the following characteristics:

1. Stable, predictable cash flows.
2. Little, if any, debt.
3. Assets that could be stripped from the company and sold.
4. Good quality management.

Later, as attractive candidates disappeared, many companies were acquired that met few or none of these characteristics. Many of these companies were the ones that, in the 1990s, had considerable difficulty repaying the debt that was used to acquire them.

It is important for the manager to understand highly leveraged transactions for three reasons. First, these transactions created some of the problems that were evident in the early 1990s in the United States. Second, the analysis of these transactions is somewhat different from the basic cash flow analysis discussed in the preceding chapters. Third, "highly leveraged" is a matter of semantics: the acceptance of higher amounts of debt financing varies by country and industry and over time within a country or industry. The good manager will understand the difference between high and excessive leverage and will

Appendix 7B Adjusted Present Value

not underutilize leverage in the future in an overreaction to the difficulties faced by some companies acquired during periods of market excess.[1]

This appendix discusses the changes in an analysis that must occur when evaluating a highly leveraged transaction. This analysis can be used whenever the analyst wants to be explicit about forecasting and valuing the operating and financing cash flows. For this discussion, we will return to an example that was used in Chapter 5, the acquisition of Tract Co. Let's evaluate the acquisition, but this time let's use significant amounts of leverage.

Lifelike Cabinet Co. management agreed to pay the full value, $3.7 million, for Tract Co. Management approached lenders about financing the acquisition. A group of lenders has agreed to provide $2.4 million in debt, 65 percent of the price of the acquisition. With timely principal repayments, the debt would be fully repaid by 2005. Would the value of the acquisition change if significant amounts of debt were used in its acquisition?

To determine this value, we will use a two-step process, separating the residual cash flows from the cash flows associated with the leverage. This method is called adjusted present value, since it adjusts the residual cash flow value of the investment by the positive or negative debt-derived value. The first step is to forecast the residual cash flows for the investment, in this case the acquisition of Tract Co. We showed the cash flow forecasts in Chapter 5, but repeat them here so you may see the process.[2] (See Exhibit 7B-1.)

EXHIBIT 7B-1   Tract Co.

RESIDUAL CASH FLOWS AND VALUE (in thousands)

	2000	2001	2002	2003	2004
Sales	$10,300	$10,300	$10,300	$10,300	$10,300
Operating expenses	(9,476)	(9,476)	(9,476)	(9,476)	(9,476)
Depreciation	(50)	(50)	(50)	(50)	(50)
Income before taxes	774	774	774	774	774
Taxes	(263)	(263)	(263)	(263)	(263)
Income after taxes	511	511	511	511	511
Depreciation	50	50	50	50	50
Change in PPE	(50)	(50)	(50)	(50)	(50)
Annual residual cash flow	511	511	511	511	511
Terminal value	—	—	—	—	3,703
Residual cash flow	$ 511	$ 511	$ 511	$ 511	$ 4,214

Net present value @ 13.8% discount rate = $3,704

---

[1] Some of the difficulties can be traced to over-leveraging companies that were not good candidates for high leverage. Other difficulties can be traced to the fact that the euphoric 1980s had not prepared many managers for the unexpectedly deep and protracted recession that followed.

[2] Actually, in Chapter 5, Exhibit 6, we showed only one year of cash flows and used the perpetuity method of valuation. Here we extend the analysis to 5 years to match the debt financing's life.

Appendix 7B Adjusted Present Value

The next step is to forecast the debt related cash flows. The interest rate on the debt will be high since it finances so much of the acquisition. At an interest rate of 11 percent, and five annual equal payments, the debt repayment schedule is forecasted.[3] This analysis is shown in Exhibit 7B-2.

The debt has a cost and a benefit to Lifelike Cabinet Co. The cost is the interest payments, the benefit is the tax shields from the interest payments. The tax-shield is shown in Exhibit 7B-3. The discount rate that is used for the debt-tax shields reflects their risk: the lenders require an 11 percent return, thus the discount rate should be 11 percent.

The present value of the acquisition of Tract Co., including the value of the debt-derived tax shields is

$$\text{Adjusted present value} = \text{Present value of residual cash flows} + \text{Present value of debt-tax shields}$$
$$= \$3.7 \text{ million} + 0.225 \text{ million}$$
$$= \$3.925$$

We could include in the debt value calculations below market rate debt, special financing advantages from government authorities, and other financing advantages. All of these truly increase the value of the investment.

There are a few problems that we have created with our simple analysis. First, we used the residual cash flow analysis just as we had done it in Chapter 5. However, we know that the shareholders are going to worry about the amount of leverage that is used in making the acquisition. Thus their required returns will be impacted. At first, when leverage is 65 percent of the financing,

EXHIBIT 7B-2 Tract Acquisition Debt Repayment Schedule (in thousands)

Debt Payment Schedule					
Debt—beginning of year	$2,400.0	$2,014.6	$1,586.8	$1,112.0	$585.0
Payments	649.4	649.4	649.4	649.4	649.4
Interest	264.0	221.6	174.6	122.3	64.4
Principal	385.4	427.8	474.8	527.0	585.0
Debt—end of year	$2,014.6	$1,586.9	$1,112.0	$ 585.0	$ 0.0

EXHIBIT 7B-3 Tax Shield from Debt (in thousands)

Interest	$264.0	$221.6	$174.6	$122.3	$64.4
Tax shield (taxes @ 34%)	$89.8	$75.3	$59.3	$41.6	$21.9
Present value of tax shield @ 11% = $225.050					

---

[3] Note that after the five years the company has returned to a normal capital structure.

the shareholders' required return will be higher. As leverage declines, the required return will return to that for an all-equity-financed investment. In our example we used a single rate, 13.8 percent. Doing year-by-year discount rates result in a required return in the first year that would be over 23 percent. That was calculated using the beta releveraging formula from Chapter 7. Changing discount rates would impact the value. However, in large transactions every detail should be carefully calculated and assessed.

In this evaluation of a leveraged transaction, we used very high leverage. However, it is not excessive if the company can service its debt (pay its interest and principal payments). Using the cash flow forecasts and doing some simple interest coverage ratios, we can determine that Tract is able to cover its interest payments, and appears to have considerable flexibility in case of an economic or business downturn. The cash flows from Tract alone cannot cover the principal payments. This may be an issue for Lifelike management. In essence, the limits on leverage depend on the supply of willing lenders and the buyer's appetite for risk.[4]

CONCLUSION

In this chapter we have discussed leveraged transactions. These are the ultimate example of the interaction of financing and investment decisions. We used an adapted version of net present value, and included all the costs and benefits of financing into the residual cash flow analysis. The analysis of leveraged transactions shows the attraction of using considerable debt in the financing of acquisitions. Unfortunately, some of those who made such acquisitions in the 1980s failed to evaluate fully the highly leveraged company's ability to service its debt, particularly in an economic downturn. Leverage is not the problem; the problem is that the analyst must evaluate both the potential return and the risks.

REFERENCES

For more on leveraged buyouts, see:

Brealey, Richard A., and Stewart C. Myers. *Principles of Corporate Finance.* 5th ed. New York: McGraw Hill, 1996, chap. 33.

Brigham, Eugene F., and Louis C. Gapenski. *Financial Management.* Fort Worth, TX: Dryden, 1994, chap. 24.

---

[4] We have not included study questions at the end of this appendix. The analytical techniques used are like those used in Chapter 5.

Clark, John J., John T. Gerlach, and Gerard Olson. *Restructuring Corporate America*. Fort Worth, TX: Dryden, 1996.

Donaldson, Gordon. "Corporate Restructuring in the 1980s—and Its Import for the 1990s." *Journal of Applied Corporate Finance*, Winter 1994, pp. 55–69.

Ferenbach, C. "Leveraged Buyouts: A New Capital Market Evolution." *Midland Corporate Finance Journal*, Winter 1983, pp. 56–62.

Fridson, Martin S. "What Went Wrong with the Highly Leveraged Deals?" *Journal of Applied Corporate Finance*, Fall 1991, pp. 57–67.

Rock, Milton, and Robert H. Rock. *Corporate Restructuring*. New York: McGraw Hill, 1990.

Ross, Stephen A., Randolph W. Westerfield, and Jeffrey F. Jaffe. *Corporate Finance*. 4th ed. Homewood, IL: Richard D. Irwin, 1996, chap. 17.

For a good explanation of adjusted present value, see:

Brealey, Richard A., and Stewart C. Myers. *Principles of Corporate Finance*. 5th ed. New York: McGraw Hill, 1996, chap. 19.

APPENDIX
Solutions to Study Questions

CHAPTER 1

1a. To calculate the ratios, use the formulas in the chapter and the data provided in the problem. To determine the sustainable growth rate, both the return on equity and the earnings retained must be computed. You can compute every ratio in the sustainable growth rate framework, as shown below, or use the simple formula ROE × Retention Ratio. Using the latter formula, however, leaves you with no easy way to answer the second part of the question.

Step 1. The return on equity for 1998 is net income divided by the total equity ($26.5/$178.8 = 0.148, or 14.8 percent).

Step 2. To determine earnings retained, subtract the dividends from the net income and divide the result by net income. Make sure that the amounts are either company totals or the amounts on a per-share basis.

The following table provides the results of these calculations for 1996 to 2000. As you can see, the company's sustainable growth rate has declined over the 5-year period.

	EASY CHAIR CO. FINANCIAL RATIOS				
	1996	1997	1998	1999	2000
Return on sales	6.7%	5.9%	5.4%	5.0%	4.8%
Sales/assets	146.7	155.6	144.6	158.5	163.7
Return on assets	9.9	9.2	7.9	7.9	7.8
Assets/equity	158.5	163.3	188.3	179.6	168.6
Return on equity	15.6%	14.9%	14.8%	14.2%	13.2%
Earnings per share	$1.26	$1.34	$1.45	$1.54	$1.58
Dividend payout	31.8%	29.8%	27.6%	32.5%	31.6%
Retention ratio	68.2	70.2	72.4	67.5	68.4
Sustainable growth rate	10.7	10.5	10.7	9.5	9.0

The main thing that has changed for *EASY* Chair is the profit margin (the return on sales). It has declined from 6.7 percent in 1996 to 4.8 percent in 2000. The analyst would obviously want to look further into the expense ratios, perhaps doing a common-size income statement to determine what is the primary cause of the decline—expense increases, or price declines. The answer to question 1b should help shed light on the question of price declines: If the whole industry is experiencing pricing squeezes, then all companies, including Hannaford, should have seen dropping ROSs and thus ROEs. The ROEs are examined in 1b.

1b. To compare EASY to the industry, the simplest approach is to subtract the industry's ratios from those of the company. The result is shown in the table that follows.

EASY CHAIR CO.
DIFFERENCES BETWEEN EASY AND HOME FURNISHINGS INDUSTRY RATIOS

	1997	1998	1999	2000
Return on equity	−0.8%	−0.5%	−1.3%	−1.9%
Retention rate	−1.8	1.4	−3.5	−2.6
Sustainable growth rate	−0.8	−0.2	−1.5	−1.7

EASY's return on equity and sustainable growth rate have been below the industry average. In 1999 and 2000 the differences widened. Thus, EASY's problem is not the result of an industry-wide decline.

2. Because there have been changes in the EASY Chair Co. ratios over the past five years, the next thing the analyst should examine is the income statements. To do this, first do a percentage of sales analysis by dividing each income statement item by the sales for that year. The results are shown on the next page.

This analysis shows that the biggest change is in the cost of goods sold. Either costs have risen or prices have declined. In addition, EASY's interest costs have increased in all but the last year.

EASY CHAIR COMPANY
PERCENTAGE OF SALES—INCOME STATEMENTS

	1997	1998	1999	2000
Net sales	100.0%	100.0%	100.0%	100.0%
Cost of sales	−69.0	−72.3	−71.9	−72.7
Gross profit	31.0	27.7	28.1	27.3
Selling, general, and administrative expense	−20.4	−18.8	−19.3	−18.8
Income from operations	10.6	8.9	8.8	8.5
Interest expense	−0.5	−0.8	−1.4	−1.2
Other income	0.5	0.6	0.6	0.4
Income before taxes	10.6	8.7	8.0	7.7
Taxes	−4.8	−3.2	−3.0	−2.9
Net income	5.8	5.5	5.0	4.8

Next calculate the change in each item from year to year. To calculate the growth rates, divide the difference in an account from one year to the next by the first year's total. For example, to calculate the change in sales from 1997 to 1998 do the following:

$$\text{Change in sales 1998} = \frac{(\$486.8 - 420.0)}{\$420.0}$$
$$= 0.159 \text{ or } 15.9\%$$

EASY CHAIR COMPANY
INCOME STATEMENT PERCENTAGE CHANGES

	1998	1999	2000
Net sales	15.9%	13.6%	7.1%
Cost of sales	21.5	13.0	8.2
Gross profit	3.5	15.4	4.2
Selling, general, and administrative expense	6.9	17.0	4.4
Income from operations	−3.1	12.0	3.7
Interest expense	110.5	90.0	−5.3
Other income	28.6	14.8	−19.4
Income before taxes	−6.5	4.8	3.6
Taxes	−23.6	6.5	4.8
Net income	7.7	3.8	2.9

Here we have a slightly different story. Sales growth has declined each year, and while cost of sales increased more than sales in 1998, the growth in these two items is closer in 1999 and 2000. It appears as if the increase in sales in 1998 was accompanied by production inefficiencies (e.g., cost of goods sold rose more than sales). In addition, *EASY's* income from operations declined in 1998 and rose less than sales in 1999 and 2000. Interest costs in 1998 and 1999 showed major increases. The negative impact on net income of these items has been offset somewhat by lower growth rates in selling, general, and administrative expenses in two of the three years. While the positive changes have offset some of the negative effects, the changes should be of real concern for the management of *EASY* Chair Co. A good analyst, and management, will want to know what happened in 1998 and whether it is under control.

3. To forecast financial statements for *EASY* Chair Co. based on Ms. Hampton's target ratios, the following process is used.
   a. To calculate dividends of $0.78 per share, multiply the market price of $15.00 by the dividend yield of 5.2 percent.
   b. Since the dividend payout ratio is 45 percent, divide it into the dividend to calculate the net income of $1.73 per share, or a total net income of $31,200 (with 18,000 shares).
   c. With net income of 5.1 percent and operating profit of 8.7 percent of sales, return on assets (net income/ assets) of 9.4 percent, and a return on equity of 13.7 percent, the equity, sales, and assets amounts can be determined by dividing the net income by the relevant ratio.
   d. To calculate the cost of sales, multiply the sales by the gross margin of 27.6 percent and subtract the sales from the product.
   e. Selling, general, and administrative expenses are the operating profit less the gross profit.
   f. Once the sales are determined, the accounts receivable can be calculated. To do so, divide the sales of $611,765 by 365 and multiply by the days in accounts receivable. The payables is cost of sales divided by 365 times the payables payment period.
   g. Inventory is calculated by dividing cost of sales by the inventory turnover of 733 percent.
   h. Debt is 27.3 percent of equity.
   i. Current liabilities are total assets minus debt and equity.
   j. Current assets are 573.2 percent of current liabilities.
   k. Cash is current assets minus inventory and accounts receivable.
   l. Other current liabilities are the difference between the accounts payable and the total current liabilities.
   m. Earnings before taxes (EBT) are the net income divided by (1 − tax rate) and the taxes are the difference between the net profit and the EBT.
   n. Interest is EBT less operating profit.

The statements that result from this analysis follow.

EASY CHAIR COMPANY
FINANCIAL STATEMENTS
(in millions)

Income Statement

Sales	$ 611,765
Cost of sales	(442,918)
Gross profit	168,847
Selling, general, and administrative expense	(115,623)
Operating profit	53,224
Interest	(5,951)
Earnings before taxes	47,273
Taxes	(16,073)
Net income	$ 31,200

Balance Sheet

Cash	$ 16,013
Accounts receivable	155,036
Inventory	60,401
Total current assets	231,450
Net property, plant, and equipment	100,465
Total assets	$ 331,915
Accounts payable	$ 25,240
Other current liabilities	16,766
Total current liabilities	42,006
Long-term debt	62,172
Total liabilities	104,178
Owners' equity	227,737
Total liabilities and owners' equity	$ 331,915
Dividends per share	$0.78

4. To determine Peterson's position relative to the industry, estimate the ratios using the formulas described in the chapter. The result is shown in the following table.

PETERSON'S CHEMICALS
FINANCIAL RATIOS RELATIVE TO INDUSTRY

	Industry	Peterson's 1999	Peterson's 2000
Current ratio	150%	163.7%	112.9%
Acid-test ratio	90%	108.0%	72.8%
Receivables collection period	65 days	111.2 days	106.7 days
Payables payment period	60 days	139.8 days	154.4 days
Debt/equity	110%	75.0%	78.8%
Return on assets	7%	−9.5%	−14.3%
Return on equity	19%	−28.8%	−77.0%

From the analysis of the ratios, Peterson's is not in a good position relative to its industry on any dimension except its leverage in 1999 and 2000 and its liquidity ratios in 2000.

5. To revise the statements, recalculate the sales, cost of goods sold, accounts payable and receivable, and debt as described in the problem. The only challenge is the debt. To estimate the debt, determine the 2000 equity account (the 1999 equity account balance added to the change in earnings from the actual to the pro forma of $62 [$174 − $112]). Since the debt/equity ratio is 100 percent, equity and debt are both $288.

The revised 2000 statements are as follows.

PETERSON'S CHEMICALS
ACTUAL AND PRO FORMA FINANCIAL STATEMENTS
(in millions)

Income Statement	Actual	Pro Forma
Sales	$ 1,478	$ 1,434
Cost of goods sold	(1,182)	(1,076)
Gross profit	296	358
Selling and administrative expenses	(443)	(443)
Operating profit	(147)	(85)
Interest expense	(27)	(27)
Net income	$ (174)	$ (112)

(continued)

Balance Sheet	Actual	Pro Forma
Cash and equivalent	$ 120	$ 120
Accounts receivable, net	432	306
Inventory	324	324
Other current assets	37	37
Total current assets	913	787
Plant, property, and equipment	300	300
Total assets	$ 1,213	$ 1,087
Accounts payable	$ 500	$ 202
Other current liabilities	309	309
Total current liabilities	809	511
Long-term debt	178	288
Total liabilities	987	799
Owners' equity	226	288
Total liabilities and owners' equity	$ 1,213	$ 1,087

The ratios, calculated in the usual way, follow:

PETERSON'S CHEMICALS
FINANCIAL RATIOS RELATIVE TO INDUSTRY

		Peterson's		
	Industry	1999	2000	Pro Forma
Current ratio	150%	163.7%	112.9%	154.1%
Acid-test ratio	90%	108.0%	72.8%	90.7%
Receivables collection period	65 days	111.2	106.7	78.0
Payables payment period	60 days	139.8	154.4	68.5
Debt/equity	110%	75.0%	78.8%	100.0%
Return on assets	7%	−9.5%	−14.3%	−10.3%
Return on equity	19%	−28.8%	−77.0%	−38.8%

If Peterson management had implemented the changes in 2000, Peterson's would still have lost money, but the ratios would have been stronger.

6. a. To calculate the common-size analysis of the income statements for THE FASTNER CO., divide each item by the sales. Note: Whether the most current date flows from the left or the right depends upon the country and the management's practice. In this case the most recent date is to the left.

THE FASTNER CO.
COMMON SIZE INCOME STATEMENTS

	1999	1998	1997	1996	1995
Revenues	100.0%	100.0%	100.0%	100.0%	100.0%
Cost of goods sold:					
Labor	22.3	21.2	22.5	23.3	25.0
Material	45.3	43.1	40.6	38.7	40.0
Gross profit	32.4	35.5	36.9	38.0	35.0
Marketing expenses	8.6	8.6	8.6	8.6	8.6
Administrative expenses	5.3	5.2	5.2	5.1	5.0
Operating profit	18.5	21.7	23.1	24.3	21.4
Taxes	6.1	7.1	7.6	8.0	7.1
Net income	12.4	14.6	15.5	16.3	14.3

THE FASTNER CO.'s net income had been declining since 1996. While labor costs seem to be under control since their high point in 1995, material costs are rising and are the primary culprit in the net income decline. In addition, administrative expenses, albeit a very small proportion of the overall expenses, are nonetheless creeping up. This is something on which management should keep watch.

b. To calculate the price per unit, divide the revenues by the number of units. The result is shown in the exhibit that follows.

c. Calculate the growth in the various income statement items as was done with *EASY* Chair, Problem 2, making certain you work right to left. The result is shown below.

THE FASTNER CO.
GROWTH OF INCOME STATEMENT ITEMS

	1999	1998	1997	1996	1995
Price per unit	$0.19	$0.15	$0.12	$0.09	$0.08
Growth Rates:					
Volume	−2.0%	2.0%	1.0%	8.0%	N.A.
Revenues	22.0	28.0	35.0	20.0	N.A.
Cost of goods sold:					
Labor	28.0	21.0	30.0	12.0	N.A.
Material	28.0	36.0	42.0	16.0	N.A.
Gross profit	11.1	23.5	30.9	30.3	N.A.
Marketing expenses	22.1	27.9	35.0	20.0	N.A.
Administrative expenses	24.0	30.0	37.0	22.0	N.A.
Operating profit	3.7	20.3	28.2	36.4	N.A.
Taxes	3.7	20.3	28.1	36.5	N.A.
Net income	3.7%	20.3	28.3	36.3	N.A.

The price per unit has been on a steady increase. This indicates that THE FASTNER CO. has raised prices, and has the market power to do so, has introduced new products. In looking at the cost of goods sold growth rates, it appears that the price increases have not outpaced cost increases, leading to declines in the gross profit. These uneven cost increases are reflected in the rest of the statement. This situation may lead an analyst to examine the impact that uneven price increases are having on the company, and an analysis of inflation might be in order. This leads logically to the inflation analysis in 6d.

d. To calculate the real growth rates in the income statement items, subtract the inflation rate for the year from each item. The table that follows shows the result of the analysis.

THE FASTNER CO.
REAL GROWTH OF INCOME STATEMENT ITEMS

	1999	1998	1997	1996
Revenues	−6.0%	2.0%	−5.0%	8.0%
Cost of goods sold:				
Labor	0.0	−5.0	−10.0	0.0
Material	0.0	10.0	2.0	4.0
Gross profit	−16.9	−2.5	−9.1	18.3
Marketing expenses	−5.9	1.9	−5.0	8.0
Administrative expenses	−4.0	4.0	−3.0	10.0
Operating profit	−24.3	−5.7	−11.8	24.4
Taxes	−24.3	−5.7	−11.9	24.5
Net income	−24.3	−5.7	−11.7	24.3

In drafting the report to Mr. Rickki, Lacey would certainly want to note that the profit growth the company appeared to be achieving was in fact an illusion when inflation is taken into account: in 1999 the growth rates were negative for all the income statement items. When this information is coupled with the fact that in unit terms the growth was adequate until 1999, THE FASTNER CO. is being hurt by inflation. If more inflation is expected, Mr. Rickki should certainly determine how the company will position itself to weather inflation's ravages. In addition, you will note that in real terms, the company's employees wages and the cost of materials have kept pace with inflation, but only in 1999. In the previous years materials suppliers appear to have raised prices in advance of inflation, while employees did not fare as well.

CHAPTER 2

1. To create pro forma financial statements for Top C. Company (statements that are adapted for changes in assumptions), a number of steps are needed:

   Step 1. To create the changes that Mr. Duncan suggests are possible:
   a. Multiply the current sales by 1.2 to obtain Mr. Duncan's estimate of sales.
   b. Multiply sales per day by 45 [($10,320/365) × 45] to calculate accounts receivable.
   c. Multiply the net sales by 40 percent for cost of goods sold.
   d. Multiply the sales by 2 percent for the bad debt expense (0.2 × $1,320).
   e. Divide Mr. Duncan's estimate of inventory turnover (600 percent) into cost of goods sold.
   f. Increase the operating expenses by 20 percent.
   g. Recalculate the taxes, using the 40 percent tax rate.
   h. Add the new net income to the old retained earnings.
   i. Increase the cash balance by 20 percent.
   j. Take the difference between total assets and total liabilities and equity to determine the net financing needed.
   k. Accounts payable are 114 days of cost of goods sold, and all else remains the same.

   Step 2. To create the changes Ms. Fisher suggests:
   a. Multiply current sales by 10 percent.
   b. Multiply revised sales by 5 percent to calculate bad debt expense.
   c. Multiply the net sales by 40 percent for cost of goods sold.
   d. Maintain operating expenses at $3,000.
   e. Multiply revised sales by 15 percent to estimate cash.
   f. Take 30 days of average sales for accounts receivable.
   g. For inventory, use 1/3 of cost of sales.
   h. Take the difference between total assets and total liabilities and equity to determine the net financing needed.
   i. Take the difference between total assets and total liabilities and equity to determine the net financing needed.
   j. Recalculate the taxes, using the 40 percent rate.
   k. Accounts payable are 114 days of cost of goods sold, and all else remains the same.

   The current and revised financial statements are as follows:

TOP C. COMPANY
CURRENT AND REVISED FINANCIAL STATEMENTS AND RATIOS
(dollars in millions)

Income Statements	Historic	Duncan	Fisher
Sales	$ 8,600.0	$10,320.0	$ 9,460.0
Bad debt	(430.0)	(206.4)	(473.0)
Net sales	8,170.0	10,113.6	8,987.0
Cost of goods sold	(3,500.0)	(4,128.0)	(3,784.0)
Gross profit	4,670.0	5,985.6	5,203.0
Operating expense	(3,000.0)	(3,600.0)	(3,000.0)
Operating income	1,670.0	2,385.6	2,203.0
Taxes	(668.0)	(954.2)	(881.2)
Net profit	$ 1,002.0	$ 1,431.4	$ 1,321.8

Balance Sheets	Historic	Duncan	Fisher
Assets			
Cash	$ 1,200.0	$ 2,064.0	$ 1,419.0
Accounts receivable	850.0	1,272.3	777.5
Inventory	800.0	688.0	1,261.3
Total current assets	2,850.0	4,024.3	3,457.8
Net property, plant, and equipment	4,000.0	4,000.0	4,000.0
Total assets	$ 6,850.0	$ 8,024.3	$ 7,457.8
Liabilities and Equity			
Accounts payable	$ 1,400.0	$ 1,289.3	$ 1,181.9
Short-term debt	1,500.0	1,500.0	1,500.0
Total current liabilities	2,900.0	2,789.3	2,681.9
Long-term debt	550.0	550.0	550.0
Common stock	420.0	420.0	420.0
Retained earnings	2,980.0	4,411.4	4,301.8
Total equity	3,400.0	4,831.4	4,721.8
Subtotal	6,850.0	8,170.7	7,953.7
New financing needed	0	(146.4)	(495.9)
Total liabilities and equity	$ 6,850.0	$ 8,024.3	$ 7,457.8
Net short-term debt	$ 1,500.0	$ 1,353.6	$ 1,004.1

Ratios			
Net working capital	$(50.0)	$1,235.0	$775.9
Current ratio	98%	144%	128%

Step 3. After reviewing the financial statements that you have created, you can see that both of the analysts' plans result in greater profits for the company. Under both plans, the current ratio is improved from its marginal position, net working capital is positive, and there is no new capital needed. In spite of the positive results, however, the forecasts raise issues:
  a. Mr. Duncan's plan of relaxing credit policy would actually result in a 20 percent increase in sales. This increase is substantial, and it would not be accompanied by significantly increased bad debts. Is it likely?
  b. Ms. Fisher's concerns regarding Mr. Duncan's forecasts seem warranted. Her forecasts contain increased bad debts and a smaller increase in sales because of the recession. She also includes an increase in inventories to service the new sales. However, she does not increase the company's liquid cash reserves as did Mr. Duncan.

The question of which plan to follow depends largely on your view of the impact of the widespread recession on the company's markets. At the time, a recession appeared to be affecting Asian and European countries. However, the time might have been right for the company to lure new customers to its products with increased credit availability.

2. To create the financial statements for Honda, follow these steps.

   Step 1. Sales. Increase the 1990 U.S. sales by 25 percent and the sales in Japan by 5 percent. To do this for Japan, multiply the 1990 sales by 1 plus the rate of growth. However, because the U.S. sales reported in 1990 are in yen:
   a. Translate the 1990 U.S. sales into dollars by dividing by the exchange rate of ¥154:$1.00,
   b. Multiply the U.S. dollar sales by 1 plus the rate of growth (25 percent) to determine the estimated 1991 sales in the United States,
   c. Convert the 1991 sales in the United States in dollars to yen by multiplying the U.S. sales in dollars by the estimated yen/dollar exchange rate of ¥140:$1.00.
   d. The total sales figure for Honda in 1991 is the sum of the yen-translated U.S. sales and the sales in Japan.

   Step 2. Cost of Sales. Cost of sales is expected to be 75 percent of total U.S. and Japanese sales, in yen terms. Operating costs grow at a simple rate of 10 percent, and research stays at ¥200.

   Using this information, the following income statement is created.

HONDA MOTOR COMPANY
1990–1991 INCOME STATEMENT
(in billions of yen)

	1990	1991
Net sales		
Japan	¥ 1,300.0	¥ 1,365.0
United States	2,200.0	2,500.0
Total sales	3,500.0	3,865.0
Cost of goods sold	(2,625.0)	(2,898.8)
Research and development	(200.0)	(200.0)
Gross profit	675.0	766.2
Operating expenses	(500.0)	(550.0)
Operating profit	175.0	216.2
Taxes	(70.0)	(86.5)
Net profit	¥ 105.0	¥ 129.7

Step 3. Balance Sheet. To estimate the 1991 balance sheet, the following steps must be taken:
a. Calculate the average daily sales:

$$\text{Average daily sales} = \text{Total sales}/365$$
$$= ¥3865/365$$
$$= ¥10.59 \text{ million}$$

b. Multiply the average daily sales by the collection period of 45 days to obtain the value of the accounts receivable.
c. Inventory is 1/6 of cost of sales.
d. Cash is 10 percent of sales.
e. Payables are 60 days × (Cost of sales/365).
f. Retained earnings are the sum of the 1990 retained earnings and the 1991 profit after taxes.
g. The short-term debt is the "plug" or balancing figure for the balance sheet. The total liabilities and equity, with no change in short-term debt, are ¥2,831.2 million, and the assets are ¥2,846.1 million. Thus, the new short-term debt will be ¥14.9 million.

The balance sheet is as follows.

HONDA MOTOR COMPANY
1990–1991 BALANCE SHEET
(in billions of yen)

Assets	1990	1991
Cash	¥ 250.0	¥ 386.5
Accounts receivable	400.0	476.5
Inventory	475.0	483.1
Total current assets	1,125.0	1,346.1
Net property, plant, and equipment	1,500.0	1,500.0
Total assets	¥ 2,625.0	¥ 2,846.1
Liabilities and Equity		
Accounts payable	¥ 400.0	¥ 476.5
Other short-term debt	350.0	350.0
Total current liabilities	750.0	826.5
Long-term debt	1,050.0	1,050.0
Common stock	75.0	75.0
Retained earnings	750.0	879.7
Total equity	825.0	954.7
Subtotal	2,625.0	2,831.2
New short-term financing	—	14.9
Total liabilities and equity	¥ 2,625.0	¥ 2,846.1

Step 4. Net Working Capital. To determine the change in net working capital, first subtract the current liabilities from the current assets in 1990 and 1991. The change of ¥145 billion is divided by the 1990 net working capital of ¥375 to determine the change of 38.7 percent.

Step 5. Current Ratio and Working Capital.

$$\text{Current ratio} = \text{Current assets}/\text{Current liabilities}$$

For 1990, the current ratio is:

$$\begin{aligned}\text{Current ratio} &= ¥1,125/¥750 \\ &= 1.50, \text{ or } 150 \text{ percent}\end{aligned}$$

The current ratios and net working capital changes are as follows:

HONDA MOTOR COMPANY
CURRENT RATIOS AND CHANGES IN WORKING CAPITAL
(currency in billions)

Working Capital

Net working capital	¥375	¥520
Change in net working capital	N.A.	39%
Current ratio	150%	163%

3. To revise your balance sheet, use the assumptions detailed in the problem and follow the steps described in the solution to Study Question 1. The revised statement is as follows:

HONDA MOTOR COMPANY
REVISED BALANCE SHEET
(currency in billions)

Assets	1990	Revised 1991
Cash	¥ 250.0	¥ 270.6
Accounts receivable	400.0	635.3
Inventory	475.0	483.1
Total current assets	1,125.0	1,389.0
Net property, plant, and equipment	1,500.0	1,500.0
Total assets	¥2,625.0	¥2,889.0
Liabilities and Equity		
Accounts payable	¥ 400.0	¥ 357.4
Other short-term debt	350.0	350.0
Total current liabilities	750.0	707.4
Long-term debt	1,050.0	1,050.0
Common stock	75.0	75.0
Retained earnings	750.0	879.8
Total equity	825.0	954.8
Subtotal	2,625.0	2,712.2
New short-term financing	—	176.8
Total liabilities and equity	¥2,625.0	¥2,889.0

The current ratios and net working capital changes are as follows:

HONDA MOTOR COMPANY
CURRENT RATIOS AND CHANGES IN WORKING CAPITAL
(currency in billions)

Net working capital	¥375	¥682
Change in net working capital	N.A.	82%
Current ratio	150%	196%

As you can see from your analysis, the changes that occur if Honda Motor Company extends its collection period (relaxes its credit terms) and pays its suppliers more quickly include a greater need for financing. This need results from the increase in accounts receivable. While the changes in accounts receivable and payables ought to have a net negative impact on the working capital and the current ratio, they do not in this case: the decrease in cash and increase in financing from short-term sources offset the increase.

Thus, the impact on Honda of these changes appears to be neutral. If Honda management decided not to reduce its cash position, and if it financed the changes from long-term sources of capital, the change would not be neutral.

This analysis reveals Honda's financial strength. Its current ratio exceeds the average for the industry. If payables lengthened and receivables were to be collected more slowly in economic downturns, Honda could easily endure the changes. This should concern Honda's competitors.

4. With a change in the dollar:yen exchange rate, the following statements would result.

HONDA MOTOR COMPANY
REVISED FINANCIAL STATEMENTS—¥85:$1.00
(currency in billions)

Income Statements	1990	1991
Net sales		
Japan	¥ 1,300.0	¥ 1,365.0
United States	2,200.0	1,517.9
Total sales	3,500.0	2,882.9
Cost of goods sold	(2,625.0)	(2,162.1)
Research and development	(200.0)	(200.0)
Gross profit	675.0	520.8
Operating expenses	(500.0)	(550.0)
Operating profit	175.0	(29.2)
Taxes	(70.0)	11.6
Net profit	¥ 105.0	¥ (17.6)

Balance Sheets	1990	1991
Assets		
Cash	¥ 250.0	¥ 201.8
Accounts receivable	400.0	355.4
Inventory	475.0	360.4
Total current assets	1,125.0	917.6
Net property, plant, and equipment	1,500.0	1,500.0
Total assets	¥ 2,625.0	¥ 2,417.6
Liabilities and Equity		
Accounts payable	¥ 400.0	¥ 266.6
Other short-term debt	350.0	350.0
Total current liabilities	750.0	616.6
Long-term debt	1,050.0	1,050.0
Common stock	75.0	75.0
Retained earnings	750.0	732.4
Total equity	825.0	807.4
Subtotal	2,625.0	2,474.0
New short-term financing	—	(56.4)
Total liabilities and equity	¥ 2,625.0	¥ 2,417.6
Working Capital		
Net working capital	¥375	¥301
Change in net working capital	N.A.	−20%
Current ratio	150%	149%

Honda would be hurt by the change and might raise its U.S. prices, thus making G.M. products more price competitive.

5. To forecast a monthly cash budget for Mary's Ski Chalet for 2001, first create 12 columns headed by the months of the year beginning with January. Then determine the cash receipts and disbursements.

Step 1. Cash receipts are determined as follows:
a. Cash is received from cash sales and collections from accounts receivable. Credit sales—75 percent of sales—are collected 30 days after the sale is made. The sales forecasts and beginning accounts receivable are provided in the problem.
b. Cash collections are the total of cash sales—25 percent of sales—plus the collections from accounts receivable.

Step 2. Disbursements are determined as follows:

a. Purchases are cost of goods sold plus 8 percent (83 percent of sales), and are paid 30 days after the goods are ordered. The accounts payable account at the end of the month is the beginning accounts payable less the accounts payable payments plus the purchases.
b. The disbursements are the payments of accounts payable plus the selling, general, and administrative expenses of 19 percent of sales and lease and interest expenses of $2,000 per month ($24,000 for the year).

Step 3. Net receipts are the receipts less the disbursements.

Step 4. The cash balance is the beginning cash account plus the net receipts.

The forecasts for Mary's Ski Chalet are shown in the following table. As you can see, although Mary's Ski Chalet will have to pay out more than it receives for most months until August, the beginning cash balance of $65 plus the receipts in January will provide sufficient cash to operate through the difficult spring and summer months.

MARY'S SKI CHALET
CASH RECEIPTS AND ACCOUNTS RECEIVABLE ACCOUNT
(in thousands)

	Jan.	Feb.	Mar.	Apr.	May	June	July	Aug.	Sept.	Oct.	Nov.	Dec.
Sales	$210.0	$175.0	$160.0	$140.0	$ 50.0	$30.0	$30.0	$75.0	$90.0	$125.0	$165.0	$230.0
Cost of goods sold	$157.5	$131.3	$120.0	$105.0	$ 37.5	$22.5	$22.5	$56.3	$67.5	$ 93.8	$123.8	$172.5
Accounts Receivable Schedule												
Beginning accts. receivable	$184.0	$157.5	$131.3	$120.0	$105.0	$37.5	$22.5	$22.5	$56.3	$ 67.5	$ 93.8	$123.8
Credit sales	157.5	131.3	120.0	105.0	37.5	22.5	22.5	56.3	67.5	93.8	123.8	172.5
Collections on accts. receivable	184.0	157.5	131.3	120.0	105.0	37.5	22.5	22.5	56.3	67.5	93.8	123.8
Ending accts. receivable	$157.5	$131.3	$120.0	$105.0	$ 37.5	$22.5	$22.5	$56.3	$67.5	$ 93.8	$123.8	$172.5
Accounts Payable Schedule												
Beginning accts. payable	$173.0	$170.1	$141.8	$129.6	$113.4	$40.5	$24.3	$24.3	$60.8	$ 72.9	$101.3	$133.7
Purchases	170.1	141.8	129.6	113.4	40.5	24.3	24.3	60.8	72.9	101.3	133.7	186.3
Payments on accts. payable	173.0	170.1	141.8	129.6	113.4	40.5	24.3	24.3	60.8	72.9	101.3	133.7
Ending accts. payable	$170.1	$141.8	$129.6	$113.4	$ 40.5	$24.3	$24.3	$60.8	$72.9	$101.3	$133.7	$186.3
Receipts												
Cash sales	$ 52.5	$ 43.8	$ 40.0	$ 35.0	$ 12.5	$ 7.5	$ 7.5	$18.8	$22.5	$ 31.3	$ 41.3	$ 57.5
Collections on accts. receivable	184.0	157.5	131.3	120.0	105.0	37.5	22.5	22.5	56.3	67.5	93.8	123.8
Total receipts	$236.5	$201.3	$171.3	$155.0	$117.5	$45.0	$30.0	$41.3	$78.8	$ 98.8	$135.1	$181.3
Disbursements												
Payments on accounts payable	$173.0	$170.1	$141.8	$129.6	$113.4	$40.5	$24.3	$24.3	$60.8	$ 72.9	$101.3	$133.7
Selling, general, and administrative expenses	39.9	33.3	30.4	26.6	9.5	5.7	5.7	14.3	17.1	23.8	31.4	43.7
Lease and interest expenses	2.0	2.0	2.0	2.0	2.0	2.0	2.0	2.0	2.0	2.0	2.0	2.0
Total disbursements	$214.9	$205.4	$174.2	$158.2	$124.9	$48.2	$32.0	$40.6	$79.9	$ 98.7	$134.7	$179.4
Cash Account												
Beginning cash	$ 65.0	$ 86.6	$ 82.5	$ 79.6	$ 76.4	$69.0	$65.8	$63.8	$64.5	$ 63.4	$ 63.5	$ 63.9
Receipts less disbursements	21.6	(4.1)	(2.9)	(3.2)	(7.4)	(3.2)	(2.0)	0.7	(1.1)	0.1	0.4	1.9
Ending cash	$ 86.6	$ 82.5	$ 79.6	$ 76.4	$ 69.0	$65.8	$63.8	$64.5	$63.4	$ 63.5	$ 63.9	$ 65.8

Note: shaded boxes are beginning balances.

6. Once the cash balance has been determined, the income statement and balance sheet are simple.

   Step 1. Income Statement.
   a. The sales are the sum of the monthly sales for the year.
   b. Cost of goods sold is 75 percent of sales.
   c. Selling, general, and administrative expenses are 19 percent of the total sales.
   d. Interest and lease expenses are $24,000.
   e. Depreciation is $12,000.

   The income statement for 2001 follows.

MARY'S SKI CHALET
2001 INCOME STATEMENT FORECAST
(in thousands)

Sales	$ 1,480.0
Cost of goods sold	(1,110.0)
Gross income	370.0
Selling and general expenses	(281.2)
Depreciation	(12.0)
Lease and interest expenses	(24.0)
Net income	$ 52.8

   Step 2. Balance Sheet.
   a. The cash, accounts receivable, and accounts payable accounts are those for the ending balances from the cash budget.
   b. Inventory is the beginning inventory account given in the problem, plus the purchases of $1,199, less cost of goods sold.
   c. Property, plant, and equipment is the account at the beginning of the year, less the depreciation of $12,000.
   d. Equity is the beginning equity plus the net income for the year.

   The balance sheets for 2000 and 2001 follow.

MARY'S SKI CHALET
ACTUAL 2000 AND FORECASTED 2001 BALANCE SHEETS
(in thousands)

Assets	2000	2001
Cash	$ 65.0	$ 65.8
Accounts receivable	184.0	172.5
Inventory	50.0	138.8
Current assets	299.0	377.1
Net property, plant, and equipment	345.0	333.0
Total assets	$644.0	$710.1
Liabilities and Equity		
Accounts payable	$173.0	$186.3
Current liabilities	173.0	186.3
Equity	471.0	523.8
Total liabilities and equity	$644.0	$710.1

7. To make forecasts for Aries Corporation you must use the information in the problem and information from the 1998 and 1999 actual financial statements. The first step is to do a percentage of sales analysis of the 1998 and 1999 financial statements. This analysis is shown next to the "Actual" columns on the statements that follow. Once the analysis is done, the forecasts can be made. These forecasts, shown in the "Forecast" columns in the following statements, are made like those in preceding problems. When ratios were different in 1998 and 1999, we used the ratio for 1999. You may have chosen to use an average.

ARIES CORPORATION
HISTORIC AND PROJECTED FINANCIAL STATEMENTS

	HISTORIC						FORECAST		
	1998	Percent	1999	Percent	2000	2001	2002	2003	2004
Income Statements									
Sales	$ 221.0	100.0%	$ 266.0	100.0%	$ 320.0	$ 352.0	$ 390.7	$ 437.6	$ 494.5
Cost of goods sold	(145.0)	65.6	(166.0)	62.4	(167.7)	(177.4)	(197.9)	(220.5)	(249.2)
Gross profit	76.0	34.4	100.0	37.6	152.3	174.7	193.8	217.1	245.3
Operating expenses	(38.0)	17.2	(35.0)	13.2	(42.2)	(46.5)	(51.6)	(57.8)	(65.3)
Operating profit	38.0	17.2	65.0	24.4	110.1	128.1	142.2	159.3	180.0
Taxes	(19.0)	50.0*	(33.0)	50.8*	(55.9)	(65.1)	(54.0)	(60.5)	(68.5)
Net profit	$ 19.0	8.6%	$ 32.0	12.0%	$ 54.2	$ 63.0	$ 88.2	$ 98.8	$ 111.6
Sales growth				20.3%	20.3%	10.0%	11.0%	12.0%	13.0%
*Taxes as percent of operating profit.									
Balance Sheets									
Assets									
Cash	$ 22.0	10.0%	$ 37.0	13.9%	$ 44.5	$ 49.0	$ 54.4	$ 60.9	$ 68.8
Accounts receivable	49.0	80.9 days	31.0	42.5 days	37.3	41.0	45.6	51.0	57.7
Inventory	47.0	118.3 days	45.0	98.8 days	21.0	22.1	32.8	36.8	41.6
Total current assets	118.0		113.0		102.8	112.1	132.8	148.7	168.1
Fixed assets	70.0		122.0		265.0	291.0	323.0	403.0	513.0
Total assets	$ 188.0		$ 235.0		$ 367.8	$ 403.1	$ 455.8	$ 551.7	$ 681.1
Liabilities and Equity									
Accounts payable	$ 19.0	47.8 days	$ 34.0	74.8 days	$ 27.6	$ 29.2	$ 32.4	$ 36.3	$ 41.0
Total current liabilities	19.0		34.0		27.6	29.2	32.4	36.3	41.0
Equity	169.0		201.0		255.2	318.2	406.4	505.2	616.8
Subtotal	188.0		235.0		282.8	347.4	438.8	541.5	657.8
New notes payable	—		—		85.0	55.7	17.0	10.2	23.3
Total liabilities and equity	$ 188.0		$ 235.0		$ 367.8	$ 403.1	$ 455.8	$ 551.7	$ 681.1

CHAPTER 3

1. Forecasting the 2001 financial statements for Chateau Royale requires several steps:

   Step 1. Income Statement.
   a. Sales for 2001 are 160 percent of 2000 sales.
   b. Cost of goods sold is 75 percent of 2001 sales.
   c. Operating expenses are 110 percent of 2001 operating expenses.
   d. Depreciation is $8,000.
   e. Operating profit is sales minus cost of goods sold, operating expenses, and depreciation.
   f. Taxes are 34 percent of operating income.
   g. Net profit after taxes is operating profit minus taxes.

   The resulting income statements follow.

   CHATEAU ROYALE INTERNATIONAL
   2000–2001 INCOME STATEMENTS
   (in billions)

	2000	2001
Sales	$ 375,000	$ 600,000
Cost of goods sold	(276,150)	(450,000)
Gross profit	98,850	150,000
Operating expenses	(75,000)	(82,500)
Depreciation	(5,100)	(8,000)
Operating profit	18,750	59,500
Taxes	(7,500)	(20,230)
Net profit	$ 11,250	$ 39,270

   Step 2. Balance Sheet.
   a. Long-term debt and common stock remain unchanged from 2000.
   b. Property, plant, and equipment assets are the 2000 account less the 2001 depreciation of $8,000.
   c. Inventory turnover is 3 times.
   d. Retained earnings are the prior year's retained earnings plus net profit from 2001.
   e. Accounts receivable are 45/365 times 2001 sales, and inventory is one-third of cost of goods sold.
   f. Accounts payable are 30/365 times 2001 cost of goods sold. We use cost of goods sold since no information about purchases is given.
   g. Cash is 20 percent of 2001 sales.
   h. Since we do not know what Chateau Royale management expects to do about short-term debt, we enter a zero.

i. Forecasted assets will not balance with liabilities and equity. The best way to balance the assets and liabilities is to put in a balancing account called "net financing needed." Net financing needed is total assets less the subtotal.

The balance sheets for Chateau Royale follow.

CHATEAU ROYALE INTERNATIONAL
2000–2001 BALANCE SHEETS
(in billions)

Assets	2000	2001
Cash	$ 75,000	$ 120,000
Accounts receivable	46,233	73,973
Inventory	93,750	150,000
Current assets	214,983	343,973
Net property, plant, and equipment	115,000	107,000
Total assets	$ 329,983	$ 450,973
Liabilities and Equity		
Accounts payable	$ 23,116	$ 36,986
Short-term debt	51,867	—
Current liabilities	74,983	36,986
Long-term debt	125,000	125,000
Common stock	100,000	100,000
Retained earnings	30,000	69,270
Subtotal	329,983	331,256
Net financing needed (excess cash)	—	119,717
Total liabilities and owners' equity	$ 329,983	$ 450,973

Step 3. The net working capital is current assets minus current liabilities. To calculate the current ratio divide the two accounts. The net working capital and current ratios for 2000 and 2001 follow.

CHATEAU ROYALE INTERNATIONAL
WORKING CAPITAL RATIOS

Ratios	2000	2001
Current ratio	287%	930%
Net working capital change	N.A.	$166,987

2. In revising the statements for Chateau Royale International, only these assumptions change:
   a. Cash/sales is reduced to 15 percent.

b. Days of cost of goods sold in payables is increased to 45 days.
c. Inventory turnover is increased to 400 percent.

While the income statements stay the same, the following balance sheets reflect these changes.

CHATEAU ROYALE INTERNATIONAL
2000–2001 REVISED BALANCE SHEETS
(in billions)

Assets	2000	2001
Cash	$ 75,000	$ 90,000
Accounts receivable	46,233	73,973
Inventory	93,750	112,500
Current assets	214,983	276,473
Net property, plant, and equipment	115,000	107,000
Total assets	$ 329,983	$ 383,473
Liabilities and Equity		
Accounts payable	$ 23,116	$ 55,479
Short-term debt	51,867	—
Current liabilities	74,983	55,479
Long-term debt	125,000	125,000
Common stock	100,000	100,000
Retained earnings	30,000	69,270
Trial balance	329,983	349,749
New financing needed (excess cash)	—	33,724
Total liabilities and owners' equity	$ 329,983	$ 383,473
Ratios	**2000**	**2001**
Current ratio	287%	498%
Net working capital change		$80,993

As a result of the lower cash balance and more rapid inventory turnover, the current ratio is above the industry average of 320 percent. Chateau Royale management must take into consideration that the increase in the payables period may result in higher supplier costs, such as interest on unpaid balances, or may result in increased prices. Management should also consider whether lower cash and inventory could result in insufficient inventory to service customers or insufficient cash to transact business.

3. The process used in forecasting the statement revisions according to Mr. Dine and Mr. Triano is similar to the process used in solving Study Questions 1 and 2. The assumptions are those provided in the problem and are used to create the following financial statements:

KURZ CORP.
FINANCIAL STATEMENTS
(Canadian dollars in thousands)

Income Statements	Original	Triano	Dine
Sales	CD$505,000	CD$757,500	CD$505,000
Bad debt	(5,000)	(15,150)	0
Net sales	500,000	742,350	505,000
Cost of goods sold	(375,000)	(568,125)	(378,750)
Gross profit	125,000	174,225	126,250
Operating expenses	(90,900)	(90,900)	(90,900)
Operating profit	34,100	83,325	35,350
Taxes	(11,935)	(29,164)	(12,373)
Net profit	CD$ 22,165	CD$ 54,161	CD$ 22,977

Balance Sheets	Original	Triano	Dine
Assets			
Cash	CD$ 90,000	CD$148,470	CD$ 75,750
Accounts receivable	61,644	124,521	41,507
Inventory	62,500	81,161	75,750
Current assets	214,144	354,152	193,007
Net property, plant, and equipment	130,000	130,000	130,000
Total assets	CD$344,144	CD$484,152	CD$323,007
Liabilities and Equity			
Accounts payable	CD$ 30,822	CD$ 46,228	CD$ 30,819
Short-term debt	86,322	—	0
Current liabilities	117,144	46,228	30,819
Long-term debt	110,000	110,000	110,000
Common stock	75,000	75,000	75,000
Retained earnings	42,000	73,996	42,812
Subtotal	344,144	305,224	258,631
New financing needed (excess cash)	—	178,928	64,376
Total liabilities and owners' equity	CD$344,144	CD$484,152	CD$323,007

Ratios	Base	Triano	Dine
Current assets	CD$214,144	CD$354,152	CD$193,007
Current liabilities	117,144	46,228	30,819
Net working capital	CD$ 97,000	CD$307,924	CD$162,188
Current ratio	183%	766%	626%

Based on these statements, Ms. Brittain should implement Mr. Triano's plan. Despite the higher cost, this plan results in a higher net profit and higher asset growth. However, this policy also results in having to borrow much more short-term money and thus increases the risk of financial distress if sales decline substantially.

4. THE CRESCENT is a typical short-term working capital problem. The steps followed in making the forecast for THE CRESCENT are similar to those followed in the problems in Chapter 2. The only special challenges that this problem presents are as follows:

   a. Some of the payments are made in Philippine pesos and some in dollars. You must be careful to denominate expenses in the proper currency.

   b. The dollar/Philippine peso exchange rate is expected to change as early as February, and that exchange rate change must be built into the forecasts.

   c. Some of the goods ordered require a funded letter of credit before delivery. Thus, some of the expenses are incurred at the time the letter of credit is funded, and that is well before the goods arrive. For instance, the letter of credit for the cement purchases must be opened one month prior to delivery. Thus, the first payment for cement is for the letter of credit in January. These are non-recourse letters of credit are the same as paying for the goods.

The full forecasts are in the following table. These forecasts show that Mr. Dizon will need to have a credit line with United Coconut, which will be rapidly paid down as revenues are received. Mr. Lucas should ask the United Coconut Planters' Bank for a revolving line of credit of at least P10,732,000. This is the total needed by July, the month before the expenses begin to decline and the revenues begin to offset the costs of building materials for THE CRESCENT. Mr. Dizon will need the credit line from March until September 2001.

THE CRESCENT
MONTHLY CASH FLOW FORECASTS
(in millions of Philippine pesos)

	Jan.	Feb.	March	April	May	June	July
Cash Receipts							
Cash receipts	4,500				9,000		
Cash Disbursements							
Cement	3,402		3,645		3,645		3,645
Granite tiles					5,000		
Window frames			120	120	120	120	120
Elevators		600					
Generator					2,000		
Bathroom fixtures							
Salaries and benefits	375	375	375	375	375	375	375
Overhead	10	10	10	10	10	10	10
Total disbursements	3,787	985	4,150	505	11,150	505	4,150
Cash Balance							
Beginning cash balance	1,000	1,713	728	(3,422)	(3,927)	(6,077)	(6,582)
Net cash flow	713	(985)	(4,150)	(505)	(2,150)	(505)	(4,150)
Ending cash balance	1,713	728	(3,422)	(3,927)	(6,077)	(6,582)	(10,732)

THE CRESCENT (cont.)

	Aug.	Sept.	Oct.	Nov.	Dec.	Jan.	Feb.	March
Cash Receipts								
Cash receipts	9,000		9,000		9,000			4,500
Cash Disbursements								
Cement								
Granite tiles		585						
Window frames	120	120	120	120	120			
Elevators								
Generator								
Bathroom fixtures								
Salaries and benefits	375	375	375	375	375			
Overhead	10	10	10	10	10			
Total disbursements	505	1,090	505	505	505			
Cash Balance								
Beginning cash balance	(10,732)	(2,237)	(3,327)	5,168	4,663	13,158	13,158	13,158
Net cash flow	8,495	(1,090)	8,495	(505)	8,495	—	—	4,500
Ending cash balance	(2,237)	(3,327)	5,168	4,663	13,158	13,158	13,158	17,658

CHAPTER 4

1. The following steps are taken to solve this problem.

   Step 1. The first thing the analyst must do to determine whether Metalwerk's management should develop a new assembly line is to forecast the residual cash flows for the project. Here they are forecast in thousands. These cash flows are straightforward. If the pattern in the chapter is followed, only two tricky things must be considered—depreciation and calculating the payback period.

   a. To calculate the double-declining-balance depreciation, take the balance left to be depreciated and calculate double the straight-line depreciation rate. For instance, in the first year, the machinery is valued at DM 1,400. The double-declining-balance depreciation is twice the 5 percent rate of straight-line depreciation times the remaining balance to be depreciated. The table calculating the depreciation follows the residual cash flow forecast.

   b. The depreciation for any year is either the double-declining-balance amount or the straight-line value if the latter is larger. Straight-line depreciation would be the undepreciated balance divided by the number of years remaining in the equipment life. Straight-line depreciation is equal in the 11th year. The depreciation for years 11–20 is the straight-line value that depreciates the equipment in the remaining 10 years, or DM 49 per year.

   Step 2. To determine the payback, subtract the annual residual cash flow from the initial cost of DM 1,400. By the fourth year, the remainder to be covered is DM 220, while the fourth year's residual cash flow is DM 385. This means that the equipment will be fully covered by the residual cash flow in an additional 0.57 years (DM 220 /DM 385). Because the payback is more than the four years the management requires, the project should not be accepted. However, to analyze this project fully, management should estimate the net present value using an appropriate discount rate.

   Step 3. The benefit/cost ratio is simply the sum of all the benefits, DM 7,482, divided by the initial cost, DM 1,300.

   The full forecasts and calculations for payback and depreciation are shown in the following table.

METALWERKS
ANALYSIS OF NEW ASSEMBLY LINE—RESIDUAL CASH FLOWS
(in thousands of deutsch marks)

	0	1	2	3	4	5	6	7	8	9
Income Statement Changes										
Sales		1,625	1,625	1,625	1,625	1,625	1,625	1,625	1,625	1,625
Raw materials		(601)	(601)	(601)	(601)	(601)	(601)	(601)	(601)	(601)
Gross profit		1,024	1,024	1,024	1,024	1,024	1,024	1,024	1,024	1,024
Repairs and utilities		(13)	(13)	(13)	(13)	(13)	(13)	(13)	(13)	(13)
Salaries and benefits		(480)	(480)	(480)	(480)	(480)	(480)	(480)	(480)	(480)
Depreciation		(140)	(126)	(113)	(102)	(92)	(83)	(74)	(67)	(60)
Profit before taxes		391	405	418	429	439	448	457	464	471
Taxes		(133)	(138)	(142)	(146)	(149)	(152)	(155)	(158)	(160)
Net profit		258	267	276	283	290	296	302	306	311
Noncash Charges										
Depreciation		140	126	113	102	92	83	74	67	60
Balance Sheet Changes										
New equipment	(1,400)									
Residual net cash flow	(1,400)	398	393	389	385	382	379	376	373	371
Payback										
Unrecovered investment value	1,400	1,002	609	220	(165)					
Partial year calculation				57.1%						
Payback (years)	3.57									
Benefit/cost ratio	5.34									
Depreciation Schedule		1	2	3	4	5	6	7	8	9
Value yet undepreciated		1,400	1,260	1,134	1,021	919	827	744	670	603
Straight-line rate depreciation		5%								
Double-declining balance depr.		140	126	113	102	92	83	74	67	60
Straight-line depr. for remaining life		70	66	63	60	57	55	53	52	50
Depreciation to be taken		140	126	113	102	92	83	74	67	60

(continued)

METALWERKS (cont.)
PERIOD

	10	11	12	13	14	15	16	17	18	19	20
	1,625	1,625	1,625	1,625	1,625	1,625	1,625	1,625	1,625	1,625	1,625
	(601)	(601)	(601)	(601)	(601)	(601)	(601)	(601)	(601)	(601)	(601)
	1,024	1,024	1,024	1,024	1,024	1,024	1,024	1,024	1,024	1,024	1,024
	(13)	(13)	(13)	(13)	(13)	(13)	(13)	(13)	(13)	(13)	(13)
	(480)	(480)	(480)	(480)	(480)	(480)	(480)	(480)	(480)	(480)	(480)
	(54)	(49)	(49)	(49)	(49)	(49)	(49)	(49)	(49)	(49)	(48)
	477	482	482	482	482	482	482	482	482	482	483
	(162)	(164)	(164)	(164)	(164)	(164)	(164)	(164)	(164)	(164)	(164)
	315	318	318	318	318	318	318	318	318	318	319
	54	49	49	49	49	49	49	49	49	49	48
	369	367	367	367	367	367	367	367	367	367	367

	10	11	12	13	14	15	16	17	18	19	20
	542	488	439	391	342	293	244	195	146	97	48
	54	49	44	39	34	29	24	20	15	10	24
	49	49	49	49	49	49	49	49	49	49	49
	54	49	49	49	49	49	49	49	49	49	48

2. The single biggest difficulty in making the BELLA LUNA forecasts is dealing with the depreciation associated with the two investments. The cash flow forecasts show that depreciation is important in this case since the largest portion of the net present value is directly related to the high depreciation allowances. However, given the magnitude of the net present value, management of Bella Luna should pursue this investment. The forecasted residual cash flows are as follows:

BELLA LUNA
RESIDUAL CASH FLOW ANALYSIS
(in thousands of lira)

	\multicolumn{6}{c}{PERIOD}				
	0	1	2	3	4	5
Income Statement Changes						
Sales		120.0	138.0	158.7	182.5	209.9
Production expenses		(46.8)	(53.8)	(61.9)	(71.2)	(81.9)
Depreciation—initial investment		(30.0)	(44.0)	(42.0)	(42.0)	(42.0)
Depreciation—additional investment		—	—	(15.6)	(19.2)	(25.2)
Profit before taxes		43.2	40.2	39.2	50.1	60.8
Taxes		(19.4)	(18.1)	(17.6)	(22.5)	(27.3)
Net profit		23.8	22.1	21.6	27.6	33.5
Noncash Charges						
Depreciation		30.0	44.0	57.6	61.2	67.2
Capital Investments						
Property, plant, and equipment	(200.0)		(60.0)			
Residual net cash flow	(200.0)	53.8	6.1	79.2	88.8	100.7
Net present value (at 10%)	36.6					

The IRR, by the way, is 15.8 percent.

3. In general, the solution to this problem follows that of the previous problems in this chapter. Project 1 is the most straightforward of the two projects. The cash flows are forecasted on the basis of data in the problem and are shown in the following project evaluation. The depreciation schedule requires that the larger of the double declining balance or straight-line methods be used on the undepreciated balance. The schedule to calculate the depreciation follows the residual cash flow forecasts.

For Project 2, three things may be a problem in making the forecasts: market research expenses have already been spent and, thus, are irrelevant to this project's value; production training is an expense at the beginning of the project life; and tax credit of $68,000 is expected to offset income received by Cloud Frame from other parts of its business. For the tax credit, if Cloud Frame had no other business, the tax credit could be carried forward; if no income were ever earned, the tax credit would be useless. The tax credit reduces the asset value that can be depreciated by the amount of the tax credit.

The net present value, benefit/cost ratio, and payback are calculated as demonstrated in the chapter.

Chapter 4 373

CLOUD FRAME COMPANY
ANALYSIS OF TWO PROJECTS
(in thousands of libras)

Project 1

Income Statement Changes	0	1	2	3	4	5	6	7	8	9	10
Sales		500.0	500.0	500.0	500.0	500.0	500.0	500.0	500.0	500.0	500.0
Cost of goods sold		(245.0)	(245.0)	(245.0)	(245.0)	(245.0)	(245.0)	(245.0)	(245.0)	(245.0)	(245.0)
Gross income		255.0	255.0	255.0	255.0	255.0	255.0	255.0	255.0	255.0	255.0
Advertising		(50.0)	(50.0)	(50.0)	(50.0)	(50.0)	(50.0)	(50.0)	(50.0)	(50.0)	(50.0)
Depreciation		(160.0)	(128.0)	(102.4)	(81.9)	(65.5)	(52.5)	(52.5)	(52.4)	(52.4)	(52.4)
Operating income		45.0	77.0	102.6	123.1	139.5	152.5	152.5	152.6	152.6	152.6
Taxes		(15.3)	(26.2)	(34.9)	(41.8)	(47.4)	(51.9)	(51.9)	(51.9)	(51.9)	(51.9)
Net income		29.7	50.8	67.7	81.3	92.1	100.6	100.6	100.7	100.7	100.7
Noncash Charges											
Depreciation		160.0	128.0	102.4	81.9	65.5	52.5	52.5	52.4	52.4	52.4
Capital changes:											
New machinery	(800.0)										
Residual cash flow	(800.0)	189.7	178.8	170.1	163.2	157.6	153.1	153.1	153.1	153.1	153.1
Payback											
Investment to recover	800.0	610.3	431.5	261.4	98.1						
Partial year calculation					62.3%						
Payback period in years	4.62										
Benefit/cost ratio	2.03										
Net present value at 10%	217.7										

Depreciation Schedule	1	2	3	4	5	6	7	8	9	10
Double-declining-balance depreciation	160.0	128.0	102.4	81.9	65.5	52.4	41.9	33.6	26.8	21.5
Straight-line depreciation	80.0	71.1	64.0	58.5	54.6	52.4	52.4	52.4	52.4	52.4
Remaining balance	640.0	512.0	409.6	327.7	262.1	209.7	157.3	104.9	52.4	—
Depreciation to be taken	160.0	128.0	102.4	81.9	65.5	52.5	52.5	52.4	52.4	52.4

Depreciation in years 6 and 7 larger by 0.1 to compensate for rounding errors.

(continued)

Appendix Solutions to Study Questions

CLOUD FRAME COMPANY (cont.)

Project 2

Income Statement Changes	0	1	2	3	4	5	6	7	8	9	10
Sales		350.0	385.0	423.5	465.9	535.7	616.1	708.5	779.3	857.3	943.0
Cost of goods sold		(175.0)	(192.5)	(211.8)	(232.9)	(267.9)	(308.0)	(354.2)	(389.7)	(428.6)	(471.5)
Gross income		175.0	192.5	211.8	232.9	267.9	308.0	354.2	389.7	428.6	471.5
Advertising		(87.5)	(96.3)	(105.9)	(100.0)	(100.0)	(100.0)	(100.0)	(100.0)	(100.0)	(100.0)
Production training	(200.0)										
Depreciation		(120.0)	(96.0)	(77.0)	(61.0)	(49.0)	(39.0)	(39.0)	(39.0)	(40.0)	(40.0)
Income before taxes	(200.0)	(32.5)	0.2	28.9	71.9	118.9	169.0	215.2	250.7	288.6	331.5
Taxes or tax credit	68.0	11.1	(0.1)	(9.8)	(24.4)	(40.4)	(57.5)	(73.2)	(85.2)	(98.1)	(112.7)
Net income	(132.0)	(21.5)	0.1	19.1	47.5	78.5	111.5	142.0	165.5	190.5	218.8
Noncash Charges											
Depreciation		120.0	96.0	77.0	61.0	49.0	39.0	39.0	39.0	40.0	40.0
Balance sheet changes:											
New equipment	(600.0)										
Net residual cash flow	(732.0)	98.5	96.1	115.1	108.5	127.5	150.5	181.0	204.5	230.5	258.8
Payback											
Investment to recover	732.0	633.5	537.4	422.3	313.8	186.3	80.8				
Partial year calculation							0.4				
Payback period in years	5.4										
Benefit/cost ratio											
Benefits	1,571.0										
Benefit/cost ratio	2.1										
Net present value at 10%	147.5										

Chapter 4

CLOUD FRAME COMPANY (cont.)

Project 2

Depreciation Schedule	0	1	2	3	4	5	6	7	8	9	10
Initial cost	600.0										
Remaining balance		600	480	384	307	246	197	158	119	80	40
Double-declining-balance depreciation		120	96	77	61	49	39	32	24	16	8
Straight-line depreciation		60	53	48	44	41	39	39	39	40	40
Depreciation to be taken		120	96	77	61	49	39	39	39	40	40

Based on two measures of attractiveness, Project 2 is dominant. However, on the NPV, the preferred method of analysis, Project 1 is superior and management should choose to buy the new machinery.

CHAPTER 5

1. The maximum price that Magnus' management should be willing to pay to acquire Carr is the value of Carr plus the value of the synergies that result from the merger. To determine this total, first determine the value of Magnus, then the value of Carr, and finally the value of the combined companies. Because the problem states that there will be no growth, the value of each of the entities can be estimated using the shortcut perpetuity method:

$$\text{Value} = \frac{\text{Residual net cash flow}}{(\text{Required return on equity} - \text{Growth in residual cash flow})}$$

Step 1. Using the formula above to calculate the value of Magnus is $355,556 [$40,000/(0.1125 − 0.0)],

Step 2. The value per share is $7.11 ($355,556/50,000).

Step 3. Repeat steps 1 and 2 for Carr and the combined companies.

Step 4. Subtracting the values of Magnus and Carr from the combined companies shows that the value of the synergies is $164,444.

These values are shown in the following table.

CARR-MAGNUS VALUATION
(dollars in thousands)

	Magnus Corp.	Carr Co.	Combined Companies
Profit after taxes	$48,000	$30,000	$92,000
Residual net cash flow/year	60,000	40,000	120,000
Required return on equity	12.50%	11.25%	12.00%
Value	$480,000	$355,556	$1,000,000
Number of shares	N.A.	50,000	N.A.
Value per share	N.A.	$7.11	N.A.
Equity book value	N.A.	297,500	N.A.
Book value per share	N.A.	$5.95	N.A.

From the analysis you can see the absolute maximum price that Magnus' management should offer for Carr is the value of the synergies, $164,444, plus the value of Carr, $355,556. This is a total of $520,000, or $10.40 per share price. Magnus' shareholders would prefer that the price be lower so they may reap the benefits from the synergies. The minimum price that Carr should accept from Magnus' management for the sale of Carr is the value of Carr in the marketplace, that is, its share price. Carr management should target a price equal to the value of Carr, however, because this value is higher than the current stock price. The current stock market equity value is $300,000 ($6/share with 50,000 shares). The value from the perpetuity-shortcut valuation is $355,556, $7.11 per share, or $1.11 per share higher. Book value ($5.95 per share), often considered the floor value, is lower than the current market valuation and thus should play no role in determining the minimum acceptable price. While the minimum price is the current stock market value, Carr management should price the sale at the value of the company and bargain for Carr's shareholders to gain some of the $164,444 in synergies. Thus, the final price of this acquisition should be above $355,556, and between $7.11 per share and $10.40 per share.

2. To estimate the price Smythe should offer for Robinson Research, the first step is to estimate the value of each of the entities—Smythe, Robinson, and the combined companies. The simple shortcut perpetuity method of valuation can be used in Study Question 1 adjusting the cash flow and discount rate for growth [CF × (1 + g)/Re − g]. The only problem in dealing with this analysis is the net residual cash flow/year for the combined companies. That cash flow is management's estimate of the cash flow that would have been earned had they been merged.

Using this data, the following table shows the values of each of the three companies.

SMYTHE ACQUISITION OF ROBINSON LABS
(in millions of Canadian dollars)

	Smythe Instrument Co.	Robinson Research Lab	Combined Companies
Net residual cash flow/year	CD $6.45	CD $2.20	CD $10.92
Expected real growth in residual cash flow	4.0%	4.0%	4.0%
Expected nominal growth in residual cash flow	8.0%	8.0%	8.0%
Required return on equity (nominal)	16.2%	14.5%	15.5%
Value of company	CD $84.95	CD $36.55	CD $157.25

Once the value of each of the companies has been found, use the following formula to estimate the maximum price that Smythe could pay and still maintain value for its shareholders.

Maximum value of merger to Smythe = Value of combined companies − Value of Smythe
= CD $157.25 − CD $84.95
= CD $72.30

Robinson Research Lab management should accept a price no lower than its current value of CD $36.55 million. Any price above that will result in value being created for the Robinson shareholders. The difference between the combined values of Smythe and Robinson operating separately of CD $121.50 (CD $84.95 + CD $36.55) and the value of the combined companies of CD $157.25 is CD $35.75. This is the value of the synergies. Smythe management can pay up to the value of Robinson plus the value of the synergies before it risks losing value for its shareholders.

3. To determine the value of Action, and the price for which the company should be sold, first forecast the 2001 residual net cash flow:
   a. Forecast the 2001 sales at a growth of 5 percent from 2000 sales of $250 million. Sales from 2001 to 2007 grow at 5 percent per year, sales after 2007 grow at 3 percent.
   b. Cost of sales and selling, general, and administrative expenses are 75 percent and 10 percent of sales, respectively, and are deducted from sales.
   c. Depreciation of $7 million is deducted from sales.
   d. To calculate the profit before taxes, deduct all expenses except taxes from sales. Taxes are 34 percent of the profit before taxes.
   e. Once net income has been estimated, add back the noncash expense (depreciation) and deduct the $7 million spent on additions to working capital and property, plant, and equipment.
   f. Because the rate of growth slows after 2007, the perpetuity shortcut can be used to estimate the value of Action from then on. Because the cash flows in this level-growth world will be different from those when the company was growing more rapidly, however, first estimate the 2008 residual cash flow (a "steady-state" cash flow) and then estimate the terminal value from then on.
   g. The terminal value is the 2008 cash flow divided by the required return on equity of 11.2 percent, less the permanent growth rate of 3 percent. The resulting terminal value is $379.3 [$31.1/(0.112 − 0.03)].

The value of the company is $292.4 million as shown in the forecasted residual cash flows that follow:

ACTION CORPORATION
RESIDUAL CASH FLOWS 1996-2004
(in millions)

	Historic 2000	2001	2002	2003	Forecasted 2004	2005	2006	2007	2008
Income Statement Changes									
Sales growth	N.A.	5%	5%	5%	5%	5%	5%	5%	3%
Sales	$ 250.0	$ 262.5	$ 275.6	$ 289.4	$ 303.9	$ 319.1	$ 335.0	$ 351.8	$ 362.3
Cost of sales	(187.5)	(196.9)	(206.7)	(217.1)	(227.9)	(239.3)	(251.3)	(263.9)	(271.9)
Gross profit	62.5	65.6	68.9	72.3	76.0	79.8	83.7	87.9	90.4
Selling, general & admin.	(25.0)	(26.3)	(27.6)	(28.9)	(30.4)	(31.9)	(33.5)	(35.2)	(36.3)
Depreciation	(7.0)	(7.0)	(7.0)	(7.0)	(7.0)	(7.0)	(7.0)	(7.0)	(7.0)
Profit before taxes	30.5	32.3	34.3	36.4	38.6	40.9	43.2	45.7	47.1
Taxes	(10.4)	(11.0)	(11.7)	(12.4)	(13.1)	(13.9)	(14.7)	(15.5)	(16.0)
Profit after taxes	$ 20.1	$ 21.3	$ 22.6	$ 24.0	$ 25.5	$ 27.0	$ 28.5	$ 30.2	$ 31.1
Noncash Charges									
Depreciation	7.0	7.0	7.0	7.0	7.0	7.0	7.0	7.0	7.0
Balance Sheet Changes									
PP&E and working capital changes	(7.0)	(7.0)	(7.0)	(7.0)	(7.0)	(7.0)	(7.0)	(7.0)	(7.0)
Annual residual cash flow	20.1	21.3	22.6	24.0	25.5	27.0	28.5	30.2	31.1
Terminal value	—	—	—	—	—	—	—	—	379.3
Net residual cash flow	$ 20.1	$ 21.3	$ 22.6	$ 24.0	$ 25.5	$ 27.0	$ 28.5	$ 30.2	$ 410.4
Present value @ 11.2% =	$292.4								

4. It does not matter what the domicile of the acquiror is, Action is still worth $292.4 million. The source of the acquiror's capital, the currency in which it wishes to convert its earnings, and the economy in which it operates does not change the value of what it will acquire. Only potential positive or negative synergies would change the valuation.

CHAPTER 6

1. The following data are provided in the problem:
    - Dividend $2.86
    - Market price $25.00
    - Beta   1.32
    - Long-term dividend growth   4.9%
    - 10-year Treasury bond yield   8.9%
    - 90-day Treasury bill yield   6.5%
    - Market risk premium above:
        - Treasury bonds   6.0%
        - Treasury bills   8.5%

    To determine the cost of equity, two methods can be used.

    Method 1. Dividend-Discount Model.

    $$\text{Required return on equity} = \frac{\text{Dividend} \times (1 + \text{Dividend growth})}{\text{Market price}} + \text{Dividend growth}$$

    The dividend yield, the dividend divided by the market price, is 12.0 percent ($2.86 × (1 + .049)/$25.00). To the dividend yield, add management's estimated growth rate of 4.9 percent, for a total required return on equity of 16.9 percent.

    Method 2. Capital Asset Pricing Model.

    Required return on equity = Risk-free rate + (Beta × Market risk premium)

    Using the 10-year Treasury bond rate as the nominal risk-free rate of 8.9 percent and the matching market risk premium of 6.0 percent yields a required return on equity of 16.8 percent [8.9 percent + (1.32 × 6.0 percent)]. This required return on equity is very close to that estimated by the dividend-discount model. Because an equity is a long-term instrument, the short-term Treasury bill rate and its matching premium are not appropriate to use.

2. Using the following data and the pattern used in the answer to Study Question 1, the dividend-discount model required return on equity for

Kelly Services is 12.5 percent [($3.00/36.00) + 4.2 percent]. We do not multiply the dividend by the growth rate since the dividend is what is expected to be paid next year.

Growth rate	4.2%
U.S. Treasury bill yield	3.8%
U.S. Treasury bond yield	6.3%
Beta	0.95
Dividend	$3.00
Market price	$36.00

The capital asset pricing model is

$$\text{Required ROE} = \text{Risk-free rate of return} + \text{Beta} \times (\text{Market rate of return} - \text{Risk free rate of return})$$

The problem says that the market return is expected to be 8.9 percent above the yield on U.S. Treasury bills, or a total of 12.7 percent. Using this as the market rate of return, we subtract the U.S. Treasury bond return of 6.3 percent to get the market premium. We use the 6.3 percent as the risk-free rate of return, and a beta of 0.95, to get the required return on equity of 12.4 percent [6.3 percent + 0.95 × (12.7 percent − 6.3 percent)]. Note, our use of the market rate of return of 12.7 percent is an approximation of the premium over the Treasury bond rate. However, since the beta for Kelly is almost 1.0, it is an approximation that is unlikely to be misestimated. You should also note that by adding the U.S. Treasury bill rate to the premium to create a market estimate does not mean that the Treasury bill rate is being used as the risk-free rate of return.

3. To be honest, the Grupo Mercado Tropical problem is a bit of a trick. While the problem suggests you might want to return to the data in Chapter 1, in fact, all the information that you need is contained in the problem. Since Grupo is valuing Hannaford, the data should be that of Hannaford operating in the U.S. market. Thus the required return on equity would be 13.7 percent [6.0% + (1.02 × 7.5%)].

CHAPTER 7

1. In order to determine the EPS-EBIT break-even table,

   Step 1. Calculate the earnings per share at two different levels of earnings before interest and taxes. The most logical choices for the two EBIT levels are Zumar's current revenues and the revenues when the store is expanded, $100 million and $120 million, respectively.

Step 2. Calculate the profit after taxes. To do this, you must account for $2.8 million in interest expense on existing debt ($40 million at 7 percent), and the costs of new financing. The cost of debt financing is 10 percent, and the cost of equity financing is dilution, or the increase in the number of shares from 2.0 million to 2.75 million. The following table provides the EBIT and EPS under the two financing schemes for two levels of revenue.

ZUMAR, INC.
EARNINGS WITH EXISTING AND EXPECTED REVENUES
(in millions, except per share)

	Debt Financing		Equity Financing	
	Old Revenues	New Revenues	Old Revenues	New Revenues
Revenues	$100.0	$120.0	$100.0	$120.0
Earnings before interest and taxes	13.0	15.6	13.0	15.6
Interest:				
Old	(2.8)	(2.8)	(2.8)	(2.8)
New	(1.5)	(1.5)	0.0	0.0
Profit before taxes	8.7	11.3	10.2	12.8
Taxes	(3.0)	(3.8)	(3.5)	(4.4)
Profit after taxes	$ 5.7	$ 7.5	$ 6.7	$ 8.4
Number of shares	2.00	2.00	2.75	2.75
Earnings per share	$2.85	$3.75	$2.44	$3.06

Step 3. To determine the equivalency point, the following data are used:

Debt (millions):	
Old	$40.0
New	$15.0
Interest rate:	
Old	7.0%
New	10.0%
Number of shares (millions):	
Debt financing	2.00
Equity financing	2.75

The formula for the EBIT break-even or equivalency point is in the chapter. The result of the analysis with no preferred dividends is:

$$\text{EBIT Break-even} = \frac{(2.0 \times \$2.8) - (2.75 \times \$2.8) - (2.75 \times \$1.5)}{2.0 - 2.75}$$

$$= \$8.3$$

Graphically, the result is shown below.

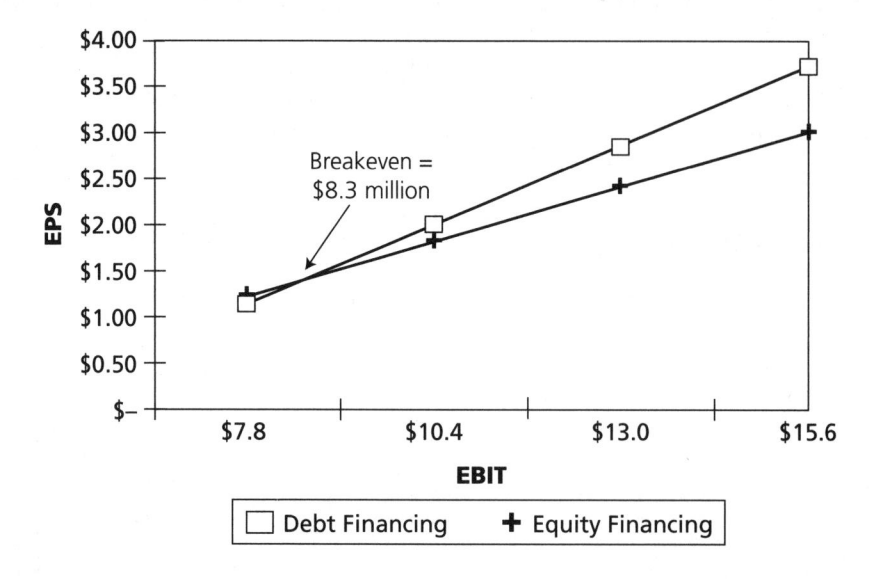

If Zumar management expects to earn more than $8.3 million in earnings before interest and taxes, the debt alternative results in a higher EPS for the shareholders.

2. To determine the dividend coverage, the dividends per share to be paid by Zumar are divided into the earnings per share for each alternative method of financing, as follows:

ZUMAR, INC.
DIVIDEND COVERAGE WITH EXISTING AND EXPECTED REVENUES
(in millions)

	Debt Financing		Equity Financing	
	Old Revenues	New Revenues	Old Revenues	New Revenues
Revenues	$100.0	$120.0	$100.0	$120.0
Earnings before interest and taxes	13.0	15.6	13.0	15.6
Interest:				
Old	(2.8)	(2.8)	(2.8)	(2.8)
New	(1.5)	(1.5)	0.0	0.0
Profit before taxes	8.7	11.3	10.2	12.8
Taxes	(3.0)	(3.8)	(3.5)	(4.4)
Profit after taxes	$ 5.7	$ 7.5	$6.7	$ 8.4
Number of shares	2.00	2.00	2.75	2.75
Earnings per share	$2.85	$3.75	$2.44	$3.05
Dividends per share	$0.75	$0.75	$0.75	$0.75
Dividend coverage	380%	500%	325%	407%

Regardless of the financing method used, Zumar has sufficient earnings to cover dividend payments generously.

3. Using the dividend-discount model and the following data:

Dividends =	$0.75
Dividend growth =	5.00%
Required return on equity:	
Debt alternative =	15.40%
Equity alternative =	16.90%

The value of the company under the two financing alternatives is:

$$\text{Debt alternative value per share} = \frac{\text{Dividends} \times (1 + \text{Dividend growth})}{\text{Required return on equity with debt financing} - \text{Dividend growth}}$$

$$= \frac{\$0.75 \times (1.05)}{0.154 - 0.05}$$

$$= \$7.57$$

$$\text{Equity alternative value per share} = \frac{\text{Dividends} \times (1 + \text{Dividend growth})}{\text{Required return on equity with equity financing}} - \text{Dividend growth}$$

$$= \frac{\$0.75 \times (1.05)}{0.169 - 0.05}$$

$$= \$6.62$$

The value per share when debt is used to finance the expansion is higher than if equity were used. Thus, Zumar should finance with debt, unless there are other factors that mitigate the added value from debt financing.

4. To determine which scheme would allow Zumar the most flexibility, we can look at the leverage and interest coverage ratios calculated below. The "Without Financing" retained earnings are as shown in the problem. The retained earnings for the Debt and Equity columns were the additional net income added to the base case retained earnings. Those net income figures are from Problem 2.

ZUMAR DEBT RATIOS WITH AND WITHOUT NEW FINANCING
(dollars in millions)

Balance Sheet	Without Financing	New Financing	
		Debt	Equity
Current liabilities	$ 40.0	$ 40.0	$ 40.0
Long-term debt	40.0	55.0	40.0
Common stock	4.0	4.0	19.0
Retained earnings	50.0	50.7	51.7
Total liabilities and equity	$134.0	$149.7	$150.7
Debt/total capital	42.6%	50.1%	36.1%
Equity/assets	40.3%	36.5%	46.9%
Net income	$6.73	$7.46	$8.45
Interest expense	$2.80	$4.30	$2.80
Interest coverage	240%	173%	302%

Clearly financing with equity allows Zumar the most flexibility in how to finance any Internet venture: the debt/total capital ratio is the lowest and the interest coverage ratio is the highest.

APPENDIX 7A

1. *Step 1.* This problem is an extension of Study Question 1, Chapter 6. In this problem Bakelite Co. has debt financing the company. Thus, it is the weighted-averaged cost of capital that must be determined. In Chapter 6,

you first determined the required return on equity using the following steps. The following data are provided in the problem:

Dividend	$3.00
Market price	$25.00
Beta	1.32
Long-term growth	4.9%
7-year Treasury bond yield	8.9
90-day Treasury bill yield	6.5
Market risk premium above:	
Treasury bonds	6.0
Treasury bills	8.5%
Bakelite bond coupon	17.3%
New B-rated bond yield	14.5%

To determine the cost of equity, two methods can be used.

Method 1. Dividend-Discount Model.

$$\begin{aligned}\text{Required return on equity} &= (\text{Dividend}/\text{Market price}) + \text{Dividend growth} \\ &= ((\$3.00 \times 1.049)/\$25.00) + 0.049 \\ &= 0.175 \text{ or } 17.5 \text{ percent}\end{aligned}$$

Method 2. Capital Asset Pricing Model.

$$\text{Required return on equity} = \text{Risk-free rate} + \text{Beta} \times (\text{Risk premium})$$

Using the 7-year Treasury bond rate of 8.9 percent as the nominal risk-free rate and the matching market risk premium of 6.0 percent results in a required return on equity of 16.8 percent [8.9% + (1.32 × 6.0%)]. This is a required return on equity that is very close to that estimated by the dividend-discount model. Since an equity is a long-term instrument, the short-term Treasury bill rate and its matching premium are not appropriate to use.

Step 2. The next step is to determine the cost of debt for Bakelite. The marginal cost of debt is best estimated from the current yield-to-maturity on newly issued B-rated bonds of 14.5 percent. The coupon of 17.3 percent on the company's bonds reflect their cost of borrowing in an economic environment where rates were higher. The cost of this debt to the company is partially offset by the tax deductibility of the interest expense on the debt. With a tax rate of 34 percent the after-tax cost of debt is 9.57 percent [14.5 percent × (1 − 0.34)].

Step 3. Finally, the required return on equity and the company's after-tax cost of debt should be weighted by the proportions in which management expects to raise capital. Since management expects to raise capital in the same proportions as they have in the past, the debt/total capital proportion on the balance sheet must be calculated. The debt/total capital ratio is currently 35 percent:

a. Since debt is $1.3 and equity is $2.4, total capital is

$$\begin{aligned} \text{Total capital} &= \text{Debt} + \text{Equity} \\ &= \$1.3 + \$2.4 \\ &= \$3.7 \end{aligned}$$

b. As a proportion of the capital structure:

$$\begin{aligned} \text{Debt/Total capital} &= \frac{\$1.3}{\$3.7} \\ &= 0.35 \text{ or } 35\% \end{aligned}$$

$$\begin{aligned} \text{Equity/Total capital} &= \frac{\$2.4}{\$3.7} \\ &= 0.65 \text{ or } 65\% \end{aligned}$$

Step 4. Weighting the debt cost and required return on equity by their proportions, the weighted-average cost of Bakelite's capital is 14.27 percent.

Source	Cost	Proportion	Weighting
Debt	9.57%	35%	3.35%
Equity	16.80	65	10.92
Weighted average capital cost			14.27%

2. For the Select Company, perform the following steps:

Step 1. The dividend-discount model required return on equity is:

$$\begin{aligned} \text{Required return on equity} &= (\text{Dividend/Market price}) + \text{Dividend growth} \\ &= (\$0.43/\$6.90) + 0.058 \\ &= 0.062 + 0.058 \\ &= 0.120 \text{ or } 12.0\% \end{aligned}$$

Where:
a. The dividend yield (dividend/market price) is 6.2 percent with a market price of $6.90 and a dividend that is 24 percent of earnings per share, or $0.43. Note, next year's earnings of $1.78 ($1.68 × 1 + 0.057) should be used, not the 2000 earnings in calculating the dividend expected. The dividend is 24 percent on the earnings.
b. The growth rate is 5.8 percent when calculated using:

$$\begin{aligned}
\text{Growth rate} &= (1 - \text{Payout}) \times \text{ROE} \\
&= (1 - 0.24) \times 0.077 \\
&= 0.058 \text{ or } 5.8\%
\end{aligned}$$

This is a bit higher than the growth rate for sales and earnings.

Step 2. The capital asset pricing model required return on equity is

Required return on equity = Risk-free rate + (Beta × Risk premium)

Given the data in the problem and the *expected* market return, the result is

$$\begin{aligned}
\text{Required return on equity} &= 1.10 \times 11.0\% \\
&= 12.1\%
\end{aligned}$$

Step 3. For the weights in 2000, debt is $2.26 million, equity is $4.2 million, and total capital is $6.46 million. Thus, in book value terms, the debt is 35 percent of total capital, and equity is 65 percent. In 2001 the weights are the same. However, the market value of the equity is below the book value: the value is $6.90 per share for 300,000 shares. This makes the market value capital structure 52 percent debt in 2000 and 54 percent in 2001.

Step 4. Using the same process as in Study Question 1, the weighted-average cost of capital using the book value capital structure and the dividend-discount model is 10 percent [(35% × (9.6% × (100 − 34%)) + (65% × 12%)]; using the capital asset pricing model it is it is almost identical.

Using the market value capital structure the weighted average cost of capital is 9.1 percent for 2000. Before we conclude the weighted average cost of capital is 9.1 or 10.0 percent, we would want to investigate why the book and market values of the equity are so different and what capital structure management has as its target.

INDEX

A

Abandonment options, 190
Accelerated depreciation, 150
Accounts payable to cost of sales ratio, 28
Accounts payable to purchases ratio, 28
Accounts receivable, 26
    cash management and, 135–36
Accounts receivable aging, 135
Accounts receivable/net sales ratio, 26
Accrual accounting, 89
Acid-test ratio, 35–36
Acquisitions. *See also* Mergers
    cross-border, 233–34
    leverage in, 317
    leveraged, 334–37
    of non-U.S. companies by U.S. companies, *illus.*, 206
    of U.S. companies by origin of acquirer, *illus.*, 207
    of U.S. companies by U.S. and non-U.S. companies, *illus.*, 205
    with growth, 218
    with synergy, 214–17
    without synergy, 211–14
Aging of accounts receivable, 27
American options, 176
Annual report, 4
Annuity, 162
Arbitrage, 112
Arbitrageurs, 112
Ask prices, 113
Asset utilization ratios, 22–30
Assets, redundant, 217
Assets to equity ratio, 30
Average payback period, 158

B

Bailout options, 190
Balance sheet, 5

Benefit/cost ratio, 156, 158
Beta, 260, 264–66
Bid prices, 113
Block, 242
Bond rating, 287
Bonds, 284
    calling, 286
    floating-rate, 284
    refunding, 286
    variable-rate, 284
    zero-coupon, 285
Book value, 229
Book value capital structure, 328
Break-even point, 300

C

Call options, 176, 192
Call protection, 286
Calling bonds, 286
Capital
    calculating weighted-average cost of, 325–29
    financing working, 137–40
    weighted-average cost of, 276
    working, 126
Capital appreciation, 245
Capital asset pricing model, 257–66
    using, 266
Capital budgeting, 146
Capital investment, 146
Capital loss, 245
Capital market estimation, 256
Capital market funds, 240
Capital markets, 240
Capitalization ratios, 30–38
Cash balances, investing, 133–35
Cash benefits of investments, 148
Cash budgets, 89–96
    developing financial statement forecasts from, 99

391

Index

steps in creating, 90
Cash flow coverage ratio, 37
Cash flow valuation models, 246–55
   discounted cash flow models, 253–55
   dividend-discount method, 246–53
   implicit required return on equity, 255
Cash flows
   discounting techniques for timing of, 160–69
   free, 323–24
   present value analysis of, in acquisitions, 211–22
   residual, 155, 323
Cash management, 132–35
   investing cash balances, 133–35
   managing disbursements, 133
   managing receipts, 132–33
Cash payments of investments, 148–52
Checks, preauthorized, 133
Commercial paper, 139
Common-size statements, 19
   profitability analysis using, 18–19
Comparative ratio analysis, 50–55
   comparisons to other companies, 53–54
   comparisons with others in the industry, 54–55
   historical comparisons, 51–53
Component percentage analysis, 18, 28; *illus.*, 19, 29
Compounding, 162
Consolidated financial statement, 69
Constant cost accounting, 74
Constant growth perpetuity, 220
Contingency, 190
Contingent claim, 176
Contingent claims analysis, 176–78
Controlled disbursement system, 133
Convertible instruments, 244, 284
Cost
   embedded, 326
   sunk, 149
Cost-benefit analysis of proposed investments, 147–52
Costs and benefits, evaluating incremental, 152–56
Costs of inputs, 309–10
Counter-party, 312
Covenants, 283
Coverage ratios, 36
Cross-border acquisition, 233–34
Cross-border ratio analysis, 63–86
Current ratio, 35
Cyclical sales activity, 130

D

Days' inventory ratio, 26
Days' sales outstanding, 27
Debt
   determining cost of, 287–91
   junk, 286
   marginal cost of, 326
   mortgage, 287
   original issue discount (OID), 286
   securitized, 287
   subordinated, 287
Debt capacity, 295
Debt financing, 307–8
   sources of, 283–87
Debt policy, 295
Debt-service coverage ratio, 37
Debt-service ratios, 36
Deposit concentration, 133
Depreciation
   accelerated, 150
   double-declining-balance, 150
   straight-line, 150
Devaluation, 113
Disbursements, managing, 133
Discount rates
   changing, 170
   danger of raising, 172
Discounted cash flow models, 253–55
Discounted cash flow techniques, 160–69
Discounted present value, 162
Dividend-discount model, 246–53
Dividend discount valuation, 231–32
Dividend payout ratio, 38
Dividend yield ratio, 45–46
Double-declining-balance depreciation, 150
Dynamic decision, 190

E

Earnings multiples, 223–27
Earnings per share, 42
Earnings retention ratio, 39
EBIT, 17
EBIT coverage ratio, 36–37
EBIT/sales ratio, 17
EBITDA, 18
EBITDA/sales ratio, 18
Efficiency ratios, 22
Efficient market, 246
Electronic funds transfer, 132–33
Embedded cost, 326
Embedded options, 177, 191
Equity
   implicit cost of, 255
   implicit required return on, 255
Equity financing, 306–7
Eurobond market, 134
European options, 176, 192

EVA analysis, 48–50
Exchange rate theories, 112–14
Exchange rates
   how forecasts are affected by, 114–18
   importance of, 111
Exercise date, 192
Exercising an option, 176
Expected value, 110–11, 175
Explicit cost of financing, 299

F

Factoring, 139
Financial distress, 281
Financial embarrassment, 281
Financial leverage, 30
Financial options, 192–95
Financial risks, 310–14
Financial statement footnotes, 10, 12
Financial statement forecasts
   analyzing assumptions, 103–11
   developing from cash budgets, 99
   developing in uncertain conditions, 99–103
   developing projections directly, 96–99
Financial statements, 3–12
   analysis of, 12–50
   impact of nondomestic transactions on, 77–81
   multi-currency, 111–18
   projected, 96–99
   projecting in uncertain conditions, 99–103
Financing
   debt, 307–8
   equity, 306–7
   explicit cost of, 299
   implicit cost of, 299
   sources of debt, 283–87
First-in, first out, 70
Fisher effect, 112
Fixed exchange rate, 113
Floaters, 284
Floating exchange rate, 112
Floating-rate bonds, 284
Forecasting financial needs
   historical comparisons, 104–7
   probability analysis, 110–11
   sensitivity analysis, 107–10
Forecasts, how exchange rates affect, 114–18
Foreign exchange transactions, 77–79
   effects of different accounting methods for, illus., 79
Foreign exchange translations, 80–81
   effects of different accounting methods for, illus., 82–83
Forward contracts, 113
Forward markets, 113

Free cash flow valuation, when to use, 329–30
Free cash flows, 323–24
Funds flow statement, 5
Future value, 160
Future value factor, 161
Futures contract, 312
Futures markets, 113

G

Gearing, 30
General price-level adjustments, 74
Gross margin, 17
Gross profit, 17
Growth options, 190
Growth rate, sustainable, 38–42

H

Hedging, 114
Hurdle rate, 164

I

Implicit cost of equity, 255
Implicit cost of financing, 299
Implicit required return on equity, 255
Implied price/earnings ratio, 226
Income statement, 3
Incremental benefits, 147
Incremental costs, 147
Incremental costs and benefits, evaluating, 152–56
Indenture agreement, 284
Independent investments, 152
Inflation, 70–77
   and growth, 221–22
   impact of, on working capital cycle, 128
   incorporating expected, on investment valuation, 183–85
   tax codes and depreciation with high, 203–4
Initial public offerings (IPOs), 241
Inputs, costs of, 309–10
Interest, 275
Interest rate parity, 112
Internal rate of return, 166–69
Intrinsic market price, 245
Inventories, cash management and, 136–37
Inventory, 69–70
Inventory methods and impact on earnings, illus., 13
Inventory turnover ratio, 25
Investment options, 190
Investments
   cash benefits, 148

cash payments, 148–52
choosing among, 156–69
cost-benefit analysis of proposed, 147–52
discounted cash flow techniques for, 160–69
evaluating incremental costs and benefits, 152–56
impact of taxes and depreciation on, 178–82
incorporating expected inflation on, 183–85
independent, 152
multiple scenario analysis, 173–76
mutually exclusive, 152
ranking, 169
replacement, 153
simple valuation methods, 156–60
size considerations, 182–83

J

Junk debt, 286

L

Last-in, first out, 70
Leasing, 315–17
Lenders, 275
    risk to, 294–99
Leverage
    in acquisitions, 317
    value of, 276–83
Leveraged acquisitions, 334–37
Line of credit, 138
    secured, 138
Liquidation value, 229–30
Lockboxes, 132
Long-term debt to equity ratio, 33
Long-term debt to total assets ratio, 33
Long-term debt to total capital ratio, 34

M

Making a market, 242
Managed balance account, 133
Marginal benefits, 147
Marginal cost of debt, 326
Marginal costs, 147
Market price of risk, 275
Market price/cash flow ratio, 44
Market price/EBIT ratio, 43
Market price/EBITDA ratio, 44
Market price/revenues ratio, 44
Market rate of return, 263–64
Market ratios, 42–46
Market-to-book value ratio, 45
Market value, 230–31
Market value capital structure, 328

Markets
    capital, 240
    efficient, 246
    over-the-counter, 242
    primary, 240
    public bond, 243
    secondary, 241
Maturity, 240, 284
Maturity date, 192
Merger activity outside the United States, *illus.*, 207
Mergers
    pooling method, 208
    purchase method, 208
    reason for, 209
Money market funds, 240
Money markets, 134
Mortgage debt, 287
Most likely scenario, 109
Multi-currency financial statements, 111–18
Multiple scenario analysis, 173–76
Mutually exclusive investments, 152

N

NASDAQ, 242
Natural hedge, 311
Net income, 4
Net loss, 4
Net present value, 164–65
Net present value profile, 166
Net working capital, 139
New equity issues, 267
Nominal growth rate, 20
Nondomestic transactions, impact on statements, 77–81

O

One-transaction perspective, 78
Operating leverage, 22
Operating profit/sales ratio, 17
Options, 176
    abandonment (bailout), 190
    American, 176
    call, 176, 192
    embedded, 177, 191
    European, 176, 192
    exercising, 176
    financial, 192–95
    growth (production), 190
    investment, 190
    put, 176, 192
    real, 195–200
Organized exchanges, 241
Original issue discount (OID) debt, 286

Over the counter (OTC), 241
Over-the-counter market, 242

P

Par value, 284
Payables payment period, 28
Payback period, 158–59
Percentage change analysis, 52
Pooling method, 208
Preauthorized checks, 133
Preferred stock, 244, 268
Present value, 162, 164
    discounted, 162
    net, 164
Present value analysis of cash flows for acquisitions, 211–22
Present value index, 165
Present value payback, 163–64
Price/earnings (P/E) ratio, 42–43
    implied, 226
Primary markets, 240
Principal, 284
Private placements, 283
Probability analysis, 110–11
Production options, 190
Production-sales cycle, 126
Profit and loss statement, 3
Profitability analysis
    using common-size statements, 18–19
    using growth rates, 19–22; *illus.*, 20, 21
    using ratios, 14–18
Profitability ratios, 14–18
Public bond market, 243
Public issues, 283
Purchase method, 208
Purchasing power, 74
Purchasing power parity, 112
Put options, 176, 192

Q

Quarterly report, 4
Quick ratio, 35

R

Rate of return
    market, 263–64
    required, 164
    risk-free, 260–63
Ratio analysis
    comparative, 50–55
    cross-border, 63–86

Ratios
    accounts payable to cost of sales, 28
    accounts payable to purchases, 28
    accounts receivable/net sales, 26
    acid-test, 35–36
    asset utilization, 22–30
    assets to equity, 30
    average payback, 158
    benefit/cost, 156, 158
    capitalization, 30–38
    cash flow coverage, 37
    coverage, 36
    current, 35
    days' inventory, 26
    days' sales outstanding, 27
    debt-service, 36
    debt-service coverage, 37
    dividend payout, 38
    dividend yield, 45–46
    earnings per share, 42
    earnings retention, 39
    EBIT coverage, 36–37
    EBIT/sales, 17
    EBITDA/sales, 18
    efficiency, 22
    gross margin, 17
    gross profit, 17
    implied price/earnings, 226
    inventory turnover, 25
    long-term debt to equity, 33
    long-term debt to total assets, 33
    long-term debt to total capital, 34
    market, 42–46
    market price/cash flow, 44
    market price/EBIT, 43
    market price/EBITDA, 44
    market price/revenues, 44
    market-to-book value, 45
    operating profit/sales, 17
    payables payment period, 28
    price/earnings (P/E), 42–43
    quick, 35
    return on assets, 24
    return on equity, 30–31
    return on sales, 14–16
    return versus risk performance, 46–50
    spread of economic value added, 46–48
    sustainable growth rate, 39–40
    total asset turnover, 22
    total liability to assets, 34
    turnover, 22
    working capital/sales, 130
Real growth rate, 20
Real options, 195–200
Receipts, managing, 132–33
Receivables collection period, 27

Index

Redundant assets, 217
Refunding bonds, 286
Relative risk premium model, 257
Replacement cost, 230
Replacement investments, 153
Required rate of return, 164
Research and development, 66–69
Residual cash flows, 155, 323
Retained earnings, cost of, 267–68
Return on assets, 24
Return on equity, 30–31
    and cost of retained earnings, 267–68
    and new equity issues, 267
    and preferred stock, 268
    required, for private, non-U.S., or companies experiencing change, 268–69
Return on sales, 14–16
Revaluation, 113
RICHS analysis, 291–317
    control, 306–8
    hedging and speculating, 308–14
    income, 299–306
    risk to lenders, 294–99
Risk
    and synergies, 216–17
    cash flow manipulation to incorporate, 172–73
    defining, 169–70
    market price of, 275
    to lenders, 294–99
Risk categories, 171–72
Risk-free rate of return, 260–63
Risk premium, 256
Risk premium models, 256–66
    capital asset pricing model, 257–66
    stock-bond yield spread, 256–57
Risks, financial, 310–14

S

Sales demand, impact on working capital cycle of variable, 130–32
Sales growth, impact of, on working capital cycle, 128–30
Same-store sales, 20
Seasonal sales activity, 130
Secondary markets, 241
Secular sales activity, 130
Secured line of credit, 138
Securitization, 139
Securitized debt, 287
Security characteristic line, 266
Self-sustainable growth rate, 39
Sensitivity analysis, 107
    one scenario, 107–9

    three scenarios, 109–10
Shareholders' required return, 239–40
Specific identification, 70
Specific price-level adjustments, 74–77
Spot market, 113
Spread of economic value added ratio, 46–48
Statement of cash flows, 5–8; *illus.*, 7
Statement of changes in financial position, 5
Statement of changes in shareholders' equity, 8, 10; *illus.*, 11
Statement of earnings, 3–5; *illus.*, 4
Statement of financial position, 5; *illus.*, 6
Statement of retained earnings, 8
Statement of sources and uses, 5; *illus.*, 9
Statements
    common-size, 19
    profitability analysis using common-size, 18–19
Static decision, 190
Stock, preferred, 244, 268
Stock-bond yield spread, 256–57
Straight-line depreciation, 150
Strike price, 192
Subordinated debt, 287
Sunk cost, 149
Sustainable growth rate, 38–42
Sustainable growth rate ratio, 39–40
Swaps, 312
Synergies, 214
    direct forecasts of, 214–15
    indirect forecasts, 215–16
    risk and, 216–17

T

Target capital structure, 328
Tax codes and depreciation in inflationary environments, 203–4
Terminal value, 218–21
Total asset turnover ratio, 22
Total liabilities to assets ratio, 34
Translation methods, 80
Turnover ratios, 22
Two-transaction perspective, 78

U

Underlying asset, 192

V

Valuation methods
    book value, 229
    dividend discount, 231–32